TURNER TO MONET

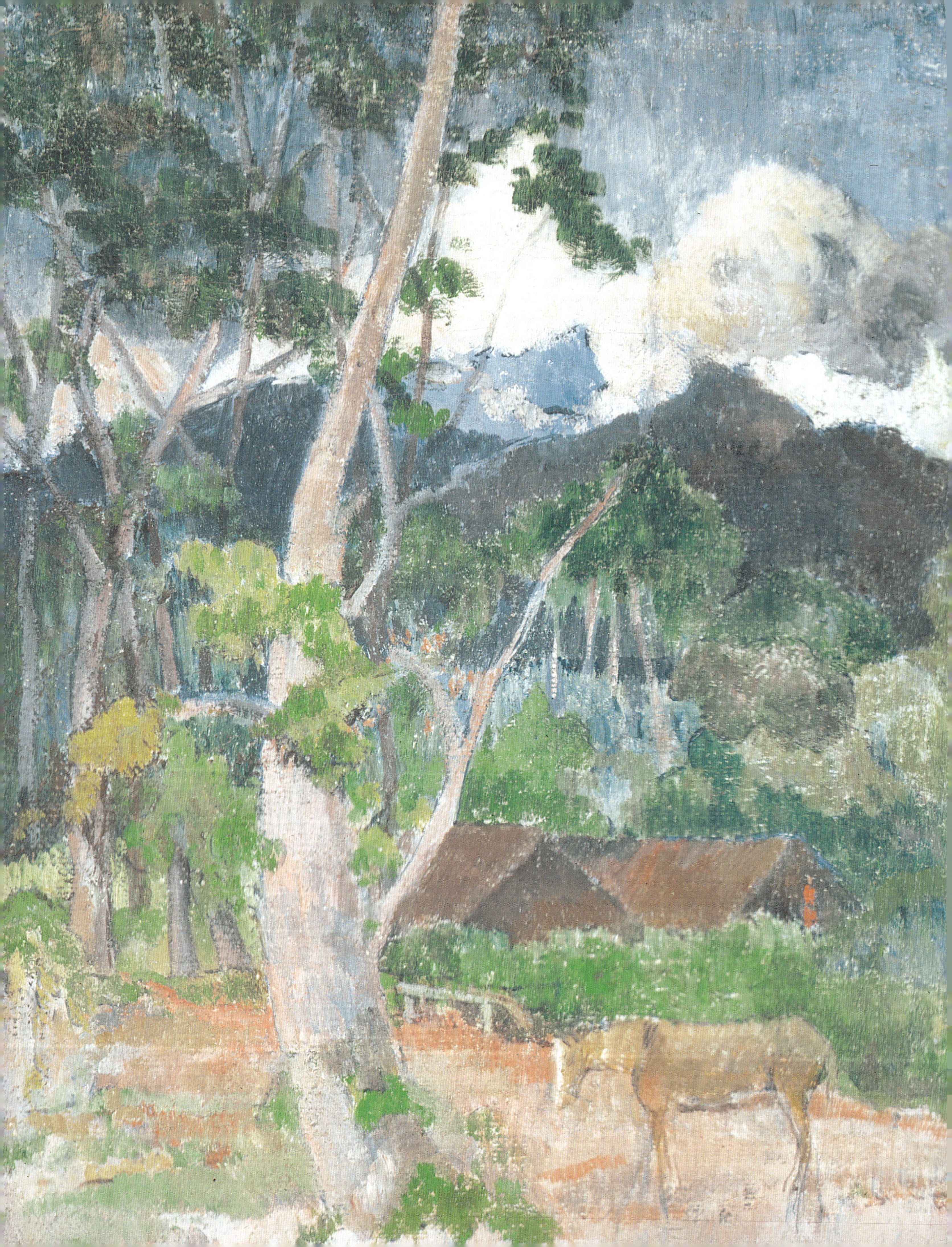

TURNER TO MONET

the triumph of landscape painting

Christine Dixon, Ron Radford and Lucina Ward

■ national gallery of **australia**

Produced by the Publishing Department of the National Gallery of Australia
nga.gov.au

The National Gallery of Australia is an Australian Government Agency

Text editing: Ariana Klepac and Eric Meredith*
Design: Kristin Thomas*
Index: Trevor Mathews
Rights and permissions: Nick Nicholson*
Print: National Capital Printing, Canberra
* National Gallery of Australia

Revised reprint, 2008

Cataloguing-in-Publication

Dixon, Christine.
Turner to Monet: the triumph of landscape
Contributing authors, Christine Dixon; Ron Radford; Lucina Ward.
1st ed.
Parkes, ACT: National Gallery of Australia, 2008
ISBN: 9780642541635 (pbk)
Landscape painting-19th century.
Radford, Ron, 1949-
Ward, Lucina.
National Gallery of Australia.
758.1

Distributed in Australia by
Thames and Hudson
11 Central Boulevard Business Park
Port Melbourne, Victoria, 3207

Distributed in the United Kingdom by
Thames and Hudson
181A High Holborn
London, WC1V 7QX

Distributed in the United States of America by
University of Washington Press
1326 Fifth Avenue, Ste 555
Seattle, WA 98101-2604

Published on the occasion of the exhibition
Turner to Monet: the triumph of landscape
14 March – 9 June 2008

The exhibition was organised by the National Gallery of Australia, Canberra

The exhibition was curated in Canberra by:
Christine Dixon, Ron Radford and Lucina Ward
Exhibition assistants: Niki van den Heuvel and Simeran Maxwell

The Nine Network is proud to sponsor the *Turner to Monet* exhibition

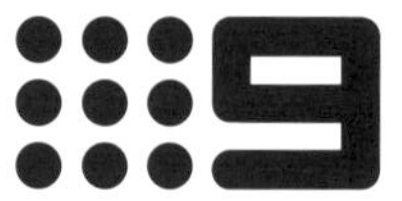

Indemnified by the Commonwealth through the Australian Government's Art Indemnity Australia program, administered by the Department of the Environment, Water, Heritage and the Arts

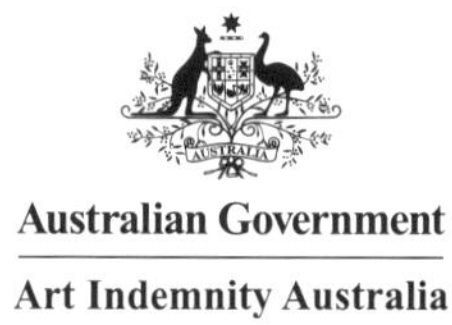

Supporting sponsor ADSHEL

Front cover: cat. 31 **J.M.W. Turner** *The Red Rigi* 1842 (detail) National Gallery of Victoria

Back cover: cat. 97 **Claude Monet** *Morning haze* 1894 Philadelphia Museum of Art

Page ii: cat. 99 **Paul Gauguin** *Landscape with a horse* 1899 (detail) Saint Louis Art Museum

Section openers: (details) cat. 19 **John Glover** *A view of the artist's house and garden, in Mills Plains, Van Diemen's Land* 1835; cat. 44 **J.M.W. Turner** *Waves breaking against the wind* c. 1840; cat. 59 **Martin Johnson Heade** *Sunlight and shadow, the Newbury Marshes* c. 1871–75; cat. 73 **Charles Daubigny** *A snow scene, Valmondois* 1875; cat. 92 **Paul Gauguin** *Haystacks in Brittany* 1890

Contents

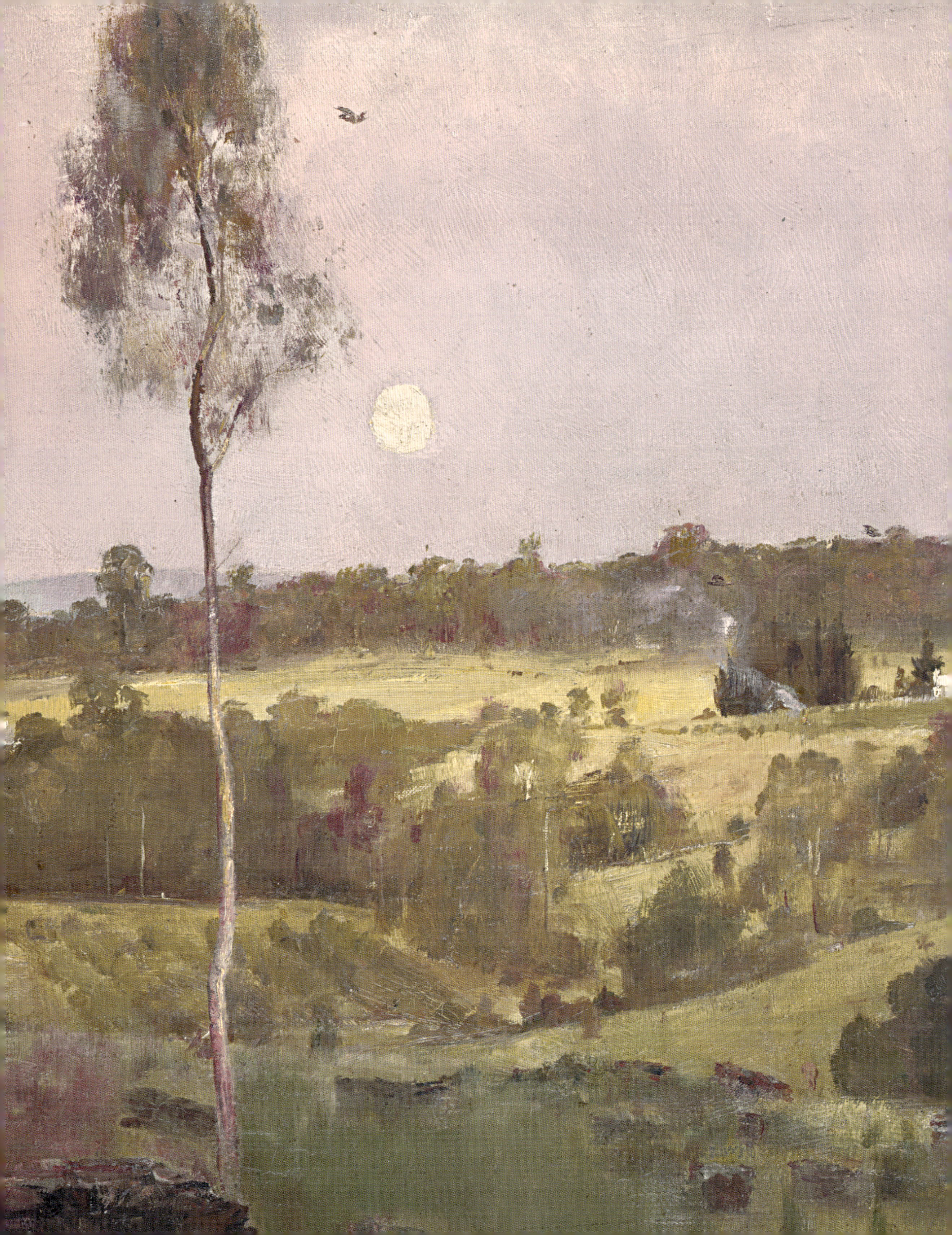

Prime Minister's foreword

Turner to Monet: the triumph of landscape is, in every sense, a landmark exhibition. It is the most comprehensive survey of nineteenth-century Western landscape painting ever assembled and showcases Australian landscape painting of the nineteenth century in an international context.

Drawn from public and private collections in Australia and abroad, this outstanding exhibition is the result of intensive research, negotiation and organisation. I commend the National Gallery of Australia for developing and presenting this important exhibition.

This exhibition also represents a milestone in the Australian Government's support for the arts. *Turner to Monet* is the 100th exhibition made possible by Art Indemnity Australia, through which the Commonwealth indemnifies major exhibitions of significant cultural material. More than 21 million visitors have accessed works covered by the scheme since it was established in 1979.

The Government is committed to supporting the creative vision of Australian artists and a vibrant and diverse arts sector. Our great national cultural institutions, including the National Gallery of Australia, make significant contributions to Australian society and identity. I am looking forward to the completion next year of the improvements and extensions to the gallery, which are currently under construction.

I hope many Australians will visit our national gallery and take this unique opportunity to experience the work of the foremost Western landscape artists to have practised in this country and the wider world.

The Honourable Kevin Rudd, MP
Prime Minister of Australia

cat. 78 **Tom Roberts** *'Evening, when the quiet east flushes faintly at the sun's last look'* 1887–88 (detail)

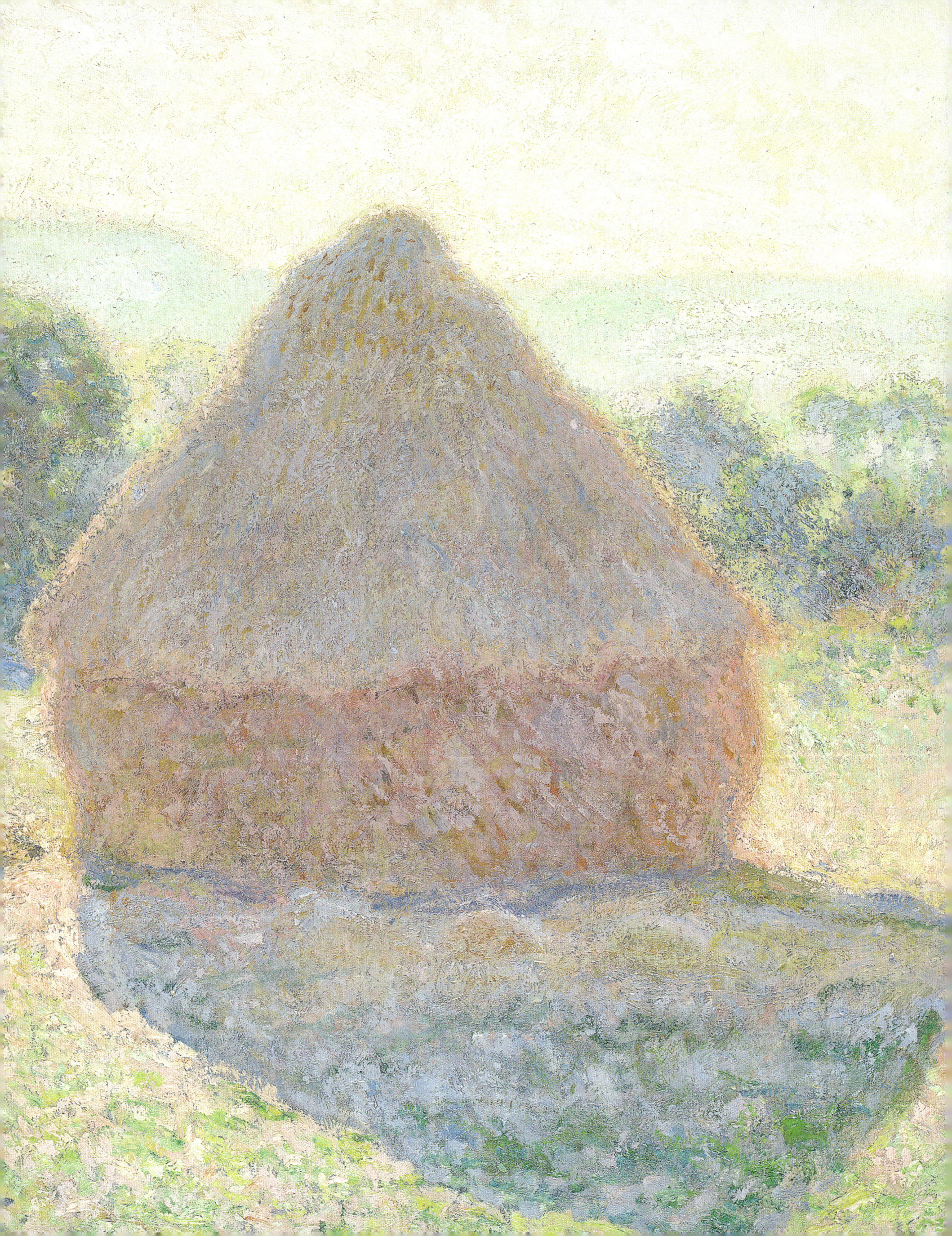

Director's foreword

The nineteenth century was the most splendid period in the history of Western landscape painting. This exhibition, *Turner to Monet: the triumph of landscape*, therefore stands for more than an analysis of nineteenth-century landscape painting; it demonstrates the triumph of landscape over other forms of art.

There are few countries in which landscape painting has been so important to the national culture as it has in this country. Since the mid nineteenth century Australia has been obsessed with its own landscape art; it is a part of our culture that has become a major force. Australia's first art museums were founded in the second half of the nineteenth century in the various British colonies that became our present-day states. From the beginning they collected major local landscapes, as well as the more conservative British landscapes of the period. From the early twentieth century the National Gallery of Victoria in Melbourne began collecting early Romantic British landscapes, and Barbizon and Impressionist French landscapes. Other state galleries did so, although less prolifically, and only after the mid twentieth century. At the mid-century, Adelaide and Melbourne also started to put together substantial collections of Italian and Dutch seventeenth-century landscapes; in the later twentieth century Sydney followed. And in the last two and a half decades, the newly established National Gallery of Australia in Canberra began to acquire Impressionist and Post-Impressionist works.

Australians have not only been great admirers and painters of their own landscape but also significant collectors of international landscape painting. Therefore, *Turner to Monet: the triumph of landscape* deliberately includes a substantial number – more than one third of the European works – from Australian public collections. The exhibition embraces the artists and the themes explored in the earlier landscape exhibitions produced by the National Gallery of Australia, but it adds other strains to show the full impact of the rise of landscape painting in Europe and the New World in the nineteenth century. It includes the early English watercolour tradition as well as oil paintings; German and Northern European Romantic landscape, not seen in Australia before; and Post-Impressionist landscape painting, which is not well represented in Australian collections. In addition to the principal European countries, America and Australia, there are landscape images of Russia, South America, Tahiti and New Zealand. Indeed, no single exhibition anywhere has hitherto attempted to explore the complex development of nineteenth-century landscape painting. We make no apology for generous inclusions of Australia's own exemplary landscapes and for placing them for the first time in the full context of international art.

For the past decade or so the National Gallery of Australia – which opened to the public as recently as 1982 – has explored important aspects of nineteenth-century landscape painting in a series of major exhibitions. The first was the great *Turner* exhibition of 1996, followed in 1998 by *New worlds from old: 19th century Australian and American landscapes*. In 2001 the National Gallery of Australia staged the ground-breaking *Monet and Japan* and in 2006 we assembled the substantial exhibition *Constable: impressions of land, sea and sky*. In 2007 *Ocean to Outback: Australian landscape painting 1850–1950* explored the dominant one hundred years of landscape art. A large national survey, including many Australian masterpieces, *Ocean to Outback*

cat. 89 **Claude Monet** *Haystacks, midday* 1890 (detail)

was designed for an extensive tour of smaller and regional galleries throughout Australia as part of the National Gallery of Australia's 25th Anniversary celebrations. At the time of the present exhibition, *Ocean to Outback* is still touring.

I would like to thank my co-curators of the exhibition, Christine Dixon, Senior Curator of International Painting and Sculpture and Lucina Ward, Curator of International Painting and Sculpture. Exhibition Assistants Niki van den Heuvel and Simeran Maxwell have also ably contributed to our project.

I would like to thank all the British, European and American art museums, who have kindly agreed to part with their works. Likewise I thank our generous Australian institutional lenders, particularly the National Gallery of Victoria, the Art Gallery of South Australia and the Art Gallery of New South Wales. We are also grateful for loans from eight private collections around the world. All lenders to the exhibition are acknowledged more specifically on the following page.

Exhibitions such as these are costly to mount, with so many international and local loans: they cannot be put on without sponsorship and government support. I would especially like to express our appreciation to Harold Mitchell, AO, and the exhibition's major sponsor, Nine Network, in particular its Chief Executive Officer David Gyngell, for their generous support of this exhibition. Qantas, for many years, has been generous with financial subsidies and continues to be a much-valued supporter of the Gallery's exhibitions. We are grateful also to Adshel for their support of the exhibition.

This extraordinarily valuable exhibition could not have taken place without the assistance of Art Indemnity Australia, the Australian Government's art indemnity scheme through which loans to the exhibition have been indemnified. We are pleased *Turner to Monet* will commemorate the one hundredth exhibition Art Indemnity Australia has supported.

Turner to Monet: the triumph of landscape is the first attempt to show the full scope of nineteenth-century landscape art in Europe and the New World throughout the full chronological range of that century, and the exhibition and its supporting catalogue should therefore be of great art-historical interest. More importantly, we hope the exhibition will bring enormous pleasure and joy to our visitors by the sheer beauty of more than one hundred landscapes.

Ron Radford, AM
Director, National Gallery of Australia, Canberra

Lenders to the exhibition

Art Gallery of South Australia, Adelaide
Christopher Menz, Director
Jane Messenger, Curator of European Art
Tracey Lock-Weir, Curator of Australian Painting and Sculpture

Ballarat Fine Art Gallery, Victoria
Gordon Morrison, Director

Queensland Art Gallery, Brisbane
Tony Ellwood, Director
Julie Ewington, Head of Australian Art

Hamilton Art Gallery, Victoria
Daniel McOwan, Director

Tasmanian Museum and Art Gallery, Hobart
Bill Bleathman, Director

National Gallery of Victoria, Melbourne
Dr Gerard Vaughan, Director
Frances Lindsay, Deputy Director

Art Gallery of Western Australia, Perth
Alan R. Dodge, former Director
Gary Dufour, Acting Director

Art Gallery of New South Wales, Sydney
Edmund Capon, AM, OBE, Director
Anthony Bond, General Manager, Curatorial Services
Barry Pearce, Head Curator, Australian Art

Staatliche Kunstsammlungen Dresden
Prof. Dr Martin Roth, Director-General

Galerie Neue Meister, Dresden
Dr Ulrich Bischoff, Director

Hamburger Kunsthalle, Hamburg
Prof. Dr Hubertus Gaßner, Director
Dr Jenns E. Howoldt, Curator

Van Gogh Museum, Amsterdam
Axel Rüger, Director
Leo Jansen, Curator of Paintings

Kröller-Müller Museum, Otterlo
Dr Evert van Straaten, Director
Dr Liz Kreijn, Head Collection Presentation

Bergen Kunstmuseum
Audun Eckhoff, Department Director and Deputy Director
Knut Ormhaug, Senior Curator

Museo Thyssen-Bornemisza, Madrid
Dr Guillermo Solana, Chief Curator

Fondation Beyeler, Basel
Ernst Beyeler
Dr Ulf Küster, Curator

Ministry of Defence Art Collection, London
Charlotte Henwood, Registrar

Royal Academy of Arts, London
Dr Charles Saumarez Smith, Secretary and Chief Executive
Dr MaryAnne Stevens, Director of Academic Affairs

Tate
Dr Stephen Deuchar, Director, Tate Britain
David Blayney Brown and Ian Warrell, Curators

Victoria & Albert Museum, London
Mark Jones, Director
Dr Mark Evans, Senior Curator of Paintings, Word and Image Department

National Galleries of Scotland
John Leighton, Director-General
Michael Clark, Director, National Gallery of Scotland, Edinburgh
Aidan Weston-Lewis, Chief Curator of Italian and Spanish Art

J. Paul Getty Museum, Los Angeles
Dr Michael Brand, Director
Dr Scott Schaefer, Curator of Paintings

Los Angeles County Museum of Art
Michael Govan, Director and Chief Executive Officer
Dr Ilene Susan Fort, Gail & John Liebes Curator of American Art

Yale Center for British Art, New Haven
Dr Amy Meyers, Director
Angus Trumble, Curator of Paintings and Sculpture

Allen Memorial Art Museum, Oberlin, Ohio
Dr Stephanie Wiles, John G.W. Cowles Director

Philadelphia Museum of Art, Philadelphia
Anne d'Harnoncourt, The George D. Widener Director and Chief Executive Officer
Joseph J. Rishel, The Gisela and Dennis Alter Senior Curator of European Painting before 1900

Saint Louis Art Museum, Missouri
Dr Brent R. Benjamin, Director
Dr Andrew J. Walker, Assistant Director for Curatorial Affairs, Curator of American Art
Dr Charlotte Eyerman, Curator of Modern and Contemporary Art

Fine Arts Museums of San Francisco
John E. Buchanan Jr, Director

California Palace of the Legion of Honor Museum
Dr Lynn Federle Orr, Curator-in-Charge of European Art

M.H. de Young Memorial Museum
Timothy Anglin Burgard, The Ednah Root Curator of American Art, Curator-in-Charge, American Art

Toledo Museum of Art, Ohio
Dr Don Bacigalupi, President, Director and Chief Executive Officer
Dr Lawrence W. Nichols, William Hutton Curator, European and American Painting and Sculpture before 1900

National Gallery of Art, Washington
Earl A. Powell III, Director
The late Philip Conisbee, Senior Curator of European Paintings
Dr Franklin Kelly, Senior Curator of American and British Painting

Smithsonian American Art Museum, Washington
Dr Elizabeth Broun, The Margaret and Terry Stent Director
Dr Eleanor Jones Harvey, Chief Curator

James O. Fairfax, AO, Australia

Asbjorn R. Lunde, New York

The Duke of Northumberland, Great Britain

Kerry Stokes Collection, Perth
Kerry Stokes, AO
The late John Stringer

John Wilmerding, USA

Galerie Paffrath, Düsseldorf
Hans-Christian Paffrath

Galerie Hans, Hamburg
Mathias F. Hans

French & Company, New York
Henry Zimet

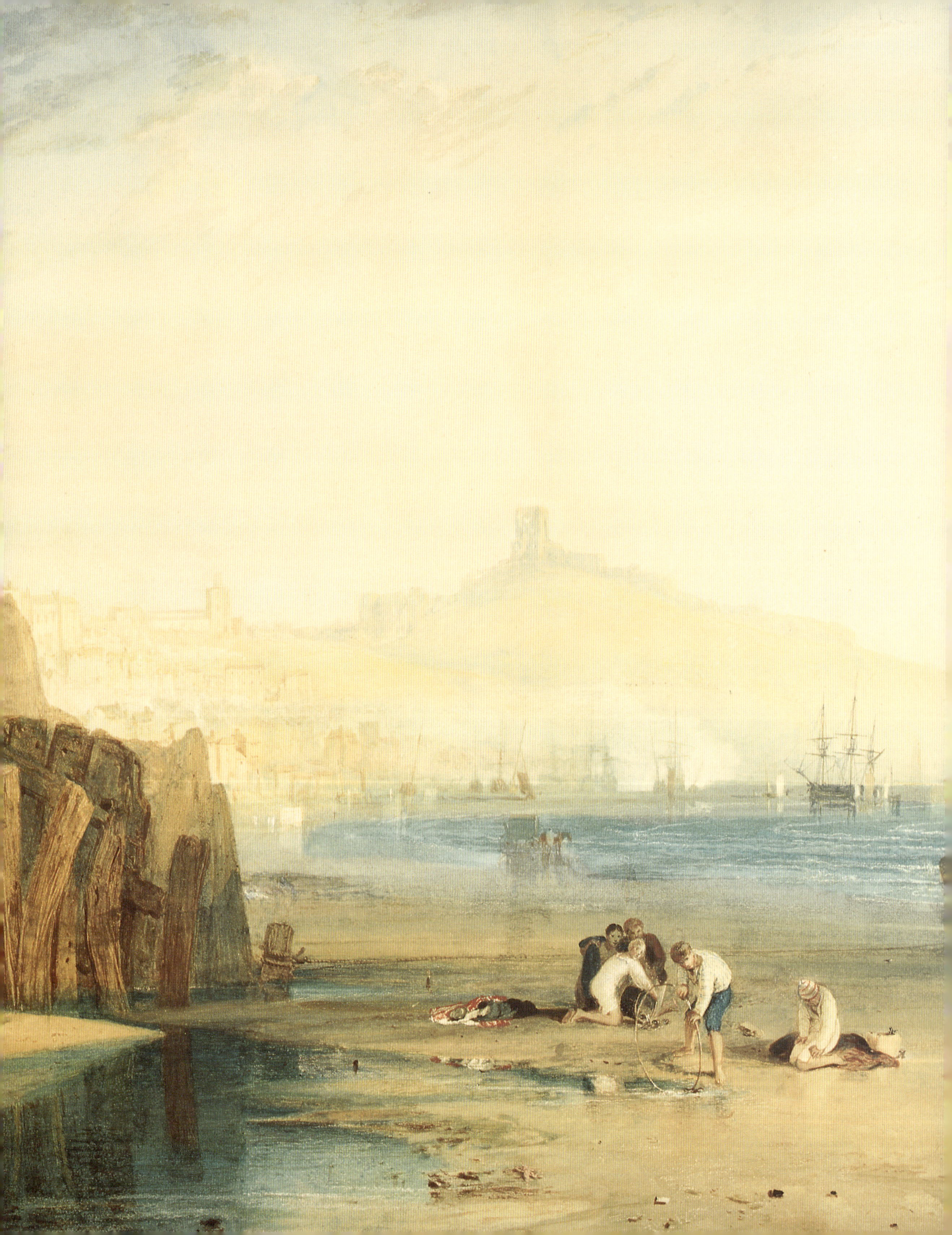

occasional landscape sales or commissions by landowner clients. He died neglected, in 1782, exactly 100 years after his Roman inspirer, Claude Lorrain. Wilson's art was not fully appreciated again until a new generation of aspiring landscape painters and collectors emerged at the beginning of the nineteenth century.

Continental landscape paintings of the past had long been collected by the British. In the eighteenth century the great art collectors of Britain, nearly all of whom had undertaken the then customary Grand Tour culminating in Rome, eventually acquired most of Claude Lorrain's Roman landscape oeuvre. By the beginning of the nineteenth century, Britain had also accumulated much of Rosa's and Dughet's oeuvre. British grandees also collected large numbers of Dutch seventeenth-century landscapes and seascapes.

Before the establishment of a National Gallery in London, private collections containing old master Dutch and Italian landscapes were usually accessible to artists and students; from 1812, old master landscape paintings could be seen at the Dulwich Picture Gallery on the outskirts of London. In 1824 the gift of Sir George Beaumont's collection helped establish Britain's National Gallery; it contained major paintings by Claude Lorrain and other seventeenth-century European landscape artists, as well as British works by Wilson. Beaumont, himself an amateur landscapist, was a mentor of artists including the young John Constable (1776–1837), but not J.M.W Turner (1775–1851). Therefore, more than their European contemporaries, British artists had remarkable access to earlier European masters of landscape.

Appreciation of Britain's own natural landscape also began to grow, especially from the 1790s to the mid 1810s, when the wars with France stifled travel on the Continent. Within Britain, increasing travel to the fashionably 'picturesque' regions of North Wales, the Highlands of Scotland and the English Lake District encouraged interest in paintings, particularly watercolours, of those and other attractive British regions. This regional particularism was paralleled and influenced by the great English Romantic nature poets, most notably William Wordsworth.

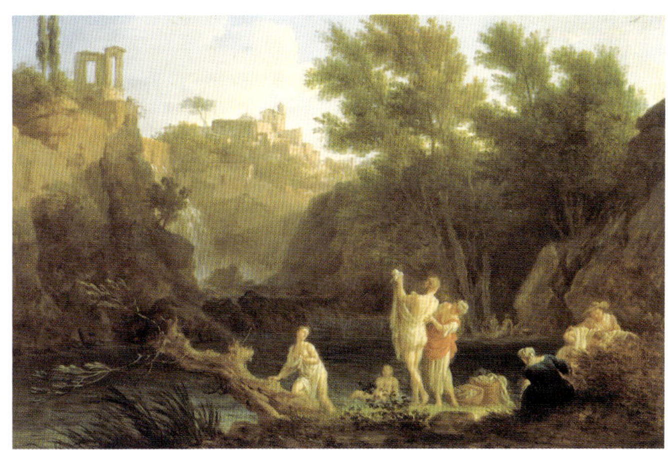

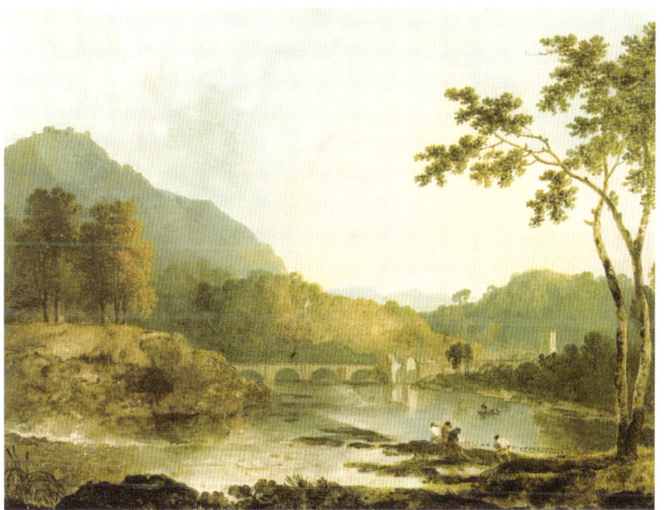

(above)
fig. 4 **Joseph Vernet** *The four times of day: evening* 1757 oil on silvered copper 29.5 x 43.5 cm Art Gallery of South Australia, Adelaide Gift of James Fairfax through the Art Gallery of South Australia Foundation 1998; fig. 5 **Richard Wilson** *Dinas Bran from Llangollen* c. 1772–75 oil on canvas 82.5 x 104.1 cm Gift of Gladys Penfold Hyland in memory of her husband Frank 1964 Art Gallery of South Australia, Adelaide

(opposite)
fig. 1 **Claude Lorrain** *Capriccio with ruins of the Roman Forum* c. 1634 oil on canvas 79.7 x 118.8 cm Art Gallery of South Australia, Adelaide Gift of the Art Gallery of South Australia Foundation assisted by the State Bank of South Australia on the occasion of the 150th Anniversary of South Australia 1985; fig. 2 **Salvator Rosa** *Romantic landscape with Mercury and Argus* c. 1655–60 oil on canvas 123.5 x 203.4 cm Felton Bequest, 1951 National Gallery of Victoria, Melbourne; fig. 3 **Jacob van Ruisdael** *Landscape with a mill-run and ruins* c. 1653 oil on canvas 59.3 x 66.1 cm Art Gallery of South Australia, Adelaide Gift of James and Diana Ramsay and the James and Diana Ramsay Fund through the Art Gallery of South Australia Foundation 1985

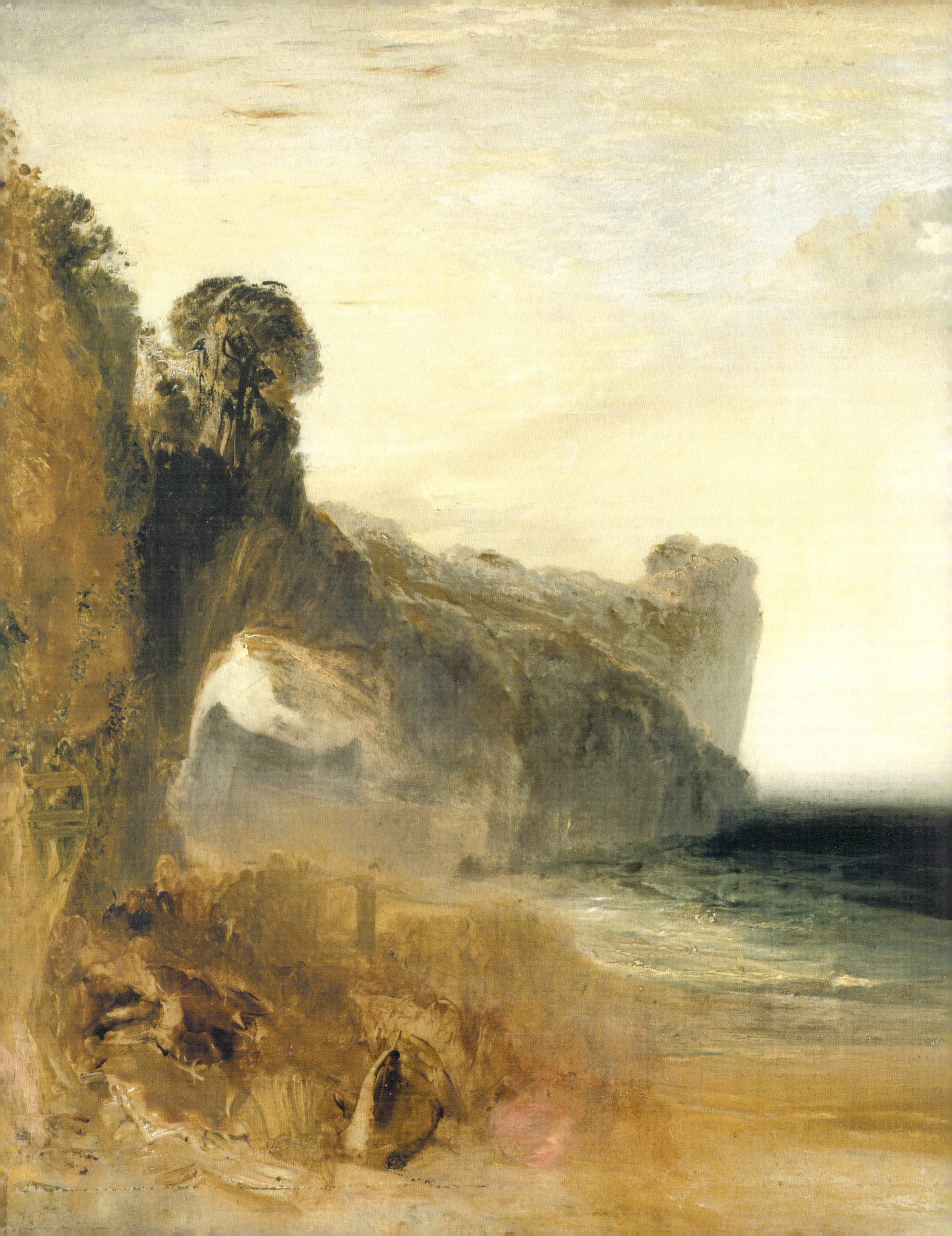

Watercolour painting, particularly of landscape, began to expand in popularity in the 1790s. Dr Thomas Monro who held a salon of artists and patrons for the appreciation of watercolours, collected fine examples as well as commissioning copies, particularly of the poetic watercolours of John Robert Cozens (1752–1797). Prominent artists who attended these gatherings (and were asked to copy Cozens's work) included the young watercolourists Thomas Girtin (1775–1802) and Turner. These two artists soon became the major pioneers of British landscape. Girtin led the way in watercolour, but died young at twenty-seven at the beginning of the century. The stippled romantic realism of his *Alnwick from Brizlee* c. 1800 (cat. 1) contrasts with the extremely dramatic 'gothic' romanticism and clear unbroken washes of another view of *Alnwick Castle* c. 1829 (cat. 30) painted much later by his early rival Turner.

An unprecedented flourishing in watercolour painting was helped by the establishment of the Society of Painters in Water Colours in 1804 and later by a number of offshoot societies for the exhibition and promotion of the medium. Britain did not invent watercolour painting but it certainly perfected and proliferated its use, and became renowned throughout Europe for proficiency in the medium. As early as the 1760s Sandby was the first whose work went beyond mere topographical recording – which was the usual earlier use for the medium – to create fully composed natural landscapes, often animated with lively figures. Many of Sandby's landscapes were large in scale to compete with oil paintings when displayed; his forest scene of 1801 (cat. 2) is a striking example, inspired, like much of his work, by Dutch realism. He lived and worked into the first decade of the nineteenth century and survived long enough to witness and benefit from the watercolour boom.

Watercolour was a more portable medium than oils, easier for artists to carry when travelling in search of picturesque local scenery. Long before the invention of photography, watercolour was also a convenient medium with which to document educational tours of the Continent or distant voyages of scientific discovery. As the world's leading maritime power in the eighteenth and nineteenth centuries, Britain led the way in its recording of new lands. It is no accident that as Britain's empire expanded around the globe, paintings of land and sea increasingly became the main focus of British art and the art of some of her colonies, including South Africa, India, Australia and New Zealand. Landscape painting was part of British nationalism, a way of relating to distinctly British scenery and also to the new possessions claimed for a growing empire.

By the late 1790s, Girtin may have been in the forefront of the new watercolourists, but Turner, his friend and rival, diversified into oil painting. In the first decade of the nineteenth century, Turner began to dazzle his contemporaries at the Royal Academy with landscapes in oil, translating the Italian Classical and Dutch realist traditions he so admired into brilliantly convincing English landscapes. The other great landscape painter in Britain in the early nineteenth century was Turner's contemporary, John Constable (cat. 7, 8, 11, 12, 14–17). He has become known as the quintessential English landscape artist of all time, but was slow to develop and inspire his English audience. Although Constable began his oil landscapes at the very start of the century they matured only after 1810 and did not become fully acceptable to his colleagues at the Royal Academy until the late 1820s.

The 1820s finally witnessed the undisputed triumph of British landscape painting. By then Turner was so confident of his popular and financial success as the nation's leading landscape artist, that he was able to experiment with paintings of light, radically abstracting his subjects almost beyond recognition. While he still continued to paint fully recognisable, and saleable, views in watercolour (sometimes as a basis for lucrative engravings) and oils, he also began to paint the fantasies of golden vapour and light which the modern eye most admires and which we see in Melbourne's almost abstract dissolving *A mountain scene, Val d'Aosta* c. 1841–45 (cat. 46). Turner was the darling of the Royal Academy, elected an Associate at the age of twenty-four, and becoming a full Academician only three years later in 1802. If his audiences were bewildered by his later experimental works, Turner had already enjoyed more than two decades of popular acclaim and success. Constable received no such early support and had to wait until 1829, when he was fifty-two, to gain full membership of the Academy. However, earlier, in 1824 he had exhibited his now iconic *The hay wain*

cat. 26 **J.M.W. Turner** *Rocky bay with figures* c. 1830 (detail) © Tate, London 2007

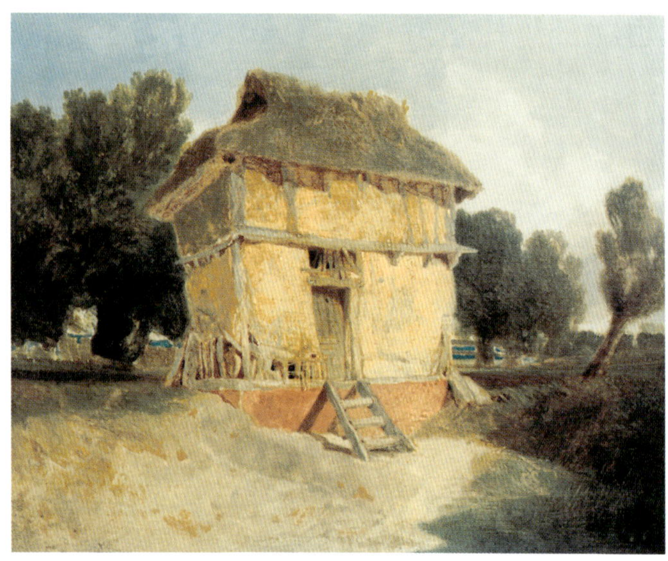

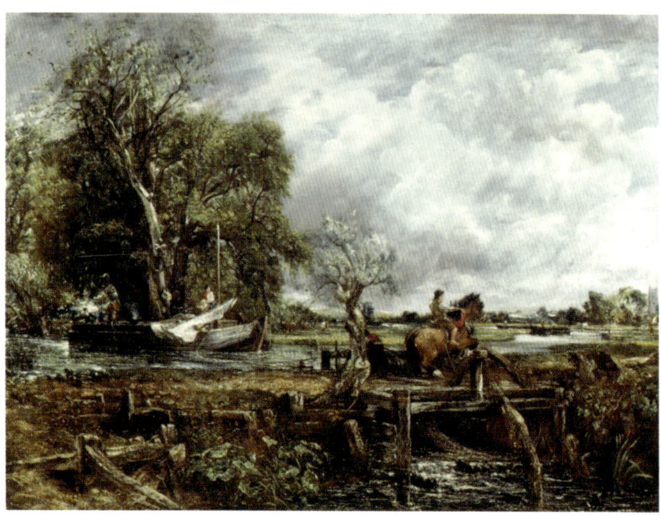

fig. 6 **John Sell Cotman** *The old pigeon house, Downham Market* c. 1810
oil on canvas 32.5 x 39.7 cm
Art Gallery of South Australia, Adelaide
Gift of William Bowmore AO OBE through the Art Gallery of South Australia Foundation 1999

cat. 7 **John Constable** *The leaping horse* 1825

(along with two other paintings) at the Paris Salon where it was much admired, notably by the Romantic artist Eugène Delacroix (1798–1863). Later, the Barbizon School painters, especially Théodore Rousseau (1812–1867), were much influenced by Constable's radical naturalism.

In the 1820s Constable's works gained greater confidence and he displayed more of his large 'six footers' (183 cm wide). Among them *The leaping horse* 1825 (cat. 7) was one of two major works he chose to leave with the Royal Academy under the terms of election to full membership. Its earthy rural dampness, black greens and sparkling white highlights contrast with Turner's golden vapours of similar date. By the 1820s, apart from Turner and Constable, there were other major and by then successful British landscape artists. Samuel Palmer (1805–1881) at the village of Shoreham in Kent executed arcadian pastorals inspired by William Blake (1757–1827), which are amongst the great works of nineteenth-century British art. *The sleeping shepherd* 1833–34 (cat. 18) is a tender example. John Sell Cotman's (1782–1842) watercolours and oils (fig. 6), and those by his contemporaries of the Norwich School, were well recognised by the 1820s as major landscapes. British watercolourists such as Anthony Vandyke Copley Fielding (1787–1855), Peter De Wint (1784–1849) (cat. 4) and John Glover (1767–1849) (cat. 6, 19, 39, 52, 53), and many others, produced some of their finest English works during the same triumphant 1820s moment.

When Sir Thomas Lawrence (1769–1830), Britain's greatest portrait painter of the time, died in 1830 with a global reputation he ended a long line of eminent British portrait painters. Reynolds's most esteemed successor, Lawrence became President of the Royal Academy in 1820, but his death ten years later sounded the death knell to the prestige of the long and venerable tradition of British portrait painting which had dominated British art for the previous 300 years. No one in the British art world or on the Continent doubted that by this time British landscape painting had indeed triumphed, and was influencing art beyond Britain.

Australia before 1850

Australia was colonised by the British in the late eighteenth century, at the very time that landscape art was on the rise in Britain. The young English painter William Westall (1781–1850) was the first professed professional landscapist to arrive in Australian waters. During 1801–03 he was part of Matthew Flinders's team sent out to circumnavigate, chart and record the coastline of Australia. The few landscape watercolours he executed here (he made many pencil drawings and coastal profiles) show the stippled influence of Girtin (fig. 7). Back in London, in 1809 he was asked to make nine oils from his Australian sketches; they are the first large Australian landscapes in oil and were exhibited at the Royal Academy to some acclaim. Westall's oils show an exotic Australia (cat. 50), just as the pictures by English artists Thomas Daniell (1749–1840) and William Daniell (1769–1837), also displayed at the Academy a little earlier, had depicted an even more exotic India (fig. 8). (William Daniell had been chosen as the artist for Flinders's voyage, but his imminent marriage to Westall's sister prevented him from sailing and he suggested to authorities that his young future brother-in-law Westall should go instead.)

Although there was a number of other resident landscape painters in Australia in the first decades of the nineteenth century, it was not until the 1830s, when John Glover arrived in Hobart and Conrad Martens (1801–1878) (cat. 34) came to Sydney, that Australia received its first long-term, resident, professional landscape painters. By that time, landscape painting was the established major art form in Britain and it was soon to become so in her Australian colonies – as it was in America, largely led by Thomas Cole (1801–1848) (cat. 51).

Glover had made his fortune in watercolour painting during the first decade of the nineteenth century, and painted in oils and watercolour into the 1820s. He was an established landscape artist when, in 1830 at the age of sixty-three, he decided to follow his sons who had settled as farmers in Tasmania. There he painted his finest and most naturalistic landscapes, often of his own farm – as vividly captured in the painting of his newly established house and flowering garden (cat. 19) – but also landscapes inhabited by the Tasmanian

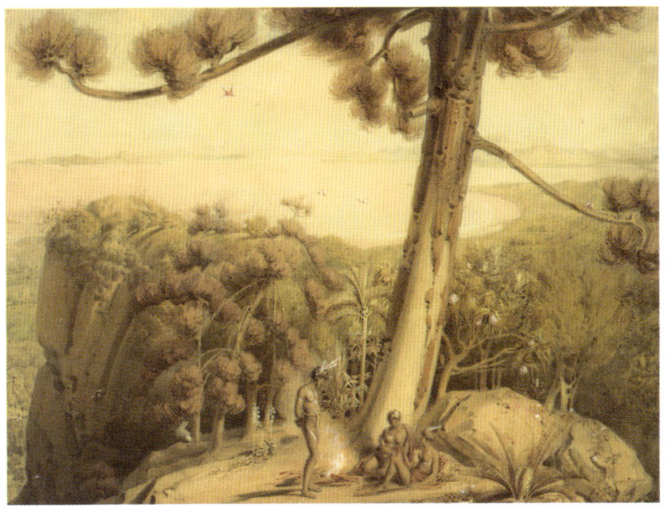

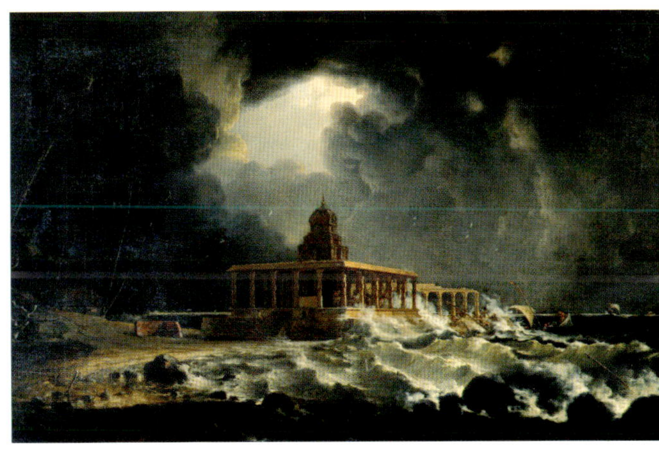

fig. 7 **William Westall** *Port Bowen* 1802?
watercolour on paper 56.0 x 77.5 cm National Library of Australia, Canberra

fig. 8 **William Daniell** *A Hindoo temple on the island of Rameswaram, with the approach of the north-east monsoon, Tamil Nadu* c. 1802
oil on canvas 76.0 x 122.0 cm
© Victoria Memorial Hall, Kolkata, India

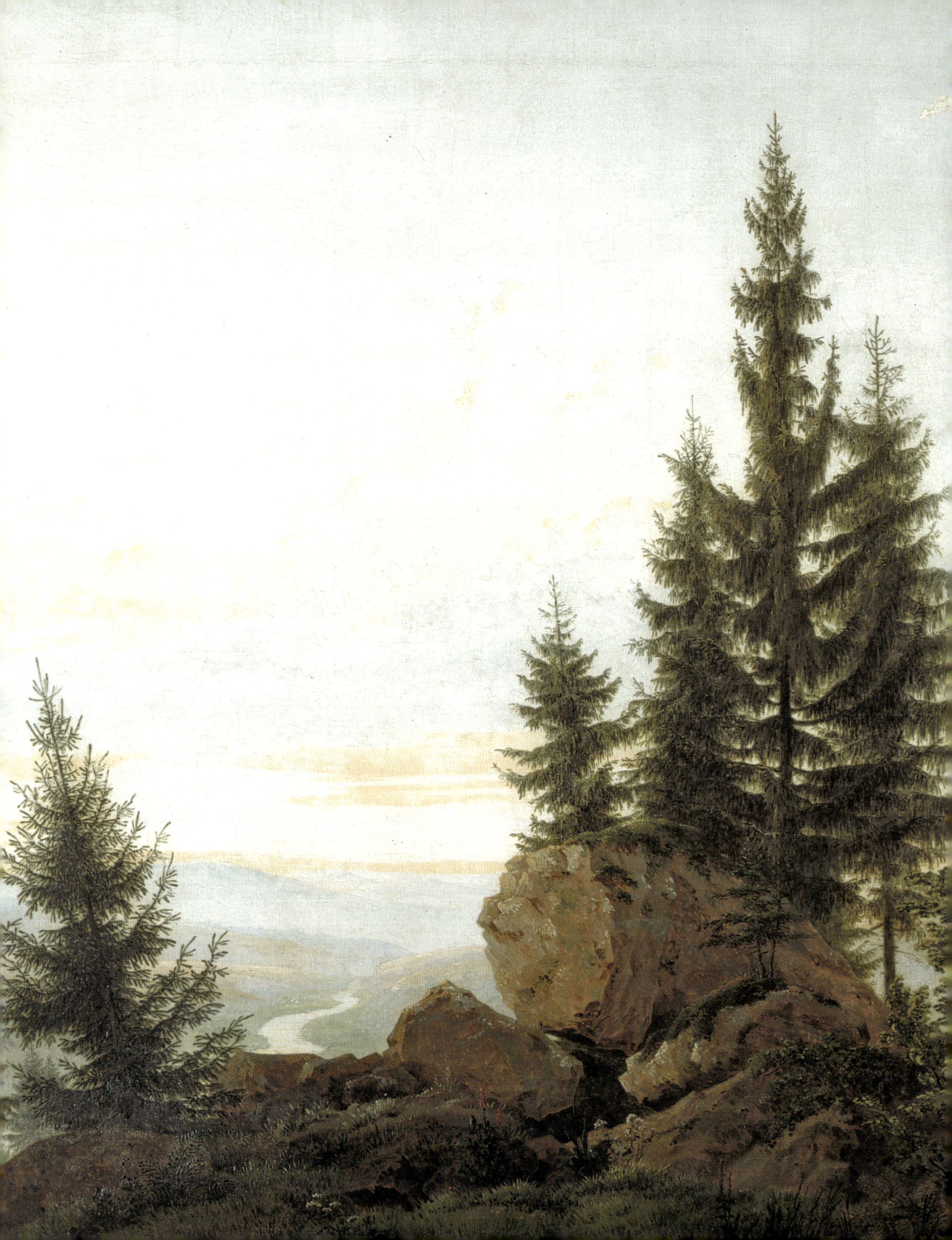

Aborigines (cat. 39), in whose 'primitive' pastoral way of life he took a serious interest. Glover sent a remarkable exhibition of these paintings (including cat. 19, 39, 52) back to Bond Street, London, in 1835. This was Australia's first major cultural exchange with the motherland.

Martens arrived in the growing mercantile city of Sydney in 1835 and painted sublime harbour views, pastoral homesteads and, later, mountain views. He had been a watercolour student of Copley Fielding's and, from his arrival in Sydney until his death in 1878, was the leading landscape painter in the colony of New South Wales. Martens brought the British Romantic watercolour tradition of Turner to Australia, as can be seen in his moody study of clouds and weather from rugged rocks in *View of Sydney from Neutral Bay* c. 1857 (cat. 34), painted more than twenty years after his arrival.

It is not surprising that in the first half of the nineteenth century it was British artists who came to Australia and influenced landscape painting. Nor is it unusual that many of them were landscape painters in watercolour. After Martens's arrival came the watercolourist John Skinner Prout (1806–1876), who worked in Sydney then Hobart, and S.T. Gill (1818–1880) and George French Angas (1822–1886), who worked in Adelaide. There was a change, however, after the gold rushes of the 1850s; most arrivals in Australia then were German and Swiss Romantic landscape artists, who painted in oil.

Germany and Switzerland

German Romantic landscape evolved early in the nineteenth century, less than a decade after it had in Britain. Of all English artists, Turner was the most aware of the art of German Romantic painters, some of whom he met on his travels to Italy and Germany. They in turn knew his works because of his exhibition in Germany, and the dissemination of his engravings. They did not appreciate his lack of detail. The greatest exponent of German Romanticism was Caspar David Friedrich (1774–1840), who worked in Dresden. His landscapes were visionary and one of his earliest oil paintings, *The Cross in the mountains* 1807–08, was designed and framed as an altarpiece. That a landscape could become an altarpiece, that nature should be worshipped in such an obvious way, gave a new status to landscape art. Friedrich's 'gothic' religious interpretations of vertical German fir trees, ancient oaks, sublime mountains and deserted coasts are intensely spiritual. Unlike Turner's later works, nothing is generalised. He was highly selective in what he chose to emphasise in nature, but he painted his selection in all its detail – God is in the detail of creation. The mountain fir trees in his early *View of the Elbe Valley* c. 1807 (cat. 27) take on the appearance and reverence of gothic church spires. His contemporary and friend, Johan Christian Dahl (1788–1857) (a Norwegian working in Germany), and the Germans Carl Gustav Carus (1789–1869) (cat. 35), Wilhelm von Kobell (1766–1853?) (cat. 64) and the architect and painter Karl Friedrich Schinkel (1781–1841), followed Friedrich's lead in their Romantic and detailed interpretation of nature.[1]

This is the German tradition in which Eugene von Guérard's (1811–1901) career had developed before he arrived in Australia in 1852, lured by the gold rushes in Victoria. By the mid 1850s he was producing sublime wilderness landscapes in great detail, such as the hard country that retains a poignant, marginalised Aboriginal presence in *Stony Rises, Lake Corangamite* 1857 (cat. 40) and later the breathtaking *North-east view from the northern top of Mount Kosciusko* 1863 (cat. 41). He also painted tamed nature in the form of commissioned homestead landscapes, which showed the harnessing of the land, for example *From the verandah of Purrumbete* 1858 and its partner, *Purrumbete from across the lake* 1858 (both cat. 21). Von Guérard brought German Romanticism to the southern hemisphere, best evinced in his paintings of the fiords and alps of New Zealand (cat. 58).

The Swiss artist Nicholas Chevalier (1828–1902) (cat. 57), whose work would have been inspired by the popular Swiss alpine artist Alexandre Calame (1810–1864) (cat. 54), arrived in Australia at the end of 1854. Probably also influenced locally by von Guérard, Chevalier painted Australian alpine landscapes and grand waterfall and river subjects in the Northern European tradition. Australia's first locally born landscape painter W.C. Piguenit (1836–1914) was born in Tasmania of a convict father. He continued the Romantic mountain and river landscapes – though with a more painterly application – from the 1870s and into

cat. 27 **Caspar David Friedrich** *View of the Elbe Valley* c. 1807 (detail)

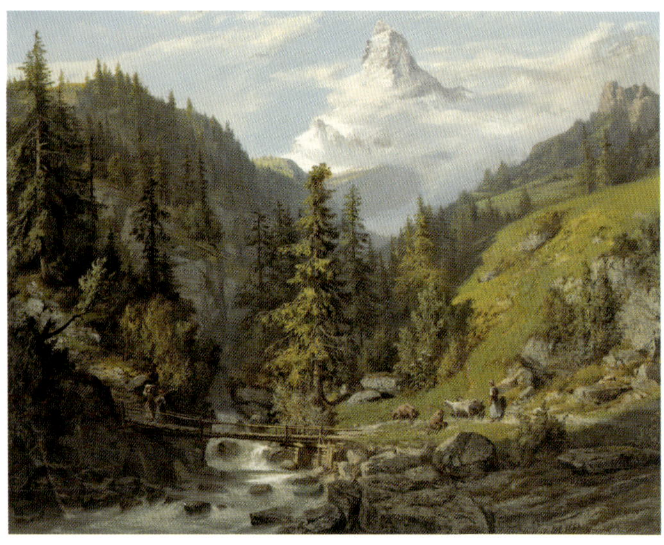

fig. 9 **Louis Buvelot** *The Matterhorn from Zermatt Valley* 1861
oil on canvas on composition board 110.3 x 145.2 cm
National Gallery of Australia, Canberra
Gift of L.A. Girardet 1941

the twentieth century. His *The flood in the Darling* 1890 (cat. 49) is the ultimate Romantic river scene, biblical in its overwhelming flood and dazzling light reflections.

Another Swiss artist who arrived in Australia in 1865, just before Piguenit's career began, was Louis Buvelot (1814–1888). Although he too, like Chevalier, was a follower of Calame's alpine scenes – as can be seen in his work *The Matterhorn from Zermatt Valley* 1861 (fig. 9) – Buvelot was also influenced by the naturalism and painterly qualities of the French Barbizon painters. In Australia, his approachable realism was a forerunner to, and an example for, the Australian Impressionism of the 1880s.

New terrains

Until the 1880s, when Australian-born and -trained artists began to predominate, nearly all Australian landscape painters came from, and were trained in, Britain or continental Europe. Unlike American landscape painters, such as Thomas Cole, Albert Bierstadt (1830–1902) and Frederic Church (1826–1900), the artists who came to more distant Australia did not have the option of easy return visits to Europe. Whereas American landscape painters regularly returned to Europe, constantly renewing their ties with past and current, but often conservative, European landscape painting, Australian artists were much more isolated. Because of this, and also due to the fact that they were faced with a remarkably different land and light, Australian artists developed a new and tougher realism, suitable for a less luxuriant country that could not be mistaken for Europe. We are aware of the landscapes that Glover, Martens, von Guérard and others painted before they came to Australia; and we can see that the transformation in their art once here was dramatic. They changed from run-of-the-mill predictable European landscape painters to strong Australian naturalistic landscape painters, perhaps more robust and less artificial than some of their American contemporaries.

But artists in America and Australia, and indeed other colonised countries, were united in the consciousness that they were painting new frontiers, landscapes that had never before been recorded. Consequently much nineteenth-century landscape painting in the New World has a sense of great wonderment.

The rise of landscape painting in the nineteenth century was of course in essence a northern hemisphere phenomenon. However, the new world of the southern hemisphere was brought into focus through the works of artists such as William Hodges (1744–1797), who accompanied Captain James Cook on his second voyage of discovery in the Pacific in the later eighteenth century, and Westall, who went on Flinders's voyage to Australian and Indonesian waters via South Africa at the beginning of the nineteenth century. The work of these two artists led a shift into scientific specificity in landscape. Hydrological, geological, botanical or ethnographic observations in the art of Hodges and Westall are part of the heyday of the natural sciences that became the context for Ruskin's admiration of Turner, and, after Charles Darwin's voyage to South America and Australia, the context for Darwin's world-changing theory of evolution by natural selection, conceived in 1838 and published in 1859. In the early to mid nineteenth century, European landscape artists frequently travelled to or settled in the southern hemisphere in South Africa, South America, Australia and New Zealand. As mentioned, von Guérard brought ideas of detailed observation as well as Romanticism to the southern hemisphere in the early 1850s. Many artists who settled in Australia had previously painted landscapes in South America, sometimes en route to Australia. These artists include Augustus Earle (1793–1838) in the 1820s and Martens in the 1830s (both of whom had separately travelled with Charles Darwin on H.M.S. *Beagle*), and Buvelot, who painted in Brazil in the 1840s and early 1850s – more than a decade before he came to Australia.

A number of artists from the United States painted the then much admired natural wonders of tropical South America, seen in this exhibition in Church's typical, almost stereotypical, view titled *South American landscape* 1856 (cat. 55). However, the most famous European artist of all who produced landscapes in the southern hemisphere was Paul Gauguin (1848–1903). He painted sensuous tropical Tahitian subjects like *Landscape with a horse* 1899 (cat. 99). He even painted decorative Tahitian landscapes on Polynesian tapa cloth that were made as fans (fig. 10). An artist who took the opposite route was Jan Toorop (1858–1928) (cat. 98). Born in Java, in the Southern hemisphere, he trained and worked as an artist in the Netherlands from the 1870s.

Patronage and the rise of the modern landscape

In seventeenth-century Rome and eighteenth-century France and Britain, landscapes had been painted for and collected by aristocratic and landed patrons. However, as in the Netherlands of the seventeenth century, in nineteenth-century Britain, Germany and France – and indeed in America and Australia – landscape painting became a subject for bourgeois patrons. The wealthy middle classes, most of whom lived in the fast-growing industrial cities, became the audience for local landscape art. City dwellers had begun to make frequent excursions to the countryside and to newly established seaside resorts, pictures of which were increasingly in demand. This development was seen as both modern and egalitarian – watercolour paintings in particular were inexpensive and accessible and they were often the basis of even more accessible landscape prints.

Although history painting was still officially seen, in the first decades of the nineteenth century, as the category of highest prestige, it was also seen as the most institutional, the most civic and, ultimately, the most foreign to the modern British audience. Landscape painting was perceived to be both more personal and national as an expression of British respect for individualism. Again, it is no coincidence that Britain, the first and most advanced industrial country, became the earliest to escape in such an enthusiastic way to unspoilt countryside and to collect landscape paintings. Moreover, as the nineteenth century progressed, naturalistic landscapes, inspired by bourgeois Dutch seventeenth-century realism, were favoured over landscapes with a Classical Italianate influence.

There were two main trends in Romantic landscape in Britain and other northern European countries in the first half of the nineteenth century. One favoured dramatically sublime mountainous landscapes, wild seascapes and other breathtaking subjects, of which Turner and Friedrich were the greatest exponents. The second favoured naturalistic views that were more approachable, domesticated and down-to-earth, such as those by Constable and the watercolourists Cotman, De Wint and Glover.

The death in 1851 of Turner, Britain's leading landscape painter, marked both the climax and thereafter the beginning

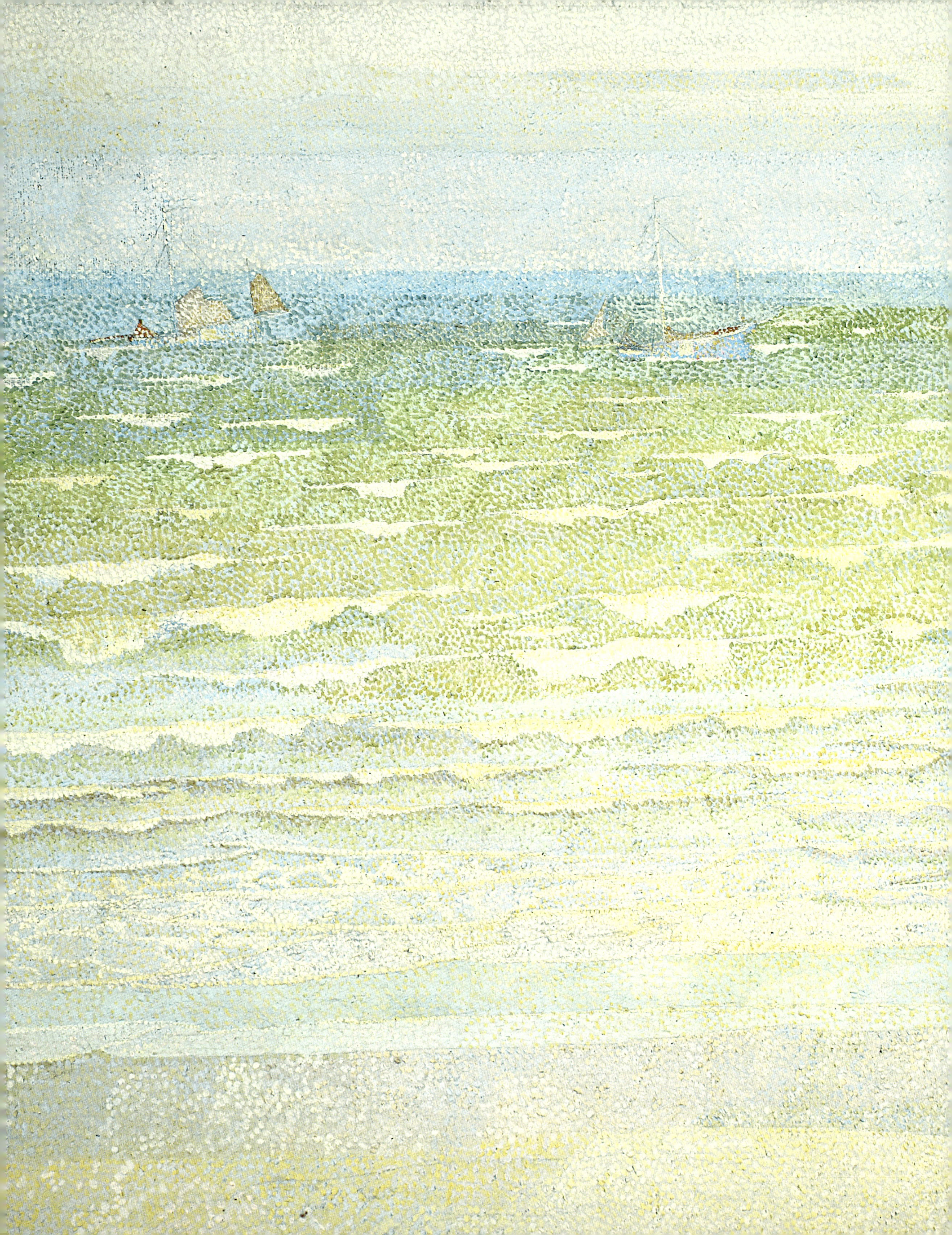

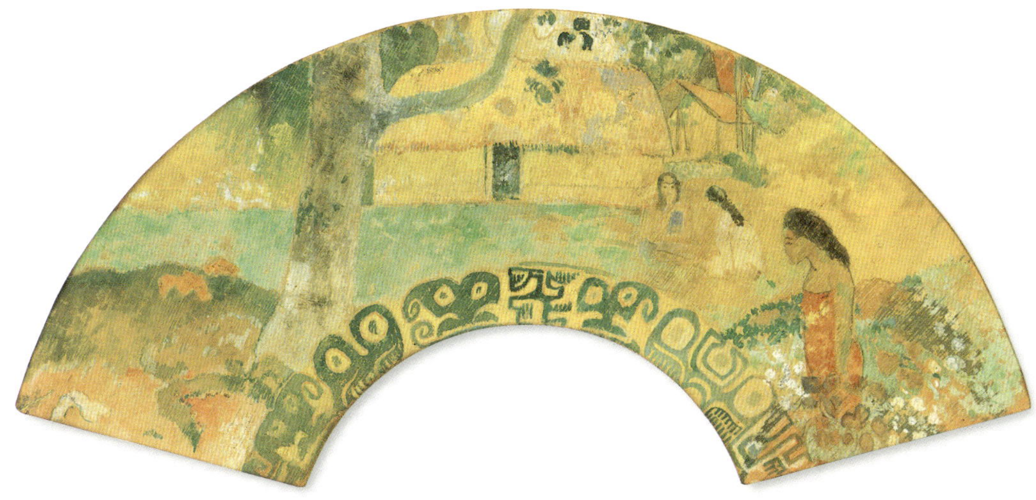

of the decline in Northern European Romantic landscape painting. Constable had died in 1837 and Friedrich did not paint after 1835. In Britain, only Palmer's late watercolours and the few pure landscapes by the Pre-Raphaelite Brotherhood successfully carried British Romantic landscape into the second half of the century. Romantic landscape still continued in its popular form, especially in countries like Switzerland, Australia and the United States.

Meanwhile, the painters of the Barbizon School, led by Camille Corot (1796–1875) (cat. 65, 66), and Realists such as Gustave Courbet (1819–1877) (cat. 69) were preferring less dramatic and more down-to-earth realistic views. Also interested in light and painterly qualities, they influenced outdoor painting around the world, including America and Australia. In Australia, the approachable light-filled landscapes of the beach and bush from the 1880s were associated with a growing nationalism, particularly in the works of Tom Roberts (1856–1931) (cat. 78), Frederick McCubbin (1855–1917) and Arthur Streeton (1867–1943) (cat. 63). In France, the Realism of the Barbizon painters inspired their immediate followers, the Impressionists, who captured with broken colour nature's flickering light and transience. Impressionism and Post-Impressionism took landscape art into new and very different realms and significantly reinvented ways of painting the subject. The late paintings of these artists culminated in what we now know as modern art.[2]

So, in the twentieth century, landscape ceased to be the main vehicle for artistic expression. Rather, it was still life and figure painting which provided the main paths towards formalist abstraction. Landscape underwent extraordinary developments throughout the nineteenth century, from being the background in history paintings, to landowner commissions, to participation in a revolutionary moment for the natural sciences, to tourism and to empire building, and finally as art for its own sake. In the late nineteenth century, the subject of landscape eventually dissolved into aestheticism, into light, colour and form, emphasising the autonomy of paint as significant in itself. Nonetheless we have seen how landscape evolved into the major subject of art in the nineteenth century, and how that century was the greatest for landscape painting in Western art.

(above) fig. 10 **Paul Gauguin** *The big tree* 1892–94 gouache on tapa
17.2 x 57.5 cm
Carrick Hill Trust, Adelaide
Hayward Bequest

(opposite) cat. 98 **Jan Toorop** *The sea* 1899 (detail)

1. The drama of German Romanticism is outlined in Lucina Ward's essay 'Science and the Sublime: nature as spectacle', pp. 14–29.
2. Their grand experiments are dealt with in the final essay, by Christine Dixon, 'Nature becomes art: landscape and modernism', pp. 30–43.

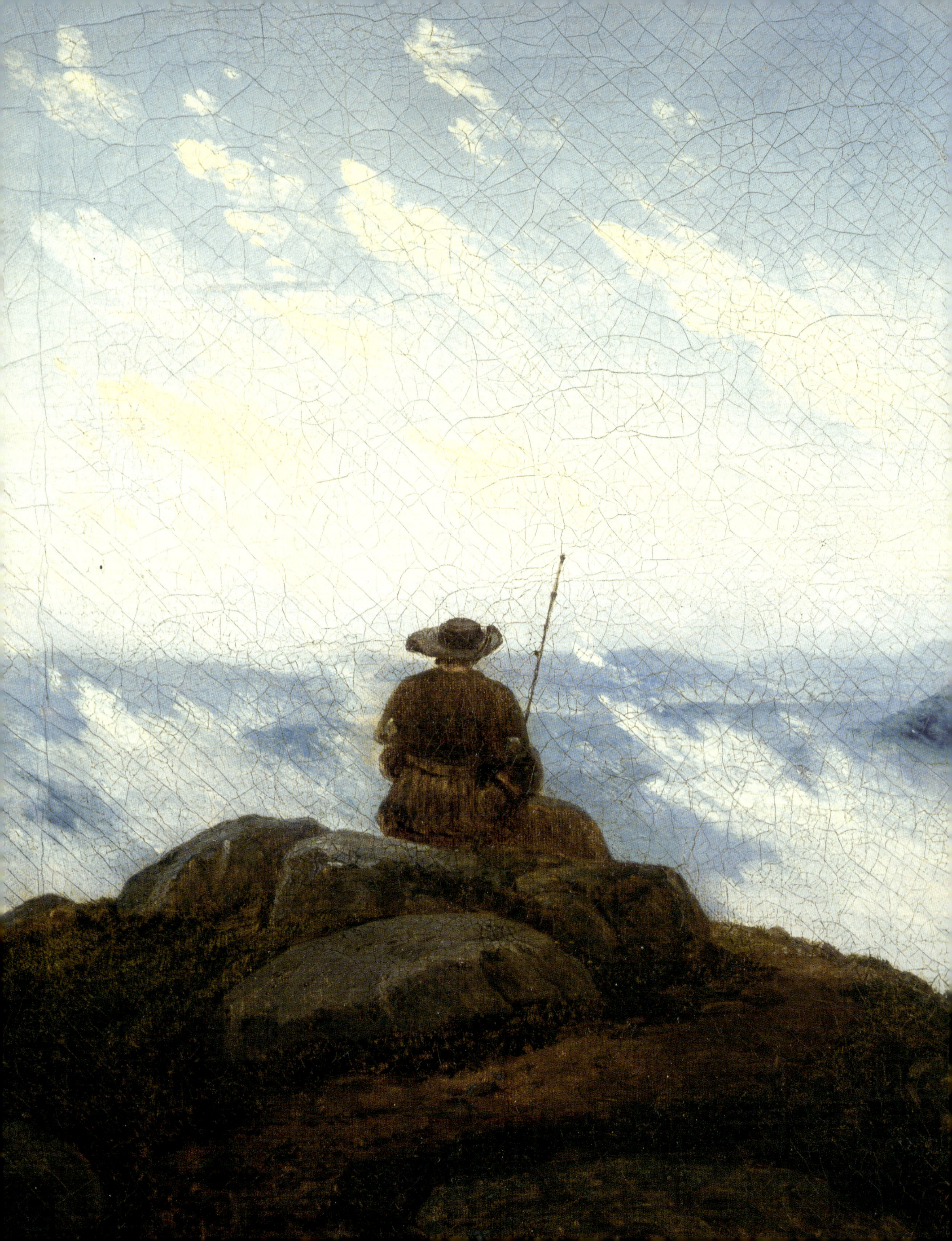

Science and the Sublime: nature as spectacle

Lucina Ward

The nineteenth century saw the triumph of new ideas. Revolutionary artists helped redefine art, science, nation and God, as Romanticism swept across the European continent. Northern Romantic concepts, German in particular, had lasting impact further afield, leading to a re-evaluation of art and attitudes to nature and to theories of art. Against a background of war, empire-building and exploration, landscape painting held special significance. The range of strategies used by artists working in the landscape genre, the ways in which landscape and concepts of Nature were harnessed to evoke feelings and express change, reveal both the impetus of scientific inquiry and struggles over religion at that time.[1]

Historically, science and philosophy were closely intertwined: until the 1800s the terms were largely synonymous. As science became a profession, new disciplines and classifications of knowledge were needed. The discovery of oxygen, the emergence of geology and geognosy, and notions of climate and environmental determinism all contributed to the development and subject matter of landscape painting.[2] Naturalism – close, methodical study of natural phenomena – was important to artists as well as scientists. The idea that the artist was an individual creative genius also came to the fore. In art, as in literature and music, Romanticism combined both ideas; indeed it is this unique relationship between art, philosophy and science that makes the period intriguing. Britain and Germany were early centres of the Romantic movement, with landscape painting as its focus.

The Napoleonic wars of 1792–1815 consumed Europe for a generation. As well as destruction and attendant loss of life, these conflicts had a profound effect on the way people travelled. James Cook's voyages to the South Seas had both scientific and political consequences, with the knowledge being pursued for overtly nationalistic ends.[3] In the circumnavigation of Australia by Matthew Flinders in 1802–03, the environment was recorded by such artists as William Westall (1781–1850) (cat. 50) and the Austrian botanical illustrator Ferdinand Bauer (1760–1826).[4] Britain and France were ever rivals on land and at sea; when Flinders attempted to return to England in 1803, he found his country again at war with France. The artists who accompanied aristocrats on their European Grand Tours also drew on topographical and illustrative traditions. Johan Christian Dahl (1788–1857) was a guest of the Danish Crown Prince Christian Frederik in Naples in 1820–21, while the physician, scientist and artist Carl Gustav Carus (1789–1869) set off for Rome in 1828 as the companion of Crown Prince Friedrich Augustus of Saxony. Dahl painted both *veduta*-style landscapes and mementoes of his stay, remarkable for their naturalism and specificity.[5] Carus's work as a scientific illustrator informed his painting in oils, as did geology, his primary passion.

As science became increasingly popular, people flocked to lectures and consumed texts on medicine and phrenology, evolution, astronomy, geology and botany. One of the most widely read books of the period, Alexander von Humboldt's five-volume *Kosmos* (1845–62), popularised the view that the Earth had an extended past and was in a state of constant transformation, albeit unperceivable. Expeditions to the Arctic in search of the Northwest Passage, journeys across the Blue Mountains of Australia, and into the western regions of North America, built on this interest. As more of the globe was charted, conversely the 'unknowable' – storms, avalanches,

cat. 35 **Carl Gustav Carus** *Wanderer on the mountaintop* 1818 (detail)

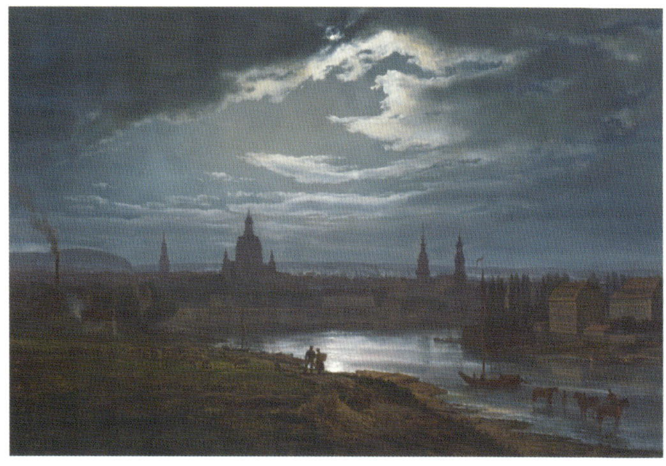

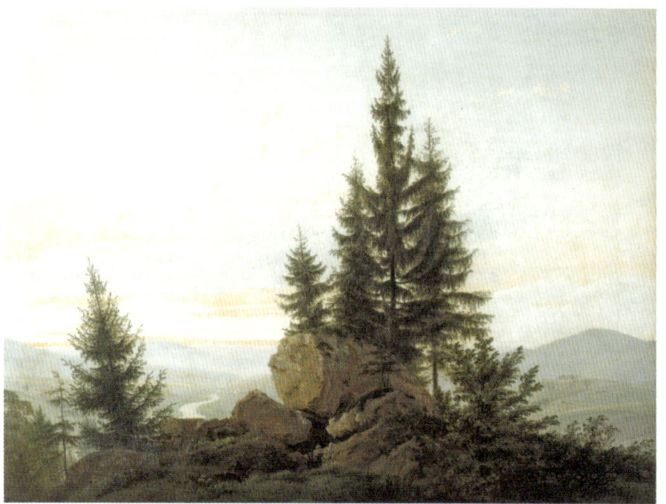

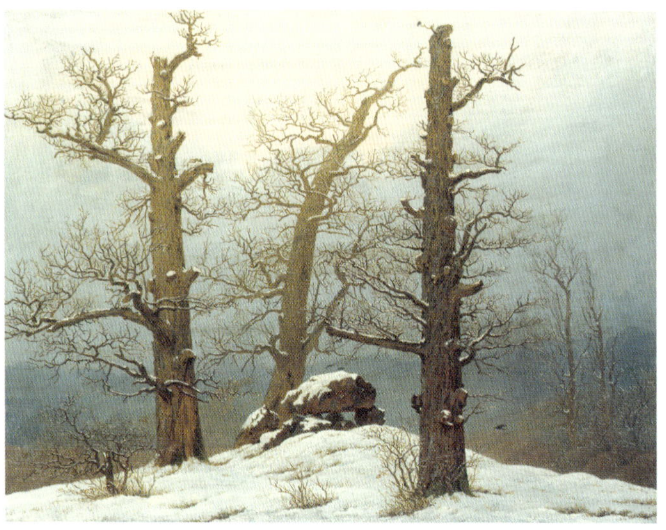

volcanoes, earthquakes – became more fascinating. Although notions of the Sublime existed long before the Romantic era, and have a long history afterwards, it was the German Caspar David Friedrich (1774–1840) and Briton J.M.W. Turner (1775–1851), as well as Eugene von Guérard (1811–1901) in Australia, and Frederic Church (1846–1900) in America, who transformed these ideas.

Reveries of a solitary walker, or, the cathedral of nature

> *When man, sensing the immense magnificence of nature, feels his own insignificance, and, feeling himself to be in God, enters into this infinity and abandons his individual existence, then his surrender is gain rather than loss. What otherwise only the mind's eye sees, here becomes almost literally visible: the oneness in the infinity of the universe.*
>
> Carl Gustav Carus[6]

On the River Elbe and surrounded by some of the most attractive German countryside, the Saxon city of Dresden is renowned for its Baroque buildings. The beauty of this 'German Florence' was captured by Dahl (cat. 38). Before unification under Prussian rule in December 1871, Germany was a set of states and principalities incorporating much of modern Poland, Slovakia and the Czech Republic. Many of the northern regions shared close ties with Sweden, Norway and Denmark. Two distinct traditions of landscape painting prevailed: Italianate landscapes, a modification of the Claudean 'formula' and, on the other hand, a more naturalistic, empirical tradition based on seventeenth-century Dutch painting. When Friedrich left his home in Greifswald on the northern Baltic coast in 1794, he studied at the Danish Academy in Copenhagen. The Neo-Classical training there – emphasising drawing, purity and order – was surprisingly liberal, incorporating aspects of topographic styles and concepts of English Romanticism as encapsulated by the Swiss-born and Swiss-trained Henry Fuseli (1741–1825).

Friedrich settled in Dresden in 1798, earning a living as a topographical artist. He gained a reputation for large compositions in sepia, often produced in day-and-night pairs, or as cycles of four or more. In Copenhagen, Friedrich worked in and around the city; from Dresden, he explored Neubrandenburg, Rügen and northern Bohemia. *View of the Elbe Valley* and *Dolmen in the snow* (cat. 27 and 28), both 1807, were composed using drawings from these field trips. The pointed trees and stone monument had strong resonances at the time, evoking distinctly 'Germanic' Gothic cathedrals and a pre-Christian, animist past. Like his compatriot Philipp Otto Runge (1777–1810), Friedrich approached landscape spiritually. As Siegel points outs, landscape epitomised all that Nature represented to the Romantics – they used it 'as the key to the eternal, as an emanation from God, as a vehicle which transports man above and beyond the earth to a realm where he is reborn, as mirror of man's soul, and as a means of returning man to an earlier purer world'.[7] This heady mix of mysticism, religiosity and creative inspiration provided ingredients for many extraordinary works of art.

Many northern German artists – especially those around Friedrich in Dresden – also approached the art of landscape with a studious approach to detail. Scientific study of nature was a way to understand God's work, and landscape provided the evidence of His project. But subjective or individualised knowledge could lead to questioning of the Bible or religious principles. Indeed, the nature of Creation was one of the most compelling intellectual controversies of the century.[8] Just as Nature was appointed by God to be humankind's friend, mentor and comforter, the artist was the intermediary who provided evidence of this message. The first clear example of a shift in thinking about art and how to respond to it can be linked to a single work: Friedrich's first major oil, *The Cross in the mountains* 1807–08, also known as the *Tetschen Altar* (fig. 11). The painting was displayed in a darkened room, on a table draped with black fabric and artificially lit, within a large gold frame of the artist's own design, shaped like a Gothic arch. It provoked a huge controversy. Friedrich Wilhelm Basilius von Ramdohr, in the January 1809 issue of *Zeitschrift für die elegante Welt* (*Journal for Elegant Society*), objected to the quality of the painting's technique, inappropriateness of subject and, in short, the subjective nature of Romanticism, 'that mysticism that is now slinking in everywhere and that wafts towards us from art and science, from philosophy and religion, like a narcotic vapour'.[9] For Ramdohr the Classicist, no

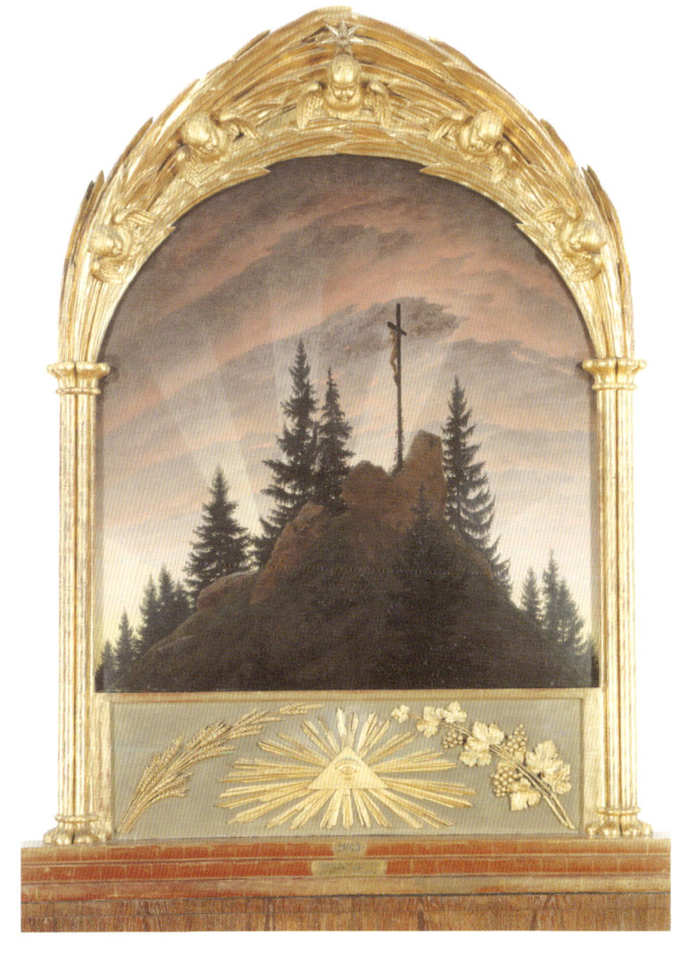

(above)
fig. 11 **Caspar David Friedrich** *The Cross in the mountains* [*Tetschen Altar*] 1807–08 oil on canvas 115.0 x 110.5 cm
Galerie Neue Meister, Staatliche Kunstsammlungen Dresden

(opposite)
cat. 38 **Johan Christian Dahl** *Dresden in moonlight* 1843

cat. 27 **Caspar David Friedrich** *View of the Elbe Valley* c. 1807

cat. 28 **Caspar David Friedrich** *Dolmen in the snow* 1807

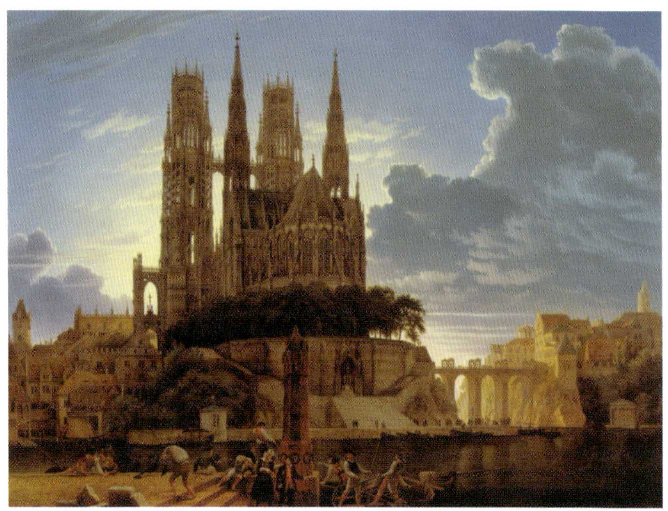

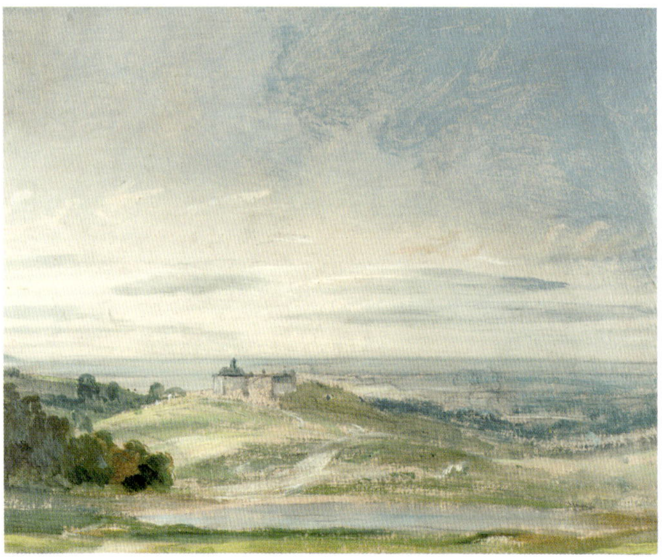

fig. 12 **Karl Eduard Biermann, after Karl Friedrich Schinkel** *Cathedral towering over a town* 1813 oil on canvas 94.0 x 125.6 cm Bayerische Staatsgemäldesammlungen, Neue Pinakothek München

cat. 14 **John Constable** *Buildings on rising ground near Hampstead* 1821

depiction of nature could be symbolical or allegorical. 'It is the greatest arrogance,' he thundered, 'when landscape painting seeks to worm its way into the churches and crawl onto the altars'. Significantly, Friedrich's composition was original, rather than a biblical scene or episode of Greek or Roman mythology specified by the Academies. Not only was the relative status of his subject matter problematic, the artist had also muddied the distinction between imitation and invention. For Ramdohr and others, however, implicit in their objections to *The Cross in the mountains* was Friedrich's transgression of the traditional boundaries of genres established in the seventeenth century.

Napoleon's invasions in Europe – and the French occupation of Dresden from 1806 – profoundly affected the lives of many artists. In Germany, especially in the kingdoms of Saxony and Prussia, the occupation privations were particularly harsh. One consequence of restrictions on travel to Italy was that many artists looked instead to local traditions. Artists examined the remnants of pagan rituals and folk customs, such as the small wooden crosses planted by peasants walking from village to village during religious festivals. Increasingly artists defined themselves and their art in opposition to France. Karl Friedrich Schinkel (1781–1841), best known as the architect of Neo-Classical Berlin, was forced to suspend his practice, instead devoting himself to painting and printmaking during the Napoleonic era. Part fairytale, part historical fantasy, *Cathedral towering over a town* 1813 (fig. 12) concentrates on the place of the built environment in humankind's relationship to God. The intensity of light behind the cathedral, in stark contrast to clouds massing over the distant town, suggests an idealised past. Whereas Neo-Classicists looked back to the ancient Greeks and Romans, Romantic artists took their inspiration from the medieval and the Gothic, although their 'fantastic pilgrimages' were imaginary.

The pleasures derived by spectators in front of landscape painting are a result of the absence of nature in daily life, according to the French Enlightenment philosopher Diderot. To sketch from nature was standard artistic training, but traditionally it meant a quick schematic rendering of a composition or the forms of specific details. In the nineteenth century, sketching developed as an independent activity. For the English painter John Constable (1776–1837) the sky was the 'organ of sentiment'. In *Buildings on rising ground near Hampstead* 1821 (cat. 14) the artist retains the foreground with pond, hill and settlement mid-ground, complete with a path to provide entry into the composition. The sky is becoming the protagonist of his paintings.

The German writer Goethe equated scientific accuracy in landscape painting with aesthetic excellence. Like his countryman and fellow polymath Carus, Goethe emphasised the importance of clear understanding of the 'mechanics' of plants. Romantic artists no longer looked for truth in the 'abstract realm of ideas', discovering it instead in tree-trunks, leaves and flowers; just as anatomy was necessary for portraitists, the landscape painter must bring together a range of disciplines in the natural sciences. Rocks, trees, sky and clouds were 'more than symbols or potential allegories' for many German landscape painters; invested with emotion, these natural phenomena exerted 'a direct influence on cultural history'.[10] Clouds, in particular, were infused with the ability to convey mutability and mood. The English meteorologist Luke Howard was extremely influential; he wrote:

> [Clouds] are subject to certain distinct modifications, produced by the general causes which affect all the variations of the atmosphere; they are commonly as good visible indicators of the operation of these causes, as is the countenance of the state of a person's mind or body.[11]

Goethe was one transmitter for these ideas to Germany where the Dresden circle of artists – Friedrich, Carus and Dahl – also made close studies of clouds. These paintings, whether working studies or finished presentation pieces, are remarkable for their naturalism and talisman-like qualities; and in Constable's case, their pinpoint, scientific, accuracy.

The Wanderer theme is common in German Romantic art and literature. Images of humans becoming one with nature, lost in silent communion with the universe, react against a cardinal thesis of the Enlightenment: man as 'a distinct and unique entity, of supreme value in his own right'.[12] From 1817, around the time of his most famous Wanderer painting (fig. 13), Friedrich began to make single or paired figures central in his works. *Staffage* provides a

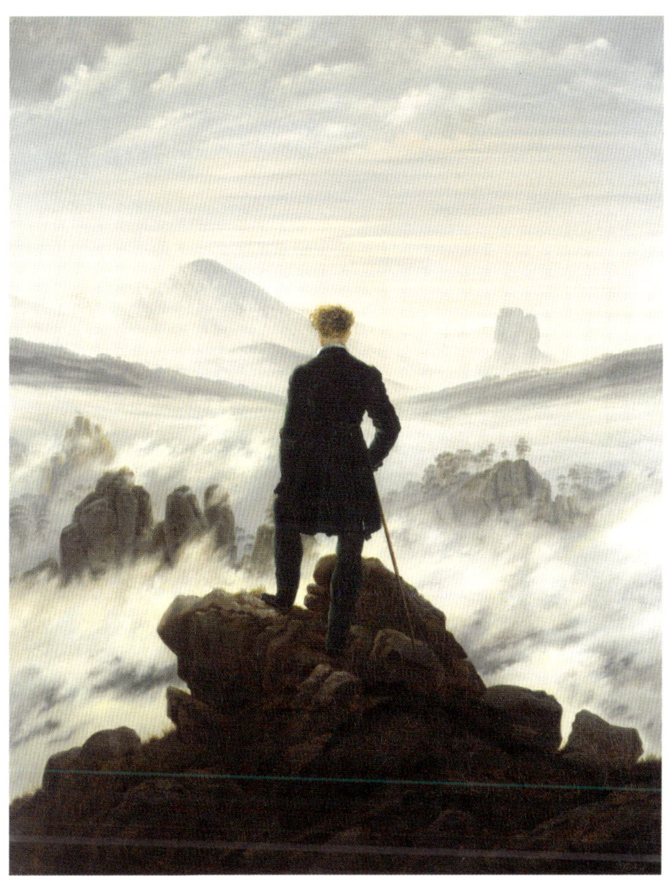

fig. 13 **Caspar David Friedrich** *Wanderer overlooking the sea of fog* 1818
oil on canvas 74.8 x 94.8 cm
Hamburger Kunsthalle, Hamburg
© bpk/Hamburger Kunsthalle/Elke Walford

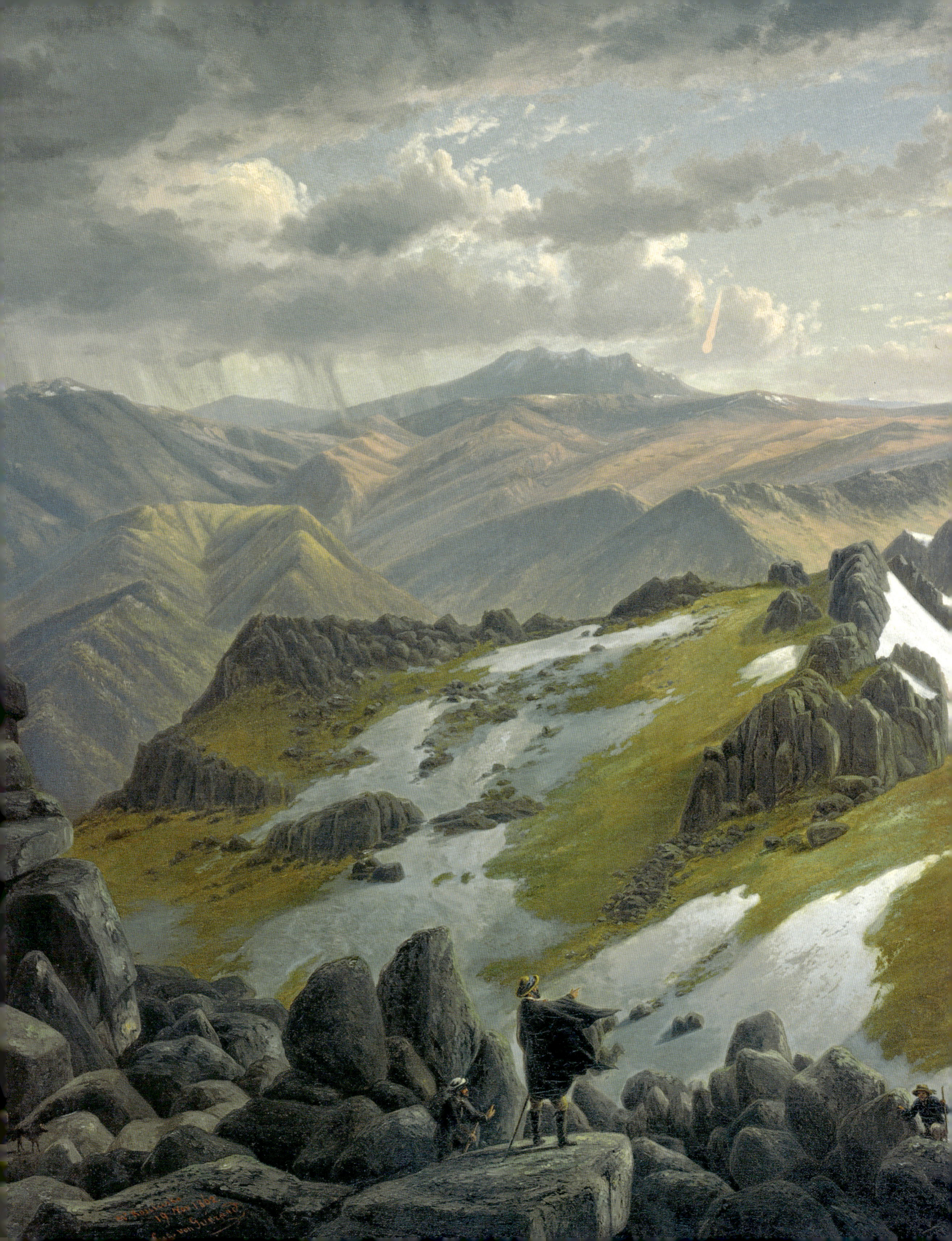

point of interest within the landscape, an element with which the viewer can associate.[13] By contrast Friedrich's and Carus's figures give us 'only the choice of remaining outside or of putting ourselves in their shoes'. Rocklike and utterly still, Carus's pilgrim–wanderer stops, staff at his side, deep in meditation (cat. 35). He, like Friedrich's paired moon-watchers (cat. 37) or trilogy of female figures, (cat. 36) seems to 'absorb the landscape' into himself.[14] We have the sense, from the pensive presence of these figures, that the space they inhabit represents their inner lives. Looking at these works we understand that humankind is an 'inferior part of the universe, a creature who can gain significance only by learning from and contemplating Nature …'[15]

The man in *Wanderer above the sea of fog* 1818 (fig. 13), seen from the back and posed in soulful isolation, is the key element of the composition. He stands for the viewer, and through him we contemplate the landscape beyond.[16] Friedrich's is not a specific place nor a landscape rendered topographically, but a scene in which landscape is reinterpreted as personalised introspection and to represent infinity. The English-born American artist Thomas Cole (1801–1848) includes a much smaller figure who looks out into a distinctive landscape in *A view of the two lakes and mountain house, Catskill Mountains, morning* 1844 (fig. 14). This artist–personage is presented as an intermediary, the foreground organised as a vantage point from whence to absorb the surrounding scenery. In a work of the Austrian-born and German-trained immigrant to Australia, von Guérard, the figure is likewise presented as an intermediary. In *North-east view from the northern top of Mount Kosciusko* 1863 (cat. 41), while we realise the explorer figure has companions, his cloak and dramatic gesture silhouetted against the snow, ensure that they are secondary.[17] Details of the vista are presented in Cole's and von Guérard's paintings, but these are composite views. They are works of art in which the artist has played his part, rather than renditions of what would be seen if we stood in his shoes. All three paintings announce a key idea of German Romantic art: how people are rendered insignificant by the vastness and grandeur of God's creation.

Mountains are another element common to these three works. Although Friedrich virtually stopped painting large-scale works after he exhibited his painting of the great German mountain, *The Watzmann* in 1825, his influence was far-reaching. German Romantic traditions travelled far, both in a geographical sense and in terms of ideas. In the Americas and in Australia, new worlds for Europeans, artists reinvented landscape traditions. The themes and broad vistas developed by painters of the Hudson River School in the United States for example, represent the parameters of a newly discovered realm in which the language of Western European landscape traditions is reinterpreted. The canvases of Cole, Church, Albert Bierstadt (1830–1902), Thomas Moran (1837–1926) and Martin Johnson Heade (1819–1904) show lush valleys and eroding peaks, fertile plains, massing of storm clouds, glorious rainbows and volcanic springs: everywhere is evidence of the Earth as an active, 'living' entity. In their explorations of the North and South American landmasses, Europeans discovered continents 'in the making'.

To be artistically effective, forms within nature were considered for landscape compositions only to the extent that they conveyed an idea. Mountains occur, according to the explanation given by geognosy, not accidentally but by design; and so their existence was ideally suited to the traditional aesthetic of landscape painting.[18] Church's early *South American landscape* 1856 (cat. 55) centres on a magnificent snow-covered peak and then travels, via a series of strong diagonals, down to the rainforest below. Attendants – a figure on the path in the centre foreground, another on the bridge on the left – and the monastery which crowns the smaller of the two peaks, function more as traditional *staffage* than the man in Cole's Catskill Mountains. The exotic scene and strong rendering of the mountain forms may have contributed to those mixed reviews which greeted the young Church's exhibition of tropical subjects in 1856. More comfortable with American, Italian and occasionally Swiss landscapes, viewers responded to the fabulous image with confusion and distrust.[19] Church painted *South American landscape* from memory, and it suggests Humboldt's enthusiasm for the Andes mountains as the supreme place to experience the different ecologies of Latin America. Cole's, Church's and von Guérard's paintings, produced a decade apart, exemplify the ways Romantic ideas and landscape conventions were remade in America and Australia.

cat. 41 **Eugene von Guérard** *North-east view from the northern top of Mount Kosciusko* 1863 (detail)

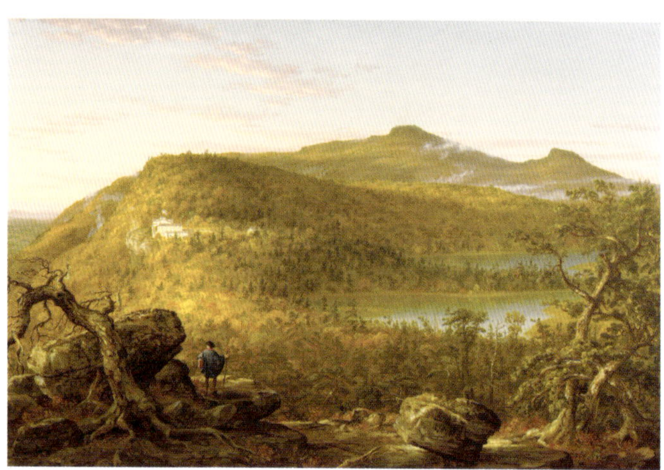

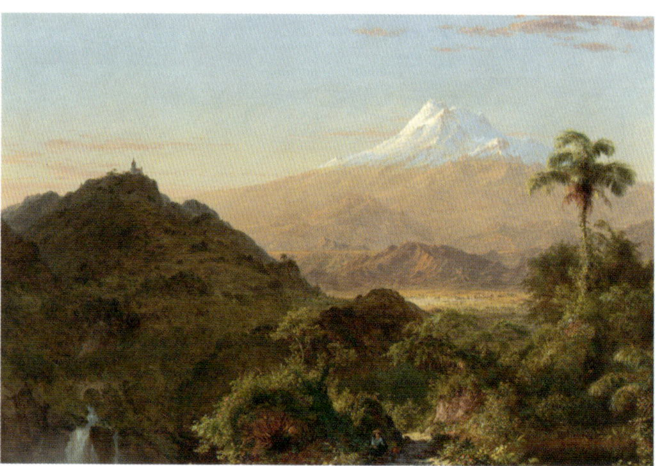

fig. 14 **Thomas Cole** *A view of the two lakes and mountain house, Catskill Mountains, morning* 1844 oil on canvas 91.0 x 136.9 cm
Brooklyn Museum, New York
Dick S. Ramsay Fund

cat. 55 **Frederic Church** *South American landscape* 1856
© Carmen Thyssen-Bornemisza on loan at the Museo Thyssen-Bornemisza, Madrid

'Awful shadow of some unseen Power'

> *A splendid conception: fancy thirty or forty [icebergs] rushing about London and Paris drunk and disorderly and throwing whole streets at each other's heads. There has been no such image since the well-known American's description of the boundaries of his country, as being 'On the East the rising sun, on the West the setting ditto, on the North the* aurora borealis, *and on the South the day of judgement'.*
>
> *Pall Mall Gazette*, London, an unnamed journalist responding to Charles Dickens's widely reported comment that the Earth was being 'overrun by an iceberg'[20]

If ideal landscapes are closely connected to a language of symbols, as Kenneth Clark has it, the challenge laid down by many artists in the first decades of the nineteenth century was to make great compositions from observed facts.[21] After Napoleon's final defeat at Waterloo in June 1815, it was again possible to travel for pleasure. Instead of being perilous hazards, mountain passes and deep woods could revert to awesome vistas for contemplation and enjoyment. Dahl's journeying in Italy not only provided him with a range of subjects, it also prompted a change of style, and seems to have encouraged greater confidence with colour. In his atmospherically charged scenes of Vesuvius (cat. 42, 43) – one composition probably painted in Italy, the second on his return to Dresden – the Norwegian artist captures the frisson of danger, the thrill of 'really being there'. Dahl's paintings are often more spontaneously executed than Friedrich's, while the influence of Carus appears in Dahl's quasi-scientific approach to the wonders of the natural world.

The 'highest thing in art', according to Fuseli, is the Sublime. 'In nature and in art,' he writes, 'the merely beautiful and good pleases us; it is agreeable or delightful; it makes a gentle impression that we enjoy in tranquillity. But the sublime deals massive blows, sweeps us away, and seizes the mind irresistibly'.[22] Bätschmann traces an increased demand for paintings with Sublime motifs – storms at sea, shipwrecked mariners, thunderous waterfalls, horrific chasms, awe-inspiring mountain ranges, fathomless caves and volcanoes belching fire – to Edmund Burke's treatise, *A philosophical inquiry into the origin of our ideas of the sublime and beautiful* 1757. He counts Turner among the specialists who painted to satisfy a desire for the Sublime.[23] The English master produced memorable works depicting crossing the Alps, buildings on fire and saturated Italy but as Brown points out, for a landscape painter Turner's lack of interest in the substance of landscape is remarkable.[24]

Romantic interest in growth and change stimulated the scrutiny of transient manifestations of light, atmosphere and water. Technical parallels exist between Turner's and Friedrich's artistic development. But in mood and in terms of pictorial strategies they could not be further apart. Storms and other extreme weather conditions are noticeably absent in Friedrich's landscapes and seascapes. In fact, as Siegel points out, his work is remarkable for its 'uncanny quietude, a stillness, and an absence of all movement'.[25] The sense of exquisite melancholy in Friedrich's masterly *The Great Preserve* c. 1832 (fig. 15) overwhelms the viewer. A tiny boat, almost imperceptible against the grove of trees, is the artist's doppelganger, into which may be poured a whole gamut of emotions. The pattern of the marshy ground, mirrored in a gorgeous dusky sky above, ensures that this painting is one of the most unforgettable of Romantic landscapes.

In the art of Friedrich and Turner, human presence is implied rather than shown, especially in late works – the intensity of feelings fascinates. As Warrell points out, in even his earliest depictions of the sea Turner sought through paint to replicate the dramatic movements of water.[26] In three magnificent late works – *Waves breaking against the wind* c. 1840, *Stormy sea with blazing wreck* c. 1835–40 and *A mountain scene, Val d'Aosta* c. 1841–45 (cat. 44–46) – we find spontaneity and directness in Turner's application of paint. Like Constable, Turner uses the sky as a vehicle for emotion, but combined with the sea, the built environment, mountains, storms or trains for extra impact. The combination of uncertain, manipulated pictorial space and a flurry of energetic marks in a painting such as *Stormy sea with blazing wreck* puts the viewer into the scene: the painting consumes our senses, as though we might actually enter it to be surrounded by the disaster. This is truly a Sublime experience, and this aspect of Turner's art appealed directly to the Impressionists.

For a painting to overwhelm the spectator, the most obvious means the artist can use is size.[27] Many of Turner's paintings are physically large, but also grand in pictorial terms. The

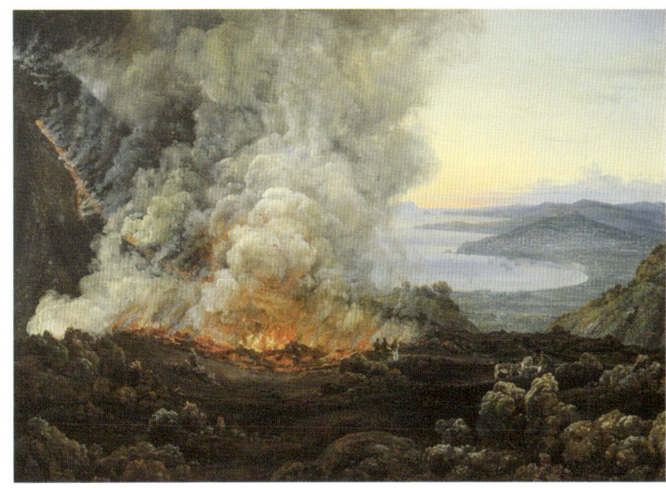

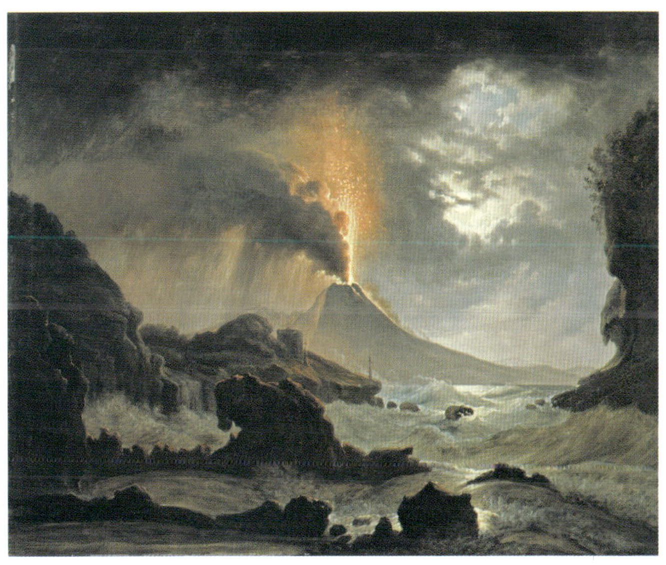

cat. 43 **Johan Christian Dahl** *Vesuvius in eruption* 1821

cat. 42 **Johan Christian Dahl** *Eruption of Vesuvius* 1823

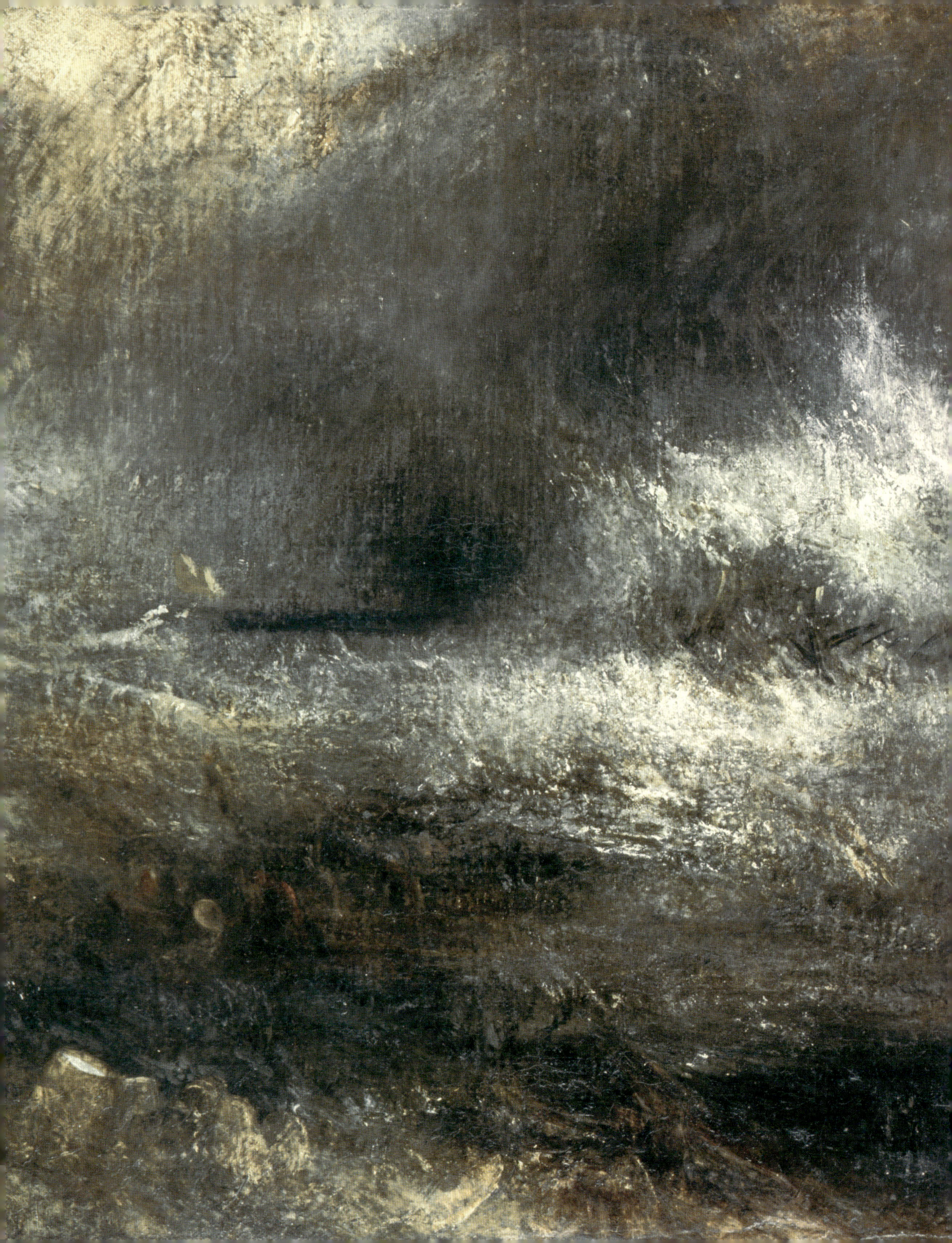

size of *The Red Rigi* 1842 (cat. 31) is no impediment to its impact. In fact, many Romantic, Realist and avant-garde artists reacted against the large history paintings, which were the apogee of the Academy; they regarded these so-called 'machines' as bombastic and irrelevant to contemporary life. The nineteenth-century public, on the other hand, disagreed. In London, Paris and the United States they flocked to Great Exhibitions, annuals shows at the Royal Academy or Salon, and a range of popular spectacles, such as Robert Barker's two-level, 360-degree panorama presented in Leicester Square.[28] The always savvy Church built on this enthusiasm for knowledge with his gigantic canvases, such as *Heart of the Andes* 1859 and *Aurora borealis* 1865 (fig. 16). He displayed single paintings with architectural frames and velvet curtains – the viewer was meant to feel as if he or she was looking out of a window – and provided descriptive pamphlets with the entry fee. For his grand Arctic painting he persuades us that we are actually part of the 1859 expedition conducted by Church's polar explorer Dr Isaac Hayes.[29]

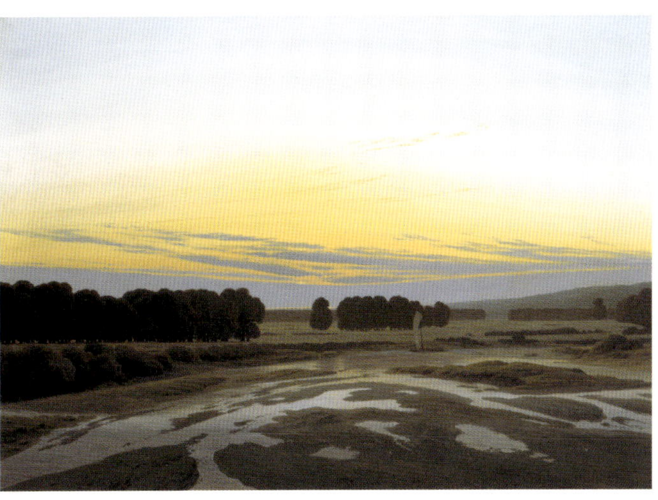

(above) fig. 15 **Caspar David Friedrich** *The Great Preserve* c. 1832 oil on canvas 73.5 x 103 cm Galerie Neue Meister, Staatliche Kunstsammlungen Dresden

(opposite) cat. 45 **J.M.W. Turner** *Stormy sea with blazing wreck* c. 1835–40 (detail) © Tate, London 2008

Artists working in the southern hemisphere also incorporated aspects of the Sublime, relying on the strategies of large size and people's thirst for knowledge. *Cape Chudleigh, Coast of Labrador* 1893/95 (cat. 48) by Isaac Walter Jenner (1836–1902) reveals the same enthusiasm for Arctic adventures as Friedrich and Church. W.C. Piguenit (1836–1914) was likewise prompted by a specific event to paint *The flood in the Darling 1890* 1895 (cat. 49). These 'history paintings' record current, often devastating, events on a grand scale. But in this new type of history painting no human hero commands the scene, rather plenty of space allows the viewers to insert their own meanings. Ultimately Nature is the hero, we conclude. As Bonyhady points out, if Piguenit saw his landscapes having a purpose, it was the practical aim of promoting tourism.[30]

Over the course of one hundred years, from the 1750s until the mid 1800s, the United States changed from vast, wild frontier territory, to a country defined by cities and industries. As in Europe, there was a new reverence and romantic longing for undisturbed, unpeopled land, fuelling demand for such images. As Hughes has it, 'Americans saw in their wilderness the very prototype of Nature, the place where the designs of God survived in their virgin and

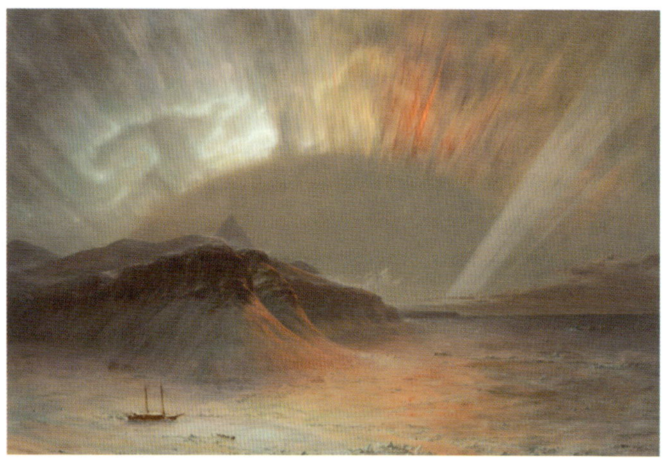

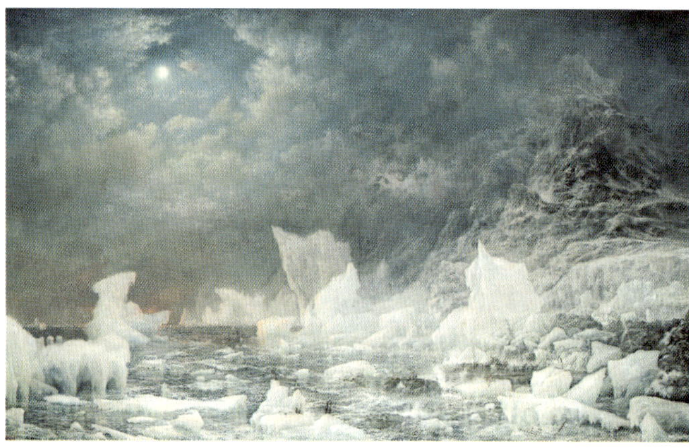

fig. 16 **Frederic Church** *Aurora borealis* 1865
oil on canvas 142.3 x 212.2 cm
Smithsonian American Art Museum, Washington
Gift of Eleanor Blodgett

cat. 48 **Isaac Walter Jenner** *Cape Chudleigh, Coast of Labrador* 1893/95

unedited state'.[31] In these vast, crystalline skies many artists construed the strong light as an embodiment of the Deity, especially sky phenomena such as so-called 'Jacob's ladders'.

Many nineteenth-century American paintings are intriguing combinations of the Sublime with underlying religious and philosophical themes, as Bedell reveals.[32] Cole's first New York exhibition in 1825 brought him to the attention of members of the American Academy of Fine Arts, prominent collectors as well as amateur and professional geologists. His portrayal of rocks and other natural formations was criticised by some scientists. They seemed to overlook the fact that Cole's choice of features in works such as *Peace at sunset (evening in the White Mountains)* c. 1827 (cat. 51) was made for the purpose of producing dramatic landscape paintings, rather than geologically or geographically accurate renderings.[33] Such criticism misconstrued the character of art.

Americans, like Australians, perceived that real art came from somewhere else. Occasionally they saw works by English artists such as John Martin (1789–1854). In New York at the Düsseldorf Gallery, opened in 1849, highly finished German paintings of academic subjects were more common. Alexandre Calame (1810–1864) was very influential and *Torrent in the Alps* 1849 (cat. 54) typifies the sort of paintings enjoyed by nineteenth-century New Yorkers. Bierstadt, for example – born in Solingen in the North Rhine–Westphalia region, who moved to the United States in 1833 – returned to Germany twenty years later to study in Düsseldorf. Emerging from the Romantic moment, the members of the Düsseldorf School tended to paint *en plein air* and to use a relatively subdued palette. Bierstadt's Yosemite paintings (cat. 61) appealed to the more literal-minded, and those who valued technical skills highly. Moran takes this aspect of 'travel painting' one step further in *Hot springs of the Yellowstone* 1872 (cat. 60), producing an extraordinary painting reminiscent of Martin's 'hysterical' or 'hyperbolic sublime'. Many commentators trace this westwards migration, as well as the rise of the national parks movement in the nineteenth century, to a conviction that the East was tainted with blood from the Civil War.

The Sublime and the spectacle of landscape are less grandiose in the 'Great South Land'. Wars were fought differently, not between armies. Nineteenth-century Australian landscape painting shows similar influences to America's: they include imported German and English models, application of the Sublime, interest in spectacular natural scenery and the impact of science. Initially lured by the promise of gold, by 1852 von Guérard settled in Melbourne and resumed his painting career. His *Bush fire between Mt Elephant and Timboon 1857* 1859 (cat. 47) looks very modern, divided almost into equal fields of red and black. All our attention is directed to the horror and heat of the terrible fire. It may have been started by lightning, but could be part of Indigenous agricultural practices. Like Bierstadt in America, von Guérard brought aspects of his training at the Staatliche Kunstakademie, Düsseldorf, to his Australian paintings.[34]

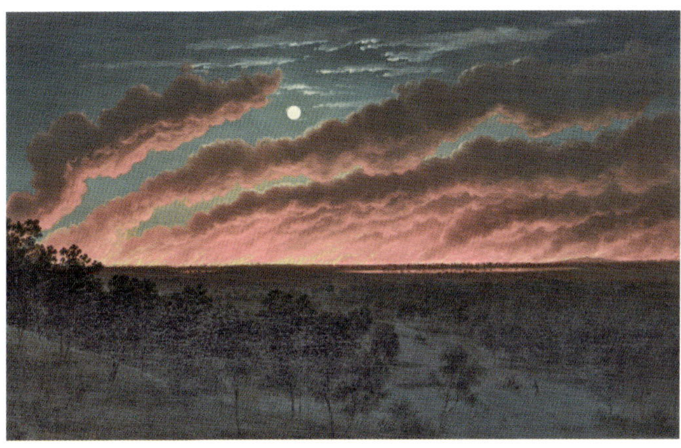

cat. 47 **Eugene von Guérard** *Bush fire between Mt Elephant and Timboon 1857* 1859

Von Guérard participated in expeditions conducted by the Bavarian astronomer, geophysicist and explorer, Georg von Neumayer. Like Humboldt, Neumayer favoured direct measurements and experimentation in the field. The party travelled Victoria's Otway Ranges in October 1859 and April 1862, and to the Australian Alps in October–November 1862 (cat. 41). The Russian-born Nicholas Chevalier (1828–1902) was official artist for the second Victorian trip (cat. 57). Like many German and American artists informed by Romanticism, von Guérard travelled extensively in Australia and further afield in search of Sublime and picturesque subjects. One of his two major New Zealand subjects (cat. 58) was exhibited widely with its companion painting. Displayed in Sydney, Melbourne, London and Paris, the pair became some of the best-known nineteenth-century antipodean images.[35]

Back in the 'old countries', the post-Napoleonic repartition of Europe was still being felt. From the 1840s borders changed, new countries defined, and nationalistic consciousness developed. In Britain the Pre-Raphaelites took their models from historic Italian art and their near-contemporaries, the Nazarenes or German Romans. British Realists produced portraits and religious subjects, painting narratives rich in moral and patriotic messages, for those who cared to read them. William Bell Scott (1811–1890), Thomas Seddon (1821–1856) and John William Inchbold (1830–1888), among others, painted exquisite and obsessively detailed landscapes. The sharp focus and

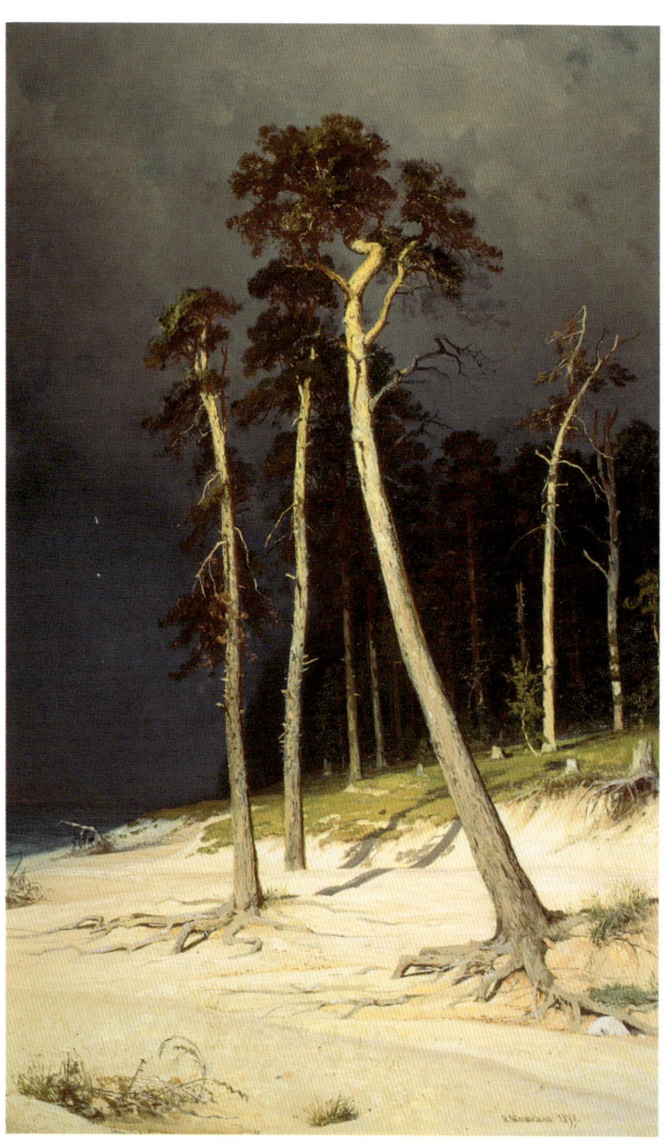

cat. 62 **Ivan Shishkin** *A sandy coastline* 1879

'photographic' exactness of their images – from city streets and parks, to scenery of Italy and Switzerland, or places as far away and exotic as Jerusalem and imagined history of the Holy Land – infused topographical traditions with new meanings. Scott's 1860 landscape of Ailsa Craig (cat. 56), on the other hand, suggests a new approach to tourism which finds appealing scenery closer to home, yet still exotic.

Building on German foundations, Russian and Scandinavian artists devised their own forms of heroic nationalism and local consciousness. Another 'wanderer,' Ivan Shishkin (1832–1898), shows fascinating details of his homeland in *A sandy coastline* 1879 (cat. 62), an aspect which may also be traced back to training in Munich, Prague and Düsseldorf. Eventually, however, the imitative functions of landscape painting were overtaken by photography, and so many of these ideas proved to be dead ends. For innovation in art, attention turned to France, where avant-garde artists again began to question the subject of art, and to engage aspects of modern life and notions of change.

'Everything strives towards landscape', wrote the artist Runge in a letter to his brother in February 1802.[36] His comments seem remarkably prophetic. Runge's *landschaft* (landscape) was an antonym of history painting. Even allowing for the defiant circumstances of their production, the originality of early Romantic work still surprises us almost two centuries later. Educational, pantheistic or political – and, as Vaughan points out, frequently all three – the meanings harnessed to landscape in the nineteenth century are many and varied.[37] Artists use a range of devices and pictorial techniques to convey meaning. In northern Europe the focus on local scenery encouraged artists in other countries to re-evaluate their own. Scrutiny of the transient manifestations of landscape, or concepts such as the soul, brought a new range of emotions to landscape painting.

1 The concurrence and symbiotic nature of this 'rewriting of the earth's history and a re-evaluation of nature's powers', and its impact on art as redefined by philosophers and aestheticians, is the central thesis of Timothy F. Mitchell's *Art and science in German landscape painting 1770–1840*, Oxford: Clarendon Press, 1993. My reading of nineteenth-century landscape painting and German Romanticism has been informed and stimulated by Mitchell's work, as well as that of Rebecca Bedell in *The anatomy of nature: geology and American landscape painting 1825–1875*, Princeton: Princeton University Press, 2001. Furthermore I have also benefited from exchanges with Ruth Pullin; her doctoral thesis 'Von Guérard and the science of landscape painting' is being considered through Melbourne University.

2 'Geognosy', meaning 'knowledge of the earth', refers to the study of the Earth's materials, its structure and layers. Geognosy was understood in the nineteenth century as a factual rather than theoretical discipline. 'Environmental determinism' refers to the theory that human characteristics are caused by birthplace, race and physical surroundings. It was important because of debates on evolution and nationalism.

3 See Paul Keen (ed.), *Revolutions in Romantic literature: an anthology of print culture 1780–1832*, Peterborough: Broadview Press, 2004, p. 125.

4 Nicolas Baudin, captain of Le Géographe on the rival French exploration of the south and west coasts of Australia, was accompanied by Nicolas-Martin Petit (1777–1804) and Charles-Alexandre Lesueur (1778–1846).

5 The *veduta* tradition – highly detailed, topographic-style paintings, usually of cityscapes or landscape vistas – originated in sixteenth- and seventeenth-century Dutch art. At the height of its popularity, in the mid eighteenth century, Venice became the centre of production for *vedute* (Italian for 'views').

6 Carl Gustav Carus, *Neun briefe über landschaftsmalerei: geschrieben in den jahren 1815 bis 1824*, Dresden: W. Jess Verlag, 1831, English translation from Lorenz Eitner, *Neoclassicism and romanticism 1750–1850: sources and documents*, vol. II, Englewood Cliffs: Prentice-Hall, 1970, p. 48; see also *Nine letters on landscape painting: written in the years 1815–1824, with a letter from Goethe by way of introduction*, Los Angeles: Getty Research Institute, 2002.

7 Linda Siegel, *Caspar David Friedrich and the age of German Romanticism*, Boston: Branden Press, 1978, p. 49.

8 James Hamilton, in *Turner: the late seascapes*, New Haven: Yale University Press, 2003, pp. 112–13, argues that Turner's friendship with scientists such as William Buckland, as well as the artist's own intellectual curiosity, meant that he would have been aware of the debates around geology and theology in the 1840s; see also James Hamilton, *Turner and the scientists*, London: Tate Gallery Publishing, 1998.

9 Both English quotations come from W.N.B. Mullan, 'Baron Friedrich Wilhelm Basilius von Ramdohr', *Grove Art Online*, Oxford University Press, viewed December 2007, groveart.com, and 'Caspar David Friedrich', *Biographies: Answers.com*, viewed December 2007, answers.com/topic/casper-david-friedrich. The so-called Ramdohr dispute (*Ramdohrstreit*) is the subject of much discussion: for a useful summary, see Mitchell, 'From vedute to vision: the importance of popular imagery in Friedrich's development of Romantic landscape painting', *The Art Bulletin*, vol. 64, no. 3, September 1982, pp. 414–24.

10 Mitchell, pp. 2, 32.

11 Luke Howard, 'On the modification of clouds', *Tilloch's Philosophical Magazine* (1803), quoted in John E. Thornes, *John Constable's skies: a fusion of art and science*, Edgbaston: University of Birmingham Press, 1999, p. 36.

12 Siegel, pp. 23–6, suggests a source for the wanderer image in Ludwig Tieck's *Der Runenberg*.

13 *Staffage*, a term derived from the French, refers to the 'peopling' of landscape with small human figures or animals.

14 Wieland Schmied, *Caspar David Friedrich*, New York: Harry N. Abrams, 1995, p. 24; see also Carus's *Pilgrim in a rocky valley* c. 1820, National-galerie, Berlin.

15 Siegel, pp. 26.

16 In this exhibition Carus's *Wanderer on the mountaintop* (cat. 35) has a similar function.

17 We find a range of figures, seen at an angle or with their backs to the picture plane, elsewhere in von Guérard's oeuvre; in *Govett's Leap and Grose River Valley, Blue Mountains, New South Wales* 1873, for example, the *staffage* is again explorer figures, but perched on the rocky viewing platform, they are minute against the vast, unknown 'wilderness'; the work is part of the National Gallery of Australia's collection.

18 Mitchell, p. 133.

19 This point is made by Katherine E. Manthone in her entry for the work, in *Nineteenth-century American painting*, London: Sotheby's Publications, 1986, (Thyssen-Bornemisza Collection catalogue).

20 *Pall Mall Gazette*, 5 May 1868, and quoted in Eleanor Jones Harvey, *The voyage of the icebergs: Frederic Church's Arctic masterpiece*, Dallas: Dallas Museum of Art, 2002, p. 16.

21 Kenneth Clark, *Landscape into art*, new edn, London: John Murray, 1976, pp. 139, 154.

22 Henry Fuseli, 'Erhaben' (Sublime), in *Allgemeine theorie derr schönen künste in einzeln*, quoted in Oskar Bätschmann, 'Introduction', in Carus, *Nine letters on landscape painting*, p. 15.

23 Bätschmann gives two others: Joseph Vernet (1714–1789) and Joseph Anton Koch (1768–1839); see introduction to Carus, *Nine letters on landscape painting*, p. 15.

24 David Blayney Brown, *Romanticism*, London: Phaidon, 2001, p. 160; in this exhibition, Turner's *Overlooking the coast, with classical building* 1828? might even announce the overthrow of the classical tradition.

25 Siegel, p. 70.

26 See Ian Warrell, in this publication, cat. 44, pp. 134–5.

27 See, for example, Andrew Wilton and Tim Barringer, *American Sublime: landscape in the United States*, London: Tate Publishing, 2002, pp. 10–37.

28 In the mid 1860s, for example, when between 4000 and 5000 works were on display in each of the annual Paris Salons, as many as 300 000 people visited the exhibition. See Jane Mayo Roos, *Early Impressionism and the French state (1866–1874)*, Cambridge: Cambridge University Press, 1996, and quoted by Belinda Thomson, *Impressionism: origins, practice, reception*, London: Thames & Hudson, 2000, p. 15.

29 Wilton reproduces a 1864 photograph of *Heart of the Andes*, on display at the Metropolitan Sanitary Fair, crowned with portraits of presidents; according to the Boston newspapers 30 000 people visited the painting in that city. See Wilton and Barringer, p. 30.

30 Tim Bonyhady, *The colonial earth*, Carlton: Miegunyah Press, 2000, p. 282.

31 Robert Hughes, *American visions: the epic history of art in America*, London: Harvill Press, 1997, p. 138.

32 Bedell also demonstrates that many American artists avoided materialist science, particularly Darwinism and, like the German Northern Romantics, favoured a Christianised geology as a means to understanding God; especially pp. 3–15.

33 Bedell, especially pp. 17–45.

34 Von Guérard also studied in Italy. In Melbourne he taught at the National School of Art, where artists such as Frederick McCubbin (1855–1917) and Tom Roberts (1856–1931) were students (see cat. 76, 78, 82).

35 *Lake Wakatipu with Mount Earnslaw, Middle Island, New Zealand* 1877–79, collection of Auckland Art Gallery Toi o T maki.

36 Phillip Otto Runge, 'Es drängtsich alles zur landschaft' (Everything strives towards landscape), in *Hinterlassene Schriften*, facsimile edn, Hamburg: Verlag von Friedrich Perthes, 1840–41, Göttingen: Vanderhoeck & Ruprecht, 1965.

37 William Vaughan, *German Romantic painting*, New Haven: Yale University Press, 1980.

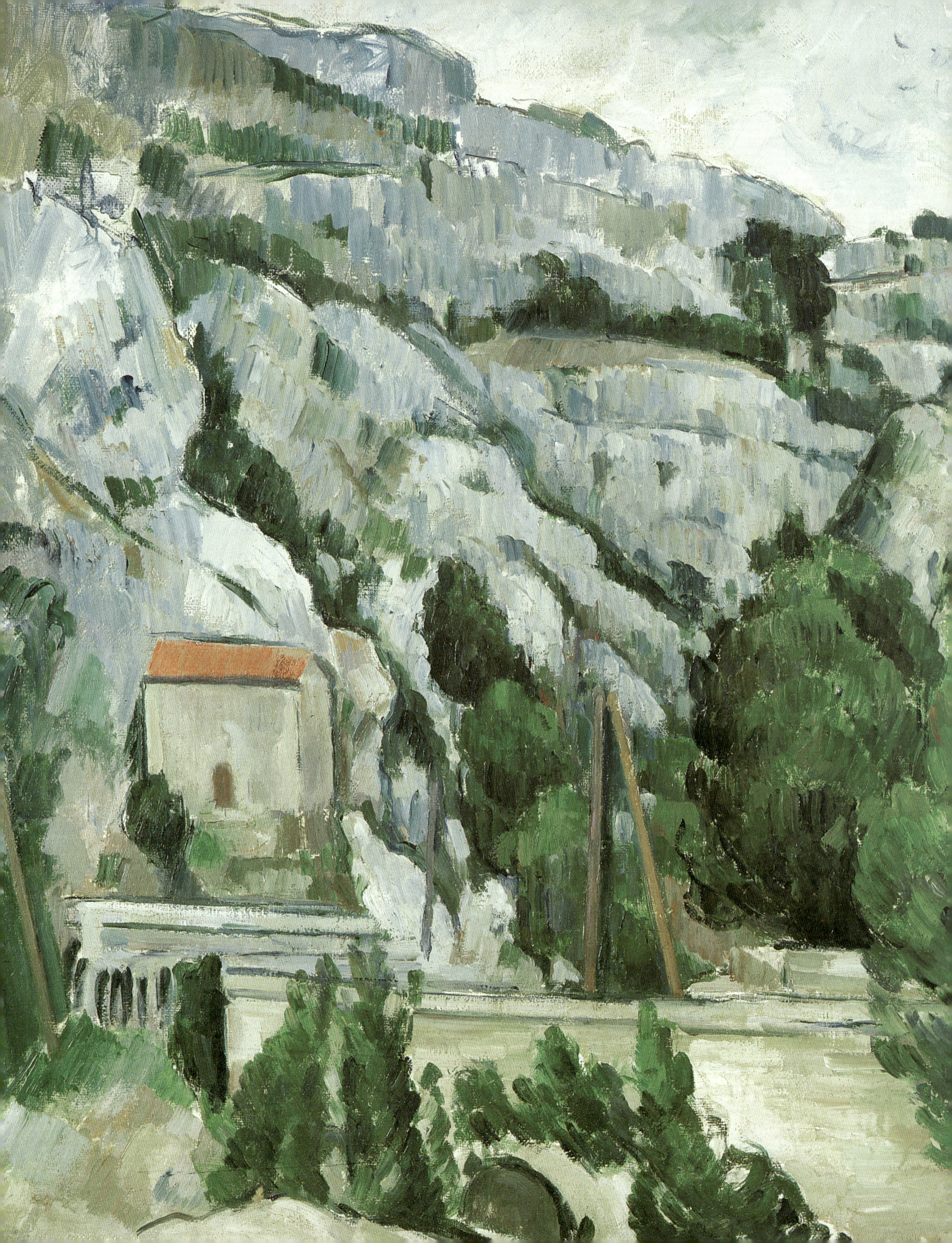

Nature becomes art: landscape and modernism

Christine Dixon

By modernity I mean the ephemeral, the fugitive, the contingent, the half of art whose other half is the eternal and the immutable.

Baudelaire, 'The painter of modern life', 1863[1]

Change implies loss of certainty, that quality so characteristic of modernity. The values that Baudelaire chooses for his definition – ephemeral, fugitive, contingent – all refer to speed, change and doubt. Painting modern life means rejecting past beliefs, especially old aesthetic conventions and rules.

Modern art began in France in the middle of the nineteenth century. There artists building on achievements of previous decades, especially those of Romantic and Realist painters in Britain, Germany and France, transformed the nature of art. The new vision can be traced in landscape paintings by Gustave Courbet (1819–1877), Paul Cézanne (1839–1906), Claude Monet (1840–1926), Vincent van Gogh (1853–1890) and Georges Seurat (1859–1891), among others.

From the turn of the nineteenth century, when landscape became a major subject for painters, theories of nature and culture competed for artists' attention. Nature won, but only just. Religion, science, poetry, philosophy and history were also contenders. In the pictorial arena, German Romantic artists – Friedrich, Carus, Dahl, Schinkel, Kobell – believed in the transformation of observed scenes to communicate larger imagined ideas, often spiritual or transcendent. On the other hand, Realist artists rejected academic and fantastic Romanticism because it implied that reality was inferior to artifice, or ideals, or invented stories. They thought that nothing trumped nature: the world itself was the most extraordinary and surprising source of artistic expression possible. In any competition between truth and beauty, *la verité*, truth or sincerity, was the victor.

To paint *en plein air* – outside, in the fresh air, in the open – became a normal activity for artists in Rome about 1800, then in Britain, France and Germany in the first decades of the next century. The state of the resulting canvas was always contested: study, sketch, or a final painting which would be submitted for exhibition. *Plein-air* works were begun outside and then, usually, finished or re-created in the studio. Those of the 1820s and 1830s made by Camille Corot (1796–1875), both in Italy and France, were lauded as an early high point of *plein-air* painting. They depended on a broad expression of minutely-concentrated attention to the whole as well as its parts. Previously, Classical and picturesque landscapes were composed of observed components. These were reassembled into a harmonious and 'correct' whole, according to academic principles of beauty. In contrast, Corot's *Bridge on the Saône River at Mâcon* 1834 (cat. 65) is unified by daylight playing across its constituent and real elements of stone, water and air. The artist has witnessed this scene. No part is privileged over any other in order to dramatise the composition; indeed, the artist constructs the painting from pale yellow light.

Unusually in such a rivalrous cultural history, the French immediately recognised the jolting effect of an English painter, when three works by John Constable (1776–1837) were exhibited in the 1824 Paris Salon. *The hay wain* 1821 – awarded a gold medal – breathed fresh air into the almost moribund academic and Neo-Classical official tradition. More of Constable's paintings were shown and collected in

cat. 84 **Paul Cézanne** *Viaduct at l'Estaque* 1882 (detail)

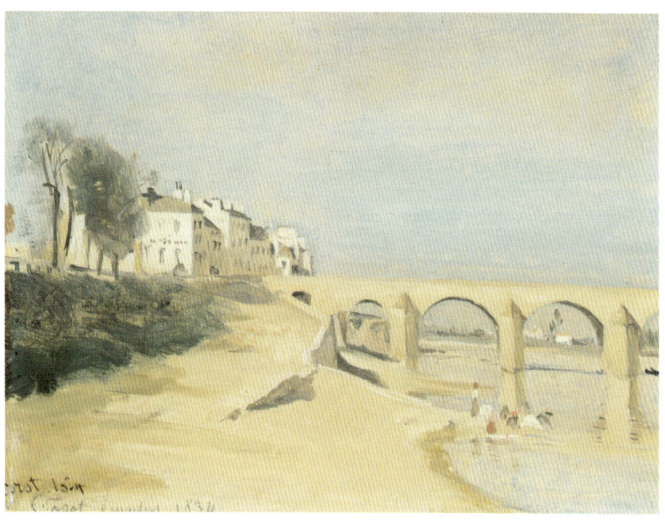

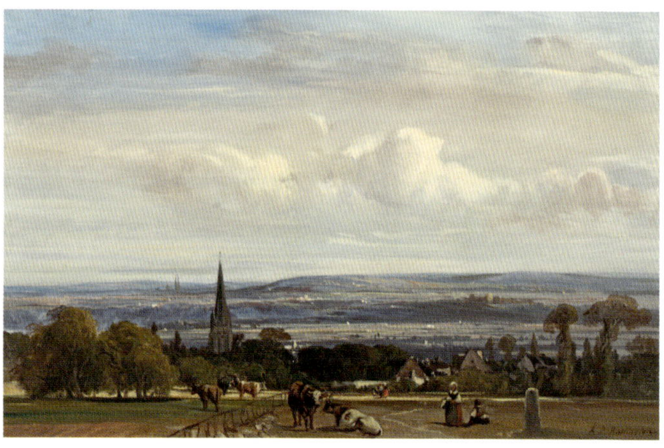

cat. 65 **Camille Corot** *Bridge on the Saône River at Mâcon* 1834

cat. 10 **Richard Parkes Bonington** *Normandy landscape near Lillebonne* 1823

Paris in his lifetime. Ironically, the conservative English artist refused to travel to decadent France, where his radical paintings inspired artists to look at nature anew. Richard Parkes Bonington (1802–1828), in particular, admired the immediacy with which paint could be applied. His *Normandy landscape near Lillebonne* 1823 (cat. 10) used similar strategies to those of Constable: a dominant sky occupies two-thirds of the canvas and horizontal layers of light define the countryside. A human element is often included, here two women. An implied narrative remains, of the eternal harmonious rhythms of rural work and village life, which may imply the beneficence of God's Creation.

Plein-air painting, seen in Constable's oil sketches, was also employed in France by Corot and then, most significantly, by artists based at the village of Barbizon in the forest of Fontainebleau. The activity was regarded as preparation until Impressionists broke down the division between sketch and finished painting in the 1860s and 1870s. Working in the open air became practicable and widespread only when oil paints could be pre-mixed and packed into portable tubes. Before John G. Rand, an American artist working in London, patented his squeezable tin tube in 1841 and 1842, cumbersome leather bladders were standard. New tools, including collapsible easels and paintboxes, and lightweight supports such as readymade academy and canvas boards, allowed easier transport of materials, making them more convenient out of doors.

Théodore Rousseau (1812–1867), doyen of the Barbizon school, used a specially-made easel and portable lean-to, so that he could remain outside to observe every change of weather or varying condition of atmosphere. In such paintings as *Under the birches, evening* 1842–43 (cat. 67), Rousseau naturalised his study of earlier Dutch landscape and his English contemporary Constable into an expression of French nationalism. The Prix de Rome – a long-valued award by the Academy of travel to Italy to absorb the Classical past – lost its importance. It was displaced by what artists came to see as an urgent necessity to explore the 'truth' of the French countryside. This subject was imbued with historical and aesthetic associations, best realised after close observation, rather than the imaginative re-creation of symbolic or mythic events.

It seems paradoxical that the most naturalistic artists of their time, whose fidelity to observed truth was paramount, are regarded now as conservative, or even reactionary. Constable, Corot and Alexandre Calame (1820–1864) all painted preparatory studies *en plein air*, it seems with the underlying assumption that painstaking studies of the natural world produced both beauty and truth. Indeed, they may have believed that nature was identical with beauty, that faithfully reproducing the effects of nature created art. But the factor that such artists ignored, discounted or literally could not see, was the newly unstable character of beauty itself. It changed at some time during the nineteenth century: exact depictions of sublime mountains, verdant valleys or picturesque clouds and glorious foliage no longer defined beauty. In fact, its meaning was no longer constant, nor ever again agreed upon in modern times.

The camera was invented at the end of the 1830s, a new mechanism for capturing the visual world. Photographs reproduced the world in monochrome, mainly in black-and-white, for the rest of the century. The camera required time and stillness to create images. What photography meant for landscape painting was conventionalising the view. Photographers established a single viewpoint: for the painter Charles Daubigny (1817–1878) this allowed a central and radiating position where the artist stood (or sat). In *Banks of the Seine* 1855 (cat. 68) he probably positioned himself mid-stream in a boat, which was to become an Impressionist motif of pleasure. Photography's conventions combined with revelations of other novel visual schema. Chinese and Japanese works of art were seen in Paris and London in the 1850s and 1860s, at the same time that dramatic photographs of Paris by Nadar (1820–1910) were for sale. It is no coincidence that the first Impressionist exhibition of 1874 was displayed in Nadar's studio, due to the sympathy of this first photographer of aerial and underground city views.

The French novelist and critic Emile Zola noticed a painting by Camille Pissarro (1830–1903) in the Salon of 1868. 'C'est là la campagne moderne', he wrote – 'It's there, the modern countryside'.[2] What did he see? Perhaps it was the beginning of change, an acute observer's recognition of new realities. The speed of life increased, as animal transport and walking were augmented by mechanical means, such as railways and

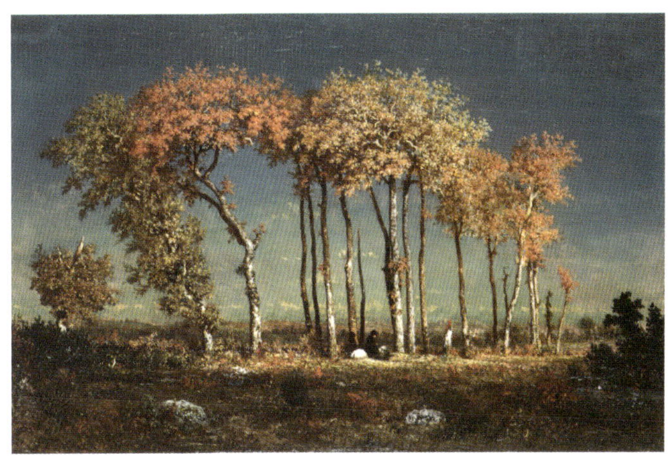

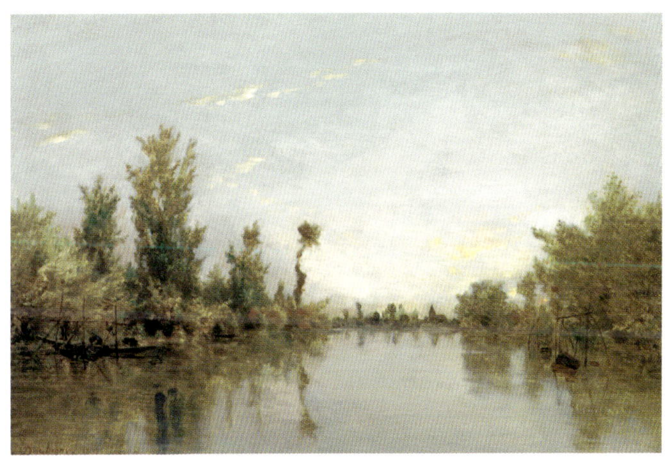

cat. 67 **Théodore Rousseau** *Under the birches, evening* 1842–43

cat. 68 **Charles Daubigny** *Banks of the Seine* 1855

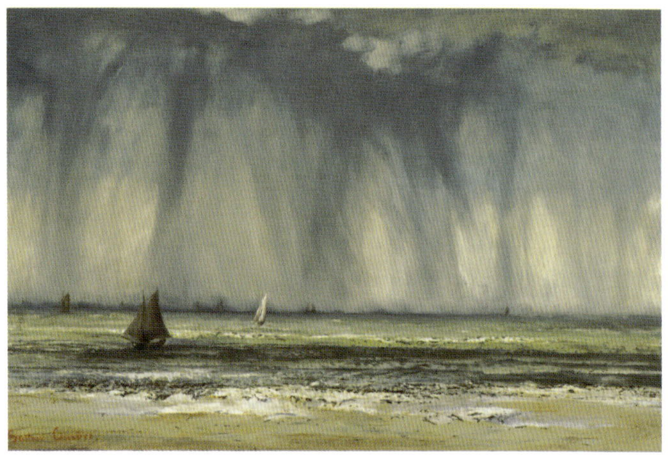

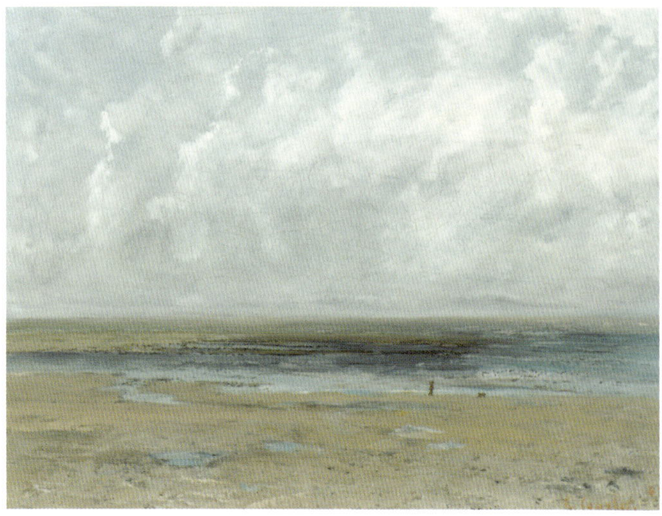

fig. 17 **Gustave Courbet** *The waterspout: marine* 1866 oil on canvas on gypsum board 43.2 x 65.7 cm
Philadelphia Museum of Art, Philadelphia
John G. Johnson Collection, 1917

cat. 70 **Gustave Courbet** *Low tide, the beach at Trouville* 1865

steamships. Millions of country-dwellers came to live in towns and cities after the Industrial Revolution took hold in Europe at the beginning of the century. In France especially, artistic production was concentrated in the capital. The city of Paris is where art schools, grand Salon exhibitions, government patronage and public honours lay. Now the wealthy bourgeoisie – merchants and financiers – became the private buyers and collectors of art.

Venturing outdoors marked a change of condition: that is, for most people in cities and towns, being indoors was their usual experience. Domestic and urban life were now 'natural'. Subjects for art increasingly were interiors or still lifes, as well as portraits. Living in towns became normal, an experience recounted daily and weekly in newspapers and journals, then in novels, plays and operas. It was inevitable that cityscapes became a common landscape subject for painters. Nature was now solace, a means of escape from the pace and dirt of the city, and seemed to be beneficial, both morally and physically. Paris is the setting for sin in *La dame aux camélias* (1848), the famous popular novel written by Alexandre Dumas, which he made into a play in 1852. Verdi renamed Marguerite, the courtesan, Violetta for his 1853 opera version *La Traviata*. The countryside is the place where innocence reigns, and where the heroine's redemptive sacrifice occurs.

No such emotive parallels are rendered by Courbet or James McNeill Whistler (1834–1903) in their attempts to catch a passing moment in the immediate effect of a storm, or night in the city. It seems obvious to us now that such images as *The waterspout: marine* 1866 (fig. 17) prefigure attempts by Impressionist artists to capture a fleeting moment. Courbet's instant is a unique, spectacular, and dramatic phenomenon, rather than that everyday experience realised by Monet and his colleagues as coloured light. More routine is the Realist artist's observation in his unassuming scene portraying *Low tide, the beach at Trouville* 1865 (cat. 70), although in its modesty and simplicity the beach seems almost a non-subject. Perhaps Courbet was influenced by Whistler, at the time his fellow painter on the Norman shores, who experimented with less paint and fewer narrative devices.

Whistler's highly original night scenes, such as *Nocturne in blue and silver* c. 1871–72 (fig. 18), seem to have a different intention, to evoke poetic thoughts in the viewer. In his 'Ten o'clock' lecture of 1885, the artist described how the 'evening mist clothes the riverside with poetry, as with a veil, and the poor buildings lose themselves in the dim sky, and the tall chimneys become campanili, and the warehouses are palaces in the night, and the whole city hangs in the heavens and fairy-land is before us'.[3] While his breathless rhetoric seems old-fashioned now, the artistic means Whistler employs are revolutionary: flattened planes, reduced colour, the image radically cropped, while he depicts the calm, transcendent night through city fog and reflections on the polluted River Thames. His debt to Japanese woodblock prints is acknowledged also in reeds which double as calligraphy, and a signature seal. Similar *japoniste* tactics can be seen in later landscape paintings, notably in those by Monet and van Gogh.

Perhaps the most extraordinary cultural transfer from state dominance to private patronage occurred in France in the last decades of the century. Those in charge of funds for commissions and public purchases would not support modern art. By denying legitimacy in the Salon to any new or experimental artists – Rousseau, Manet, Courbet, Monet and other Realists and Impressionists – the French state allowed its cultural authority to be undermined, then ignored, and finally mocked. The Salon had always been the major patron of art, the venue for exhibitions and supplier of paintings to public museums. It was vitiated by the forces of aesthetic and political reaction, so that when art moved on, official culture ossified.

Courbet, famous in Paris for his peasant coarseness, was the son of a wealthy farmer in deeply rural France. It seems extraordinary now that his transgressive communist political opinions, values he often realised on canvas, could permit an offer of the Legion of Honour and Cross in 1870. He refused, but the Academy's aim was to co-opt Courbet into the French government's regime of culture. So long as an artist gained official recognition at the Salon, automatic exhibition selection, state commissions and purchases followed, including acquisition of his works for the Louvre. Previously no other path to success in a French artist's career existed.

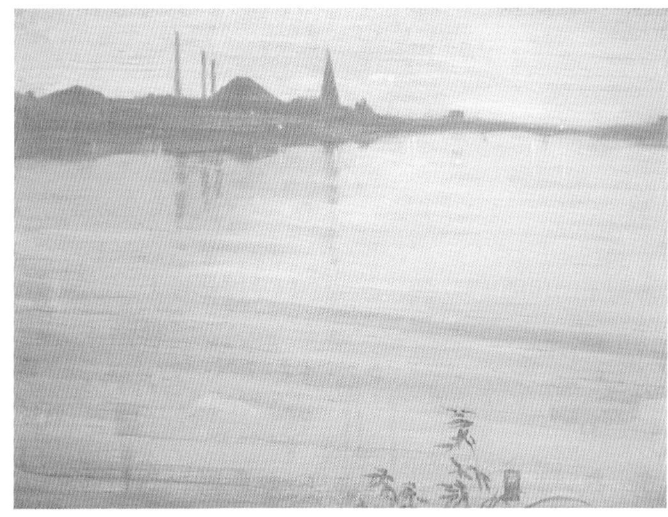

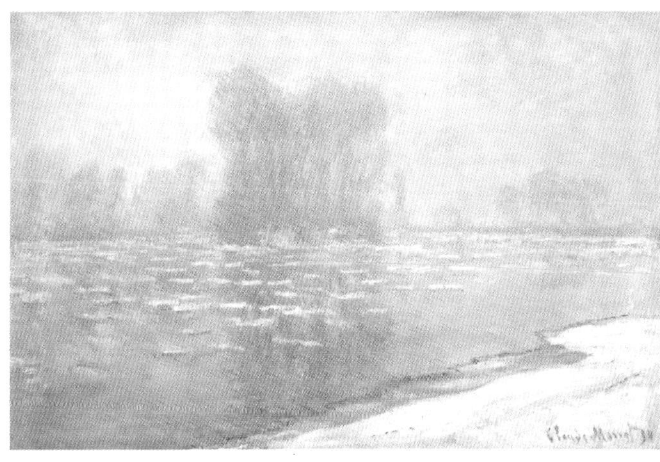

fig. 18 **James McNeill Whistler** *Nocturne in blue and silver* c. 1871–1872
oil on panel 44.1 x 61.0 cm
Harvard University Art Museums, Fogg Art Museum
Bequest of Grenville L. Winthrop

cat. 97 **Claude Monet** *Morning haze* 1894

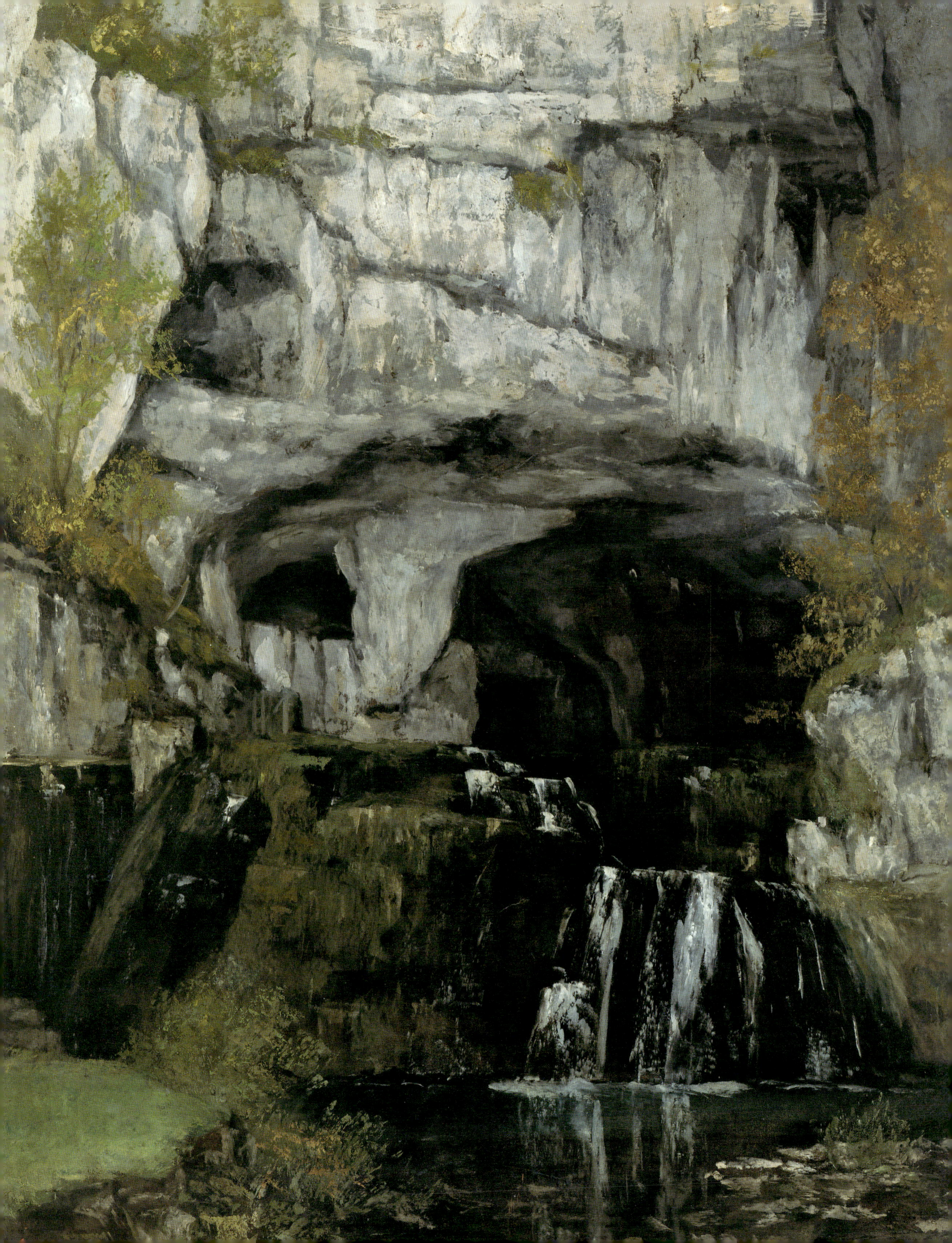

Capitalism and its new art market awaited. Private dealers with galleries burgeoned; the Galerie Durand-Ruel began in the 1820s as a stationery shop which sold art supplies, while the still active auction house Drouot was established in 1852. Such agencies at first hovered around arts margins, but eventually prevailed over the state monopoly. By 1861, 104 art dealers were open for business in Paris.[4] Now private representatives could offer exhibitions, sales and public auctions, and supply a burgeoning market in the United States. Vigorous American buyers, seemingly more accepting of the modern landscape because less hidebound, provided artists with financial security. By the 1890s, his American patrons gave Monet the freedom to experiment without fear of privation; in exchange, the *nouveau riche* gained much-desired cultural capital.

One significant group of artists, however, still did not make art in the open air. Why were there no female landscape painters? Excluded from life classes and therefore from heroic figure painting, women artists were also largely absent from the landscape.[5] Probably the major reason was social: contemporary morality implied the world outside the home was sexually unsafe. Women, married or single, could not venture into the countryside to paint *en plein air*, either alone or in mixed company. Even accompanied by a female servant or relative, a woman's reputation was at risk. Another, mainly practical, factor lay in the obstructive and heavy costumes worn by 'ladies' in the nineteenth century. How could a woman climb a mountain in a bustle? Go on an expedition? Spend all day in a meadow?

Realities of social class also affected who could become an artist: one needed a private income or patron, or the ability to mix easily with aristocratic and bourgeois buyers of paintings. This is why Turner established his own gallery in Harley Street, London, in 1804, although the issue of unfavourable verdicts by the judgment of conservative official juries also arose. Courbet set up his own exhibition in 1855 in a venue he called the Pavillon du Réalisme, opposite the Exposition Universelle, after having paintings rejected by its jury: the display was among the earliest independent shows by an artist. The same experience inspired Edouard Manet (1832–1883) to go it alone in 1867: both ventures were financially unsuccessful, although some of the greatest oils of the century were shown there.

Who were the bedrock supporters of modernist painting in France? Surprisingly, in the nineteenth century it was all those financially comfortable but usually disapproving fathers, who nonetheless underwrote their stubborn sons' anti-bourgeois careers.[6] Sometimes the artist's father was disappointed and fearful, vehemently opposed, or perhaps uncomprehending – although his philistine view was sometimes undermined by a sympathetic mother. Corot, Courbet, Manet, Cézanne, Monet, Whistler, Seurat and others all repudiated a family trade, profession, or middle-class occupation in order to attempt the highest artistic career possible: as a painter in oils. Occasionally a posthumous financial legacy allowed the painter to marry his mistress and continue to work.

A rupture occurs in landscape art some time in the 1860s, perhaps when artists no longer seek beauty as an aim in itself. Figure painters such as the Spanish master Goya (1746–1828), who decades earlier made images of horror and terror, had renounced many concepts about the necessity for beauty. But lovers of nature became searchers after truth as well as earthly momentary pleasures, rather than attempting to remake the world into a state of perfection. The Classical ideal of beauty had been lost decades earlier, when awkward reality was preferred to Arcadia: nymphs no longer dwelt in the forests of France.

Brutal, rocky landscapes by Courbet and Cézanne are specific to locations in their native regions of the Jura and Aix-en-Provence (cat. 69 and 100). Obdurate and boldly frontal, the compositions of these two rebels brought a new materiality to painting. Like Turner, Courbet builds up impasto, thick layers of paint on the canvas, so that the artistic trick of representing three dimensions in two is challenged, even subverted. Unlike the English artist however, Courbet insists on earthy materials for both paint and the landscape he depicts. *Source of the Lison* 1864 (cat. 69) reveals no light horizon: we cannot see past the cliff, nor up into a mutable sky, but can only look into the dark mysteries of the earth, or flow down with the river.

In *The Rue Mosnier with flags* 1878 (fig. 19), Manet used some of the disruptive techniques seen in photography. A central passage of the most banal Parisian street is portrayed in the painting as a contained avenue, with a crippled

cat. 69 **Gustave Courbet** *Source of the Lison* 1864

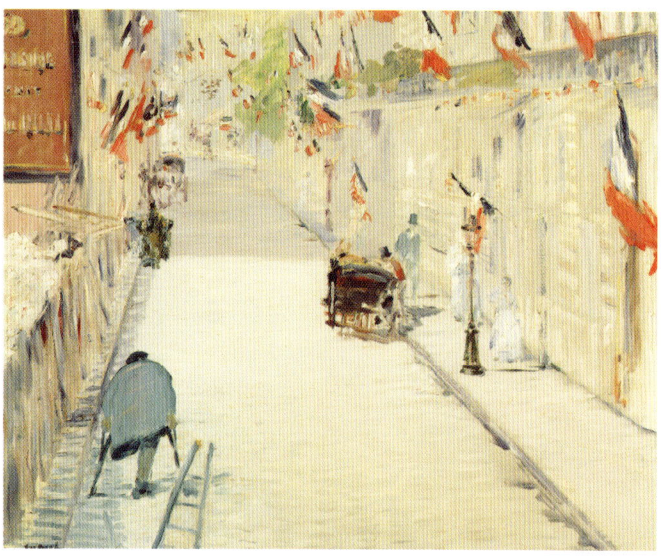

fig. 19 **Édouard Manet** *The Rue Mosnier with flags* 1878
oil on canvas 65.5 x 81.0 cm J. Paul Getty Museum, Los Angeles

(opposite)
cat. 88 **Claude Monet** *Port-Goulphar, Belle-Île* 1887

fig. 20 **Winslow Homer** *Cannon Rock* 1895 oil on canvas 101.6 x 101.6 cm
Metropolitan Museum of Art, New York
Gift of George A. Hearn, 1906
Photograph © 1983 The Metropolitan Museum of Art, New York

veteran as the protagonist of a discomfiting narrative of the here-and-now. There is no conventional beauty here, only an extraordinary display of modernity. These white-hot Parisian streets on 30 June 1878 challenge any sentimental views of the first French celebration of their Republic in the aftermath of the disastrous Franco–Prussian War, the Siege of Paris, defeat of the Commune and the consequent uneasy compromise of a restored republic.[7] Manet questions all the old certainties here, political as well as pictorial. In contrast, Monet's picturing of the same day is purely visual, his fluttering strokes of coloured pigment making flags seem to move in the breeze in the *Rue Saint-Denis, fête du 30 juin* 1878.

Impressionist painters denied the narrative or stories, and therefore consequences, in their depiction of immediate experience. Critics were dismayed by their erasure of didactic and moralising content from art, along with their flouting of aesthetic rules. If the incident portrayed is ephemeral – walking across a meadow, seeing haystacks one afternoon, watching a city street – then the grandiose aims of traditional art are fatally undermined. Impressionist canvases could not contain eternal, unchanging truths, because the moment was passing, or indeed had already passed while the artists tried to capture serial, changing realities.

Perhaps because photography could frame a view forever (or so it seemed), now landscape artists pursued the moment when it alters. In *Port-Goulphar, Belle-Île* 1887 (cat. 88), Monet captures the instant a wave breaks onto the rocks; the coincident demonstration of the power of Nature is no longer the point nor meaning of the work. Instead, light glitters on the cliffs and sea, breaking up the visual field with white on dark brown, blue and green, forcing us to look at paint instead of scenery. In his strikingly similar composition of *Cannon Rock* 1895 (fig. 20), the American artist Winslow Homer (1836–1919) does not understand the aesthetic transformation which had occurred in France. Instead, he renders the waves' energy by a mimetic realisation of the drama.

The French countryside no longer separates into views of pasture or wilderness: places are either worked and shaped by humans, or exist untouched except by travellers. There are few farmers, shepherds or explorers in modern landscapes. Artists instead show sites of leisure for city-dwellers. As well as the Impressionists in France, Australians Tom Roberts (1856–1931) and Charles Conder (1868–1909) reveal casual, haphazard beauty on suburban beaches such as Mentone and Bronte (cat. 76 and 77). On the fringes of large cities – perhaps Melbourne or Sydney now within easy reach of many people by public transport – seaside visitors are portrayed as temporary inhabitants of a kind of earthly paradise, previously available only to the rich or aristocratic.

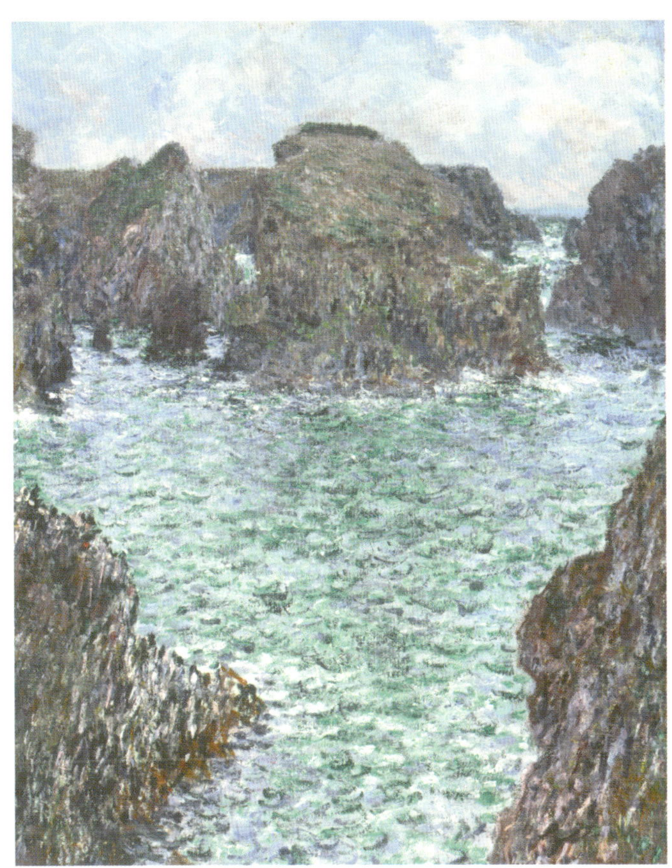

In the last years of the nineteenth century, artists used the genre of landscape to experiment with colour and form, questioning the nature of painting. Van Gogh paints *Tree trunks in the grass* 1890 (cat. 91) as an extraordinary close-up rendition of an urban park, which is in fact the garden at his asylum. He reinvigorates the landscape format by looking down – inward, not outward – thus eliminating both horizon and sky. Characteristically short and sharp paint strokes, delicate in the flowers and thick grass, become longer and more definite in the rugged bark of the trees. This landscape is no longer continuous, part of a journey through scenery. It has been fractured by the disruptive elements of modernity: constant change, abrupt dislocations, new disbeliefs, and aesthetic theories which describe art anew.

By the 1870s the countryside had become unusual, even exotic: it was the place where urban people ventured in order to escape the worries and congestion of town life. They sought a cleansing breath of naturally fresh air, wishing for cool greenery and blue waters instead of hot stone streets, a place of leisure rather than work. Aesthetic pleasure in nature replaced the smells, dirt and mechanical ugliness of the city. Although secular in character rather than the religious yearnings of German Romanticism, French landscape painters of the mid nineteenth century looked mainly to exceptional rural scenes rather than to the urban everyday. When a young group of artists attempted that new subject, the city, late in the nineteenth century, it seems appropriate that they tried a scientific and modern approach.[8]

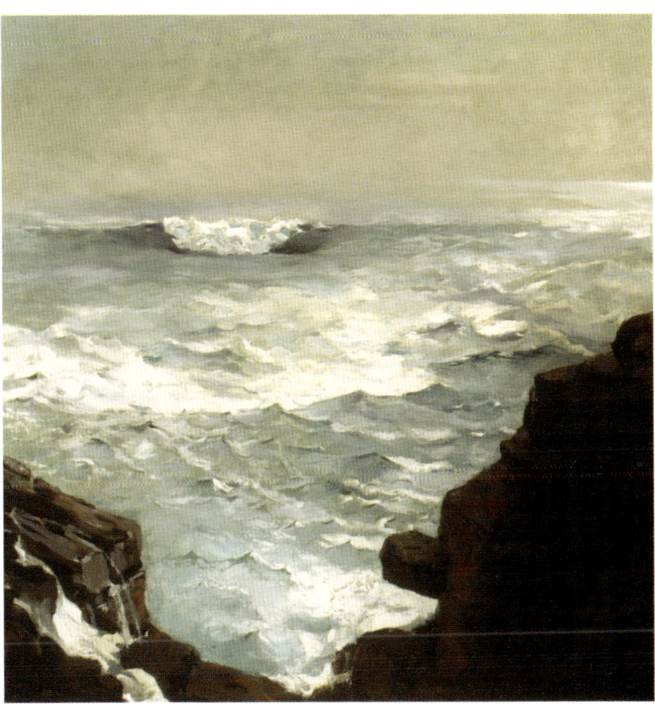

Seurat's heroic expositions of colour and perception, influenced by such writers as Chevreul, Blanc and Henry,[9] are based on the optical effects of opposing colours: for

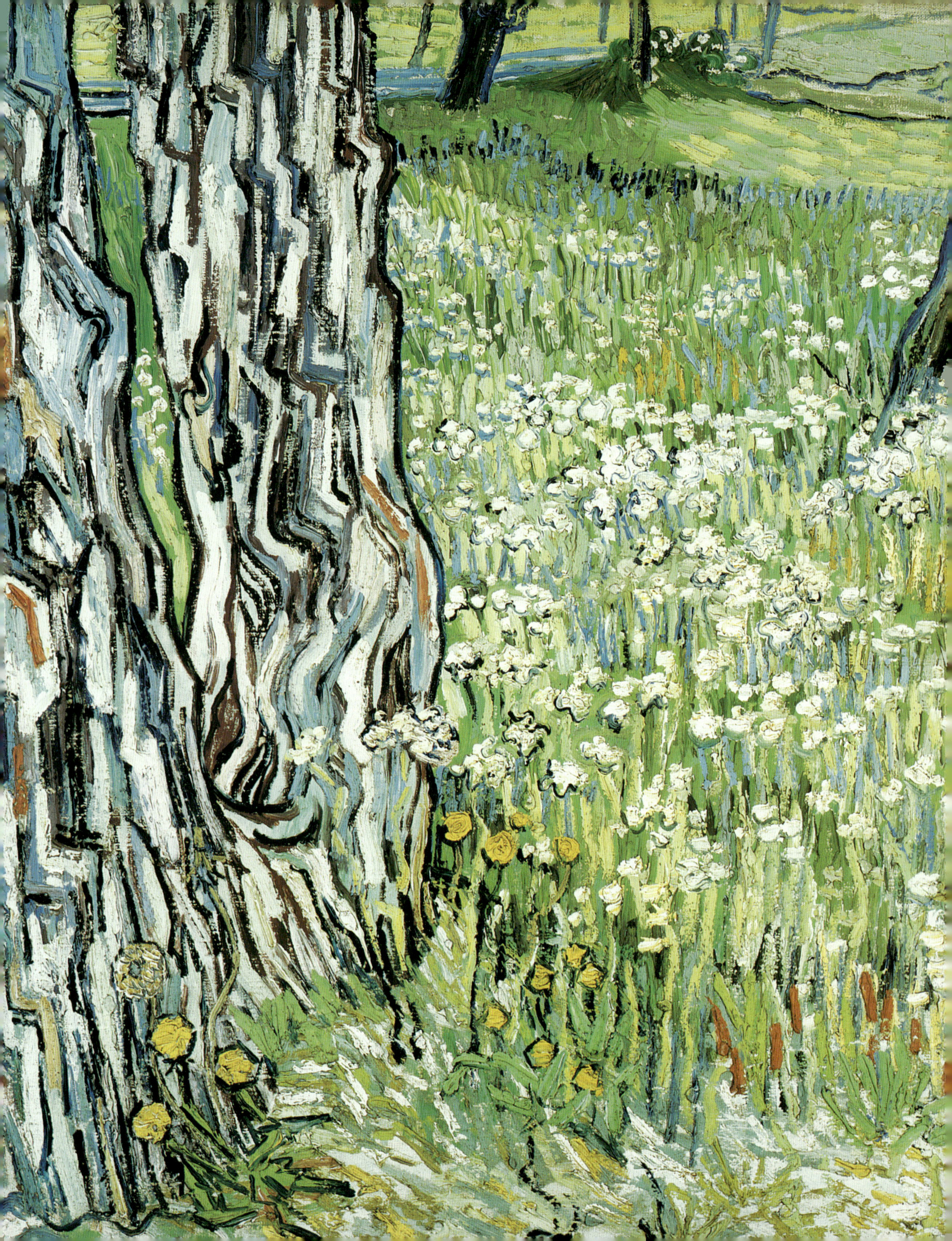

example, we perceive brown when patches of pure red are placed next to green. Many small brushstrokes or dots of paint of differing hues make up large areas of the canvas, the 'divisionist' strategy of the Neo-Impressionists. Colour has an emotional impact also: Seurat's various cool and warm harmonies intensify the expressive content of his paintings. *Lucerne, Saint-Denis* 1885 (cat. 86) instances how the strongest colour combinations are calmed and unified by the artist's small and lively brushstrokes, to delightful effect.

Another contemporary intellectual element is an interest in synaesthesia, where the senses are intertwined so that a musical note may evoke a colour or a scent, or vice versa. Wagnerian and Symbolist theories about the moral and social imperatives of the arts and society also affected the Neo-Impressionists. When Paul Signac (1863–1935) painted the high-keyed, almost blond values of city buildings in *Gasometers at Clichy* 1886 (cat. 87), he also employed the pictorially useful red roof tiles and blue summer sky to best advantage. But it was an aesthetic revolution to show an industrial building, such as a factory, at all. This is a cathedral for the late nineteenth century, addressed frontally, even baldly. But where are the people, the city's inhabitants, the workers? For Neo-Impressionists such as Seurat, Signac, Maximilien Luce (1858–1941) and Jan Toorop (1858–1928), aesthetically radical and politically Anarchist in their sympathies, the city surely implies workers. Yet they are often absent. Instead, Seurat depicted Parisians at play: bathing in the river, at the circus, walking in the park.[10]

As modern art developed into a fresh way of thinking about the world, artists such as Monet and Cézanne returned to the same motifs, with endless variations. In *Morning haze* 1894 (cat. 97) Monet's subject is the disappearance of form and colour under nature's wintry grey and white coverings of snow and fog on the river Seine. Like Turner, Monet attempts to paint the ineffable effects of light and water on infinite arrays of land and sky. Cézanne's obsession with the mountain of Saint-Victoire – he painted it more than fifty times – points to those differences of approach now recognised as the transition from Impressionism to Post-Impressionism. When artists recognised that painting is only the arrangement of liquid pigment on a flat surface, they experimented with those other, formal, qualities which underlay physical appearances.

Even now, more than a century after his death, few artists provoke such an equivocal response as Cézanne, in whose paintings human presence is naturalised as equivalent to the surrounding scenery, or as part of it. He uses high or low viewpoints, either distant or impossibly close, diagonal or layered structures, and reduced forms which serve to emphasise this conflation of human and natural construction. As Rishel noted, the imminent disintegration of *The house with the cracked walls* c. 1892–94 (fig. 21) accords with Cézanne's own abandonment of conventional perspective in this architectural stacking of planes. He analysed how the 'large fissure that rends the upper part of the house and continues below into the attached, projecting outbuilding declares a slow but persistent collapse of the entire structure'.[11]

Eventually, as the century ends, oil paint need not even fully obscure the canvas ground. In *Forest scene (Path from Mas Jolie to Château Noir)* 1900–02 for instance (cat. 100), each constituent patch of paint making up stairs or leaves or shadows is equal in value; they are tentative markers of the material world. Cézanne wrote of this unfinished quality to a fellow artist: '… the sensations of colour, which give light, are the reasons for the abstractions which prevent me from either covering my canvas or continuing the delimitation of the objects when their points of contact are fine and delicate; from which it results [that] my image or picture is incomplete'.[12] Landscapes no longer need render a specific place; they rather encompass their creators' aesthetic theories.

As wilderness receded as a possible or normative subject, artists still tended to show evidence of human intervention in the landscape. Haystacks, pastures and crops, domesticated animals, paths and even plain village houses became central subjects for many painters. Little unexplored country was left. Gauguin lived in Tahiti in the 1890s and reveals, in his *Landscape with a horse* 1899 (cat. 99), the house and stock of local people, with a beautiful, dramatic volcano in the background. None of us – artist, Tahitians, the viewer – is unduly threatened by the violence of Nature, although all perhaps recognise the fecundity of Pacific vegetation. The intensity of experience, however, is newly presented by Gauguin in rich hues of secondary colours: dark green, purple, orange. Simpler primaries, of blazing red and yellow

cat. 91 **Vincent van Gogh** *Tree trunks in the grass* 1890 (detail)

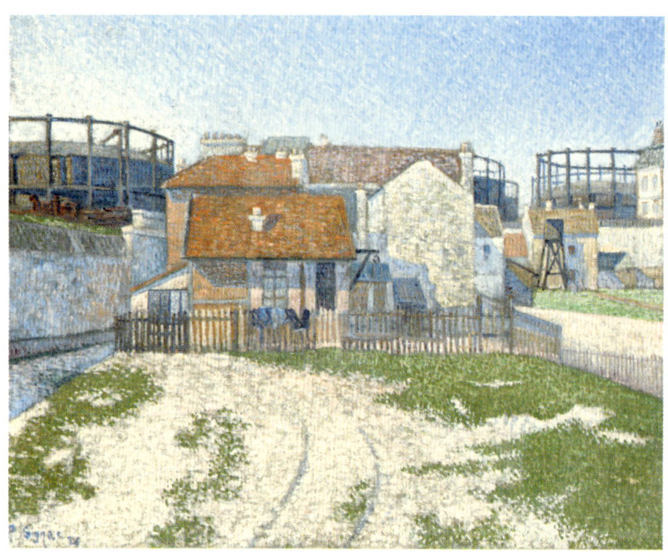

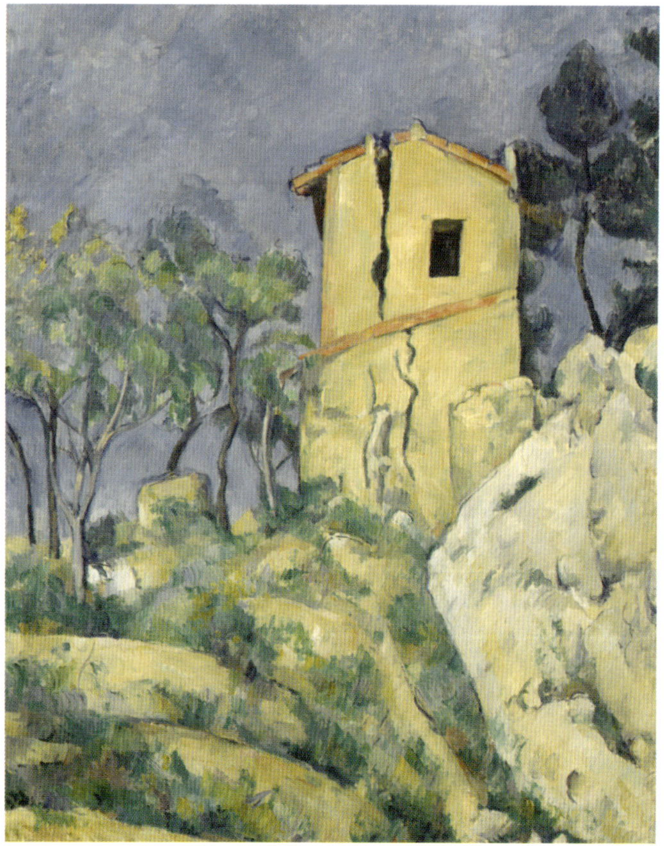

or intense blues and greens are preferred by van Gogh, in order to illuminate the duller northern hemisphere.

When the nature of art changed in the nineteenth century, many things previously regarded as ugly, and thus unpaintable, are depicted in new ways. Modern artists show how almost anything can be beautiful, or marvellous, or strange. In 1897 Pissarro recognised a new beauty – banal city streets as a suitable subject for art. He wrote to his son Lucien that his hotel room had:

> … a superb view over the avenue de l'Opéra and that corner of the place du Palais-Royal! It is beautiful to paint. Perhaps it is not very aesthetic, but I am delighted to be able to try to do these Paris streets which are customarily called ugly, but which are so silvery, so luminous and so lively and which are so different from the boulevards – it's completely modern!!![13]

By the turn of the twentieth century, the lives of ordinary people are modern also: reality is faster, lived in urban rather than rural surrounds, labour is based on machines, while women encroach into the public sphere. Art too is ever-changing, and filled with doubt. In Monet's *Waterlilies* 1914–17 (fig. 22) the surface of the pond is interrupted, so that we read the image at once vertically (looking down into the translucent water) and horizontally (looking over the iris bed and past a flowering frond over the opaque water). What we as modern viewers do, automatically, is accept that the artist's ambiguity adds both meaning and beauty to contemplation of his depthless blue paint, where light diffuses from the canvas into our uncertain world.

cat. 87 **Paul Signac** *Gasometers at Clichy* 1886

fig. 21 **Paul Cézanne** *The house with the cracked walls* c. 1892–94
oil on canvas 80.0 x 64.1 cm
The Metropolitan Museum of Art, New York
The Walter H. and Leonore Annenberg Collection, Gift of Walter H. and Leonore Annenberg, 1993, Bequest of Walter H. Annenberg, 2002
Photograph © 1994 The Metropolitan Museum of Art, New York

(opposite)
fig. 22 **Claude Monet** *Waterlilies* [*Nymphéas*] c. 1914–17
oil on canvas 181.0 x 201.6 cm
National Gallery of Australia, Canberra
Purchased 1979 NGA 1979.2858

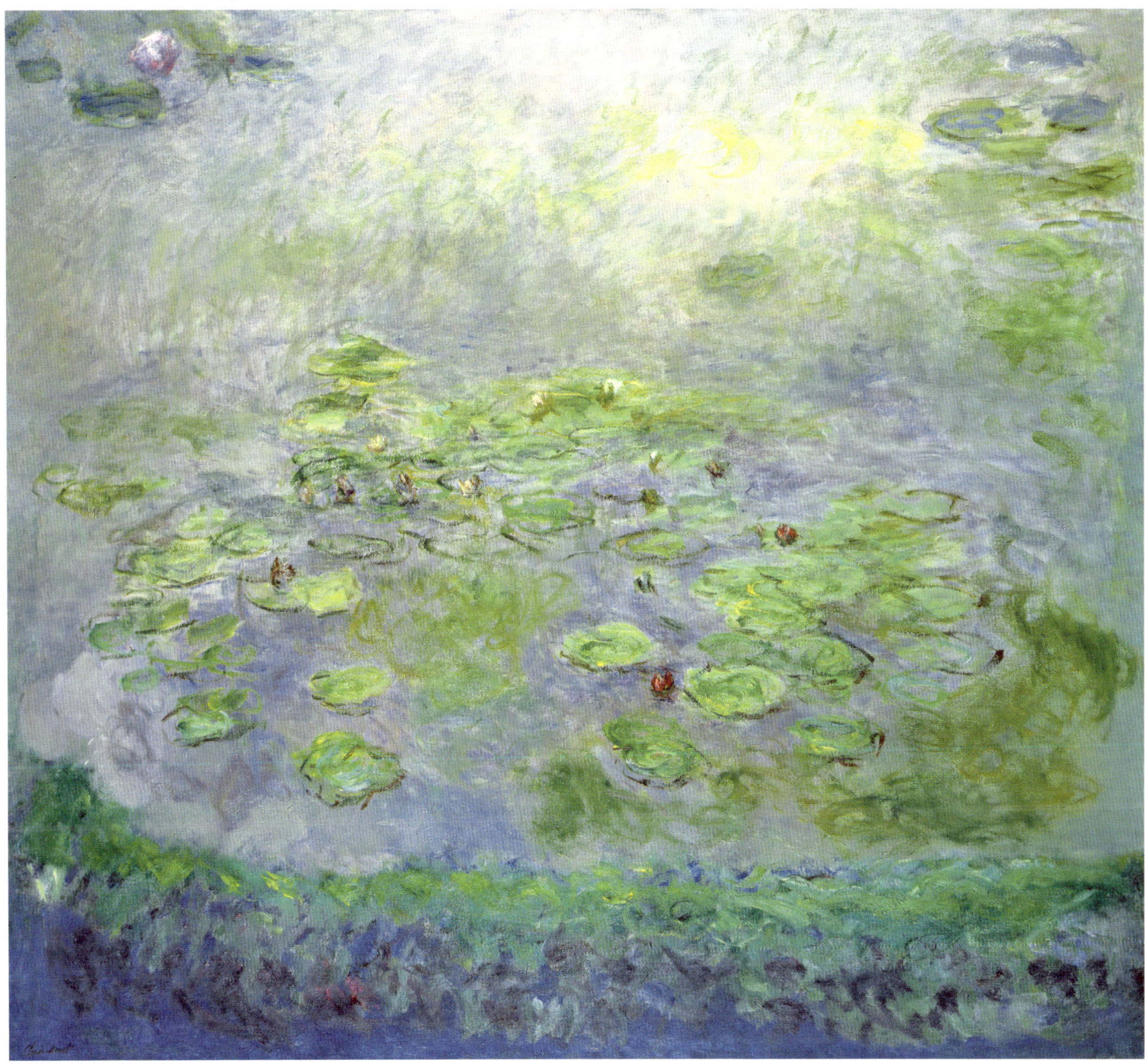

1. Charles Baudelaire (1821–1867), poet and critic of literature and art, published his review of the annual Salon exhibition as 'Le Peintre de la vie moderne' in the newspaper *Le Figaro* on 29 November 1863.
2. Cited by Linda Nochlin in 'Camille Pissarro: The unassuming eye', in *The Politics of vision: Essays in nineteenth-century art and society*, New York: Harper and Row, 1989, p. 63.
3. First published as *Mr Whistler's '10 o'clock'*, London: Chatto & Windus, 1888.
4. Paul Lacroix, *L'Annuaire des artists et des amateurs*, Paris: Veuve J. Renouard, 1861, cited by Harrison C. White and Cynthia A. White in *Canvases and careers: institutional change in the French painting world*, rev. edn, Chicago and London: Chicago University Press, 1965, 1993, p. 97, note 19, p. 110.
5. Genre specialists such as the animal painter Rosa Bonheur (1822–1899) and painter of battle scenes Elizabeth Butler (1850–1933) were not regarded as landscape painters.
6. For an exposition of the family relationships of the artists see, for example, Belinda Thomson, *Impressionism: origins, practice, reception*, London: Thames & Hudson, 2000, pp. 70–81.
7. After 1880 France's national day was marked as Bastille Day on 14 July.
8. Paul Smith argues that Seurat in particular did not adopt a positivist, scientific approach; rather, it was Pissarro's interpretation of his philosophy that allowed the 'scientific' misinterpretation to continue. See his *Seurat and the avant-garde*, New Haven and London: Yale University Press 1997, p. 1 and passim.
9. M.E. Chevreul, *De la loi du contraste simultané des couleurs, et de l'assortiment des objets colorés …*, Paris: Pitois-Levrault et cie, 1839; Charles Blanc, *Grammaire des arts du dessin, architecture, sculpture, peinture*, Paris: Veuve J. Renouard, 1867; Odgen Rood, *Modern chromatics, with applications to art and industry*, New York, D. Appleton and Company, 1879; Charles Henry, *Cercle chromatique et rapporteur esthétique*, Paris: C. Verdin, 1888.
10. Impressionist landscapes by women, notably Mary Cassatt (1844–1926) and Berthe Morisot (1841–1895), usually depict mothers and children in municipal parks. The paintings are figure compositions, placed just outside the bounds of domestic interiors.
11. Colin B. Bailey, Joseph J. Rishel and Mark Rosenthal, *Masterpieces of Impressionism and Post-Impressionism: The Annenberg Collection*, New York: Harry N. Abrams, 1989, p. 78.
12. Letter to Emile Bernard, 23 October 1905, no. CLXXXIV, in John Rewald (ed.), *Paul Cézanne: letters*, trans. Marguerite Kay, London: Bruno Cassirer, 1941, pp. 251–2.
13. Letter to Lucien Pissarro, 15 December 1897, in Janine Bailly-Herzberg (ed.), *Correspondance de Camille Pissarro*, vol. 4, Paris: Presses Universitaires de France, 1989, p. 418.

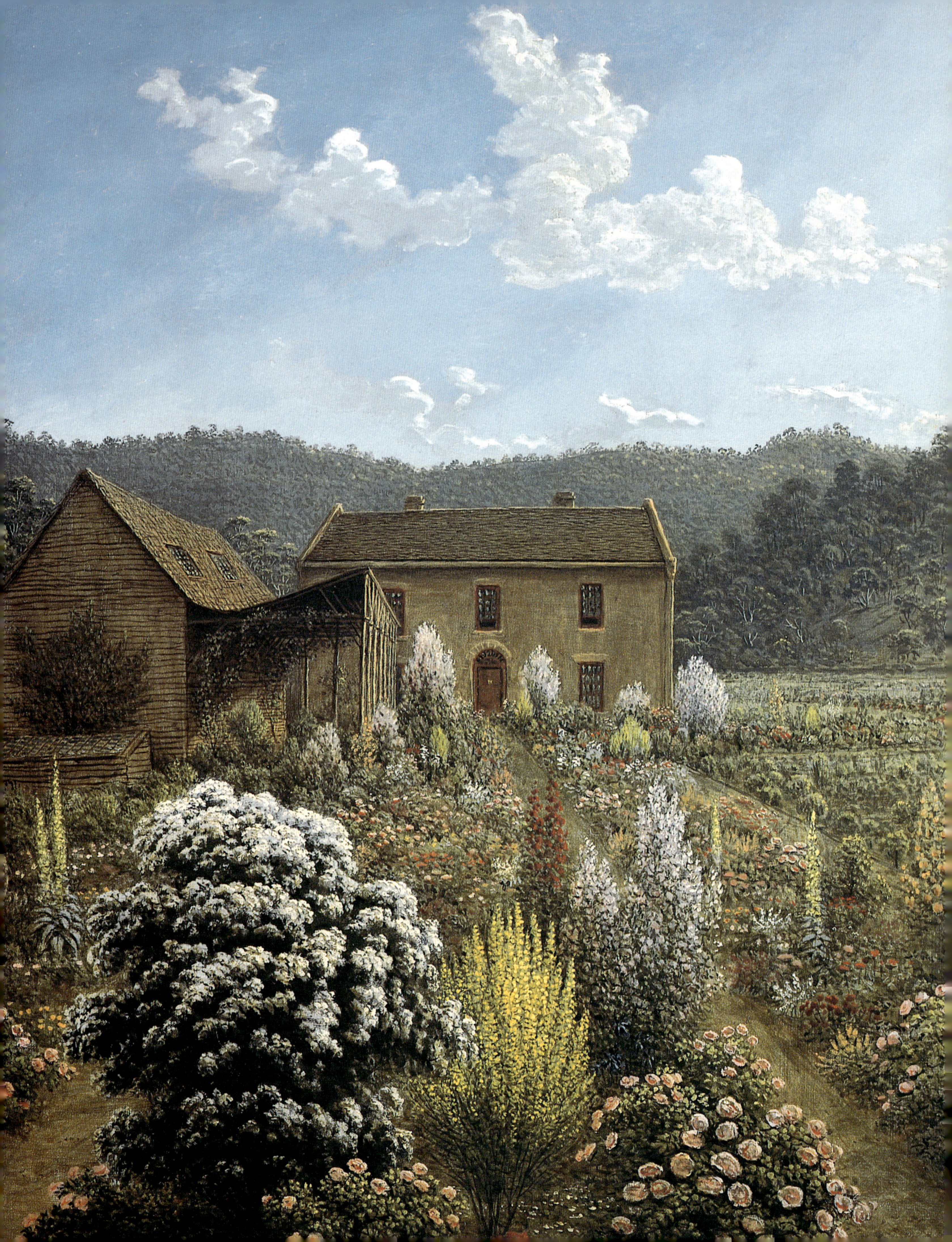

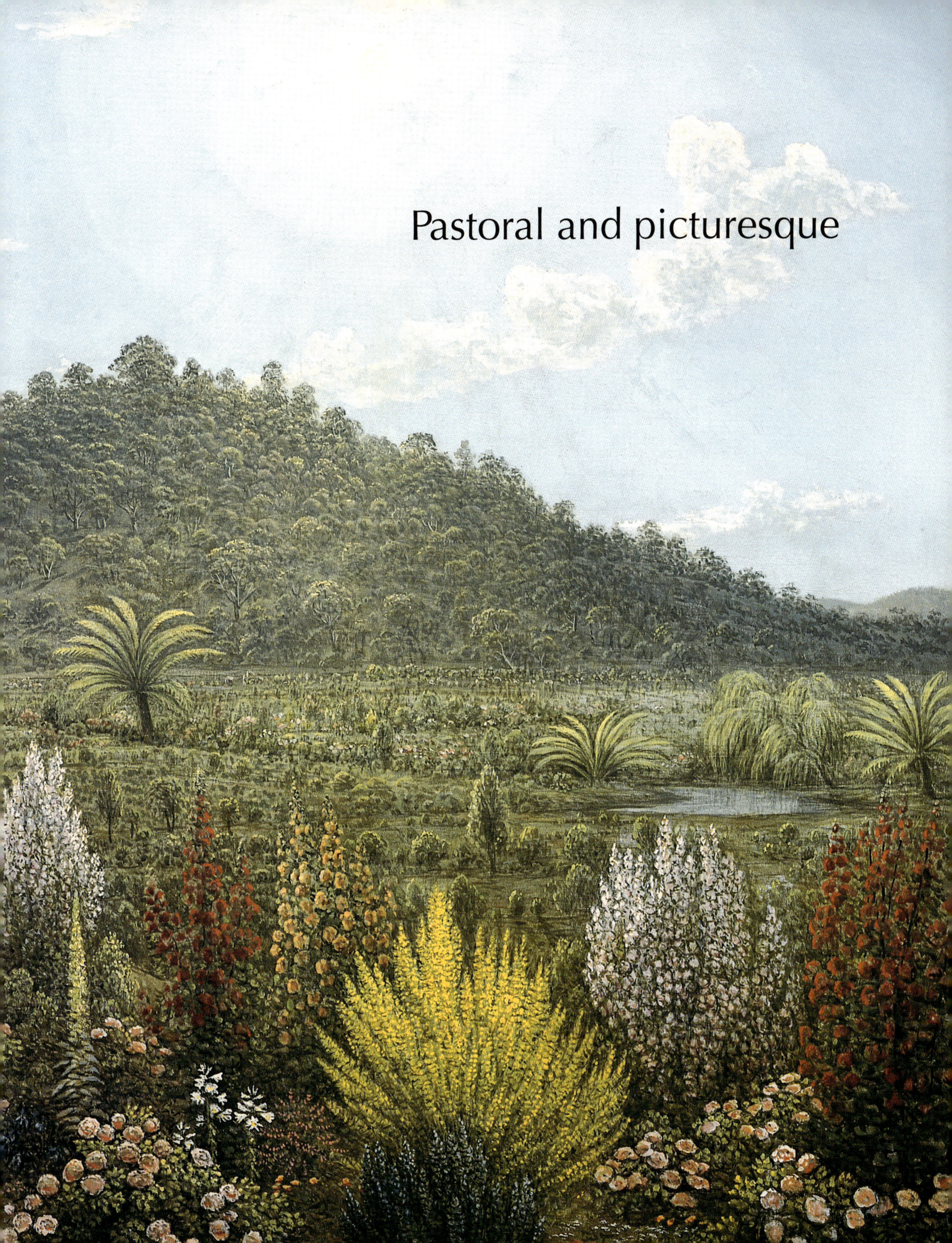

Pastoral and picturesque

1. Thomas Girtin

Great Britain 1775–1802
Alnwick from Brizlee c. 1800
watercolour and pencil on paper 40.7 x 53.0 cm
Duke of Northumberland, Alnwick Castle

Girtin is one of the most remarkable and innovatory English watercolour painters. He, together with J.M.W. Turner, revolutionised the art of watercolour. They transformed the medium from an art of tinted drawing to one that captured the moods of Nature and a range of light and weather effects, using looser handling. Girtin is known particularly for the emotional expressiveness, subtle delicacy and economy of his images. He attained a depth of colour using bold, broad transparent washes in a subdued tonal palette.

Girtin was apprenticed to Edward Dayes, a topographical watercolourist from whom he gained a sound practical training. While still a young man he became a close friend and associate of Turner – and his chief rival. From about 1794 to 1798 they worked in collaboration, copying watercolours by John Robert Cozens for the amateur collector Dr Thomas Monro, learning from Cozens's approach to landscape composition. Girtin first established his reputation with architectural and topographical sketches and drawings. He became known for his images of solitary mountains and coasts, but also painted many views of picturesque villages, rural scenes and country house portraits. He later created works aimed at a mass audience, including an enormous 360-degree circular panorama of London called *Eidometropolis*, exhibited to the public in 1802. It had a naturalistic treatment of light and atmosphere which gave the spectator the illusion of being in the location.

In *Alnwick from Brizlee* Girtin places the town and castle of Alnwick within in a sweeping vista. He viewed the landscape from above, looking over a broad, almost empty foreground, leading the eye into the space beyond, towards the distant sea. Beams of light radiate from the sky over the landscape, conveying the grandeur of Nature and evoking a sense of spiritual uplifting. The sweeping simplicity of the landscape is emphasised by the distribution of light and shade (chiaroscuro). Through the long overview of the scene and the high viewpoint, Girtin pointed to the prosperity of the landscape. Although he makes Alnwick Castle subservient to the landscape setting, beams of light fall on recent improvements to the property: Robert Adam's Lion Bridge and Robert Mylne's Denwick Bridge.[1] And by including the mother and child in the foreground he implies the Duke of Northumberland's generosity, as the bundles of sticks they are carrying indicate the Duke's acknowledgment of their customary rights.[2]

But in this impressive watercolour Girtin was not primarily interested in creating a narrative nor in making social comment. Rather, he was concerned with conveying the atmosphere of an expanse of open country – in depicting the light and dark in the sky and clouds and the way these unified the landscape, and with presenting a broad, majestic sweep of the terrain. When he died from tuberculosis at the age of twenty-seven, Girtin was described by his contemporary Joseph Farington as 'a genius'. Although Turner is said to have suggested that 'if Girtin had lived, I should have starved', this is unlikely. There is no doubt, however, that Turner greatly admired Girtin's work.

Anne Gray

1. Greg Smith, *Thomas Girtin: the art of watercolour*, London: Tate Publishing, 2002, p. 218.
2. Smith, p. 218.

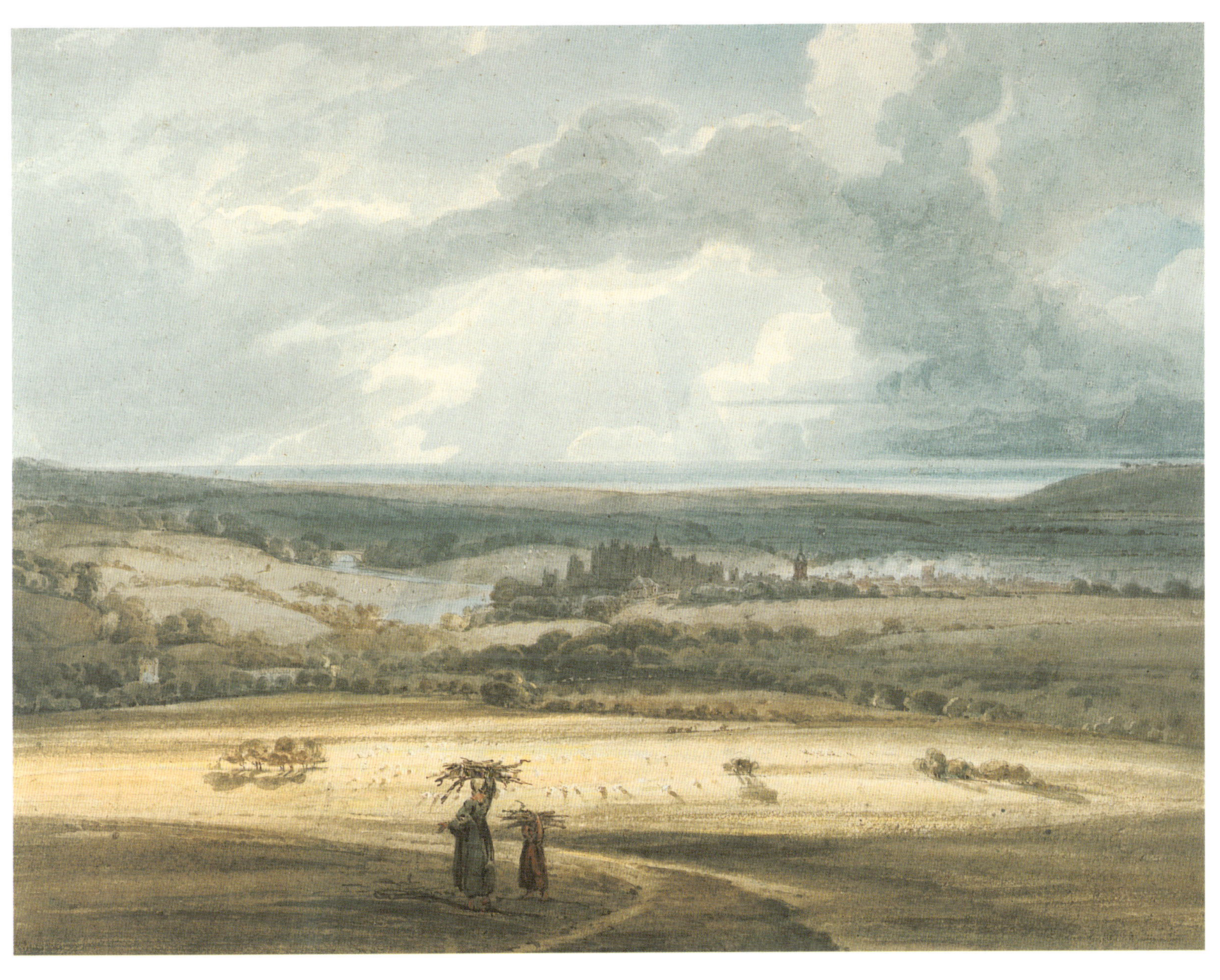

2. Paul Sandby

Great Britain 1731–1809
A scene in Windsor Forest 1801
bodycolour with wash on paper on canvas 80.6 x 107.3 cm
Hamilton Art Gallery, Victoria

The 'father of modern landscape painting in water-colours', Sandby is famous for his views of Windsor Castle and its environs.[1] The works, executed with meticulous attention to detail, reveal his early training as a topographical draughtsman. Gainsborough declared Sandby 'the only Man of Genius … who had employ'd his pencil' to produce '*real Views* from nature in this Country'.[2] Sandby was also a master of the painterly effects of bodycolour: in later life he abandoned linear treatment in favour of bolder, more expressive handling of light and shade.

Sandby's association with Windsor Forest was both personal and long-standing. His elder brother, Thomas, was Steward to the Dukes of Cumberland from 1764 until his death in 1798. This position, which encompassed Deputy Ranger of Windsor Great Park, meant that the artist enjoyed privileged access to the castle, park and forest. He was a frequent visitor, recording views there.[3]

The shadowy glade and woodland creatures depicted in *A scene in Windsor Forest* may appear highly imaginative, reflecting the Dutch and Flemish landscape tradition, or Sandby's early illustration of Tasso's *Enchanted forest*.[4] In fact, this work belongs to a series of compositions produced from the late 1770s, celebrating the fantastically gnarled and convoluted beech trees of Windsor. Sandby's son recalled the artist's careful pencil studies of trees and his proficiency in delineating their trunks and foliage. He also emphasised his father's desire to give 'his drawings a similar appearance to that seen in a camera obscura … [with] the truth in the reflected lights, the clearness in shadows. and aerial tint'.[5] Thus for all its gothic atmosphere, *A scene in Windsor Forest* conveys a sense of immediacy in its rendering of natural forms and lighting that is achieved through loose but subtle brushwork.

The herd of deer populating Sandby's dense woodland is similarly anchored in reality – namely, the Hanoverian kings' campaign to increase the deer stocks at Windsor. As Roberts has shown, the determination of George I to 'crack down' on deer poaching culminated in the notorious 'Black Act' on capital crimes in 1723, while in George III's reign, 'a number of stags became positive heroes of the hunting field' – even the names of the individual deer were well-known.[6] Sandby was intimately acquainted with the royal hunting grounds. His knowledge that 'the protection of the venison (red and fallow deer, roe and wild boar) and the vert (the timber and undergrowth that gave shelter to the venison) was paramount', pervades this painting of Windsor Forest.[7]

Windsor Castle was reinstated as the principal royal country residence, a status mirrored in its growing popularity with artists and writers. Sandby's work inspired others to portray Windsor's majestic beeches,[8] while Alexander Pope's poem, 'Windsor-Forest' 1713 extolled this British locale as a worthy alternative to classical landscape.[9] Such alignment of landscape with a nascent nationalism is discernable in Sandby's art, but it was his sensitive response to 'pure nature' that directly foreshadowed the rise of naturalistic landscape art in the nineteenth century.

Alison Inglis

1. 'Obituary: Paul Sandby', *London Review and Literary Journal*, 8 November 1809, p. 400, quoted in E. Bruce Robertson, 'Introduction', *The art of Paul Sandby*, New Haven: Yale Center for British Art, 1985, p. 12.
2. Letter from Gainsborough to Lord Hardwicke, c. 1764, quoted in Luke Herrmann, *Paul and Thomas Sandby*, London: B.T. Batsford Ltd, 1986, pp. 23, 25.
3. See Jane Roberts, *Views of Windsor, watercolours by Thomas and Paul Sandby from the collection of Her Majesty the Queen*, London: Merrell Holberton, 1995, pp. 17–18.
4. Sandby and Edward Rooker, etching after J. Collins, *The Forest as enchanted – scene from Tasso's 'Jerusalem Delivered'*, c. 1760.
5. A.P. Oppe, 'The memoir of Paul Sandby by his son Thomas Paul', *Burlington Magazine*, vol. 88, no. 519, June 1946, p. 146.
6. See Jane Roberts, *Royal landscape, the gardens and parks of Windsor*, New Haven: Yale University Press, 1997, pp. 111, 113; D.B. Banwell, *The royal stags of Windsor*, Auckland: Halcyon Press, 1994, p. 27.
7. Roberts, 1997, p. 111.
8. Robertson, 1985, p. 96.
9. Peter Dowling, *Paul Sandby, his place in the British landscape art tradition*, Hamilton, Victoria: Hamilton Art Gallery, 2004, pp. 3–4.

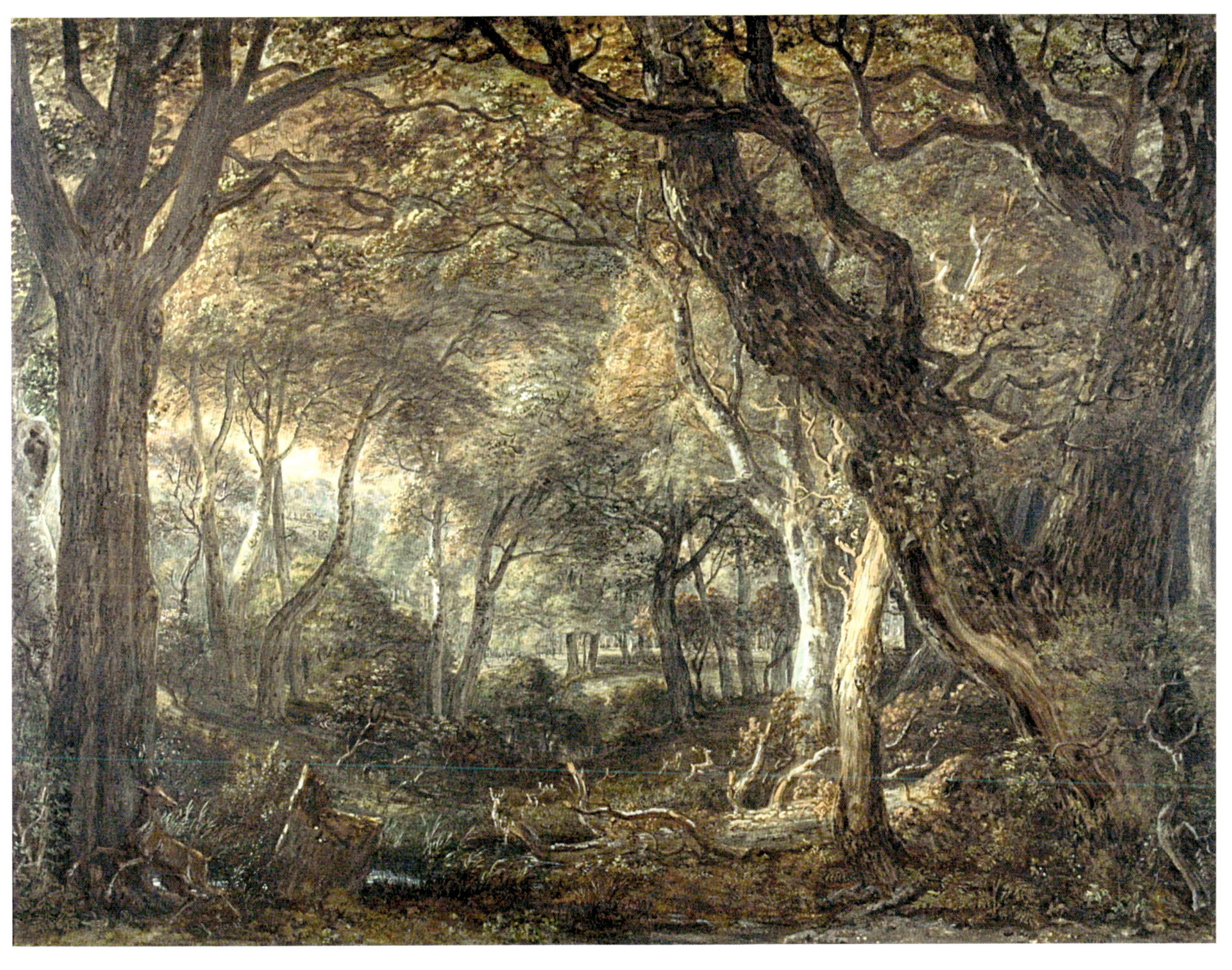

3. J.M.W. Turner

Great Britain 1775–1851
Scarborough town and castle: morning: boys catching crabs c.1810
watercolour on paper 68.5 x 101.7 cm
Art Gallery of South Australia, Adelaide
Gift from the collection of the late Mrs S.M. Crabtree by her children Rosalind, Robert, Richard and John assisted by the Roy and Marjory Edwards Bequest Fund and the Art Gallery of South Australia Foundation to commemorate the Gallery's 125th anniversary 2006

Turner's masterful watercolour depicts the seaport of Scarborough on the Yorkshire coast in north England. Scarborough here is bathed in the soft light of morning: the tide is out, the waves are purling in and the early mist has almost cleared. Nature is tranquil but the small city is busy and hard-working. In *Scarborough town and castle: morning: boys catching crabs* Turner is less concerned with the descriptive and anecdotal than in a broader cycle of continuity, a sense of place, and the richness of the everyday in a productive society.

This is a painting in which the past links with the present, an ancient Roman seaport is now also a modern spa town. In the middle distance of the painting the ruins of the town's medieval castle and Roman signal station loom above the town. The town faces the shore, the source of its fishery income and its attractions as a resort. And the beach is populated by Scarborough's working men and women with their young male offspring, their hope for the future. Catching crabs, laying washing out to dry or fishing at the water's edge, they are placed to provide interest within the landscape and also to show people working with and making a living from nature. Unified by radiant light, the scene transcends naturalism and becomes an ideal of social harmony and cyclical history.

British artists of the Romantic era painted coastal and beach scenes on an unprecedented scale, creating a thematic tradition that lasted to the end of the century. This is largely attributable to the growing attraction of beach-town health resorts which became popular particularly from the early nineteenth century.[1] Turner's beachscapes show both the busy workers of the ports as well as the recreational aspects of coastal town life. In *Scarborough town and castle: morning: boys catching crabs*, a horse-drawn bathing machine entering the shallows in the very centre of the composition hints at the recreational pleasures and health cures the town has to offer.

Turner's extraordinary energy, tireless inquisitiveness and unflagging inspiration enabled him to create hundreds of oil paintings and many thousands of watercolours, and to show an almost infinite inventiveness, especially in his miraculous effects of light. He should be regarded as Claude Lorrain's greatest follower. Nevertheless, other significant artists of the past also inspired him: Gaspard Dughet, Nicolas Poussin, and seventeenth-century Dutch masters, including Rembrandt, Aelbert Cuyp and other seascape painters.

This painting is reminiscent of Dutch seventeenth-century paintings of busy river ports at the start of a peaceful day. Its naturalism is far removed from earlier oils of the Classical coasts and seaports inspired by Claude. Nevertheless, the diffused golden glow ultimately derives from Claudean coastal scenes, albeit modified by the influence of Cuyp and Dutch seascape artists, such as Jan van de Cappelle, Willem van de Velde the Younger and Jacob van Ruisdael. Turner borrowed openly and freely from the subjects and inventions of these masters but always transformed them through his own personal vision. This composition is carefully balanced in a predictable way, and yet Turner captures, as no other artist has, a natural sense of receding distance and glowing atmospheric light.

Ron Radford

Adapted from Ron Radford, *Island to empire: 300 years of British art 1550–1850*, Adelaide: Art Gallery of South Australia, 2005, pp. 206–9.

1. Louis Hawes, *Presences of nature: British landscape 1780–1730*, New Haven: Yale Center for British Art, 1982, p. 17.

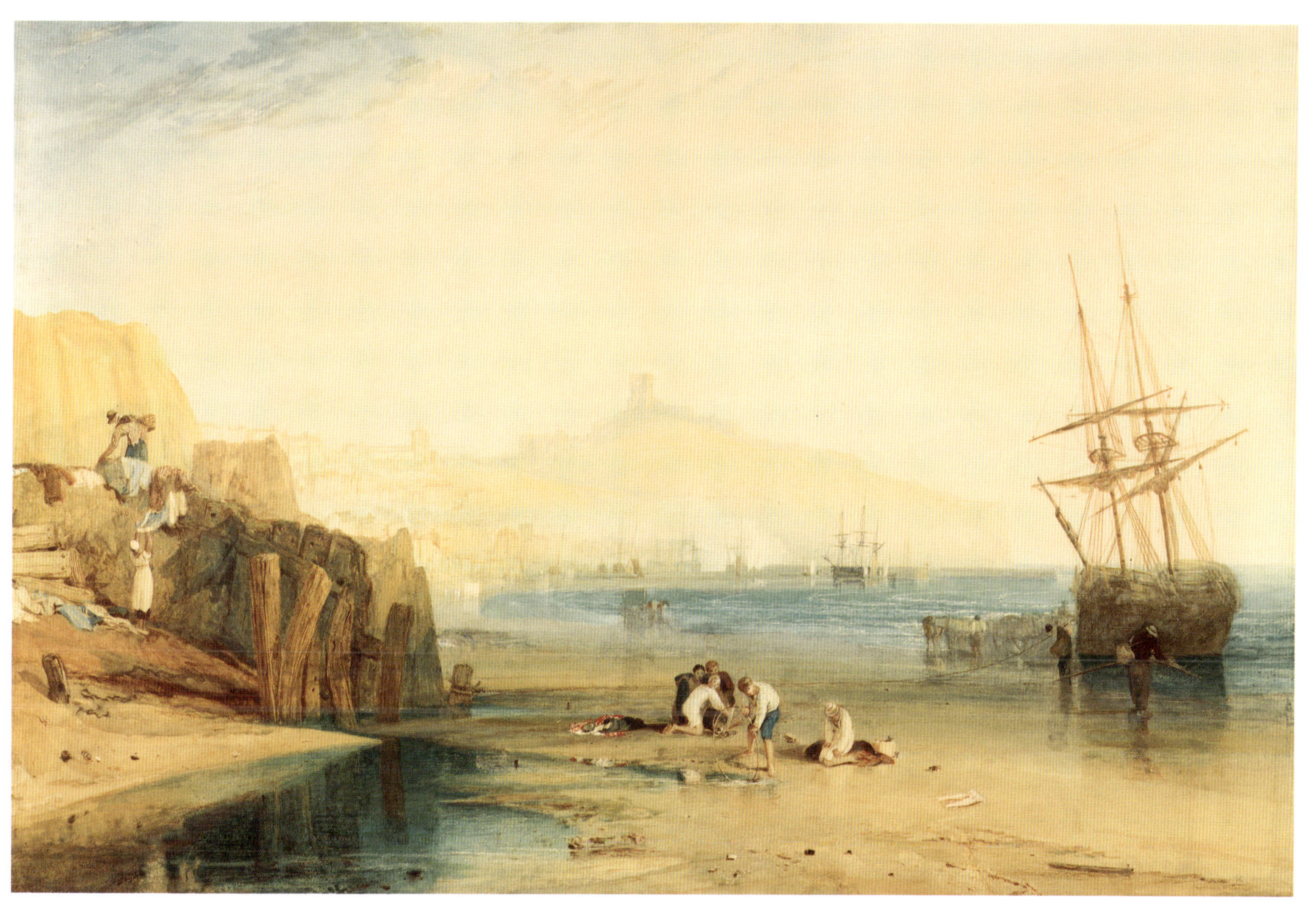

4. Peter De Wint

Great Britain 1784–1849
Kenilworth Castle c. 1827
watercolour on paper 51.4 x 70.0 cm
Art Gallery of South Australia, Adelaide
South Australian Government Grant 1955

De Wint is widely known for his expansive vistas of flat landscape executed with a confident breadth of handling. His peaceful, open, often sunny, always optimistic and productive landscapes and rural scenes seem oblivious to, or perhaps consciously avoid, the social upheavals of his time, brought about by the Industrial Revolution. As the novelist William Thackeray wrote, '[One] might have called for a pot of port at seeing one of De Wint's haymakings … everything basked lazily for him, and one wondered whether he remained torpid in winter'.[1] De Wint's works are nostalgic and romantic scenes of reaction. He produced simple watercolour sketches of Dutch-like flat landscapes, often taken around Lincoln in south-eastern England. They showed grain-harvesting and haymaking, or conventionally imposing views that included such institutional subjects as cathedrals, county houses and castles.

De Wint painted the subject of *Kenilworth Castle* many times. This is a large exhibition watercolour, the biggest and most highly worked of his known versions of Kenilworth Castle. The castle, in the midland county of Warwickshire, has romantic historical associations from early Norman to Elizabethan times, when it became the seat of Robert Dudley, Earl of Leicester, Queen Elizabeth I's favourite, who entertained her lavishly. It was immortalised in Walter Scott's popular novel *Kenilworth*, first published in 1821, only a few years before De Wint painted this watercolour. A visitors' guide to the castle published in the 1820s says, '… as we tread the ground so much famed in history as Kenilworth, the mind is naturally affected with a pleasing pensive melancholy'.[2] This is the mood evoked by the artist. John Clare, poet of the natural world and a friend of De Wint's, wrote in his 'Essay on landscape': 'The only artist that produces real English scenery in which British landscapes are seen and felt upon paper with all their poetry and exillerating [*sic.*] expression of beauty about them is De Wint'.

The balanced composition and careful rendering follows the spirit and grand style of Claude Lorrain who painted in Rome nearly two hundred years earlier. The middle-distant medieval ruins, like Claude's Roman ruins, are silhouetted against a sky radiating with the warm glow of a setting sun. This magical Claudean light is reflected up from foreground water, and it backlights the classically balanced framing foliage. By capturing the golden light De Wint transforms the subject from mere topography into a landscape of poetry, evoking the passage of time. In doing so he is stylistically linked to his great contemporary Turner, as is amply demonstrated in his Romantic castle of similar date, *Alnwick Castle* c. 1829 (cat. 30), and earlier golden *Scarborough town and castle: morning: boys catching crabs* c. 1810 (cat. 3).

Ron Radford

Adapted from Ron Radford, *Island to empire: 300 years of British art 1550–1850*, Adelaide: Art Gallery of South Australia, 2005, pp. 245–6.

1. W.M. Thackeray, *Critical papers in art*, London, 1911, p. 269.
2. F. Smith, *An historical and descriptive guide to Leamington Spa with an account of Warwick and Kenilworth*, London, first published 1820s, reprinted in 1831, n.p.

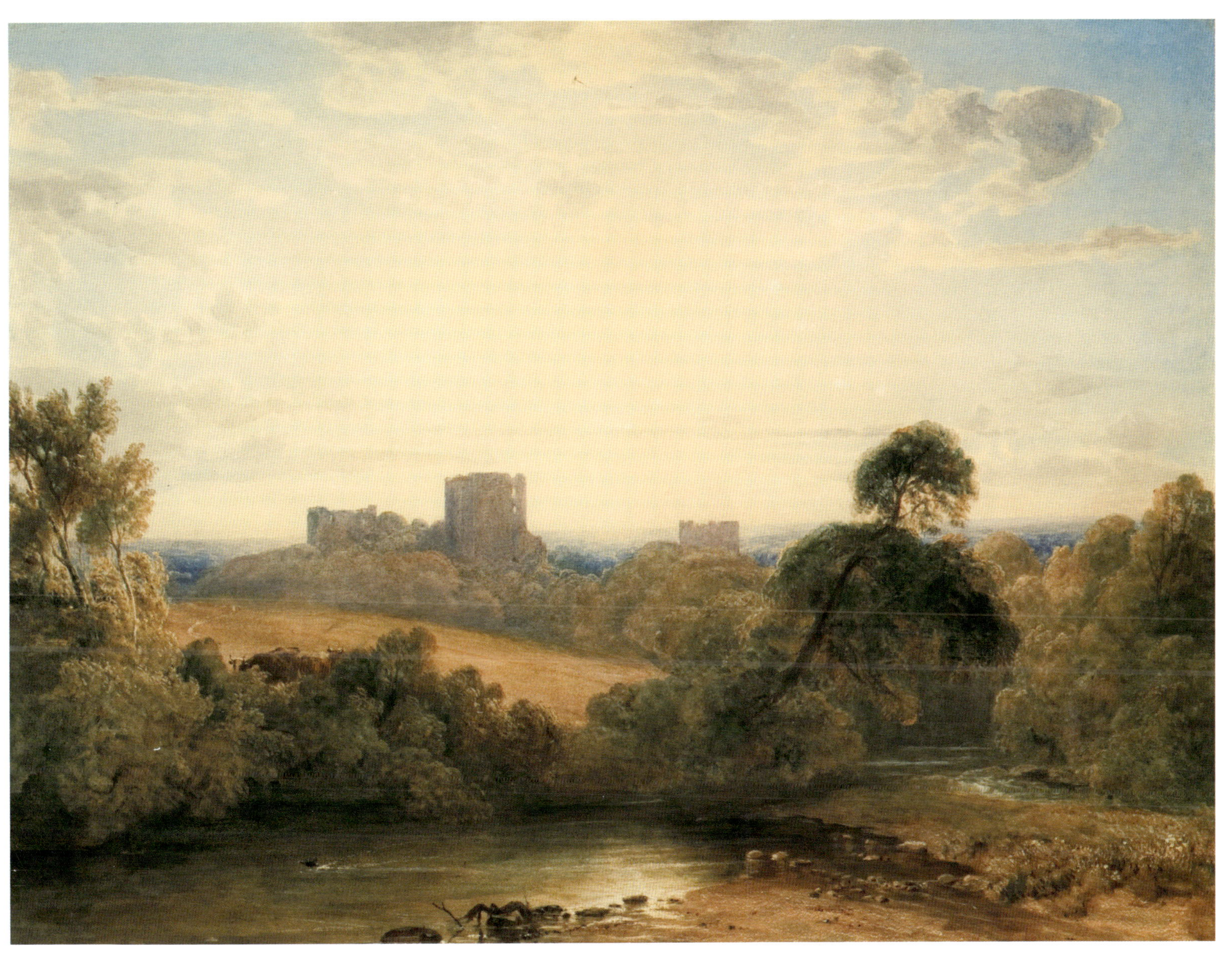

5. J.M.W. Turner

Great Britain 1775–1851
Crossing the brook exhibited 1815
oil on canvas 193.0 x 165.1 cm
Tate Britain
Accepted by the British nation as part of the Turner Bequest 1856

Turner looks to Claude Lorrain, the great artistic model of seventeenth-century Classical landscape painting, for his composition of *Crossing the brook*. Devices include framing trees to left and right, while Turner also uses light to lead the eye through a curving central valley until it meets a limpid white sky, which dissipates upwards into palest blue. Dark planes intersect in the foreground across the front of the water, down through the foliage and tunnel path on the right. A spotlight picks out three figures who ford the brook: one girl has waded across, then looks back to her dog in midstream. The animal helps by carrying her basket, while another young woman prepares on the far bank by removing her shoes and tucking up her dress.

Further along the valley are an aqueduct and large waterwheel. We are not in the Roman *campagna*, however, but rather in an equivocal English Arcadia. The brook leads into the River Tamar, which divides Devon from Cornwall, while the arches belong to Calstock Bridge. The wheel drives water for a clay pit: this is modern Britain at the end of the Napoleonic wars. War with France has lasted more than twenty years; Britain is all but bankrupt, and appears to be on the verge of revolution. Turner, always a history painter, manages to meld a Classical manner with a contemporary subject. Rural England now includes industry and urbanisation, implying a new vision of beauty.

Between 1811 and 1814 Turner made three journeys into the West Country. These were extended summer tours, primarily to make watercolours for an engraving commission, *Picturesque views of the south coast of England*, which was published in sixteen parts from 1814 to 1826. In his last trip in 1814 Turner 'sketched around the River Tamar, making studies of the river valley at Gunnislake and Calstock'.[1]

The artist exhibited two large oils, *Crossing the brook* and *Dido building Carthage*, at the Royal Academy in 1815. Despite the different scale of ambition that seems to mark their titles and subjects, an idyllic English scene could also be a grand history painting, to be shown at the season which marked Britain's final victory over Napoleon. The large vertical landscape was well received, and praised by most. Not everyone liked it, however: Sir George Beaumont, the artist's enemy, characterised it as '*weak* and like the work of an Old man, one who had no longer saw or felt colour properly; it was all of *peagreen* insipidity'.[2] Contemporary viewers may disagree with his sour verdict. *Crossing the brook* is a masterpiece of nineteenth-century landscape, which encapsulates local and national views of ideal Classical painting. It presents these views in a grand yet succinct form. In 1815 Turner summed up the hopes of a war-weary Britain in this naturalised Claudean landscape of observed incident and eternal pleasure.

Christine Dixon

1. James Hamilton, *Turner: a life*, London: Hodder and Stoughton, 1997 p. 168.
2. Kathryn Cave (ed.), *The diary of Joseph Farington: volume XIII – January 1814 – December 1815*, New Haven: Yale University Press, 1984, p. 4638, quoted in David Blayney Brown, *The art of J. M. W. Turner*, Secaucus: Wellfleet Press, 1990, p. 128.

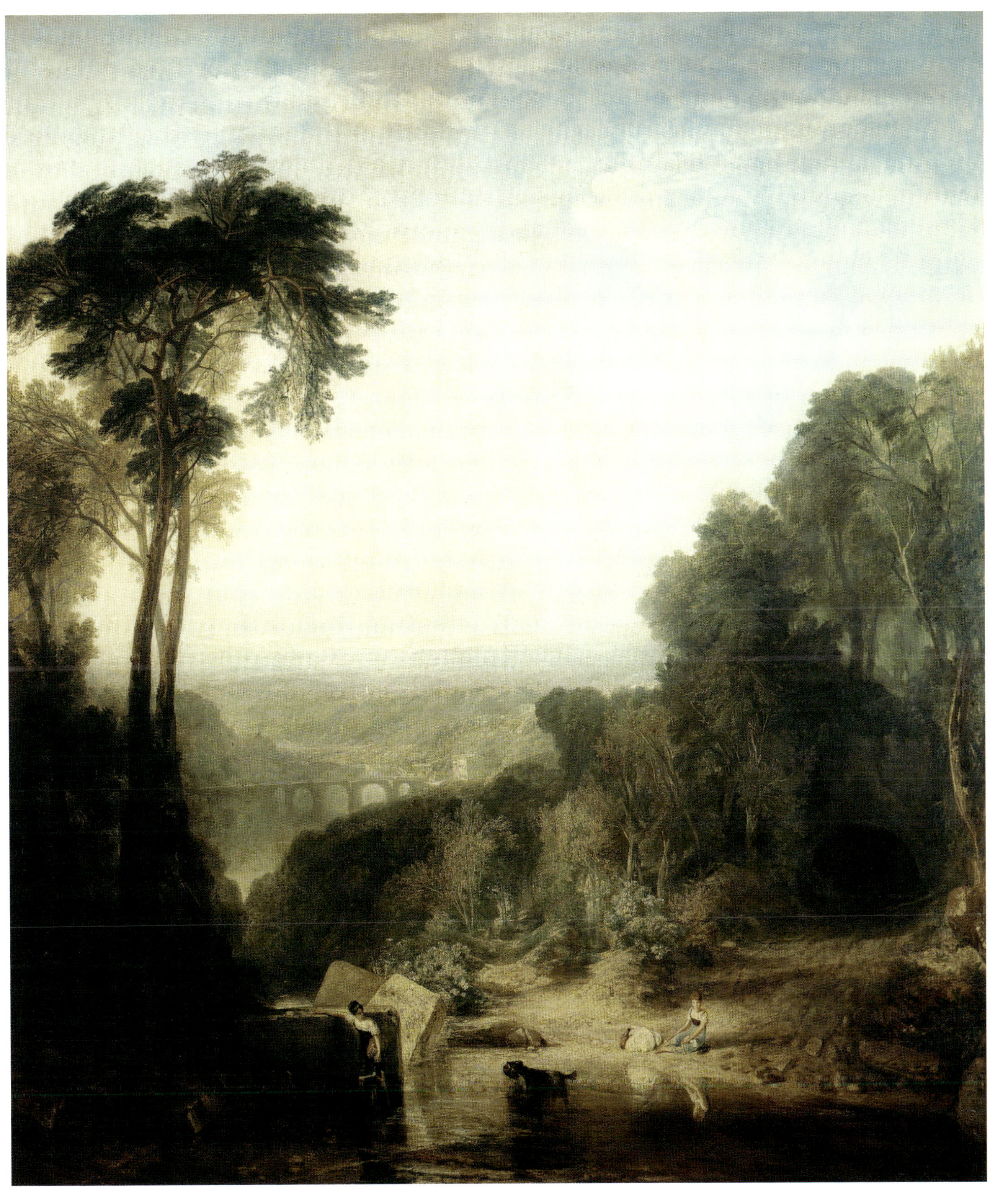

6. John Glover

Great Britain 1767 – Australia 1849
Rome with St Peter's and the Castel Sant' Angelo c. 1821
also known as ***View of Rome from the Villa Madama***
oil on oak panel 35.6 x 43.6 cm
National Gallery of Australia, Canberra
Purchased 1980 1980.3309

Despite receiving very little critical acclaim within London art circles, Glover had established himself as a successful English landscape painter before his emigration to Australia in 1830. The artist's early oeuvre includes numerous views of his native Leicestershire and its surrounds, as well as landscapes painted after sketching tours of France in 1814 and Italy in 1818. Following in the footsteps of eighteenth-century Grand Tourists, Glover's key destination during his Italian travels was Rome, where he made several sketches of the Eternal City from within its walls and the surrounding Tiburtine hills.

Rome with St Peter's and the Castel Sant' Angelo shows the city from a location on the hills of Mount Pincio.[1] From this vantage the viewer looks beyond a wooded foreground, towering umbrella pines and Italian cypresses first to the Tiber River and then the architecture of Baroque Rome. Our eye sweeps from the Castel St Angelo, at far left, to the towering dome of St Peter's Cathedral and the Vatican. Luminous under the clear open sky, the sweeping vista contrasts with the bosky woodland and darkly silhouetted evergreens of the immediate foreground. Here the sun illuminates patches of the wood, highlighting a lightly trodden path on the right and grazing goats, painted to provide interest in the immediate landscape.

Glover turned to the landscapes of various seventeenth-century masters for inspiration. In an inscription on its reverse, the painting is described as 'an imitation of Claude'.[2] *Rome with St Peter's and the Castel Sant' Angelo* departs from the Classically balanced compositions of Glover's idol. Missing from this landscape are the French master's backdrops of fading mountain vistas. Moreover, the composition lacks a counterbalance to the off-centre towering trees in the foreground. Instead this painting emulates, far more closely, the landscapes of seventeenth-century Dutch masters, such as Jacob van Ruisdael, Meindert Hobbema and Antoni Waterlo. Indeed, Carey notes how Glover '… wandered over the fields of Art, and enriched himself with her treasures', looking not only at Claude and Gaspar but at 'Ruysdael', 'Hobbima' and 'Waterloo' until he learnt how to 'behold Nature with their eyes'.[3]

These Dutch influences manifest in various ways throughout *Rome with St Peter's and the Castel Sant' Angelo*. For example, the artist's panoramic depiction of Rome is strongly reminiscent of Jacob van Ruisdael's Harlem panoramas or *Harlempjes*. Like Ruisdael, Glover has painted the city from a low viewpoint among the hills, so that the sky looms above the cityscape.[4] In the foreground the silhouetted cypresses and umbrella pines are reminiscent of Dutch landscapes, particularly those of Hobbema, which depict unconventionally arranged clusters and avenues of leafy trees. Finally, the starkly naturalistic rendering of these woods seems far closer to Dutch compositions which depict the land in colour schemes of rich greens, earthy hues and dark tones, illuminated by dappled patches of sunlight.

Niki van den Heuvel

1. Exhibited under this name in 1824, the painting has had numerous titles, including *Rome from the Villa Madama*. See Tim Bonyhady, *Australian colonial painting in the Australian National Gallery*, Canberra: Australian National Gallery, 1986, pp. 111–12.
2. Thomas Phillipps, quoted in David Hansen, *John Glover and the colonial Picturesque*, Tasmania: Art Gallery of Tasmania & Art Exhibitions Australia, 2003, p. 176.
3. William Carey, quoted in Hansen, p. 38.
4. Nils Büttner, *Landscape painting: a history*, New York & London: Abbeville, 2006, p. 208.

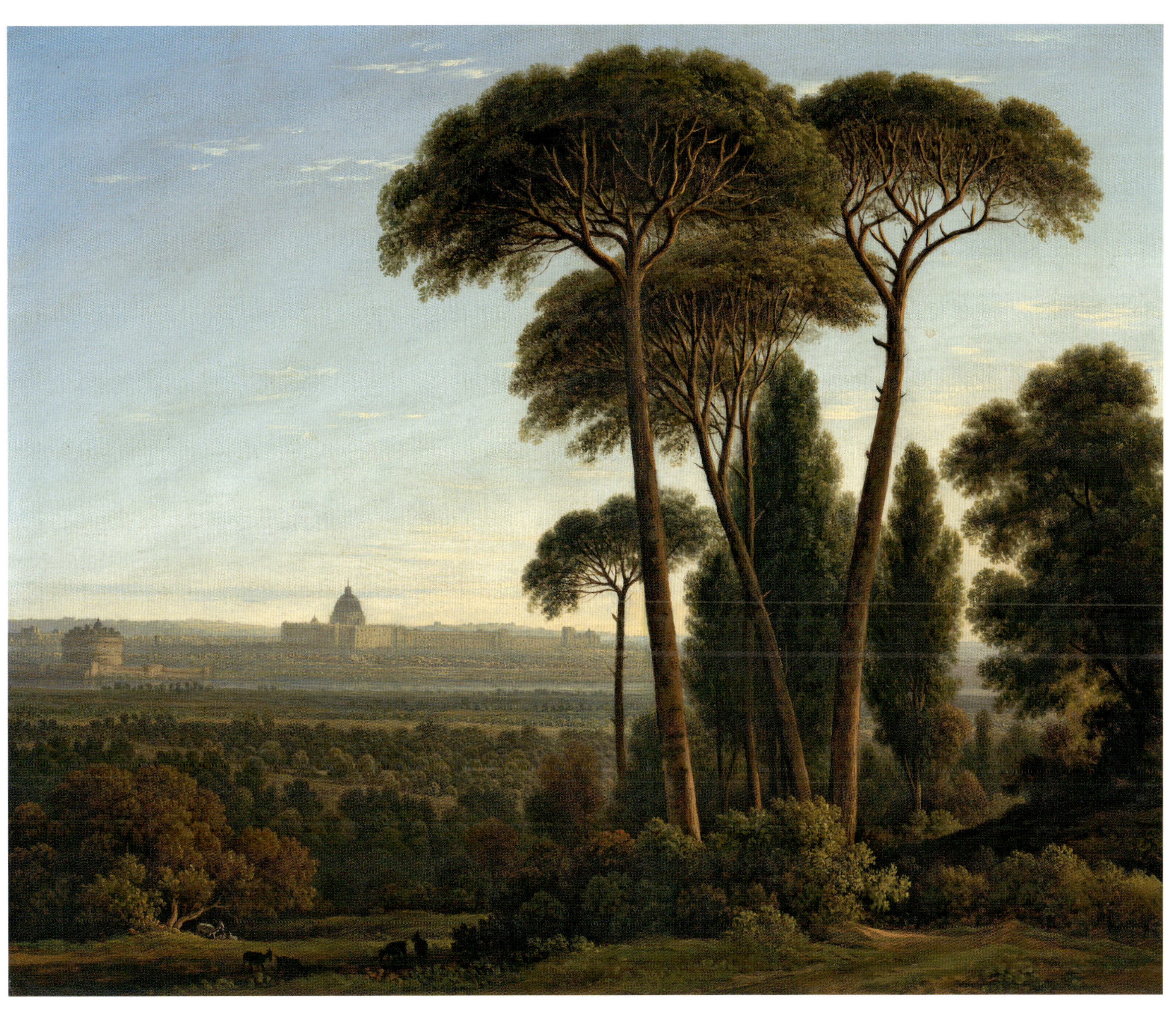

7. John Constable

Great Britain 1776–1837
The leaping horse 1825
oil on canvas 142.0 x 187.3 cm
Royal Academy of Arts, London

Constable, one of the foremost British landscape painters of the nineteenth century, first achieved success with his large canvases depicting landscape and life in and around the Stour Valley, which he exhibited between 1819 and 1825. Such was the success of the first of these large paintings, *The white horse* 1819,[1] when Constable exhibited it at the Royal Academy in 1819, that he was elected Associate of the Academy later that year.[2] Working on a scale usually reserved for history painting, Constable redefined the notion of a 'finished' picture by giving his large landscapes something of the spontaneous freedom and expressive handling of a rapidly painted sketch.

The leaping horse is the sixth and the last of these large Stour Valley landscapes and one of the most powerful. Constable chose a place called Float Jump, close to where the course of the old river temporarily left the navigable portion of the Stour. It also marked the boundary between the counties of Essex and Suffolk. The jump itself consisted of a wooden barrier a metre high, constructed across the tow path. Built to stop cattle straying, it was low enough to allow barge horses to leap over it. Constable chose the moment when the horse, mounted by a boy, was leaping the barrier, which gave vigour to the scene. He depicted it from a low viewpoint to give the horse and rider a dramatic presence.

Constable's principal concern was not, however, with the specifics of the location but rather capturing the atmosphere of place and the general feelings associated with experiencing nature. He sought to present nature as something mutable, not fixed. 'It is a lovely subject,' Constable said of *The leaping horse*, 'lively – & soothing – calm and exhilarating, fresh – & blowing'.[3]

He wanted his landscapes to create a total experience, including a sense of movement and sound as well as what can be directly observed. In this painting he wanted to convey the feel of the wind, the shimmering of light, the sense of being outdoors. And he extended the experience of the landscape by depicting a moorhen startled from her nest by the thundering of the horse's hoofs.

Constable's handling of paint is expressionist and almost abstract. He used palette knife as well as brush, with which he created a visual impression of flickering lights and shadows. The light rises as if the sun is coming out and the storm clouds are blowing away. It sparkles on the trees on the left and gives the pollarded tree in the centre a silvery look.

Constable also carried through his interest in 'skying' into all his large landscapes. In saying the sky was the 'chief organ of sentiment' in a painting, he emphasised his belief in the expressive importance of the sky, and its ability to dictate the mood of a landscape.[4] His skies are a vital part of his compositions and a main conveyor of mood, as in *The leaping horse*. They transform comfortable, stable scenes into ones of continual change and transition.

Anne Gray

1. The Frick Collection, New York.
2. Constable described this work as 'a placid representation of a serene grey morning, summer', Graham Reynolds, *The later paintings and drawings of John Constable: text*, New Haven & London: Yale University Press, 1984, p. 156.
3. R.B. Beckett, *John Constable's correspondence VI*, Ipswich: Suffolk Records Society, 1968, p. 198.
4. Beckett, p. 77.

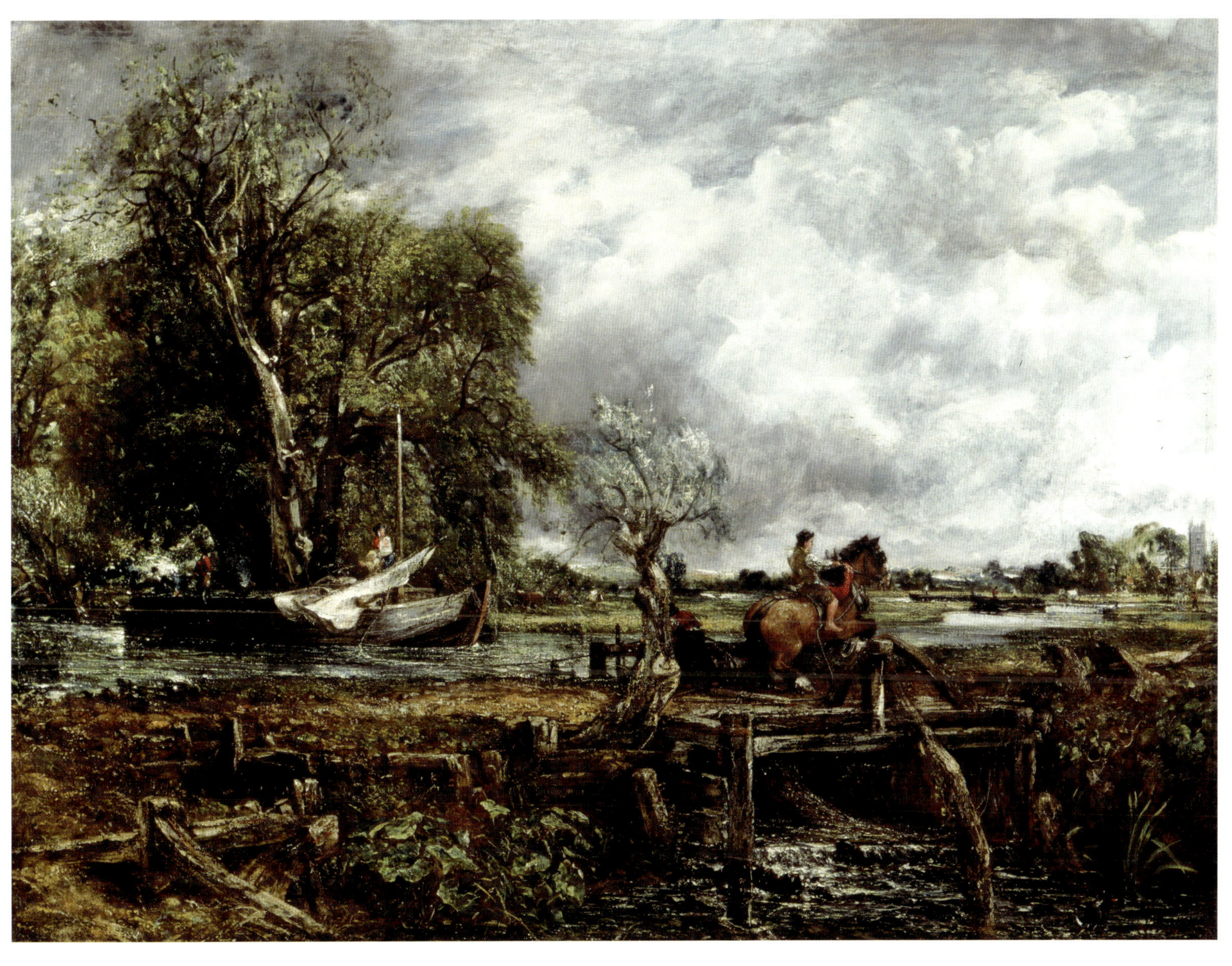

8. John Constable

Great Britain 1776–1837
Flatford Mill from the lock c. 1811
also known as ***Flatford Mill from a lock on the Stour***
oil on canvas 24.8 x 29.8 cm
Victoria and Albert Museum, London
Given by Isabel Constable, daughter of the artist 135-1888

Throughout his life Constable revisited favourite scenes from his youth, especially those in the Stour Valley, where his father owned the mill. In *Flatford Mill from the lock* the artist shows buildings on the left bank balanced by a group of trees on the right. His main consideration, however, is the passage of shining water leading to a sentinel black tree, underneath a bank of blowsy white clouds. The composition's diagonal lines all converge at this central point. The sky sets an equivocal mood: dark storm clouds mass around the bright clouds scudding across a cheerful cerulean sky. They shed dark and light reflections on the shimmering river.

Constable's painting technique is particularly lively, notable for spontaneity and seeming haste of execution. The artist has loaded his brush with paint and scribbled freely across the canvas. In the sky he barely covers a reddish ground. Holmes commented on its aesthetic function in his Slade lectures of 1909:

> A ground of middle tint is convenient for securing unity of tone … Constable, for many of his paintings, and for the majority of his sketches, employed a foundation of strong reddish-brown. In his case it served both as a connecting link between the detached touches by which his studies were built up, and as a contrast to the cool greens and blues and grays that he favoured, which might otherwise have looked cold. It must be remembered, too, that Constable generally painted with a full brush, so that his pigment was thick enough to prevent the dark foundation from lowering the tones materially.[1]

Constable's debt to seventeenth-century Dutch painters, such as Meindert Hobbema, can be detected particularly in this frontal approach: we look straight up the central watery path to the dark tree. The vignette is another compositional device he employs. Boundaries of darkness are built up around the edges, so that the centre becomes a circle of light. The small figure in red on the left draws our attention to the warm browns of the brick and wooden mill. It was these sparkling strokes of freshness and vigour that Eugène Delacroix and Richard Parkes Bonington admired when they first saw Constable's paintings in Paris in 1824, and which provoked surprised praise at the Paris Salon that same year.

Christine Dixon

1. Sir Charles J. Holmes, *Notes on the science of picture making*, London: Chatto and Windus, 1927, viewed January 2008, paulseaton.com/holmes/holmes1.htm.

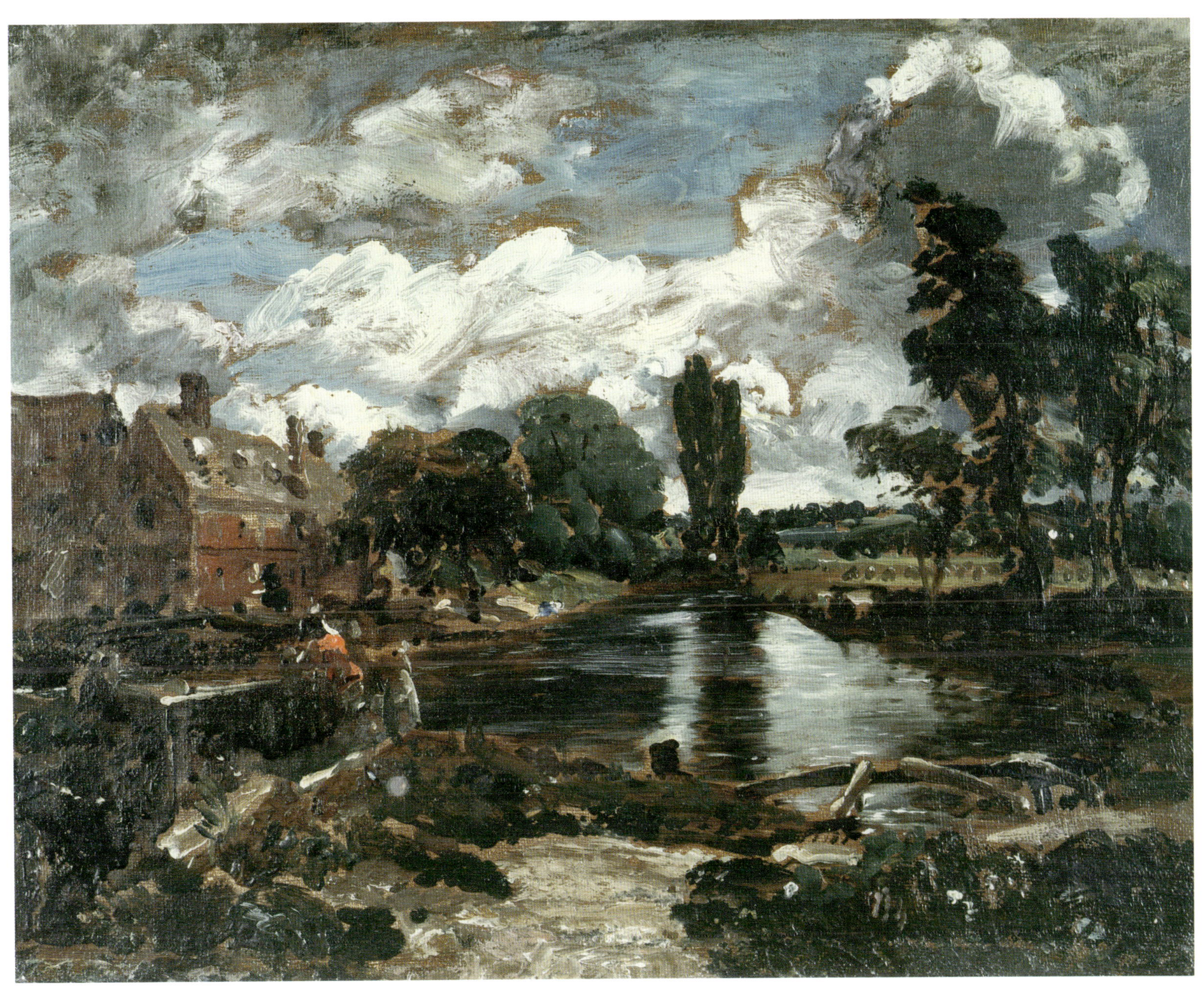

9. Caspar David Friedrich

Germany 1774–1840
***Scudding clouds* [*Ziehende Wolken*]** c. 1820
also known as ***Drifting clouds***
oil on canvas 18.3 x 24.5 cm
Hamburger Kunsthalle, Hamburg

Friedrich painted his canvases in different, standard sizes. The format of *Scudding clouds* was the smallest he used, in the Saxon measure 8 *Zoll* high and 10½ *Zoll* wide. A letter of 21 July 1821 to the collector Dr Wilhelm Körte gave the price as '4 Louisdor', or French gold coins.[1] For such a tiny painting, with its palette restricted to white, blue, green and brown, the artist achieves a large impact, both intellectually and visually.

Scudding clouds 'is based on a study from nature showing a view from the Brocken, which he made on 29 June 1811'.[2] The ten years that passed between Friedrich's original *plein-air* excursion and the finished painting demonstrate how the artist thought and rethought his conceptions of religious art. By 1820 a physical, material Christian cross was no longer needed to signal our inevitable spiritual journey through the landscape. The Brocken is the highest peak of the Harz mountains, and thus the highest in northern Germany. Here Friedrich shows a mountaintop where a small lake reflects the sky. Beyond the grass is an invisible valley that we look straight across to distant ranges. Far beyond the obstacle of mountains, obscuring clouds or mists, lies a sunlit vista. For the traveller – the artist, the viewer – to achieve this heaven, he or she must:

> … climb all the way down through the valley of death before he can reach this paradise which he can just glimpse vaguely through the clouds. The rocks in the foreground symbolize the Christian faith.[3]

Scudding clouds is a painting of great intensity, concentrated into a small space. Even the title is ambiguous, since Friedrich's intent is surely to show the arduous journey from ordinary, sensuous human life to eternal salvation. *Ziehen* in German means 'to pull'. The clouds scud or drift across the canvas: accurate translation depends on how fast they appear to move. Fluffy mist in the mountains becomes little white billows of cloud, then a grey curtain across the top of the painting. The whole is composed of horizontal fields of colour. Normal recession, from brown and green foreground to misty blue mountains, is contradicted by clouds that move through the scene, obscuring those peaks and valleys where the traveller must venture.

Christine Dixon

1. Sigrid Hinz (ed.), *Caspar David Friedrich in Briefen und Bekenntnissen*, Berlin: Henschelverlag, 1968, p. 55, quoted in *Caspar David Friedrich 1774–1840*, Munich: Prestel and Hamburger Kunsthalle, 1974, p. 241.
2. Helmut Börsch-Supan, *Caspar David Friedrich*, London: Thames and Hudson, 1973, p. 124.
3. Börsch-Supan, p. 124.

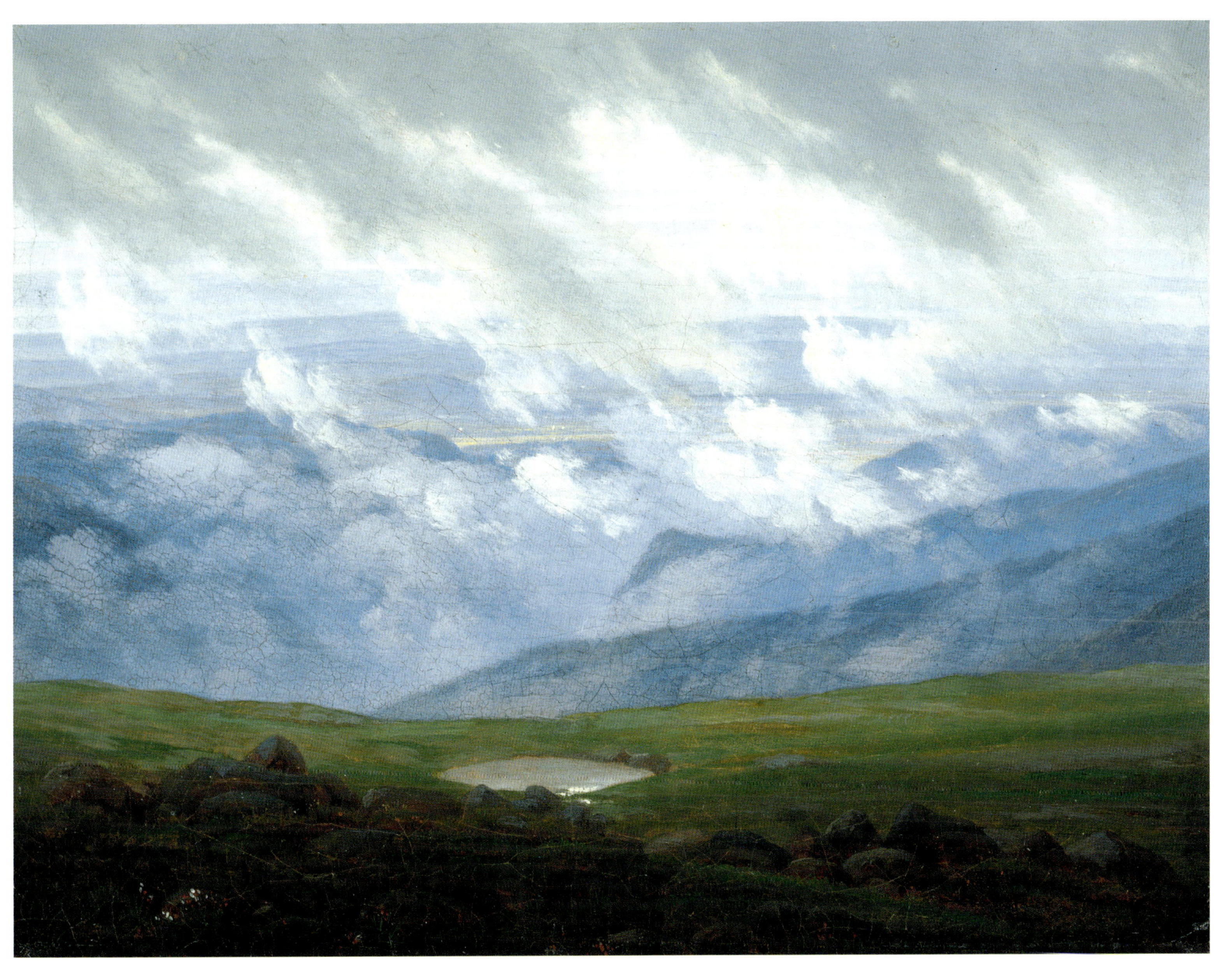

10. Richard Parkes Bonington

Great Britain 1802–1828, worked in France
Normandy landscape near Lillebonne 1823
oil on canvas 29.8 x 47.0 cm
Toledo Museum of Art, Ohio
Purchased with funds from the Libbey Endowment
Gift of Edward Drummond Libbey 1983.8

The pathos of Bonington's life – dead from tuberculosis at twenty-five – often masks the achievements of his brief career. His parents took him to live in France shortly after the Napoleonic Wars ended in 1815; he studied under Louis Francia in Calais and Baron Gros in Paris, became a friend of Delacroix's, and was an acclaimed watercolourist by the age of twenty. Because of his British origin, and admiration for Constable and Girtin, Bonington is often cited as the link between English and French Romanticism early in the nineteenth century. Corot, inspired by a Bonington watercolour shown in the dealer Schroth's window, before he himself had begun to paint, was struck by the artist's 'sincerity'.[1]

Bonington took up landscape painting in oils only about 1823, so *Normandy landscape near Lillebonne* may be among his first efforts in the medium.[2] Characteristic of his marine subjects, as well as Norman and other French scenes, is the predominance of sky over land. It takes up two-thirds of the canvas, and is the source of the bands of light and dark that serve to illuminate and enliven the landscape. The composition consists of horizontal stripes which recede from the pastoral foreground, where cows, peasant women, a stone obelisk and a fence animate the meadows. A darker belt of trees, the church and village houses stretches in front of the valley; shadows from the clouds alternate with sunny patches into the background hill and distant vista.

Freshly painted and faithfully observed in their various forms, white, grey and mauve clouds build up in a blue sky. As well as clouds being a normal outdoor source of light in Europe, both reflected and reflecting, artists studied them closely in order to convey the effects of movement in what would otherwise be a static panorama. Water has the same function, but in the calm farmland of *Normandy landscape near Lillebonne*, the dominant sky is the dramatic hero of the painting.

Christine Dixon

1. A. Dubuisson, *Richard Parkes Bonington*, trans. C.E. Hughes, London: John Lane, 1924, p.50.
2. Patrick J. Noon now disputes the signature and attribution; see his *Richard Parkes Bonington: 'On the pleasure of painting'*, New Haven and London: Yale Center for British Art and Yale University Press, 1991, p.29, note 51.

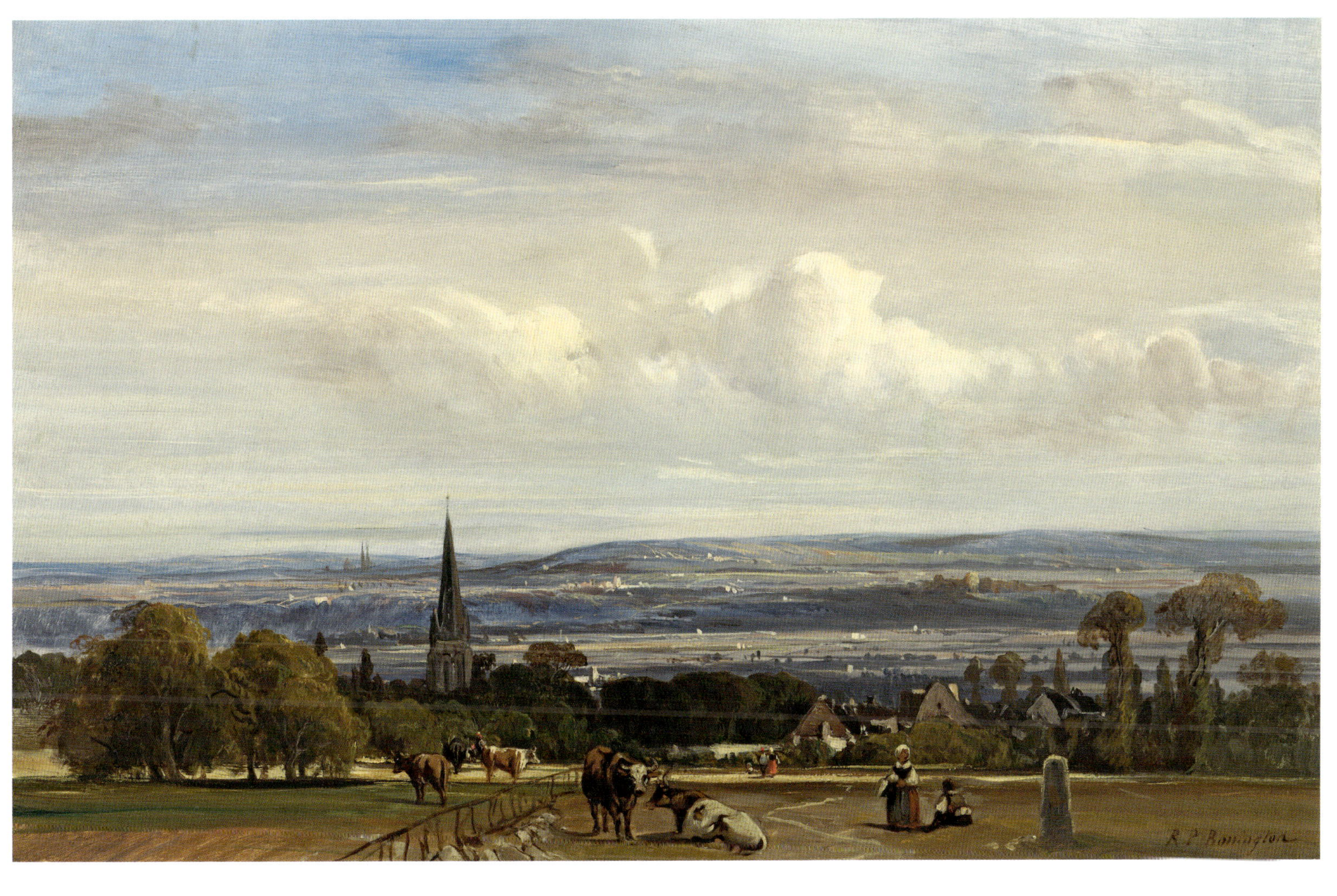

11. John Constable

Great Britain 1776–1837
Stratocumulus clouds 1821
also known as ***Cloud study with birds in flight***
oil on paper on board 25.5 x 30.5 cm
Yale Center for British Art, New Haven
Paul Mellon Collection, USA B1981.25.155

Stratocumulus clouds is typical of Constable's cloud studies, of which there are almost one hundred in existence, executed either *en plein air*, or from his house in Hampstead between 1821 and 1822. In the preceding years, he had already sought for a way to give accurate painterly expression to the phenomena of sky and its related weather patterns, but during this two-year period the artist focused on exploring the underlying fundamental principles of the representation of the sky. As a result, he painted numerous pure cloud studies that do not include any trace of landscape. He also executed a number, including this work, with unusually low-lying horizon lines, where the land is reduced to a small stripe, making the sky the main focus of interest.

From 1821–22 Constable intensified his study of clouds by undertaking several 'skying campaigns', noting on each work the time of day, date, weather conditions and wind direction. *Stratocumulus clouds* has the comments 'Sep. 28 1821 Noon – looking North West windy from the S. W. large bright clouds flying rather fast very stormy night followed'. Reynolds remarks that 'A modern typed label fixed to the new backing is inscribed, presumably copying an inscription on the original by the artist'.[1] The work fully illustrates Constable's intention: here we see the direction in which the clouds are moving; we see their coalescing and decoalescing, and the way in which their expansion in space has been captured. Constable's use of rapid, glancing brushstrokes emphasises the dynamism of the cloud forms, and the impression one has of motion, and the sense of constantly changing shapes in time and space.

It is generally accepted that Constable was aware of British meteorologist Luke Howard's system of the classification of clouds, first published in 1803. In fact, comparisons with historical contemporary weather reports reveal the remarkable accuracy of Constable's cloud studies. They accord in minute detail with existing weather records, such that they could almost be used as a basis for predicting the weather over the days that followed.

Through his close observation and systematic understanding of meteorological phenomena, Constable was able to establish the empirical basis that underpinned his handling of the sky in his great landscape paintings – the 'six footers'. In October 1821 Constable wrote to his friend John Fisher:

> It will be difficult to name a class of Landscape – in which the sky is not the 'keynote' – the 'standard scale' – and the chief 'Organ of sentiment' ... The sky is the 'source of light' in Nature, and governs everything.[2]

This statement underscores Constable's extraordinary interest in the sky, which became the dominant element in his works and simultaneously revolutionised the art of landscape painting.

Jenns Howoldt

Translated by Mark Henshaw and Christine Dixon.

1. Quoted in Graham Reynolds, *The later paintings and drawings of John Constable*, text volume, New Haven and London: Yale University Press, 1984, cat. 21.57, p. 83.
2. R.B. Beckett, *John Constable's correspondence*, VI, Suffolks Records Society, 1968, p. 77.

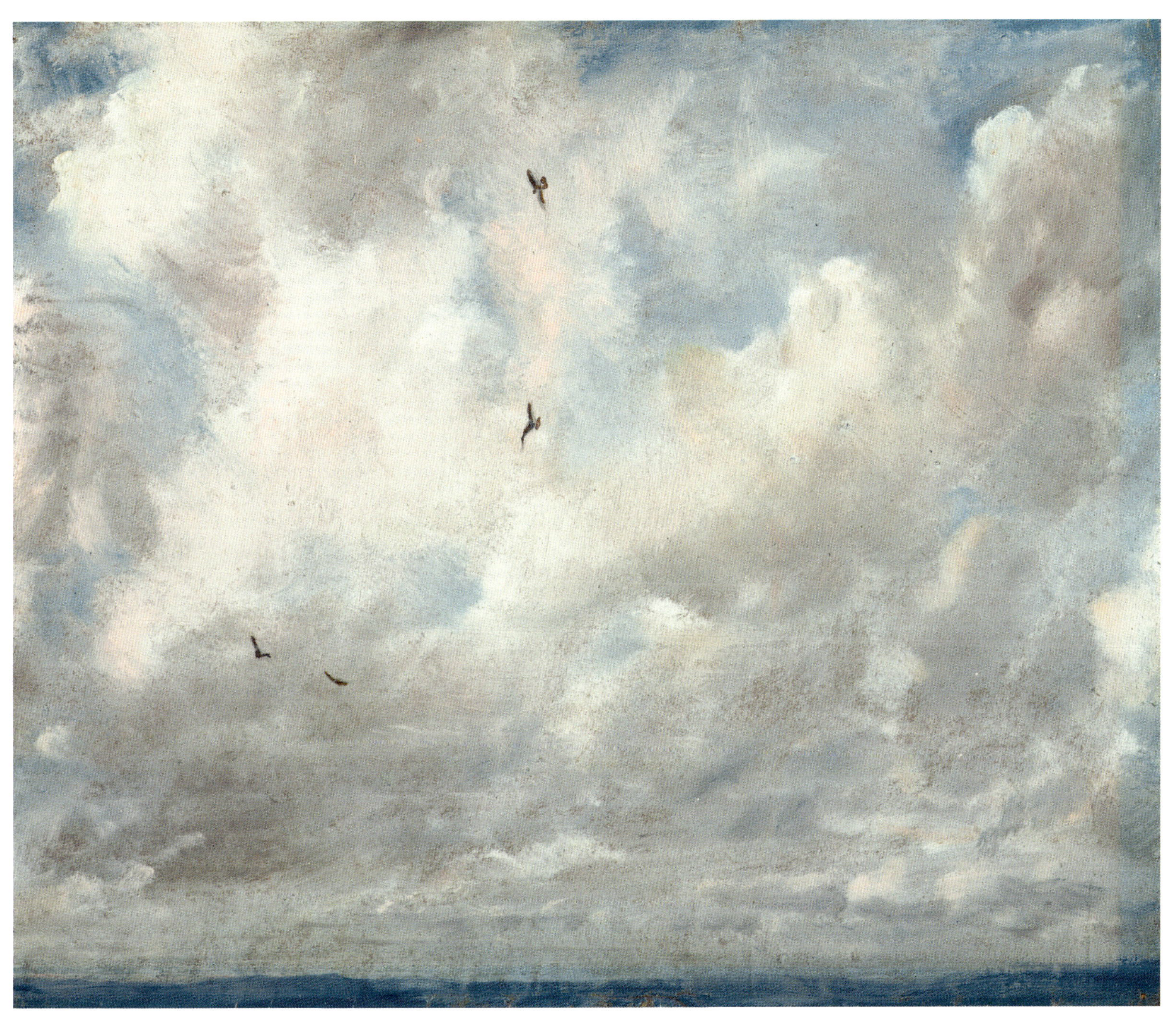

12. John Constable

Great Britain 1776–1837
A view at Salisbury from the library of Archdeacon Fisher's house 1829
oil on paper 16.2 x 30.5 cm
Victoria and Albert Museum, London
Given by Isabel Constable, daughter of the artist 153-1888

The bequest by Miss Isabel Constable in 1888 of several hundred of her father's oil paintings, watercolours, drawings and bound sketchbooks – like Turner's gift of his works to the nation – have profoundly affected the way we think about nineteenth-century British art. Artists have always prepared sketches, rapid visual notations of a first idea, details of figures or elements of a composition, or cartoons and other working drawings to aid in the scaling-up of a composition for the final painting. But these have traditionally been regarded as private works, or expendable, rarely for public display, at least in the artist's lifetime. The extensive holdings of Constable's small oils in public collections provide a unique opportunity to 'get inside' the artist's head, to examine in detail his technique and working processes.

A view at Salisbury from the library of Archdeacon Fisher's house displays Constable's ability to combine precise observation with a quality of mystery. It is an astonishingly energetic work, particularly for one contained within such small dimensions. A lovely contrast exists between the expanse of sky, conveyed in the broadest strokes with large sections of the buff-coloured ground showing through, and the fine brushstrokes of the trees, grass and water below. The left side of the painting is dominated by a large bank of storm clouds which have overtaken the clear blue sky. In the grove of trees below the clouds, we can make out a tiny figure, his torso made of lively dabs of red paint, who seems to be carrying something on his back. Tree-trunks in the foreground, with bright green new foliage, are rendered in confident flicks of black paint, while the settlement and distant hills are suggested by darker greens, grey-blues and whites. The two blocks of orange, roofs peeking through the trees at centre, link back to the figure. This is a fine example of Constable's swift and easy notation, his extraordinary facility for communicating mood, and his 'Art of seeing Nature'.[1]

Constable painted from nature all his life, and believed that exhibition pictures should connect with close study of the landscapes portrayed. The idea of working from home, of conveying the vista from an identified place or the view from a window, is also related to German Romanticism. Works by Friedrich and Carus often include a figure looking longingly out of the window or seated on a terrace, suggesting the confines of the material world and a quest for the eternal. This painting also has a personal element: Constable and John Fisher had been friends since 1811. The artist was a regular visitor to Salisbury until 1829, when his health declined. This view, looking towards Harnham Ridge, was painted on Constable's second-last visit to his friend.[2] Like others of 15, 22 and 25 July, as well as several undated works, it shows a range of weather conditions and cloud formations.[3] The artist seems to have found comfort in his work at Leydenhall following the death of his wife Maria in 1828.

Lucina Ward

1. The phrase is Sir Joshua Reynolds's, from his 'Discourse', no. 12, vol. 2, p. 104, quoted in Michael Rosenthal, *Constable*, New York: Thames and Hudson, 1987, p. 22.
2. The work is inscribed on the back, in pencil: 'Fisher's – Library – Salisbury Sunday July 12. 1829 4 o clock afternoon'.
3. See, for example, *A view at Salisbury from Fisher's house*, dated 1820 or 1829, which, by including a larger foreground section of wall, foliage and fences, emphasises the fact that the view is from a window in the south wing of the house; collection of the Victoria and Albert Museum, London [320-1888].

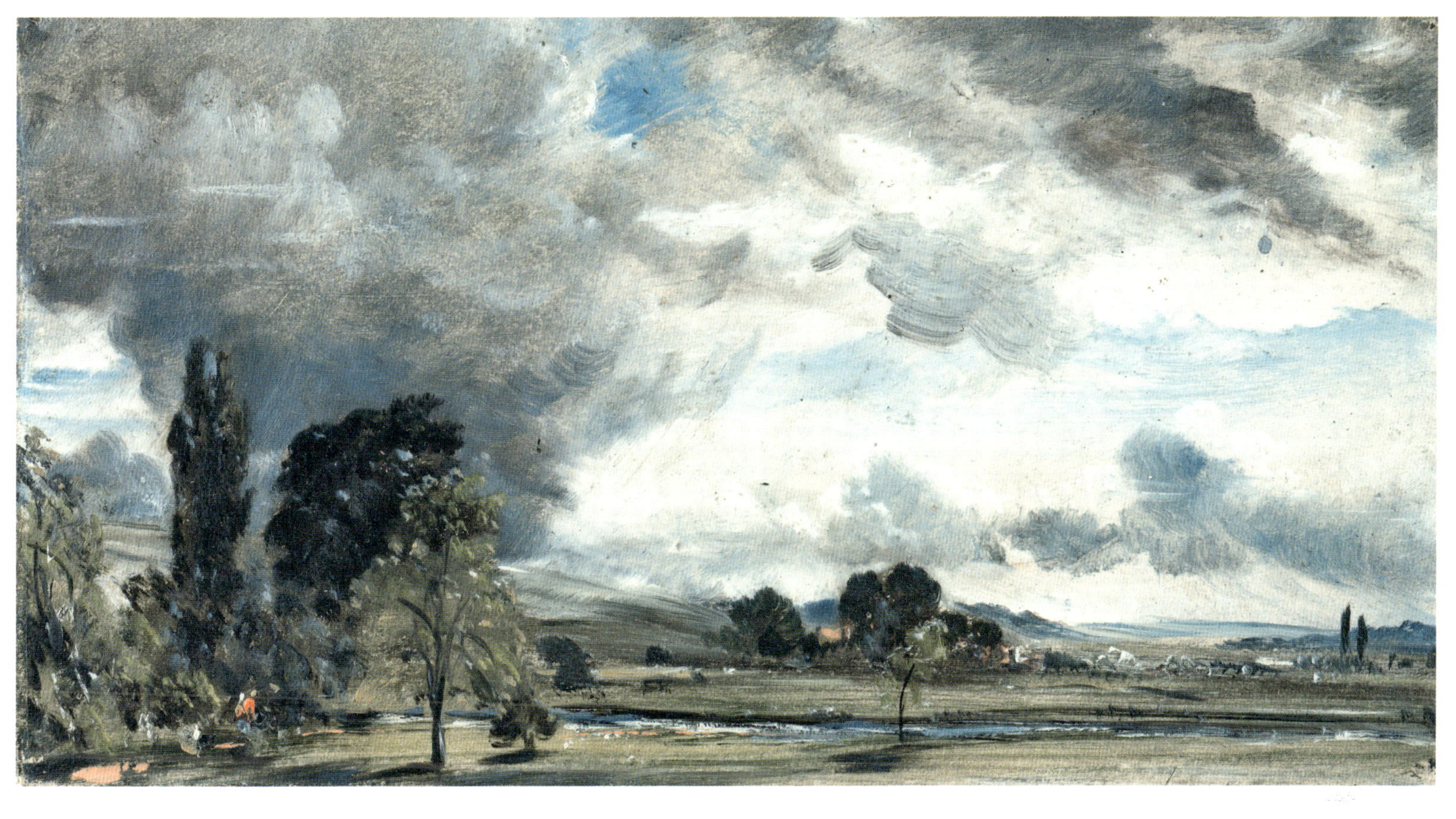

13. Johan Christian Dahl

Norway 1788 – Germany 1857
Cloud study [***Wolkenstudie***] 1832
oil on paper on card 20.3 x 20.0 cm
Hamburger Kunsthalle, Hamburg
Purchased 1910

Dahl came to Dresden in 1818 from the Copenhagen Academy. He soon joined the circle of the Dresden Romantics, centred around Friedrich and Carus. Friedrich's immediate influence can be seen clearly in Dahl's works from this period. His initial cloud studies in Dresden show the same delicate, atmospheric handling of the sky that can be observed in Friedrich's landscapes. It was not until his visit to Italy in 1820–21, however, that Dahl first found his own expressive style. From that time onwards his paintings demonstrate the characteristic use of colour and painterly freedom that even Friedrich admired and sometimes emulated.

From 1823 Dahl lived in Dresden in the same house as Friedrich. From the studio window of his apartment he had an unrestricted view over the River Elbe, a fact that was influential in stimulating his interest in cloud studies. He undertook a large series of studies of the sky at different times of day and under various weather conditions. He painted most of these studies using a smaller format than for the rest of his works, and occasionally inscribed the date on them. His interest in the accurate observation of the sky and clouds was stimulated by the discussion that had arisen amongst his fellow Dresden artists in response to Goethe's essay 'Howard's cloud forms' of c. 1820.

Goethe approached a number of artists with a view to getting them to paint visual representations of Howard's cloud classifications. While Friedrich declined the request, Carus incorporated the principles of scientific exactitude into his own theory and practice of landscape painting. He shared his enthusiasm for Goethe's work on Howard with Dahl. Shortly before Dahl's second journey to Norway in 1828, Carus lent him his own edition of Howard's 'Essay on the modification of clouds'. Howard's work intensified Dahl's scientific approach to painting and in the following years he painted more cloud studies than he had ever done before.

The small format, and use of cardboard for the support, lead us to conclude that Dahl actually painted the 1832 study *en plein air*. The study shows powerful cumulus clouds hovering over the landscape. Dahl paints their bright sunlit-defined forms using strong, muscular brushstrokes. Unlike Constable, he places more emphasis on the cloud's contours and their sense of mass.

Jenns Howoldt

Translated by Mark Henshaw and Christine Dixon.

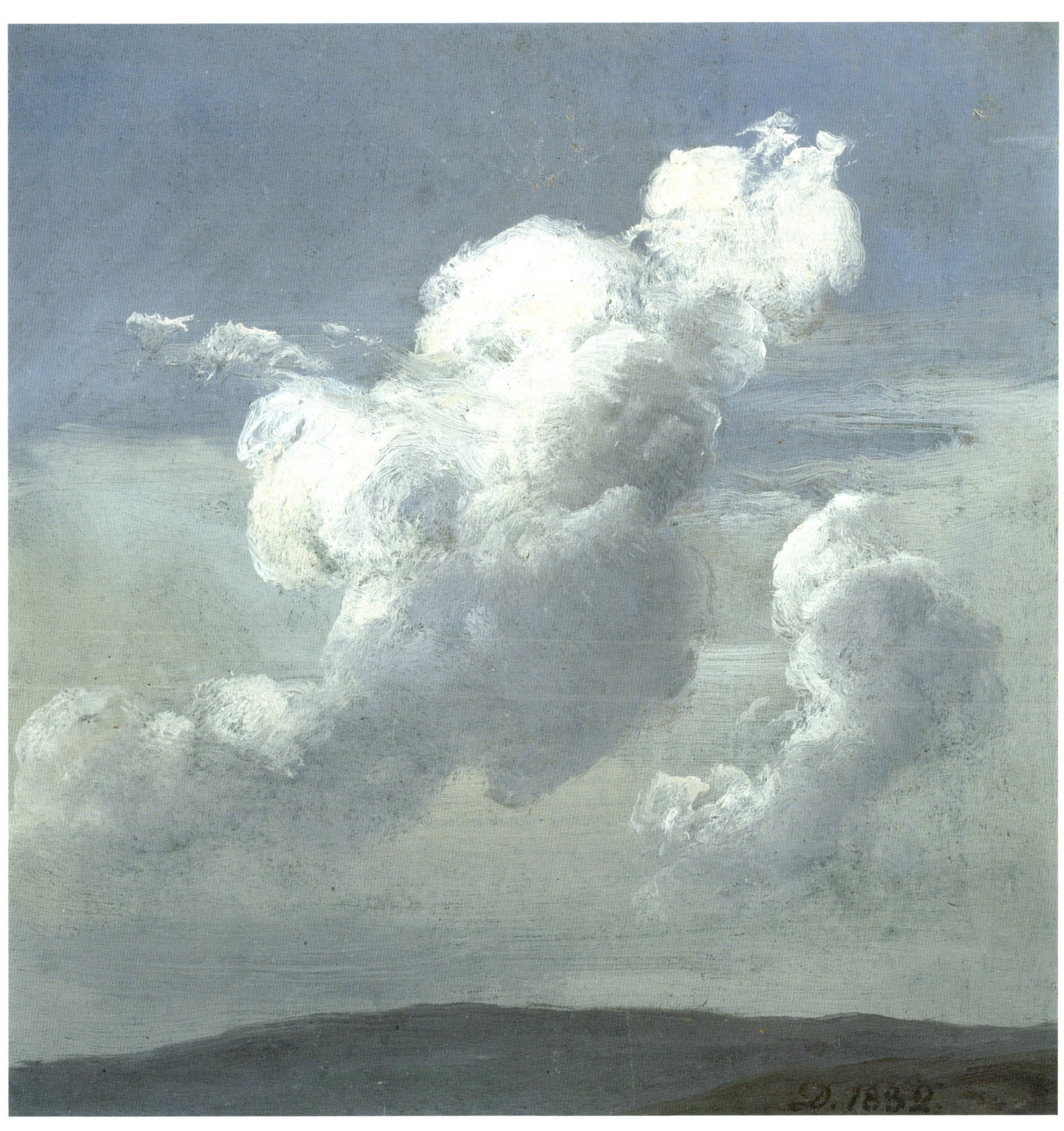

14. John Constable

Great Britain 1776–1837
Buildings on rising ground near Hampstead 1821
also known as ***'The Salt Box', Hampstead*** and
Hampstead Heath: Branch Hill[1]
oil on paper 24.8 x 29.8 cm
Victoria and Albert Museum, London
Given by Isabel Constable, daughter of the artist 781-1888

Impressively bold in its approach, *Buildings on rising ground near Hampstead* demonstrates Constable's transformation of the landscape into an evocative expression of light and atmosphere. In an otherwise unassuming landscape, the artist uses gestural strokes of paint to render the topography of Branch Hill and its surrounds. Led from a low vantage point, the eye travels past a slender blue band of water to Branch Hill and the house known as the 'The Salt Box'. Beyond this scene, another expanse of blue proffers the merest suggestion of a distant vista, that of London's Borough of Harrow, where an ethereal horizon coalesces with the vast sky.

Apart from the year 1824, Constable spent every summer from 1819 to 1826 at Hampstead Heath. The locale, with its high elevation and uninterrupted vistas, proved an important sketching ground for the artist. During the time spent at Hampstead he produced hundreds of views, scrupulously noting the time of day and meteorological phenomena such as cloud formations and wind direction. In an inscription on the reverse of this sketch, he writes the date and time, 'October 1821 at four to five in the afternoon', and records the weather as 'very fine with Gentle Wind at N.E'.[2]

Constable achieves a perfect expression of these conditions in his oil sketch. In order to capture a fleeting moment he paints quickly yet confidently. Working with a dry brush, he rapidly applies oil paint in sweeping movements. In the foreground rough brushstrokes reveal substantial areas of the artist's support. The subtle pink ground is left uncovered throughout the composition, providing warm undertones in a predominantly cool green and blue landscape. Moving upwards, brilliant streaks of paint with crisp white highlights, followed by scumbled areas of saturated blue, accentuate wispy cirrostratus clouds.

In his early Hampstead sketches, Constable increasingly began to direct his attention towards the sky. Wandering the heath, he looked upwards, sketching an extraordinary range of atmospheric phenomena. A week after this sketch was painted the artist wrote to his close friend Reverend John Fisher: 'I have done a good deal of skying', noting that 'That Landscape painter who does not make his skies a very material part of his composition … neglects to avail himself of one of his greatest aids'.[3]

Buildings on rising ground near Hampstead prefigures studies in which the artist looked entirely to the sky, eventually abandoning earthly elements altogether or reducing them to a thin band at the bottom of the painting (cat. 11). Here the undulating grounds of Hampstead and the distant horizon of London occupy only a third of the picture plane. Using the vignette's square format to his advantage, Constable flattens out the composition, reducing the sense of receding depth. In so doing the artist diverts attention from the landscape's horizontal vistas; instead he emphasises the upward-reaching panorama of land and sky.

Niki van den Heuvel

1. Graham Reynolds, *Catalogue of the Constable Collection*, 2nd edn, London: Her Majesty's Stationary Office, 1973, cat. 227, p. 143; Graham Reynolds, *The later paintings and drawings of John Constable: text*, New Haven: Yale University Press, 1984, cat. 21.61, p. 84.
2. Graham Reynolds, 1984, p. 84.
3. Quoted in Anthony Bailey, *John Constable: a kingdom of his own*, London: Chatto & Windus, 2006, p. 124.

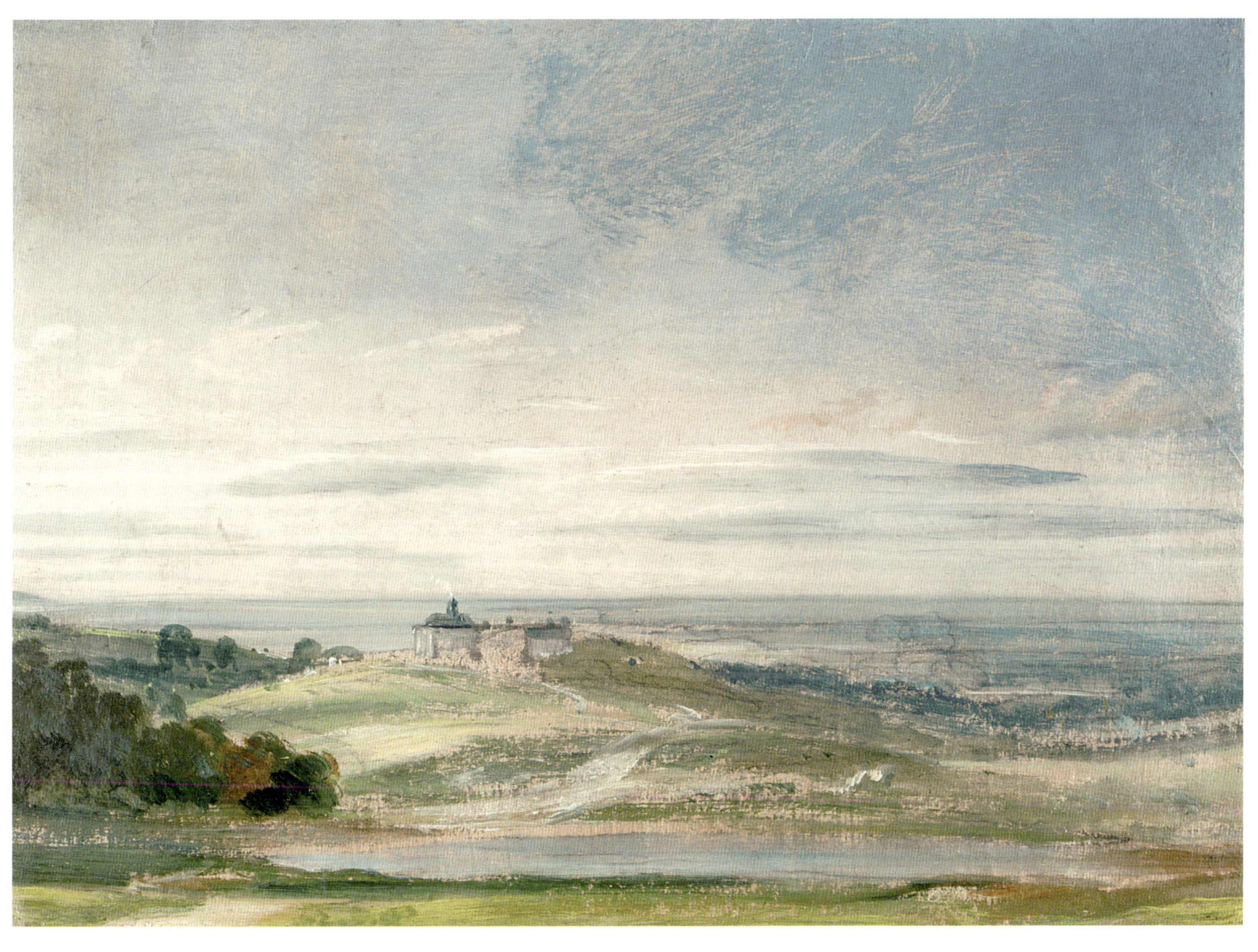

15. John Constable

Great Britain 1776–1837
Dedham from Langham c. 1812
oil on canvas 21.6 x 30.5 cm
Victoria and Albert Museum, London
Given by Isabel Constable, daughter of the artist 132-1888

Constable is one of the greatest English landscape painters of the nineteenth century, with a highly original approach to image-making. Renowned for his landscapes, his 'pure and unaffected representation of nature', he revolutionised landscape painting and placed it at the centre of Western art.

The landscapes that Constable painted were places he had lived in, with which he felt a deep personal bond and were closely bound up with his friendships. Among the places he depicted, the subject of a great proportion of his works was the Stour Valley in Suffolk, including the villages of East Bergholt, Dedham and Langham. It was the district where he was born and spent his childhood and where his family lived. Even in his lifetime it was known as 'Constable's country'.

After viewing the works on display in the Royal Academy in 1802, Constable noted that 'Nature is the fountain's head, the source from whence all originally must spring', and expressed his intention to return to the village of East Bergholt to make 'laborious studies from nature' and to get a 'pure and unaffected representation of the scenes'.[1]

Around 1812 Constable became interested in this panoramic view of the Stour Valley, seen from close to Langham church and across the Dedham Vale, which remained a favourite with him. Here, he showed an open field in the foreground and introduced a small figure disappearing over the brow of the hill, while in the foreground a cow and attendant cowherd supporting a bottle from a stick slung over his shoulder. Constable carefully balanced his composition into clear planes, building it up in carefully juxtaposed tones. He noted that 'this view of the beautiful valley of the Stour … is taken from Langham, an elevated spot … where the elegance of the tower of Dedham church is seen to much advantage'.[2]

Constable asked the printmaker David Lucas to use this sketch for his mezzotint *Summer morning*, published in *English Landscape* in 1831.[3] As a draft for the text intended to accompany Lucas's mezzotint, Constable wrote:

> Nature is never seen, in this climate at least, to greater perfection than at about nine o'clock in the mornings of July and August when the sun has gained sufficient strength to give splendour to the landscape 'still gemmed with the morning dew,' without its oppressive heat; and it is still more delightful if vegetation has been refreshed with a shower during the night.

He went on to distinguish between 'Morning and Evening effects,' writing of 'a greater depth and coolness in the shadows of the Morning' and of the lights being 'more silvery and sparkling' at that time.[4]

In paintings such as *Dedham from Langham* Constable showed the countryside as well-farmed and occupied by busy workers, but his high viewpoint emphasises the countryside itself rather than the activity represented. Nonetheless it suggests that man is in command of the view and in control of its environment. This lyrical image, with its luminous foreground and sky, also presents the landscape as one of continuing pleasure.

Anne Gray

1. R.B. Beckett, *John Constable's correspondence II*, Ipswich: Suffolk Records Society, 1964, p. 32.
2. R.B. Beckett, *John Constable's discourses*, Ipswich: Suffolk Records Society, 1970, p. 17.
3. A series of twenty-two mezzotints was engraved and published by Lucas (1802–1881) under Constable's close supervision. They were based on the painter's oil sketches as well as his exhibition paintings.
4. Beckett, 1970, p. 17.

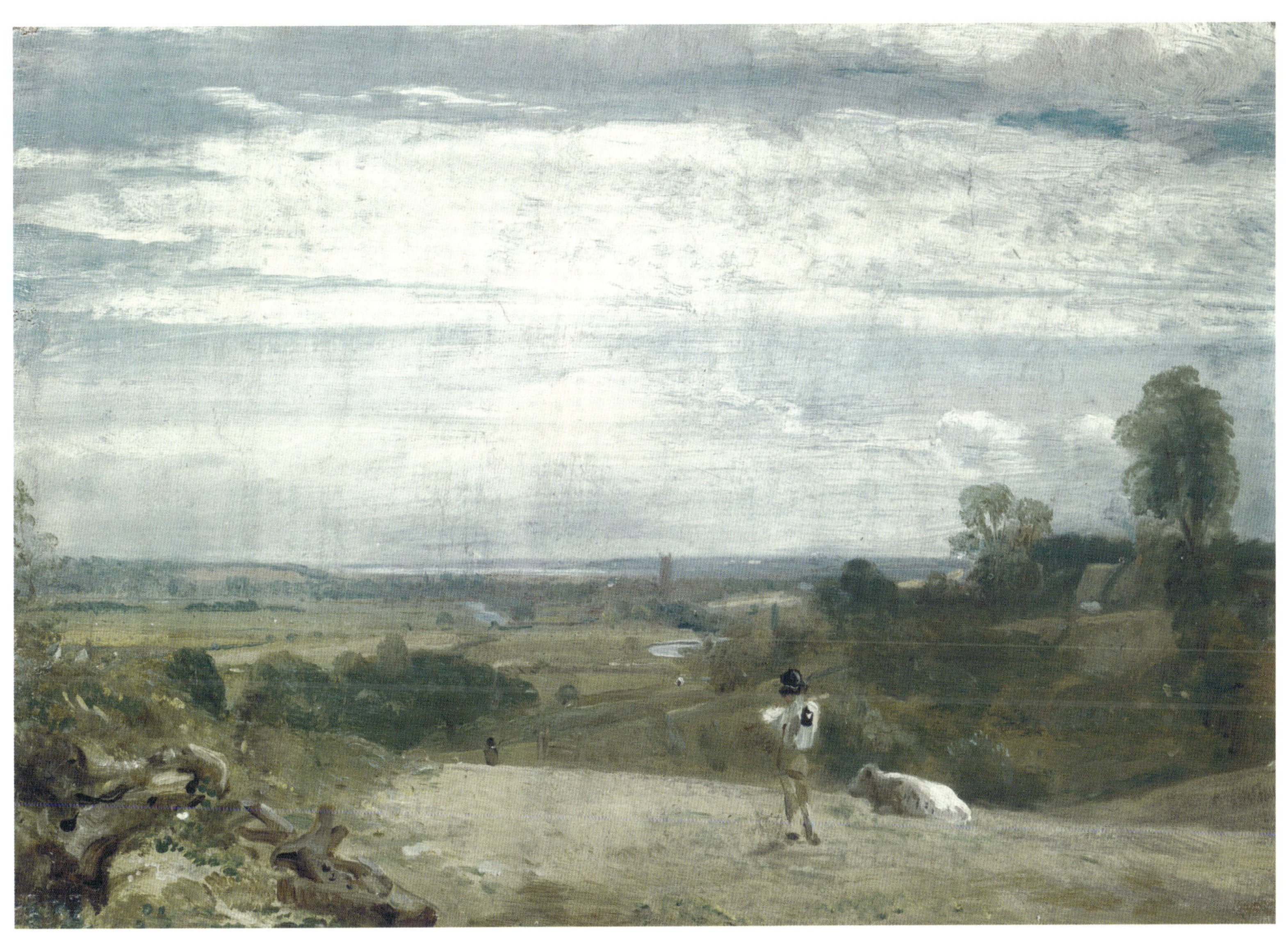

16. John Constable

Great Britain 1776–1837
Brighton Beach 1824
oil on paper 16.5 x 30.4 cm
Victoria and Albert Museum, London
Given by Isabel Constable, daughter of the artist 335-1888

In the summer of 1824, in an attempt to find a healthy environment for his wife Maria and their four young children, Constable rented accommodation at the seaside town of Brighton in south-east England. The sea air had been prescribed as a treatment for his wife's illness, tuberculosis. The family continued to visit Brighton over the next four years, and there Constable found a new stimulus for his art. Brighton was a popular health resort which advocated the benefits of sea bathing and even drinking seawater. It became particularly fashionable when the pleasure-loving Prince of Wales – later George IV – began to frequent the town in the 1780s, and members of his entourage followed.

Constable's feelings for Brighton were mixed. He was critical of the town, describing it as 'Piccadilly by the sea-side,' where there were 'Ladies dressed & *undressed* – gentlemen in morning gowns & slippers on, or without them altogether about *knee deep* in the breakers – footmen – children – nursery maids, dogs, boys, fishermen … all are mixed up together in endless & indecent confusion'.[1] Nonetheless, the artist later suggested that there was perhaps no spot in Europe 'where so many circumstances conducive to heath and enjoyment are to be found combined'.[2]

At Brighton, Constable responded to the visual aspects of the sea and the sky and to the constantly changing light. His innovative, on-the-spot sketches made there reveal his deep understanding of nature and ability to capture unique atmospheric effects. They also show the variety of his approaches to painting and the sensuality of his paint.

An annotation on the back of *Brighton Beach* indicates that this oil sketch was painted on 22 July, and that it was 'a very fine evening'. Long shadows on the ground and the rosy sky reaffirm that this is an evening study. He captured the broad expanse of beach and his use of a relatively low vantage point gives emphasis to the lively sky. Constable included a number of people promenading and sitting on the beach, and several boats on the sea. The hastily-sketched-in figures and boats create an impression of activity, a contrast to the natural elements. The knowing touches with which he created figures leaning over, strolling and sitting, are contrasted with the long strokes with which he painted shadows on the beach, and the way he breathed paint into the sky to create a sense of air.

He handled the paint expressively, working – as was usual with his Brighton sketches – on a sheet of heavy paper slotted into the lid of his paintbox, resting on his lap. He worked over a pink–grey ground, brighter than his usual priming, but a colour that Constable used for his outdoor sketches at Brighton in 1824.[3] The work, like other evocative sketches that Constable painted at Brighton, has a freshness and luminosity that anticipates the beach scenes of French painters such as Eugène Boudin in the 1860s and 1870s.

Anne Gray

1. R.B. Beckett, *John Constable's correspondence VI*, Ipswich: Suffolk Records Society, 1968, p.171.
2. R.B. Beckett, *John Constable's discourses*, Ipswich: Suffolk Records Society, 1970, p.20.
3. Sarah Cove, 'Constable's Oil Painting Materials and Techniques', in Leslie Parris and Ian Fleming-Williams (eds), *Constable*, London: Tate Gallery Publishing, 1991, p.614.

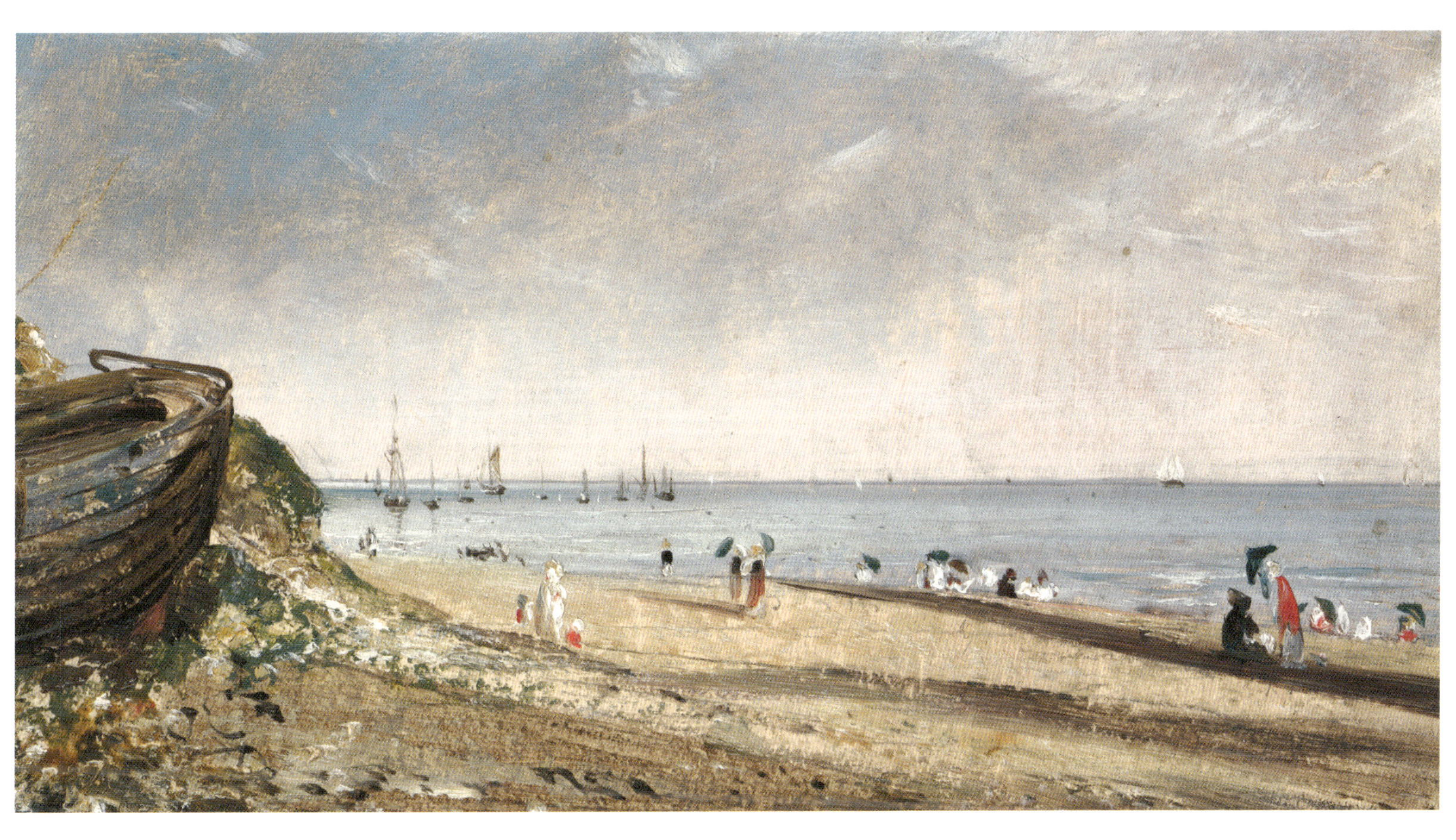

17. John Constable

Great Britain 1776–1837
West End Fields, Hampstead, noon c. 1822
oil on canvas 33.2 x 52.4 cm
National Gallery of Victoria, Melbourne
Felton Bequest, 1909 467-2

It is most likely that Constable painted *West End Fields, Hampstead, noon* in 1821 or 1822, some time during the years he rented 2 Lower Terrace Hampstead.[1] Free of London's pollution, while still close to the metropolis, the vast, rolling parkland of Hampstead Heath was one of the artist's favourite locations. He spent most summers there from 1819 onwards, moving there on a semi-permanent basis in 1827. Living in Hampstead, boasted Constable to his friend John Fisher, allowed him to '… above all see nature – & unite a town & country life'.[2] He tended to paint close to home, and this view is of West Heath, near Lower Terrace.

West End Fields is a small painting. When Constable painted works of this size, they were often quick sketches, which he did not plan to sell or exhibit. Painting out of doors, his intention was to record particular light and weather conditions, which he achieved with his canvases and boards balanced on his knees. The best known of these works are numerous studies of the sky and cloud formations, but he also painted different effects of light on trees and the landscape. He rendered these studies with a rapid brushstroke, often reducing geographical features and figures in particular, to gestural marks, painted in strong colour.

Constable's approach was so methodical that he often recorded the precise time of day of his work. He later used these sketches as aids for his larger works in his studio. In *West End Fields*, however, the artist has clearly defined the landscape, and has painted details such as the flock of sheep, the shepherd and the large tree on the right. He meticulously positions animals and people towards the middle ground, to help define the perspective.

The landscape and the atmospheric clouds are brilliantly integrated by a subdued and even light. The dramatic clouds are painted with great energy and spontaneity – no doubt drawn from one of his sky studies. The great care that Constable has taken with this work therefore places it among a group of finished 'cabinet paintings', probably executed mostly in the studio; these sit between his small experimental sketches painted *en plein air* and the large canvases for sale and exhibition, his 'six footers'. Constable clearly distinguished in his mind that his rapidly painted sketches lacked the necessary order and decorum to make them presentable in the public arena.

If the suggested date of c. 1821–22 is correct, this could be the painting of Hampstead exhibited by Constable at London's Royal Academy in 1822. He must have thought highly of the work, since it is one of the paintings he commissioned David Lucas, the mezzotint artist, to render as a print in 1830 for their series *English landscape*.

Laurie Benson

1. Leslie Parris and Ian Fleming-Williams, *Constable*, London: Tate Gallery, 1991, p. 218.
2. Letter from Constable to John Fisher dated 28 November 1826, in R.B. Beckett, *John Constable and the Fishers: the record of a friendship*, London: Routledge and Kegan Paul, 1952, p. 250.

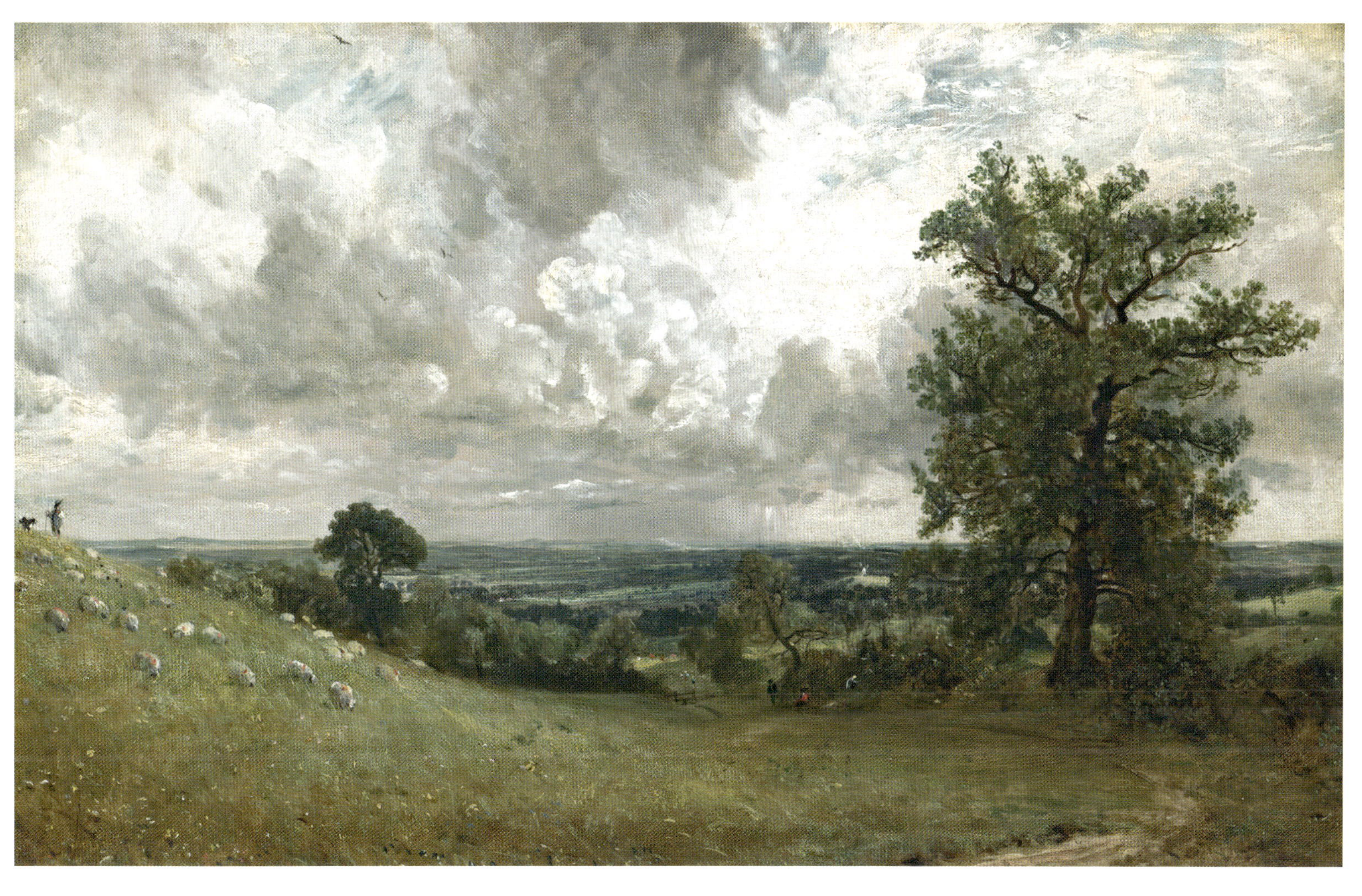

18. Samuel Palmer

Great Britain 1805–1881
The sleeping shepherd 1833–34
tempera with oil on paper on panel 38.1 x 51.4 cm
Collection of James Fairfax, AO

It pleased God to send Mr Linnell as a good angel from Heaven to pluck me from the pit of modern art.
Samuel Palmer, c. 1823–24[1]

Building on pastoral ideals, many nineteenth-century English artists were sensitive interpreters of their native scenery. The works, remarkable for their visionary qualities, were influenced by William Blake and early German woodcuts. Palmer lived in Shoreham, a village in Kent, between 1825 and 1832. Working on paper and card – and using intriguing combinations of pen and ink, tempera, gouache, watercolour, graphite, gum-arabic and varnishes – Palmer produced a range of images of the area: village churches, barns, fields and flocks, and other rural scenes under moon- and starlight. *The sleeping shepherd* was made in the artist's later period at Shoreham. He revisited the intensity and compositional devices of his earlier works but combined these with brighter colours and observations made directly from nature.

Britain was almost constantly at war with France between 1793 and 1815. The conflicts affected access to Italy, long regarded as essential for any artist's training, but war also had dramatic repercussions for the English economy in the 1820s. The mass migrations of the Industrial Revolution, the impact of mechanised threshing machines and looms, the religious crises of 1828–30: all contributed to a sense that institutional order was being questioned, and a way of life threatened. Exploitation of farm labourers by rich landowners resulted in popular protests across the agricultural south: in 1830 the countryside around Shoreham was in turmoil with wide-spread burnings and riots known as 'Captain Swing'.[2] Palmer railed against the treatment of workers by modern farmers; indeed he felt so strongly that traditional pastoral life was threatened that, in 1832, he wrote a pamphlet attacking the *Reform Act*. There is little in Palmer's work to suggest this political and social turmoil – considering the dramatic nature of the period, these events are conspicuous by their absence. It may be that his choice of subject, an arcadian English shepherd, was the artist's political gesture.

Palmer's influences and sources for *The sleeping shepherd* are many. His idyllic view of nature and notions of the pastoral are drawn from Classical antiquity and Virgil's poetry, much admired by the literary artist. Lister suggests another source, John Fletcher's play *The faithful shepherdess* 1608, while the sleeping figure is based on a Greco-Roman sculpture.[3] The whole scene is cosy. The shepherd's staff and faithful dog lie on the straw. Use of the land is suggested by an array of everyday items. The barn forms a framework for the landscape outside, including a small cottage in the valley beyond. Thus the slumbering boy is enfolded, framed on three sides by the architecture and his belongings, the outside world by foliage and protective hills. The subject remained attractive to the artist, who later reworked the pose of the shepherd in an etching.[4] Like most of his contemporaries Palmer portrayed picturesque aspects of farming; as Payne points out, depictions of labourers and actual physical work are rare in English art.[5]

Lucina Ward

1. Quoted in A.H. Palmer, *The life and letters of Samuel Palmer, painter and etcher*, London: Seeley & Co., 1892, p. 14.
2. William Vaughan, Elizabeth E. Barker and Colin Harrison, *Samuel Palmer 1805–1881: vision and landscape*, London: The British Museum Press, New York: The Metropolitan Museum of Art, 2005, p. 137; see also p. 13.
3. Raymond Lister, *The paintings of Samuel Palmer*, Cambridge: Cambridge University Press, 1985, no. 32; the marble Endymion, a late second-century sculpture, was found at Rome in 1774 or 1776, and entered the British Museum collection in 1872.
4. In *The sleeping shepherd*, a plate from *Etchings for the Art Union of London by the Etching Club* 1857, the barn is replaced by a vine-clad bower, the cosy landscape has a distant ploughman already hard at work, and a book on the floor.
5. Compare Linnell's workers (cat. 20); Christiana Payne, *Toil and plenty: images of agricultural landscape in England 1780–1890*, New Haven: Yale University Press, 1993; see also Vaughan et al., p. 161.

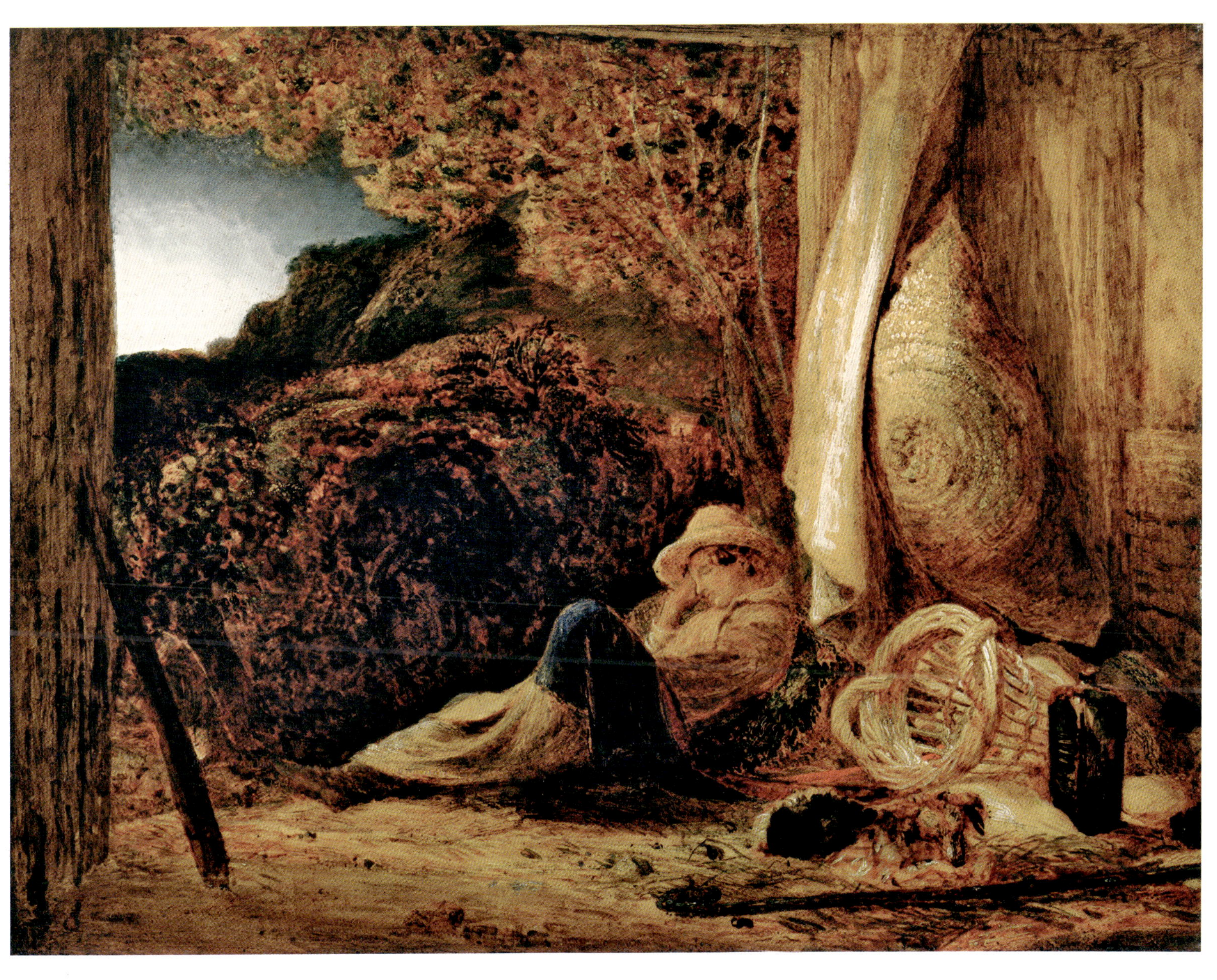

19. John Glover

Great Britain 1767 – Australia 1849
A view of the artist's house and garden, in Mills Plains, Van Diemen's Land 1835
oil on canvas 76.4 x 114.4 cm
Art Gallery of South Australia, Adelaide
Morgan Thomas Bequest Fund, 1951

The painting of Glover's house and garden in Tasmania expresses not only the artist's joy in a fresh arcadian paradise, but also a firm sense of possession for his newly built house on his own land in a new country. But although the depiction of the sun and the general idyllic mood hints at Claude Lorrain's paintings, its style is not an idealised landscape; it is realistic. The painting depicts in loving detail the artist's stone farmhouse, wooden studio–gallery and flourishing garden as they appeared at Christmas in the summer of 1834–35.[1] Glover was a farmer's son and never outgrew a passion for pastoral landscapes. *A view of the artist's house and garden, in Mills Plains, Van Diemen's Land* records the fulfilment of a childhood dream.

An extension of the Romantic view of a golden age in an innocent distant past, was the admiration of simple peasant existence in the natural countryside of one's own time and place. This owed much to the influence of the Dutch seventeenth-century masters, Claude's more naturalistic contemporaries. So it became fashionable to romanticise not only ancient ruins or Neo-Classical country houses but also rustic peasant cottages and their informal gardens. Glover's house and garden picture is, to some extent, derived from this early nineteenth-century cult of Nature and its cottage aesthetic.

As well as an observant rendering of his own planted garden, Glover accurately represents the Australian bush on the small conical hill in the painting's background. The afternoon sun, which back-lights the scene, rings the distant native trees with golden haloes. The artist, who originally portrayed English and Italian scenes according to the formulae and mannerisms of seventeenth-century landscape painting, painted Tasmania more naturalistically. In his depiction of the local bush, as seen on this hill covered with gums, there is no stylisation or generalisation of the indigenous vegetation as is the case with many colonial artists.

Australian landscape's resemblance to English park scenery had been constantly remarked upon since the 1790s. Whether or not Glover saw the hills surrounding his farm as a gentleman's park, he certainly distinguished them from his highly cultivated plain. Here the artist has exaggerated the sharpness of the pyramidal hill and the flatness of the plain, thereby making a slightly artificial stage to display his garden in bloom.

This summer garden painting is an assertive statement of a successful cultural transplant. *A view of the artist's house and garden, in Mills Plains, Van Diemen's Land* was the final painting to be completed for Glover's first London exhibition to be held since his departure from England in 1830. The first significant visual cultural exchange to occur between Australian and English art worlds, the Bond Street Exhibition of 1835 provided the artist with the opportunity to assert his new realist style to an art world that had hitherto never fully accepted him. In this painting Glover's critics, peers, and even the wider public would have read the artist's expression of his new Antipodean Arcadia and the proclamation of his joy in it.

Ron Radford

Adapted from earlier essays by the same author, 'Et in Arcadia Ego', in Daniel Thomas (ed.), *Creating Australia: 200 years of art 1788–1988*, Sydney: International Cultural Corporation of Australia, 1988, pp. 78–9, and Ron Radford and Jane Hylton, *Australian colonial art 1800–1900*, Adelaide: Art Gallery of South Australia, 1995, pp. 71–4.

1. Having successfully reared a range of northern hemisphere cuttings and seedlings brought from England, Glover often took pains to express his thriving gardens. see David Hansen, *John Glover and the colonial picturesque*, Hobart: Tasmanian Museum and Art Gallery & Art Exhibitions Australia, 2003, pp. 214–15.

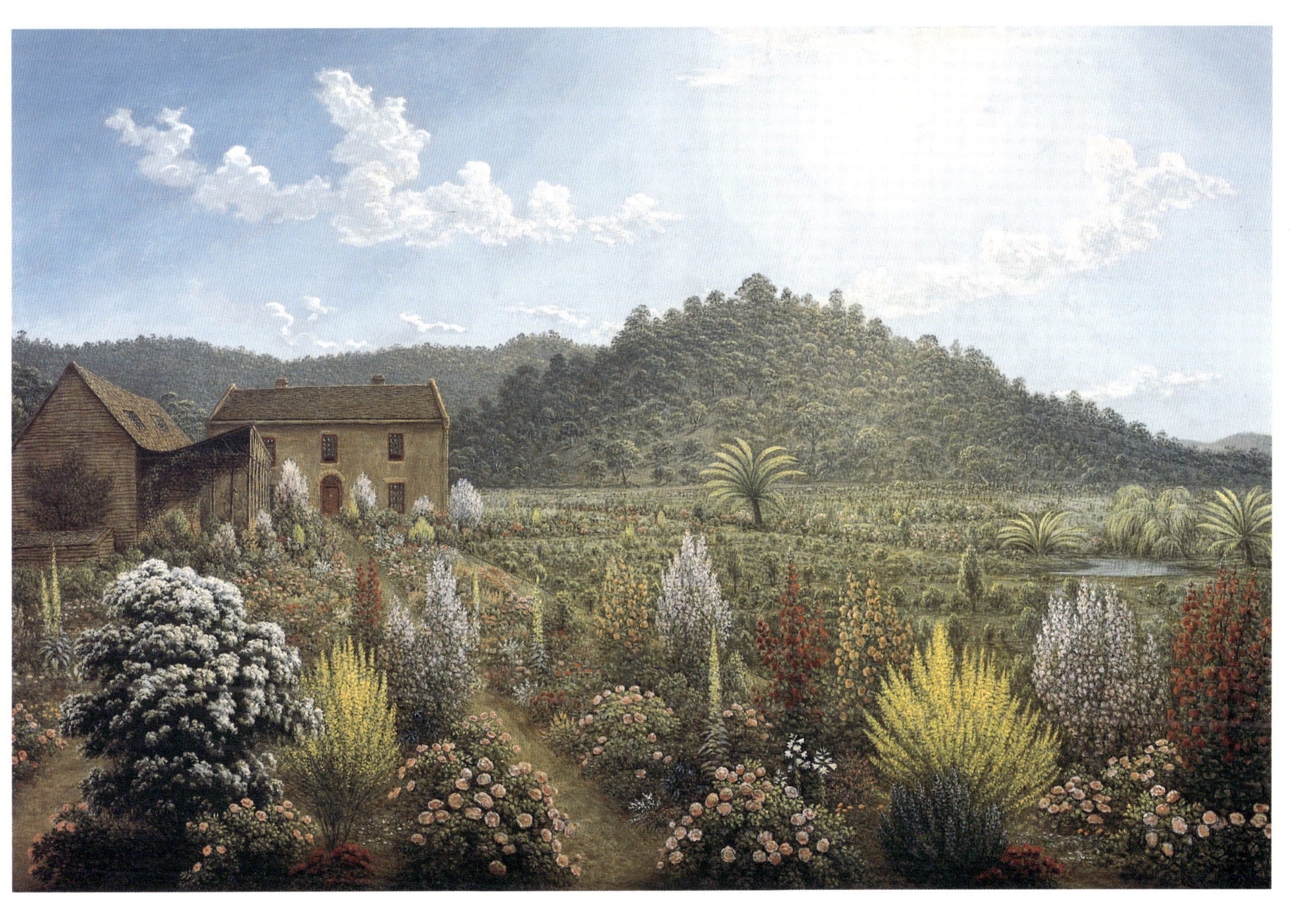

20. John Linnell

Great Britain 1792–1882
Wheat 1860
also known as ***Setting up – wheat***
oil on canvas 94.2 x 140.6 cm
National Gallery of Victoria, Melbourne
Purchased 1888 P.312.81

I hope you are aware that I consider my picture of 'Wheat' as the most artistic picture I have done. I mean by 'Artistic' – qualities which it takes the education of an artist fully to appreciate and a poetic perception to enjoy.[1]
John Linnell

Around 1845, after an extremely successful career as a portrait painter, Linnell turned exclusively to the genre of landscape. With the change of subject he also spent more time in the English countryside and, in 1851, moved permanently to Redstone Wood, Redhill, Surrey. Like several other flourishing artists of his day, Linnell bought a large area of land to which he subsequently added fields as his wealth grew. Unlike other artist landowners, however, his estate thrived and he employed many labourers. He made a careful study of the yearly harvests and the daily work of his employees. Like much of his work after 1851, the landscape and the people in *Wheat* are painted directly from his experiences at Redhill.[2] In fact many reviewers criticised the sameness of content and feel of many of his later paintings.[3]

In *Wheat* the artist depicts the harvest of golden wheat bales or stooks, as darkening clouds signal the imminent arrival of a storm overhead. In all three distinct areas of this painting – the sky, the trees and the workers amongst the wheat – Linnell creates a sense of movement. The rounded, billowing clouds seem to drift across the sky, trees move in the same imaginary breeze, while the labourers in the foreground lead the viewer's eye back and forth and around the painting. Linnell alludes to the rhythms of the seasons, and the underlying constancy of change in nature and the landscape.

As a landowner, Linnell actively resisted the industrialising trend towards faster mechanised harvesting which was growing in England and Europe, choosing instead to rely on manual labour.[4] His insistence on older methods should be seen in the light of Linnell's strong Protestant religious convictions which saw God's Earth given to humans to work with their hands. Describing the artist's landscape work, the 1883 obituary in *The Times* noted, 'John Linnell perceived the veil lifting from nature, and felt that he was consecrated to be her prophet'.[5]

Linnell's earlier biblical genre paintings failed to gain popular appeal in the art market of Victorian England. Hence he developed his landscapes into metaphorical expressions of his beliefs, since they were a perfect vehicle for displaying his religious zeal in a covert way. Biblical allusions, invariably pastoral and filled with references to farm animals, harvests and storms, could easily be reflected in Linnell's landscapes.[6]

Unlike many other landscapes of the period, people play a key role in Linnell's work. *Wheat* is a painting of labourers working a landscape rather than simply a landscape where the rustic figures are used as artistic devices. His religious philosophies are also played out in his paintings, for he held strong egalitarian views on the English class system, unlike many other artists of the period, such as Constable who wanted it to remain unchanged. Linnell highlighted what was a new lower class – the rural poor.[7]

Simeran Maxwell

1. Letter from John Linnell to William Agnew, one of his patron clients, 15 August 1860, quoted in David Linnell, *Blake, Palmer, Linnell and Co.: the life of John Linnell*, Lewes: The Book Guild Ltd, 1994, p. 283.
2. Angus Trumble, *Love and death: art in the age of Queen Victoria*, Adelaide: Art Gallery of South Australia, 2001, pp. 34–6.
3. Katherine Crouan, *John Linnell: a centennial exhibition*, Cambridge: Fitzwilliam Museum, 1982, p. xvii.
4. Trumble, p. 174.
5. Quoted in David Linnell, p. ix.
6. See Crouan, p. xv.
7. See Louis Hawkes, *Presences of nature: British landscape 1780–1830*, New Haven: Yale Center for British Art, 1982, especially Chapter V: 'Landscape with laborers'.

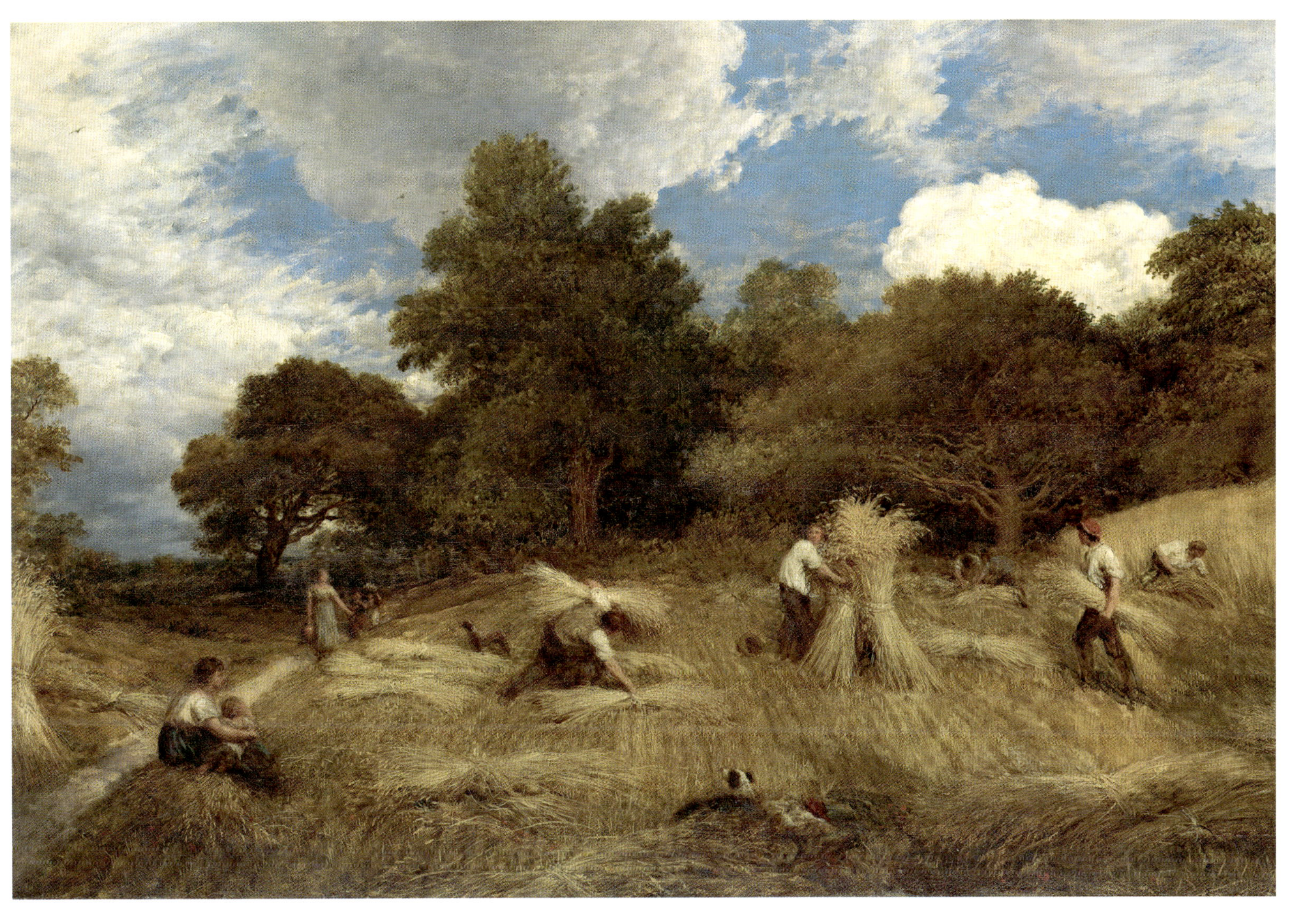

21. Eugene von Guérard

Austria 1811 – Great Britain 1901
worked in Australia 1852–81
Purrumbete from across the lake 1858
oil on canvas 51.0 x 85.5 cm
National Gallery of Australia, Canberra
Purchased with funds from the Nerissa Johnson Bequest 1998
1998.148

From the verandah of Purrumbete 1858
oil on canvas 51.4 x 86.3 cm
National Gallery of Australia, Canberra
Purchased 1978 1978.173

In two of his most inventive bucolic landscapes, *Purrumbete from across the lake* and *From the verandah of Purrumebete*, von Guérard offers a pair of alternative, yet complementary, scenes of a bountiful Victorian farm and homestead. Moving from the goldfields of Ballarat to Melbourne in the mid-1850s, the artist soon recognised the growing market for commissioned 'homestead portraits'. Based on traditions of English topographical landscapes, such views depicted wealthy country properties in the best possible light, advertising the success of the pastoralist.

Commissioned to paint the property of the Manifold brothers in 1857, von Guérard expresses the bounty of the land. Imbuing the scenes with a sense of ease and plentitude, he suggests a pastoral Arcadia. He hints at the patron's aspirations, prosperity and ownership of the land. The abundance of water, crucial to the grazier's livelihood, dominates both panoramas while, on the land, views of a well-tended home, gardens, pastures, outbuildings and livestock attest to the outcomes of intensive labour and dedication to the land.

Purrumbete from across the lake shows the Manifolds' homestead encompassed by a thriving English garden, along with the property's surrounding outbuildings and barns. Looking west from the vantage of Picnic Point, we are led into this scene of pastoral tranquillity by a grassy outcrop in the foreground where full-bellied cattle are left to graze. Small figures are placed throughout the composition to demonstrate the practical and leisurely uses of the land.[1] A solitary figure rows a boat across the glassy lake, women and young girls wander up garden steps towards the home, while men attend to the needs of the property. Von Guérard then juxtaposes these images with the majestic backdrop of Mount Leura under an expanse of open blue sky.

From the verandah of Purrumbete contrasts starkly with its companion piece. Although von Guérard repeats a number of visual motifs – we are already familiar with the outcrop of Picnic Point in the distance and the sailing boat gliding along the lake – the overall composition is dramatically different. Invited into the composition from the shady verandah, the viewer immediately experiences the beauty of a successfully transplanted English oasis. A towering willow tree, flowering rose bushes, wandering passionflower vine and other introduced plants coalesce with the architecture of the porch to frame a serene vista of land, water and sky.

This framing device is unusual in the context of the 'homestead portrait' but not at all surprising given von Guérard's European training. Initially schooled in the tradition of Salvator Rosa in Rome, the artist later trained at the renowned Düsseldorf Academy where he came under the influence of German Romanticism. Here we are reminded of compositions by Friedrich, in which the artist set up inventive framing devices to accentuate the opposing realms of contemplation against distance and departure (cat. 36, 37).[2]

Von Guérard further accentuates this opposition by back-lighting the verandah and garden to create a striking silhouette. This *contre-jour* effect was often employed by German Romantic artists. Applied to human figures and framing devices, the effect transports the viewer into the landscape. The immediate contrast of interior and outside worlds heightens our experience of the intimate and cordial domestic environment against the immensity of the outside world.[3]

Niki van den Heuvel

1. Anne Laurence, 'Space, status and gender in English topographical paintings c. 1660 – c. 1740', *Architectural History*, vol. 46, 2003, p. 84.
2. Norbert Wolf, *Friedrich 1774–1840: the painter of stillness*, Köln: Taschen, 2003, p. 41.
3. Malcolm Andrews, *Landscape and Western art*, New York: Oxford University Press, 1999, p. 111.

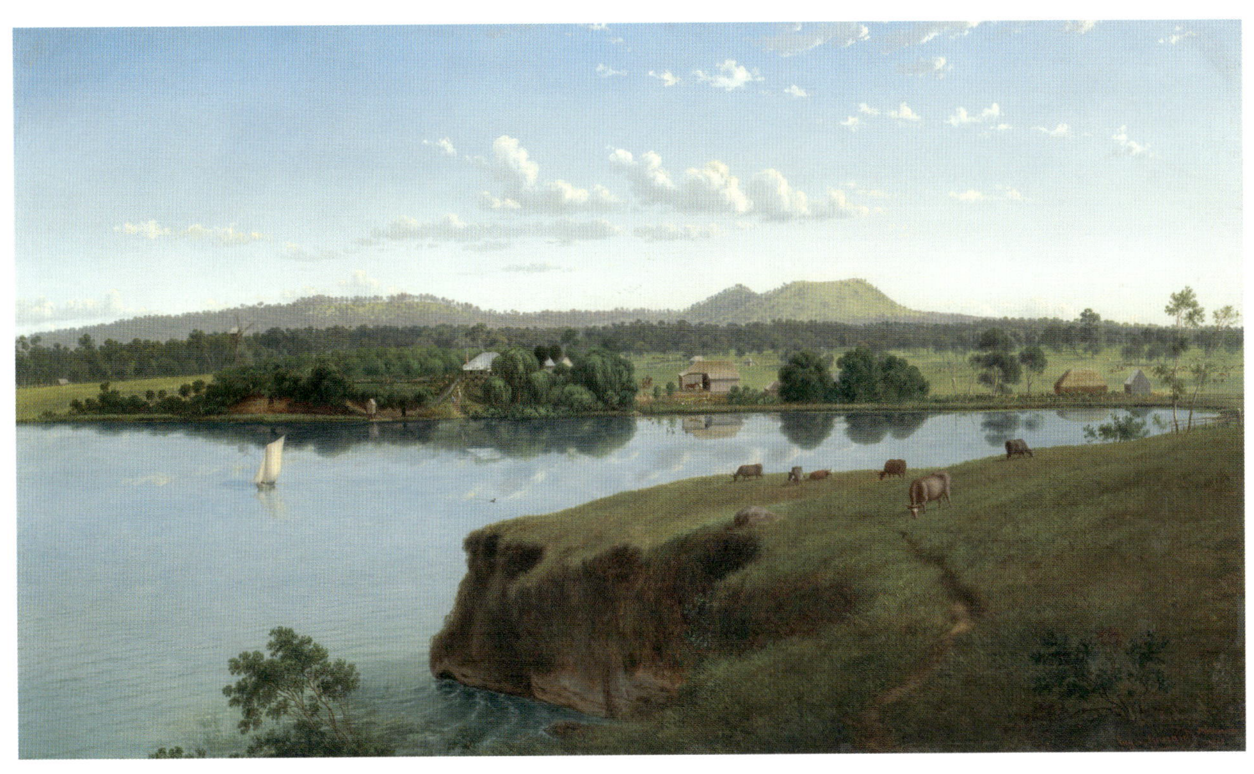

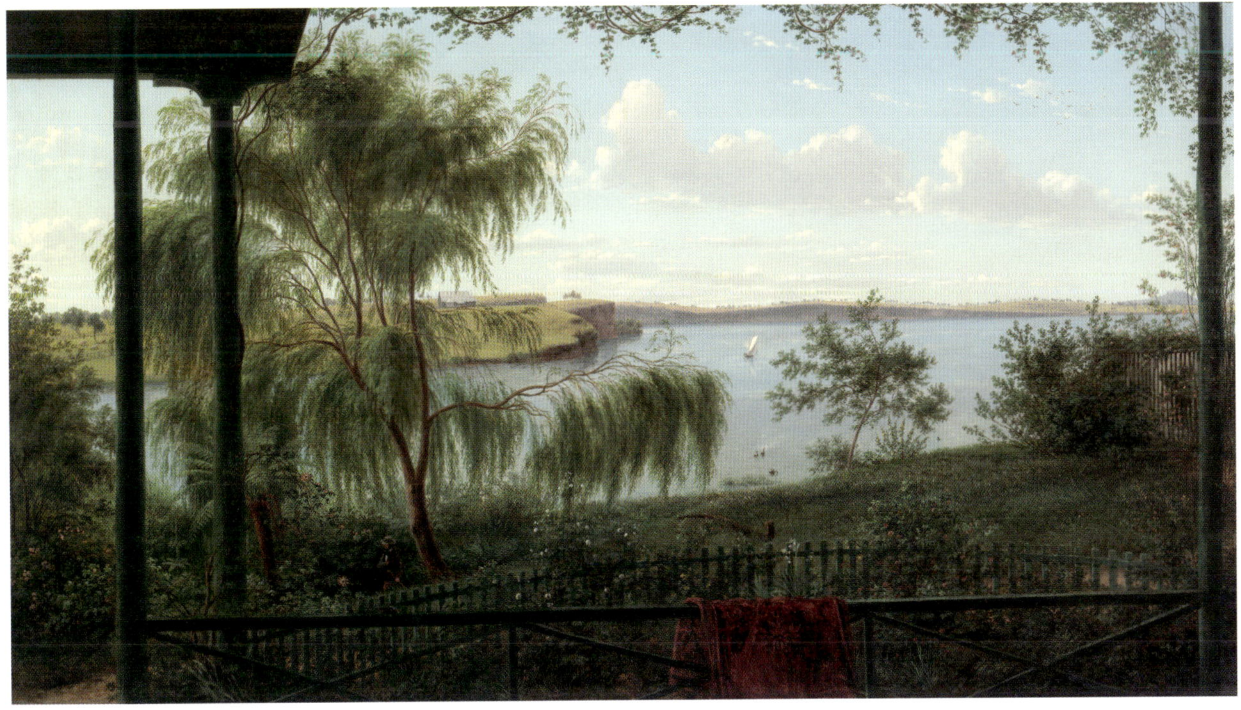

22. Camille Corot

France 1796–1875
Landscape with lake and boatman [***Le batelier (effet de soir)***] 1839
also known as ***Evening landscape*** [***Un soir; paysage***]
oil on canvas 62.5 x 102.9 cm
The J. Paul Getty Museum, Los Angeles

Corot depicts a lake at dusk, surrounded by mostly flat landscape with a small grove of trees. Two figures in simple dress go peacefully about their business. The painting is a glorious combination of sky – changing from turquoise-blue to citron and orange – set off by silhouetted trees, tinged with gold. The lower half of the canvas features modulated, blue–grey water and an energetically painted mix of solid brown rocks, sandy ground and patches of grass. The artist includes two punctuations: the red hat, and flicks of green paint that comprise the reeds on the shore. The composition is balanced, both literally and pictorially, on the horizontal axis, and by its left and right sides. The upper shape of foliage complements the lower ovoid of water. The slight curve of horizon is mirrored by the water's edges. All is just so.

The painter lived in Italy from 1825 to 1828, and thereby aligned himself within a longstanding artistic tradition. Those artists who travelled to Italy inevitably came away with strong impressions of the light, their perceptions sharpened from painting *en plein air.* They produced – according to academic conventions – carefully composed idyllic landscapes peopled by gambolling nymphs or happy peasants, adorned with picturesque ruins, views of Rome and its surrounds. From the mid-1750s, looking was increasingly mediated or viewed through the lens of art. In an urban society, we find the idea that landscape painting can stand in for nature. Travellers composed equivalent views, using small round or oval convex mirrors called 'Claude glasses'. Looking at *Landscape with lake and boatman* may prompt us to think of the seventeenth-century master Claude. Constructed from memories and drawings, the mood of this painting is evocative and dreamlike.

In response to its exhibition at the Paris Salon of 1839, the poet and critic Théophile Gautier penned a description of *Landscape with lake and boatman* in verse.[1] Like the eighteenth-century philosopher Diderot, he felt strongly that the descriptive abilities of an art writer should help his reader 'see' the work. Gautier's ability to 'paint pictures' in words was held in high regard, possibly because of his earlier training as a painter. As was customary, Corot's production was divided into open-air studies and finished compositions made in the studio, the latter being exhibited publicly at the annual Salons in Paris. Although regarded highly by his artist contemporaries, many critics complained that Corot's Italian works were unconstrained and careless. On the other hand, those many colleagues and students who had access to Corot's studio – from 1826 when he was still in Rome, and after his return to France – greatly admired the studies, and were even allowed to borrow them.[2] During a prolific career spanning half a century, Corot used his motifs again and again, and we find the figure of this boatman in many other paintings after 1839. As an individual, however, we know almost nothing about the artist. He was a blank canvas on which others have painted pictures of their own.

Lucina Ward

1. Michael Pantazzi, Vincent Pomarède and Gary Tinterow, *Corot*, New York: Metropolitan Museum of Art, 1996, pp. 180, 412.
2. See discussion in Peter Galassi, *Corot in Italy: open-air painting and the Classical landscape tradition*, New Haven: Yale University Press, 1991.

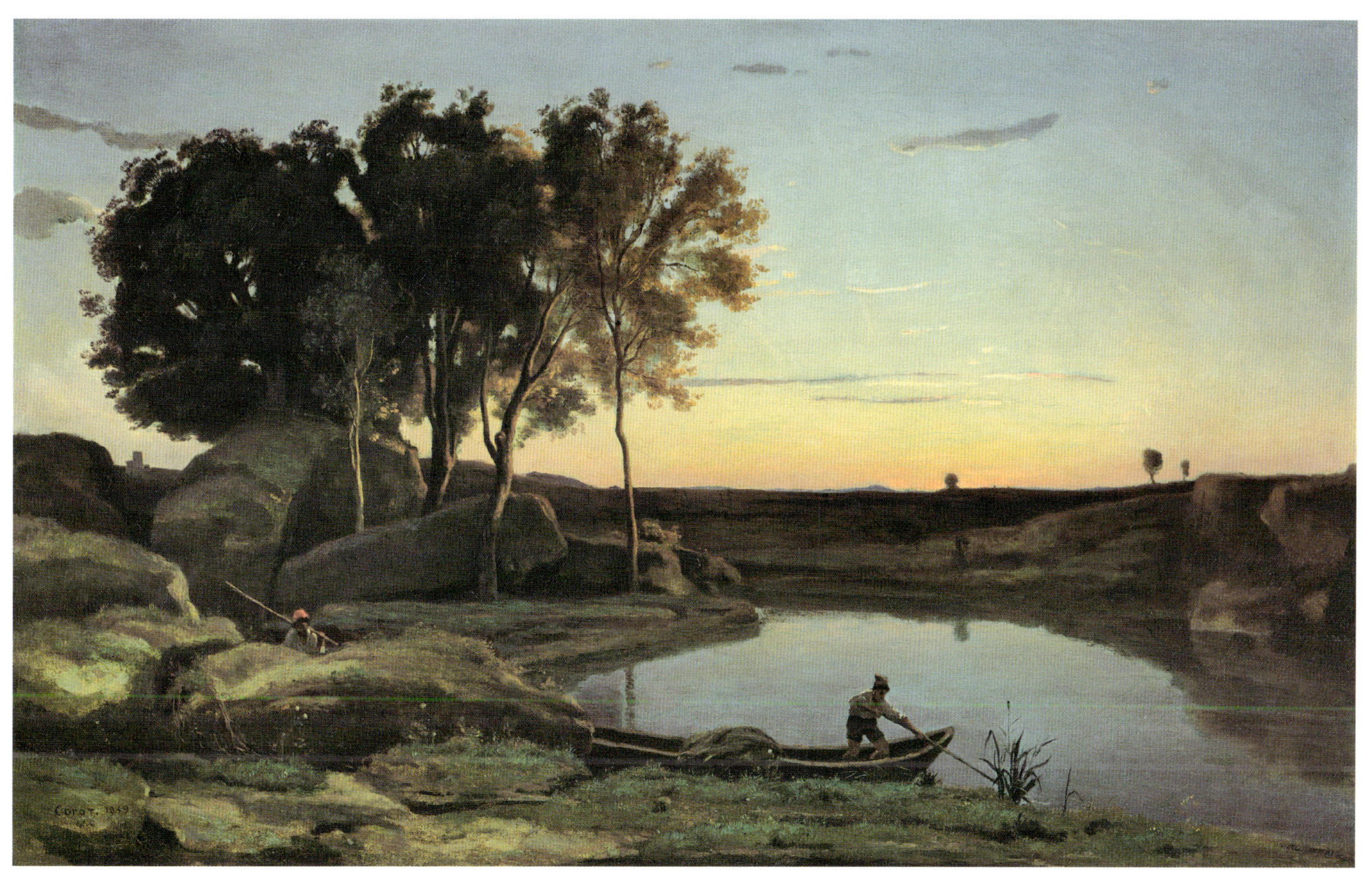

23. Camille Corot

France 1796–1875
The bent tree **[*L'arbre penché*]** c. 1855–60
oil on canvas 44.3 x 58.5 cm
National Gallery of Victoria, Melbourne
Felton Bequest, 1907 338-2

In 1857, as Baron Haussmann's program to raze old Paris gathered speed, Corot declared 'this is a new world which I no longer recognise; I am too attached to the past … I want to make a new art for myself'.[1] In this new age of the camera, evidence of change was captured in forensic detail. Corot's dismay at the human cost of modernity did not radicalise him as it did his Realist colleagues, Courbet, Jean-François Millet and Rousseau. Nevertheless, his landscapes manage to register personal regret through their sheer withdrawal from the brutal facts of contemporary France, into an exquisite past of the artist's own invention.

By 1851 both Corot's parents were dead, and he rented an apartment in Paris. Between visits to the provinces and to Switzerland, he worked up in his studio dreamlike pastoral scenes for submission to the Salon. This was a task undertaken with great seriousness, as he had pushed for reform of the Salon's selection process in 1848, and subsequently was elected to its new juries. A resulting rise in his status meant that Corot's canvases received special scrutiny. In tune with the bourgeois sentimentality of his day, Corot never shied from revealing aspects of his private self in his 'public' art. The motifs he re-used from *plein-air* sketches had personal associations, indicated by a softening of edges to render them evocative rather than topographical. The famously harsh contrasts of light and tonal values in his nature studies, so esteemed by fellow artists, Corot now modulated to an all-enveloping silvery glow. Peasants, whom he elsewhere portrays in acute detail, were reduced to vibrant dots of colour or transmuted into forest nymphs and gods.

The bent tree is a splendid example of Corot's new lyrical mode. It features a pond beside his beloved family home at the Ville d'Avray, close to Paris. The trees in the foreground are birches planted by his father, which Corot animates with two small figures and a cow, all in states of bucolic absorption. He prized these confections, which he called 'souvenirs', above his sketches painted out-of-doors. So too did his public. Despite their obvious artifice, the lingering whiff of reality clings to his arcadian idylls, which betray their *plein-air* origins. In 1853 his friend Daubigny wrote that Corot 'is now very much in fashion and … can no longer satisfy the demands that are made of him'.[2] In 1855 Napoléon III became a collector of his works.[3] Corot was happy to supply clamouring buyers with variations on his Salon pictures, writing in 1856 'I'm working like a little devil'.[4] One critic pondered:

> How many times, in thinking to retrace the pitiful contours of the hills of Ville d'Avray, [Corot] transformed them into a landscape of Arcadia! How many little white houses lost in the foliage has he disguised as ancient temples![5]

Sophie Matthiesson

1. Étienne Moreau-Nélaton, *Histoire de Corot et ses œuvres*, Paris: H. Floury, 1905, p. 180, translated in Michael Clarke, *Corot and the art of landscape*, London: British Museum Press, 1991, p. 79.
2. *Auguste Ravier 1814–1895*, Reims: Musée de Reims, 1964, p. 13, trans. Clarke, p. 96.
3. *La charrette: souvenir de Marcoussis*, 1855, Musée d'Orsay, Paris.
4. Alfred Robaut, *L'Œuvre de Corot: catalogue raisonné et illustré*, 5 vols in 4, Paris: H. Floury, 1905, vol. 1, p. 165, and vol. 4, p. 336, no. 76, trans. Michael Pantazzi, in Michael Pantazzi, Vincent Pomarède and Gary Tinterow, *Corot 1796–1875*, New York: Metropolitan Museum of Art, 1996, p. 398.
5. Charles Timbal, quoted and translated by Albert Boime, *Art in an age of counterrevolution (1815–1848)*, Chicago: University of Chicago Press, 2004, p. 480, note 100.

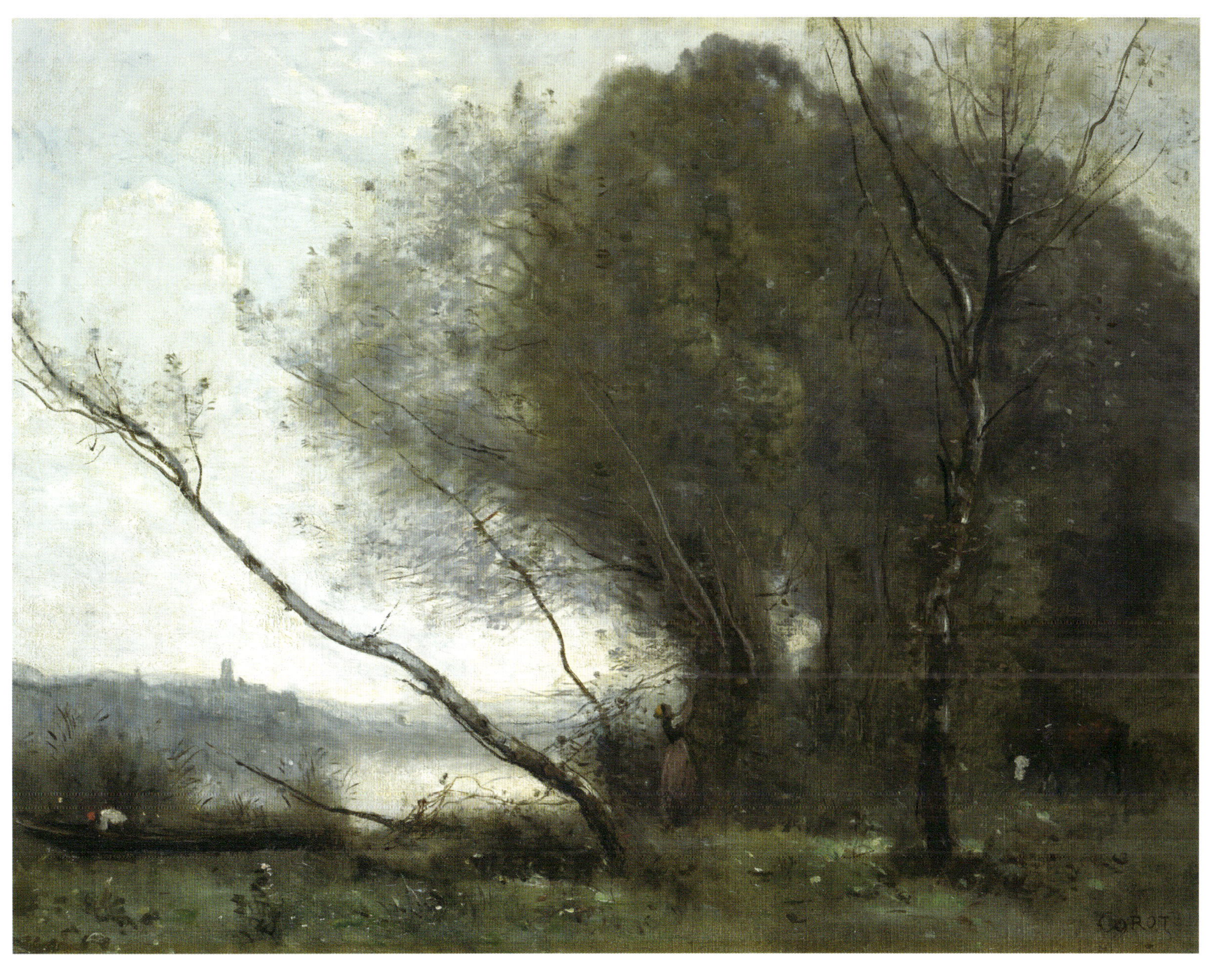
COROT

24. Samuel Palmer

Great Britain 1805–1881
The Golden City: Rome from the Janiculum 1873
watercolour, bodycolour, pencil, black chalk,
gum arabic on card 51.4 x 71.0 cm
National Gallery of Victoria, Melbourne
Presented by members of the Varley Family, 1927 340-3

In 1838 Palmer wrote home to his family from Rome, describing in lyrical terms his delight in the brilliant Italian sunlight:

> ... if I can but bring home imitations of this glorious sunshine which fuses rocks trees and ruins into amber and gold [I] shall not be unhappy. The color of the white marble ... against the blue sky is the very poetry of light[,] a light too which blends into one breadth of splendour the most intricate multitude of parts – and seems on every sunny day ... as new and magical as when it first broke upon us ... The thing we see is the brightness of poetry – not of pigments.[1]

Thirty-five years later, a much older Palmer – whose longheld hope of returning to Italy was fading – would revive this splendid 'poetry of light' in his large exhibition watercolour entitled *The Golden City*. This luminous panorama presents one of the most celebrated views of Rome, seen at sunset from the Janiculum Hill to the west of the city. Various famous landmarks, such as St Peter's and the Vatican (on the left through the pines), the Tiber, Castel Sant' Angelo and the Pantheon, shimmer in the gold and indigo haze that suffuses the middle ground and distance.

The overall impression is more realistic than Palmer's 1830s Italian views, far less accomplished in their rendering of perspective. The artist's paramount concern is not the accurate recording of this Roman vista; instead he aspires to the grander conception of landscape as the vehicle for deep emotion and poetic feeling. In his earlier Shoreham days, Palmer had adopted the Ancients' catch-cry of 'Poetry and Sentiment', and sought its embodiment in the Kentish countryside (cat. 18).[2] Now in later life, he pursued these ideals through the Classical tradition of landscape, and praised its exponents, Claude and Poussin, who: 'addressed not the perception chiefly, but the IMAGINATION, and here is the hinge and essence of the whole matter'.[3]

The Golden City illustrates Palmer's increasingly brilliant and expressive use of colour. This chromatic exuberance, as well as his preference for idyllic landscape, led many critics to declare him the successor of Turner.[4] Certainly Palmer was a great admirer of this artist who, like him, laid stress on the literary underpinnings of his art. In fact, this large and vibrant work could be regarded as an attempt by Palmer to rival Turner's great classical oil paintings, such as *Childe Harold's pilgrimage – Italy*.[5] Significantly, Palmer chose to include a verse from Byron's poem *Childe Harold's pilgrimage* – the subject of Turner's masterpiece – in the catalogue that accompanied *The Golden City* when it was exhibited at the Old Watercolour Society in London in 1873. The verse's mood of romantic yearning finds perfect expression in the elegiac image of *The Golden City*.

> Oh Rome! My country! City of the soul!
> The orphans of the heart must turn to thee,
> Lone mother of dead empires! And control
> in their shut breasts their petty misery.
> What are our woes and sufferance?[6]

Alison Inglis

1. Letter from Samuel Palmer to John Linnell, 21 January 1838, *The letters of Samuel Palmer*, ed. Raymond Lister, 2 vols, Oxford: Clarendon Press, 1974, vol.1, pp. 105–6.
2. David Blayney Brown, '"To fancy what is lost to sight": Palmer and Literature' in William Vaughan et al., *Samuel Palmer 1805–1881: vision and landscape*, London: British Museum Press, 2005, p. 23.
3. Letter from Samuel Palmer to Leonard Rowe Valpy, May 1875, quoted in Scott Wilcox and Christopher Newall, *Victorian landscape watercolors*, New York: Hudson Hill Press and Yale Center for British Art, 1992, p. 109.
4. Scott Wilcox, 'Poetic Feeling and Chromatic Madness: Palmer and Victorian Watercolour Painting' in Vaughan, p. 46.
5. Collection of the Tate Britain.
6. Canto IV, 1818; see Nicholas Williams, 'Samuel Palmer, *The golden city: Rome from the Janiculum*', in Cathy Leahy et al., *Prints and drawings in the international collections of the National Gallery of Victoria*, Melbourne: NGV, 2003, p. 87.

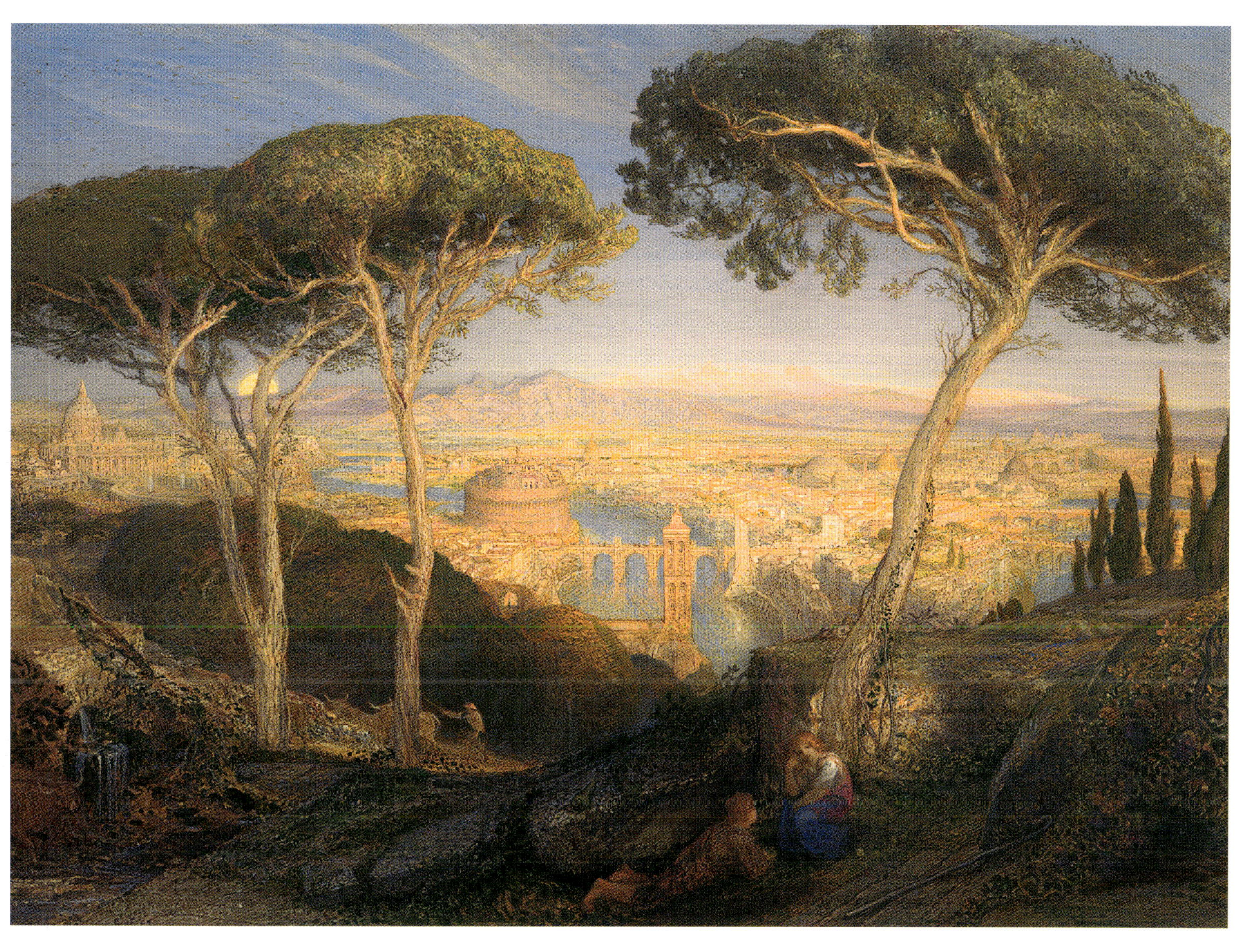

25. J.M.W. Turner

Great Britain 1775–1851
Overlooking the coast, with classical building c.1827
oil on canvas 60.3 x 84.5 cm
Tate Britain
Accepted by the British nation as part of the Turner Bequest 1856
N02991

Turner's lifelong passion for Claude Lorrain was renewed and refreshed by successive experience. His sketchbooks are full of variations on Claude's characteristic classical landscapes or seaports and, besides painting notable pictures on such themes, he trialled many others in sketches and studies. During his first visit to Italy in 1819 Turner saw for himself the landscape and light that had been painted by Claude, and looked with new eyes at his pictures in Roman collections. On his first trip to Paris in 1802 Turner had given curiously little attention to Claude's works in the Louvre – either because they were hard to see in galleries then undergoing rearrangement, or because the artist was well represented in British collections and already familiar through reproductions of his oeuvre catalogue, the *Liber veritatis*. But Turner's Italian memories sparked fresh interest during a return visit to Paris in 1821, and he copied various Claudes, several to a page in his sketchbooks, and made extensive notes.

This classical seaport is one of a group of sixteen oil sketches, roughly the same size, which have been cut from four rolls of canvas containing four designs each, Turner having worked across the canvas in linked pairs of compositions. The working process, somewhat comparable to the imprinting of successive images on a roll of film, echoes his approach in his sketchbooks. For many years it was believed that these rolls of canvas were used during Turner's second visit to Italy, in 1828, when he set up a studio in Rome, and were preferred for ease of transport. Recent research by Warrell, however, has shown that some of the subjects are French, originating in the same sketchbook that Turner used to copy Claude in the Louvre in 1821, while another relates to a picture Turner painted before leaving for Italy in 1828.[1] Thus subjects like this seaport are just as likely to be studio exercises painted in anticipation of renewed experience of Italy and Claude, as direct responses painted in Rome.

The motifs of a curving bay in the background, with trees and seated figures in the left foreground, can be traced to some pencil variations on a Claude painting that Turner saw at the Palazzo Sciarra in Rome in 1819, *Landscape with the port of Santa Marinella*. Drawn in a sketchbook mainly used on a visit to Scotland in 1822, these show him not as copyist but as improviser, absorbing the essence of a master to spur his own creativity. What seems to have been the left half of the original pair of painted sketches draws on the same sources and imagery, but also on drawings that Turner made in 1821 of the aqueduct at Arcueil, south of Paris.[2] In such ways, Turner's experience of France, Italy and Claude came together in his imagination to form an ideal vision of antiquity and the sunlit South.

David Blayney Brown

1. Ian Warrell, *Turner et le Lorrain*, Nancy: Ville de Nancy, cat. 64–71, pp. 132–3, 195–6.
2. *Landscape, with towers, trees and figures; possibly Arcueil, near Paris* c.1827, Tate N02992, Warrell, cat. 64; see Martin Butlin and Evelyn Joll, *The paintings of J.M.W. Turner*, rev. edn, New Haven: Yale University Press, 1984, cat. 307.

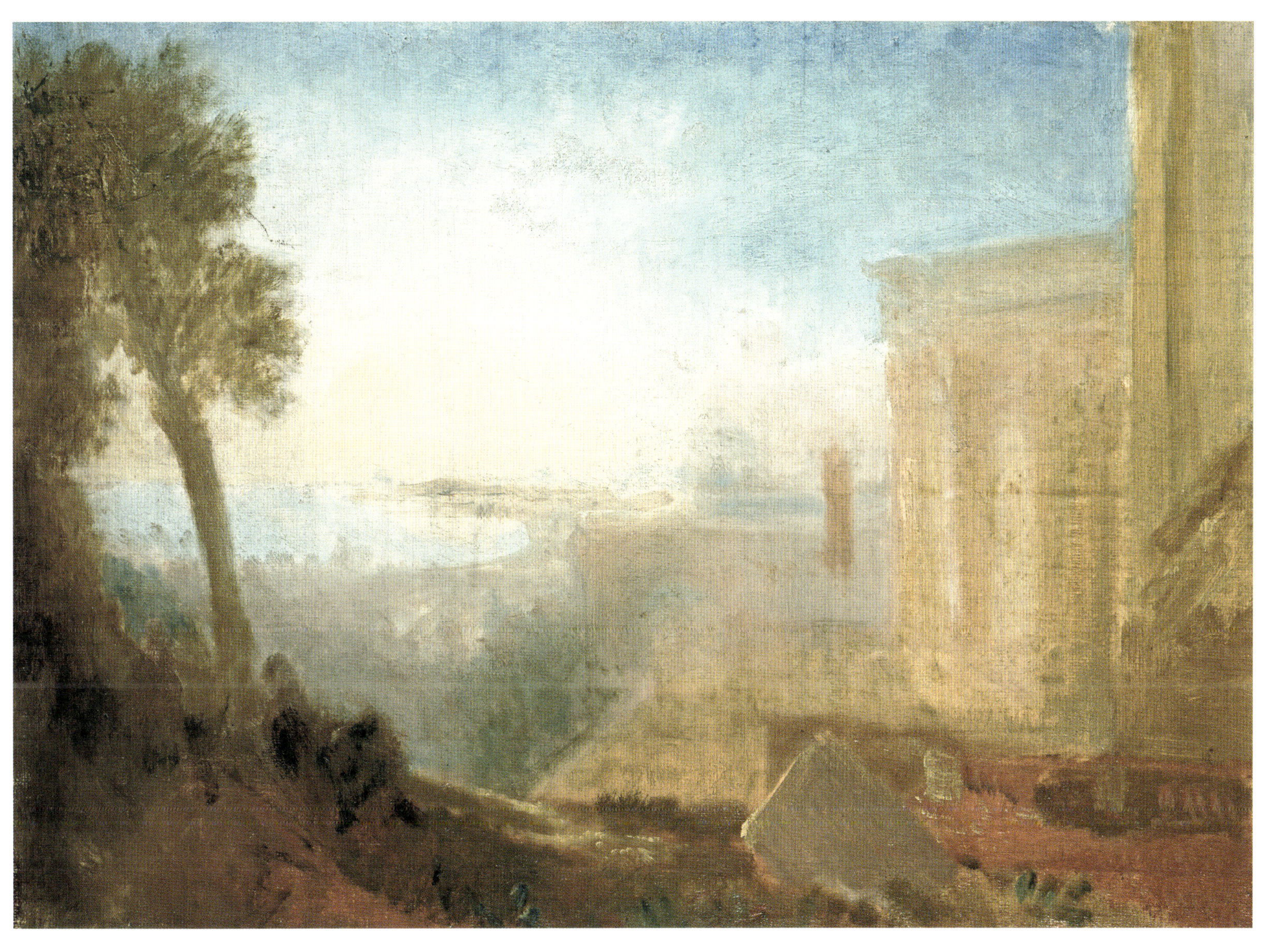

26. J.M.W. Turner

Great Britain 1775–1851
Rocky bay with figures c. 1830
oil on canvas 90.2 x 123.2 cm
Tate Britain
Accepted by the British nation as part of the Turner Bequest 1856
N01989

This beautiful canvas is not an oil sketch but an unfinished painting. Turner abandoned *Rocky bay with figures* before completing the foreground, and before clarifying the historical or mythological theme implied by the setting and the fleet of ancient ships in the distance. He was in the habit of taking such nearly finished canvases for completion during the 'varnishing days' prior to the opening of Royal Academy exhibitions.

The composition evokes ancient Greece or Rome, as in *Overlooking the coast, with classical building* 1827 (cat. 25), and the tradition of Claude Lorrain. There are already faint suggestions of figures as well as ships, but not enough to determine what the subject is. It has been suggested that the design might be for an episode in the story of Dido and Aeneas, a frequent source for Turner and indeed the one chosen for his final exhibits at the Academy in 1850. Alternatively it may be an early idea for his 1829 exhibit, *Ulysses deriding Polyphemus*,[1] a subject from Homer's *Odyssey*. If the latter, the composition would be presented in reverse, with the cave of the giant Polyphemus on the left. However, this would not account for the fleet in the background, nor for the figures grouped on the shore. One has outstretched arms, as if declaiming or pleading.

Turner's reading of classical authors was extensive and on the evidence of his sketchbooks, he often applied alternative subjects to the same designs. The closest scenic parallels for this composition, made in reverse, are dated some years earlier: a watercolour, *Chryses*,[2] exhibited at the Academy in 1811, and an unpublished design, *Glaucus and Scylla*, for his collection of landscape exemplars, the *Liber studiorum*. The first illustrated Homer's *Iliad*. It showed the priest Chryses on a beach beside a rocky bay, praying to Apollo for the return of his daughter who had been taken by the Greeks. The second, illustrating Ovid's *Metamorphoses*, depicted the Nereid Scylla fleeing her suitor. Common to both compositions are the bay and distinctive rock arch. They are traceable to the same sources, Claude's *Coast scene with Perseus and the origin of coral* and *Sea of Galilee with Christ calling Peter and Andrew*, both known to Turner from reproductions in Claude's catalogue of works, the *Liber veritatis*.

Of these four possible subjects, Turner's *Chryses* seems the most probable. The declaiming figure may remind one of the priest at his invocations, and shows the ships which took his daughter away or later returned her. Turner's drawing for *Glaucus and Scylla*,[3] however, has an alternative title *Departure of Theseus*, indicating that he associated Scylla's plight with that of Ariadne, abandoned on Naxos by Theseus. Conceivably this idea is sustained in the unfinished *Rocky bay with figures*, in which case the distant ships would be carrying Theseus away. Whatever the case, the composition is proof of the enduring power that the classical tradition, both literary and pictorial, exercised on Turner's imagination throughout his life.

David Blayney Brown

1. Collection of the National Gallery, London.
2. Private collection.
3. Collection of the Tate Britain.

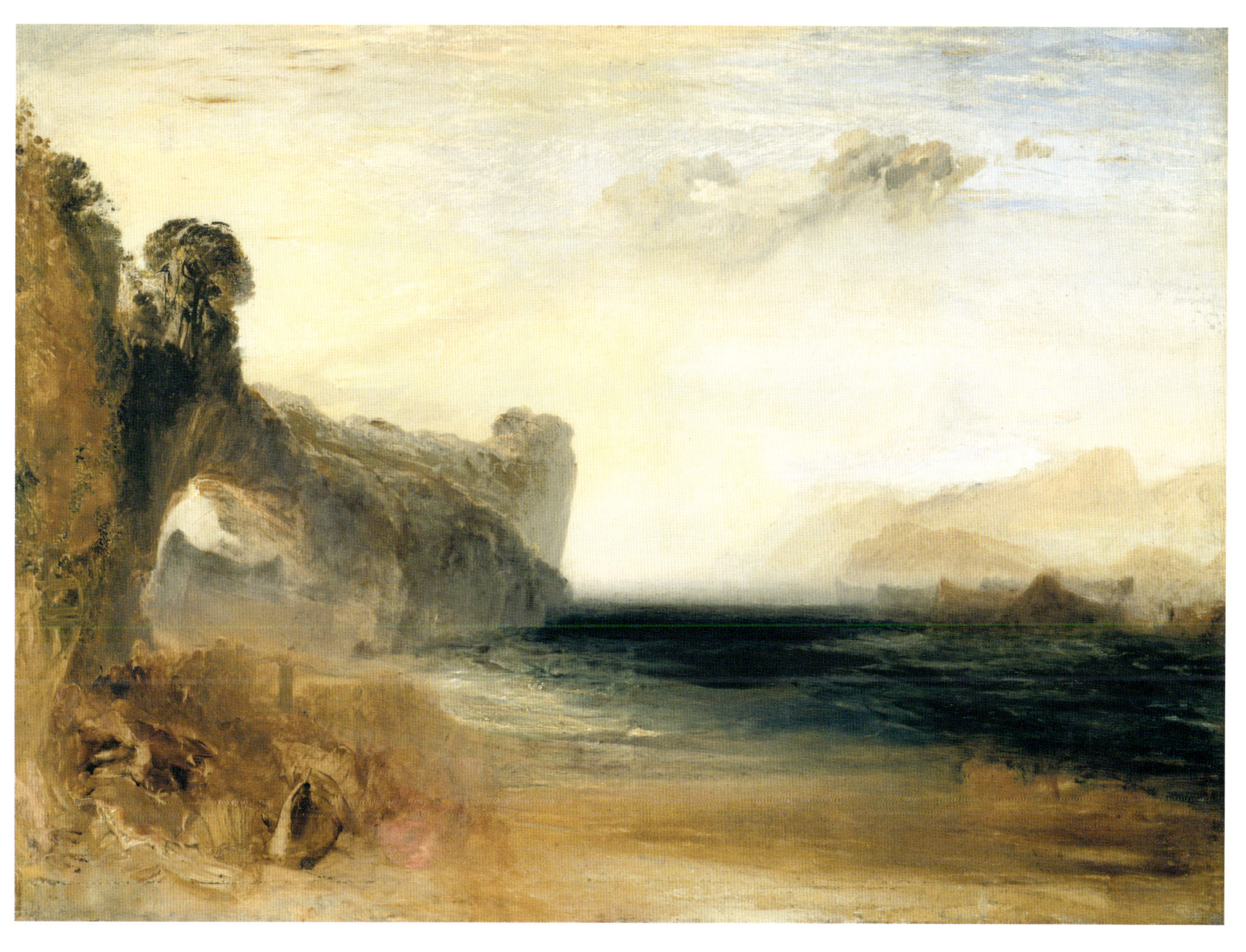

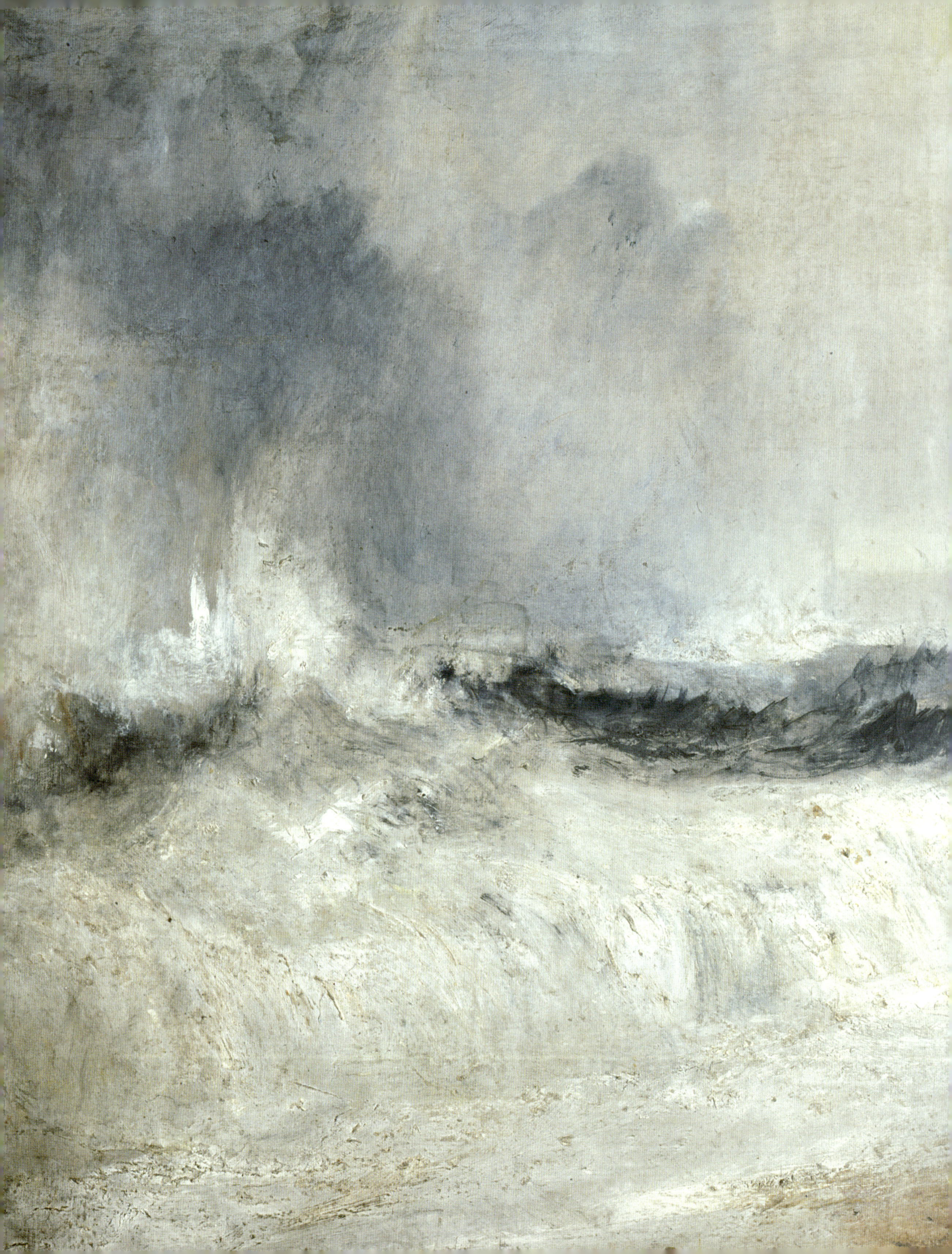

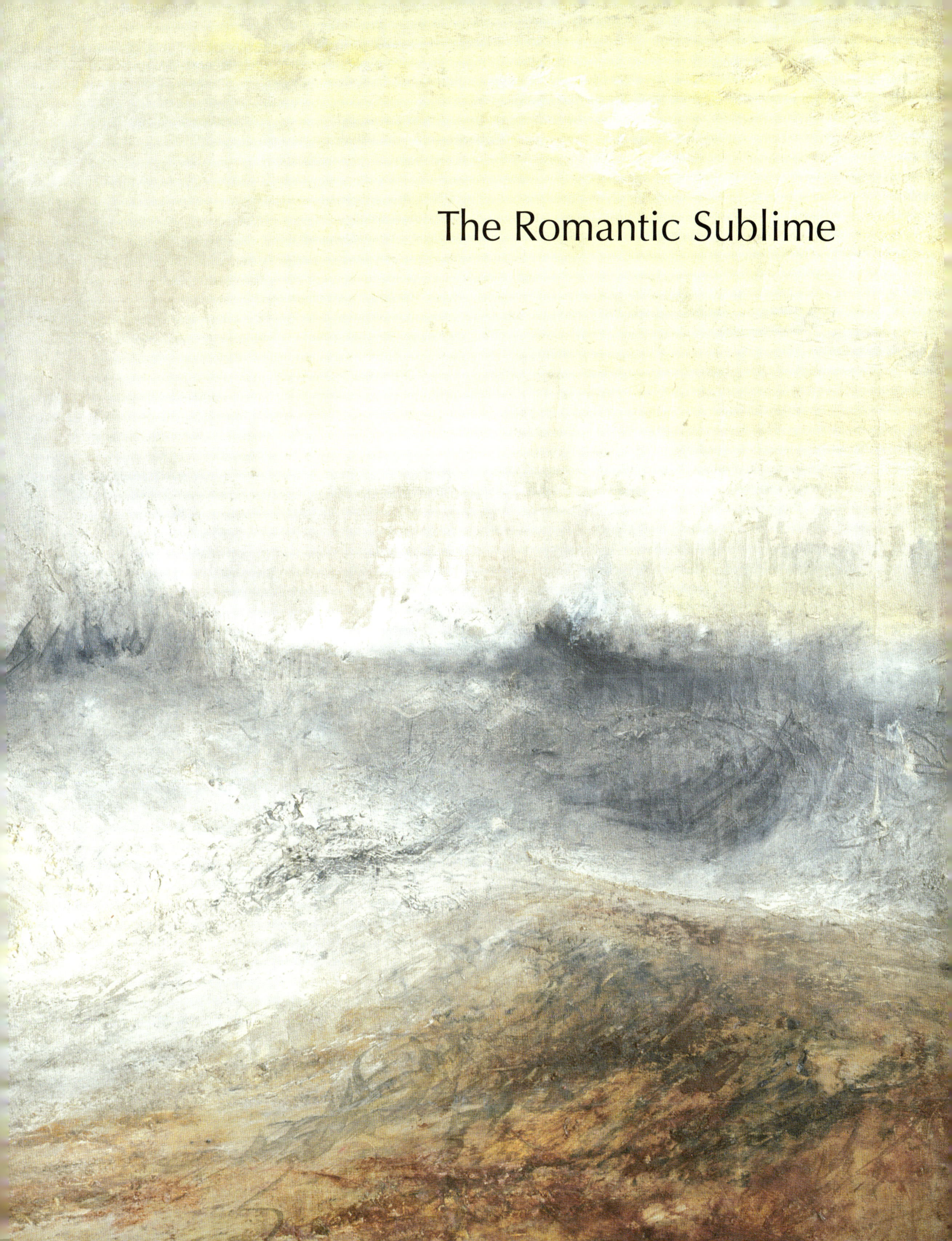
The Romantic Sublime

27. Caspar David Friedrich

Germany 1774–1840
***View of the Elbe Valley** [**Ausblick ins Elbtal**]* c. 1807
oil on canvas 61.5 x 80.0 cm
Galerie Neue Meister, Staatliche Kunstsammlungen, Dresden

In the first decades of the century Friedrich produced large topographical sepia paintings, often in pairs. They showed contrasting elements in the landscape, or differing weather conditions. In 1807, when he painted *View of the Elbe Valley*, Friedrich had just started working in oils. Although this summery scene and the wintry *Dolmen in the snow* (cat. 28) are not necessarily intended as companion pieces, the canvases are the same size, employ comparable pictorial techniques and, most importantly, capture us with their dualities. They encapsulate the idea that the Christian present, which promises eternal life, has overtaken a pagan past. Oppositions are set up: evergreen spruces or deciduous oaks, summer or winter, life or death.

From about 1805–06 Friedrich simplified his compositions radically, his pictorial methods becoming severe and hierarchic.[1] The dominant, triangular group of spruces makes *View of the Elbe Valley* a particularly dramatic painting. In structure it is similar to one of Friedrich's most famous works, *The Cross in the mountains* 1807–08 (fig. 11, p. 17). As well as the resolutely upright form of the trees, the paintings share a much-reduced palette and fine technique. The artist's clear separation of fore- and backgrounds is another characteristic element of his work in this decade. By using darker colours for the rocks, trees and other foreground vegetation in *View of the Elbe Valley*, Friedrich makes a dramatic contrast with the vista of the valley. The artist's careful control of glazes and the use of stippling to 'bring dots of colour to the brightest and most shimmering moments' reminds us of Pointillist techniques.[2]

Religiosity is rarely overt in Friedrich's paintings. Rather, his images of cemeteries, the remains of Gothic churches, scenes peopled with tiny figures, or vast empty spaces with a hint of human presence, are all deeply spiritual. *View of the Elbe Valley* incorporates intriguing symbolism: this studious reproduction of nature centres on a tomblike rock structure. Spitzer points out the special relationship between the 'evergreen spruces on the rocky slope above the steadily flowing river' and 'the bleak, frozen oak trees and prehistoric tomb'.[3] Moreover, the tension between the sharply focused foreground with silhouetted spruces and the misty, remote valley, suggests the notion of transition. But where do we stand in this painting? As Mitchell reminds us, there is no logical point of entry into many of Friedrich's works; in *View of the Elbe Valley* we are left 'hovering mid-air, like some disembodied spirit'.[4] This painting is not only a superb example of the introspective melancholy particular to Friedrich's landscapes. Like so many of the artist's best, it suggests that nature can provide a vehicle for self-awareness.

Lucina Ward

1. William Vaughan, *German Romantic painting*, New Haven: Yale University Press, 1980, p. 89.
2. Vaughan, p. 89.
3. Gerd Spitzer, *From Caspar David Friedrich to Gerhard Richter: German paintings from Dresden*, Los Angeles: J. Paul Getty Museum, 2006, p. 38.
4. Timothy F. Mitchell, *Art and science in German landscape painting 1770–1840*, Oxford: Clarendon Press, 1993, p. 182.

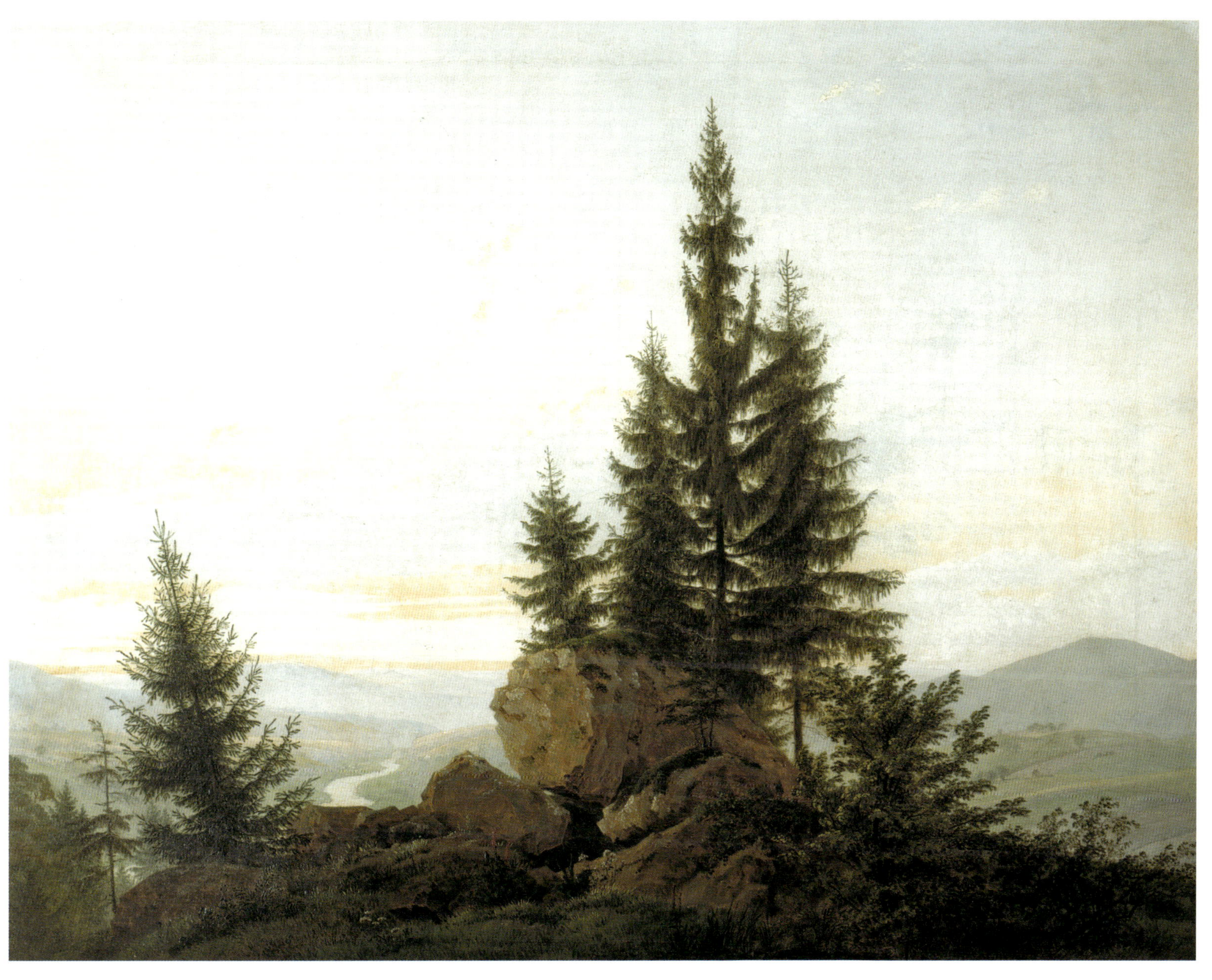

28. Caspar David Friedrich

Germany 1774–1840
***Dolmen in the snow* [*Hünengrab im Schnee*]** 1807
oil on canvas 61.0 x 80.0 cm
Galerie Neue Meister, Staatliche Kunstsammlungen, Dresden

[Friedrich is] an artist who earnestly and faithfully holds to nature, who evolves in his work his own inner being, and strives for meaning, in a word, who combines the special quality and strength of imagination with representation of the characteristics of the individual part.[1]

The unnamed reviewer was responding to Friedrich's large presentation sepia drawing, *Dolmen by the sea* 1806/08; he might easily have been writing of this canvas.[2] At thirty-three, the artist was developing a reputation for his landscapes but in 1807, the year *Dolmen in the snow* was created, he had only just begun painting in oils. Until then he worked exclusively in sepia. Friedrich honed his skills over the previous decade by using a single colour, and through his careful manipulation of tone.

Dolmen in the snow has a monumental simplicity. Oak trees are silhouetted against the icy, grey–blue sky, while mist emphasises the shallowness of the picture plane. A simple rock structure on the small rise contrasts with the upright trees. Many motifs feature elsewhere in Friedrich's oeuvre. The trees here, for example, appear in paintings from the 1810s and 1820s, in different combinations.[3] Working from Dresden, Friedrich trekked into the surrounding countryside, and toured his home region of Greifswald, then part of Sweden. There he made many beautiful and minutely accurate working drawings of fir trees, rocks and local vegetation. These drawings were sources for his presentation works, with many motifs appearing again and again.

In 1807 Dresden was occupied by the French army. As well as being interpreted as allegories of the Christian spirit, Friedrich's works were inevitably seen as expressions of nationalist sentiment in the face of the Napoleonic invasions. Indeed the reviewer described the three oaks as standing like 'great, immovable heroic characters, withstanding the elements with their own strength'. More recently, Spitzer makes an equivalent point: the stone monument in *Dolmen in the snow* was familiar to the artist from his north German homeland – and to European audiences it stood for an earlier period of Germanic history. The ancient oak trees, that have withstood the adverse storms of time, are symbols both of 'a heroic national past, and … patriotic renewal under threatening political conditions'.[4]

Friedrich's ability to unite the real and the symbolic in his landscapes has often been remarked.[5] Nature – experienced during his trips to the countryside and his mountain treks – provided the material for his paintings and presentation drawings. But in 1807, a period when artists were expected to produce their compositions from Classical sources, this creative independence carried cultural and political overtones.
Indeed the 'special quality' of Friedrich's mind, to which the anonymous reviewer drew attention, is part of what makes such apparently simple paintings as *Dolmen in the snow* resonate two centuries later.

Lucina Ward

1. *Jenaische Allgemeine Literatur-Zeitung* 1809, quoted in Timothy F. Mitchell, *Art and science in German landscape painting 1770–1840*, Oxford: Clarendon Press, 1993, p. 111–12.
2. The sepia and pencil work, dated 1807, is held in the Staatliche Kunstsammlungen, Weimar Schlossmuseum.
3. See for example, *Winter* 1807–08, formerly part of the Munich collection, destroyed 1831; *Monastery graveyard in the snow 1817–19*, formerly Berlin, destroyed during World War II; *The Solitary tree (Village landscape in the morning light)* 1822, collection of the Nationalgalerie, Staatliche Museen Preussischer Kulturbesitz, Berlin.
4. Gerd Spitzer, *From Caspar David Friedrich to Gerhard Richter: German paintings from Dresden*, Los Angeles: J. Paul Getty Museum, 2006, p. 36.
5. Mitchell, p. 111.

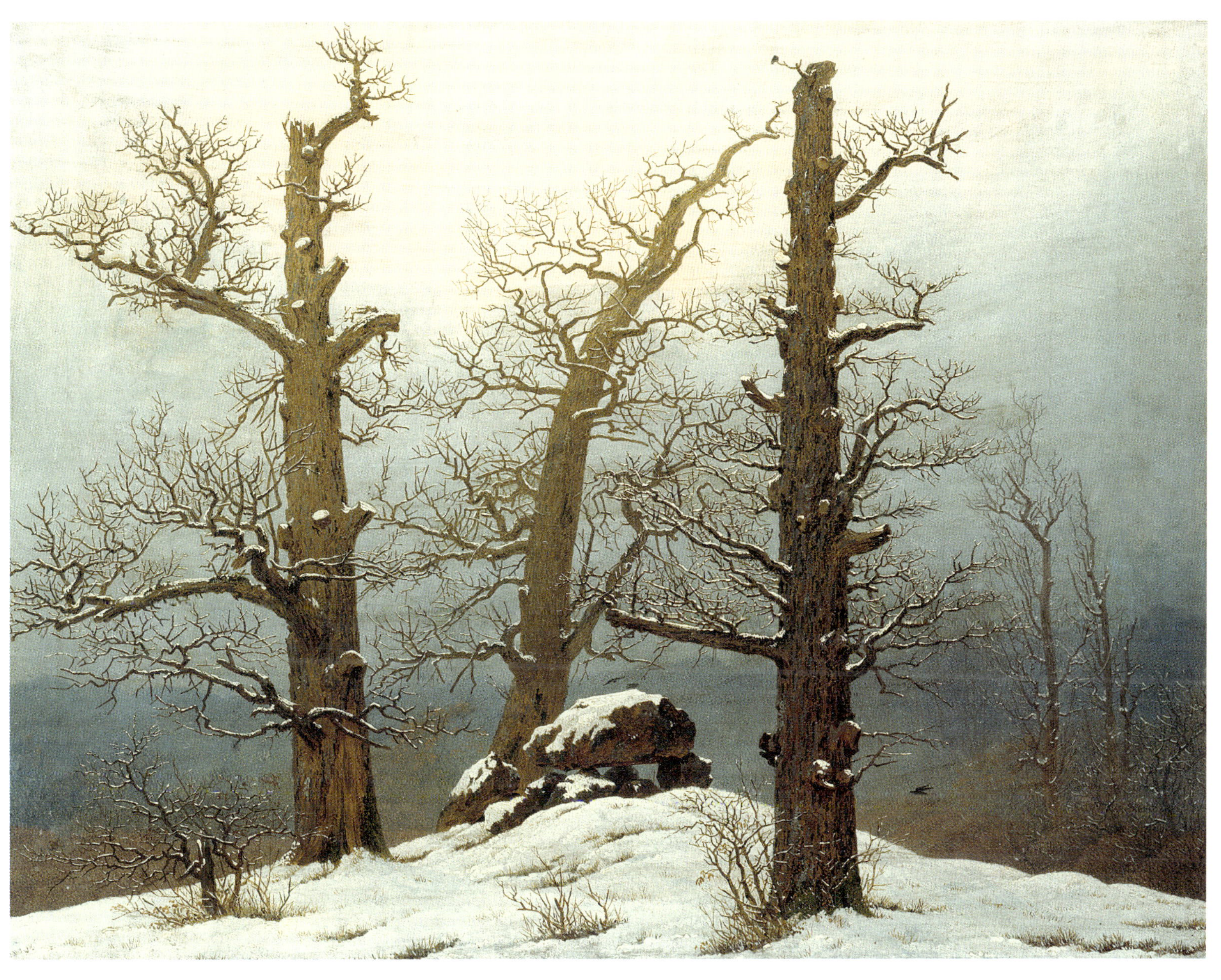

29. J.M.W. Turner

Great Britain 1775–1851
High Force, Fall of the Tees, Yorkshire 1816
watercolour on paper 28.3 x 40.3 cm
Art Gallery of New South Wales, Sydney
Purchased 1947 8030

On 3 August 1816 Turner arrived at High Force, England's largest waterfall, as part of his extended tour of Yorkshire. Four drawings of the waterfall and surrounding scenery are recorded. His sketches and subsequent watercolours of this region of northern England were to become part of a volume of 120 etchings for the *History of Richmondshire* by the Reverend Thomas Dunham Whitaker, for which Turner was to be paid the extravagant sum of 3000 guineas. The publication, however, never eventuated and Turner produced only twenty-one watercolours of the region.[1]

High Force, Fall of the Tees, Yorkshire is based on Turner's first sketch at the falls. The dramatic watercolour captures the dual cascades of the River Tees – historically the county boundary between Yorkshire and Durham – plunging over the edge of the cliff. Although not the highest waterfall in England, High Force forms the largest volume of water in vertical descent. While today the waterfall rarely has dual cascades, in Turner's time the river formed a main cascade on the left of the ravine, with smaller ribbons of water on the right and, occasionally when in flood, one huge torrent.

During his sketching tour of Yorkshire, Turner stayed with his friend and patron, Walter Fawkes, at his family seat of Farnley Hall. It was there that Turner worked on the watercolours based on each day's sketching. He completed these quickly, scraping out the paint to emphasise atmospheric effects and adding details such as figures later. *High Force, Fall of the Tees, Yorkshire* demonstrates how Turner's work was already developing into the more abstract paintings of his mature period. He highlights the mist formed as the water tumbles over the edge. He also captures the effect of the morning light, with a pronounced shadow cast across the cascade, and the rainbow rising from where the water crashes down.

The addition of two anglers in the foreground shows local flavour, a recurring device used to define a location rather than a generic landscape. This was especially the case when he was completing paintings for those illustrated histories published to capitalise on the growing middle-class tourist boom of the late eighteenth and early nineteenth centuries.[2]

Around 1825–27 Turner made a second watercolour based on another sketch from his 1816 trip to the waterfall.[3] Like the earlier watercolour, the later version was used as the basis for an etched illustration, this time for *Picturesque views of England and Wales*. There he altered the viewpoint, capturing the landscape from a position parallel to the lip of the falls looking down on the pool below. An artist sketching in the foreground, possibly representing Turner himself, has been added. Together the two watercolours and four sketches illuminate Turner's exploration of multiple viewpoints to achieve atmospheric effects. In contrast to the later watercolour, in the 1816 *High Force, Fall of the Tees, Yorkshire*, where the viewer looks up at the towering cliffs, Turner establishes the enormity and grandeur of the landscape.

Simeran Maxwell

1. For a description of Turner's tour see David Hill, *In Turner's footsteps: through the hills and dales of Northern England*, London: John Murray, 1994.
2. See Elizabeth Helsinger, 'Turner and the representation of England', in W.J.T. Mitchell (ed.), *Landscape and power*, Chicago: University of Chicago Press, 1994.
3. Hill, p.74.

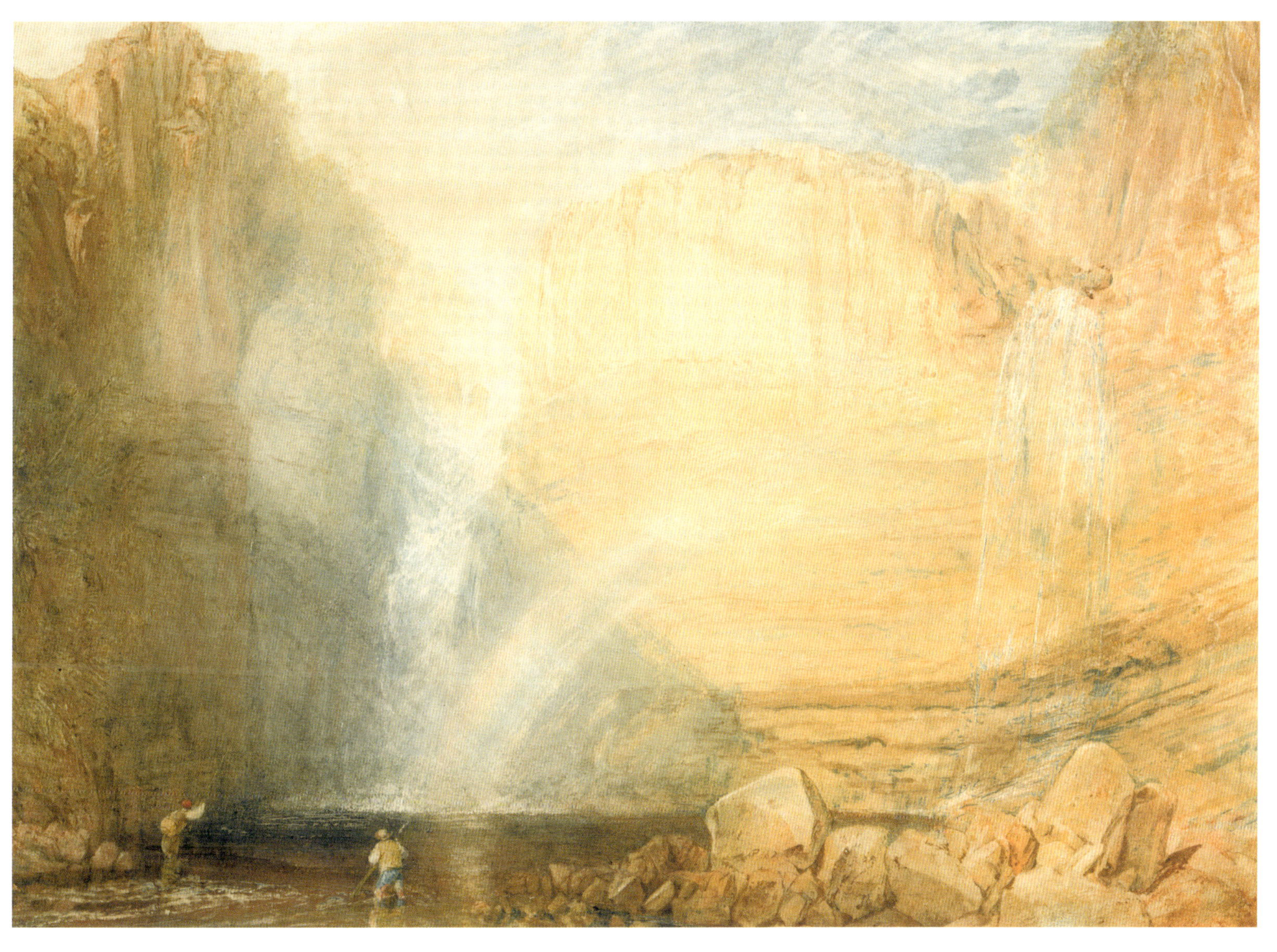

30. J.M.W. Turner

Great Britain 1775–1851
Alnwick Castle c. 1829
watercolour on paper 28.2 x 42.2 cm
Art Gallery of South Australia, Adelaide
South Australian Government Grant 1958

Turner's view of the deserted *Alnwick Castle* is a haunting riverside nocturne, showing a highly Romantic Gothic citadel guarding the river in which it is reflected. In direct contrast to his earlier watercolour, *Scarborough town and castle: morning: boys catching crabs* c. 1810, (cat. 3) where bayside activities are bathed in golden morning light, *Alnwick Castle* is illuminated only by the cold light of the moon. While *Scarborough* is open, light and golden, *Alnwick Castle* is mysterious, dark and indigo.

Turner's *Alnwick Castle* also greatly contrasts with the much earlier watercolour painted by his early friend and rival Girtin of a distant view of *Alnwick from Brizlee* c. 1800 (cat. 1). Girtin's is an expansive productive landscape, a daytime pastoral presided over by the feudal seat at the centre, applied in distinctive mottled washes. But Turner's stark close-up of the medieval pile is cloaked by night, executed theatrically in clear dark washes with scraped highlights. It was painted almost thirty years later when the Romantic movement was at its height.

Though Turner's watercolour was executed about 1829, he had first visited Alnwick Castle, the seat of the Dukes of Northumberland, in 1797.[1] Three sketches were made during his early visit in *The north of England sketchbook*,[2] which he used to develop this watercolour more than thirty years later.[3] The effect of light transforms a straightforward pictorial description of a fortress and bridge into a romantic Gothic fantasy. Moonlit towers, battlements and the arched bridge could be a moody backdrop for a stage set. Silhouettes of the deers' antlers echo the Gothic pinnacles. Painted when Romanticism and its taste for the Gothic was replacing the centuries-long European obsession with the Classical, *Alnwick Castle* is probably the most striking, theatrical and Romantic of Turner's many castle views.

Turner would have been well aware of Claude Lorrain's famous poetic painting, traditionally known as *The enchanted castle*, in which a castle at the water's edge is silhouetted against an evening sky.[4] The darkest and most mysterious of all Claude's paintings, and darkened by the crime of time, it was the one that most appealed to Gothic taste in the nineteenth century and was immortalised in 1818 by the Romantic poet John Keats. Turner's love of Claude, and knowledge of the nocturnes of his own immediate predecessor, Joseph Wright of Derby, may be the artist's starting points. His fascination with the drama of light takes *Alnwick Castle* beyond his forerunners' views and expresses the intensity of Turner's own poetic vision.

Ron Radford

Adapted from Ron Radford, *Island to empire: 300 years of British art 1550–1850*, Adelaide: Art Gallery of South Australia, 2005, pp. 210–12.

1. Turner toured the districts of England extensively from 1790, first touring the North and Lake District in 1797. Eric Shanes et al., *Turner: the great watercolours*, London: Royal Academy of Arts, 2000, p. 246.
2. Collection of the Tate Britain.
3. David Hill, *Turner in the North*, New Haven: Yale University Press, 1996, p. 70.
4. Collection of the National Gallery, London.

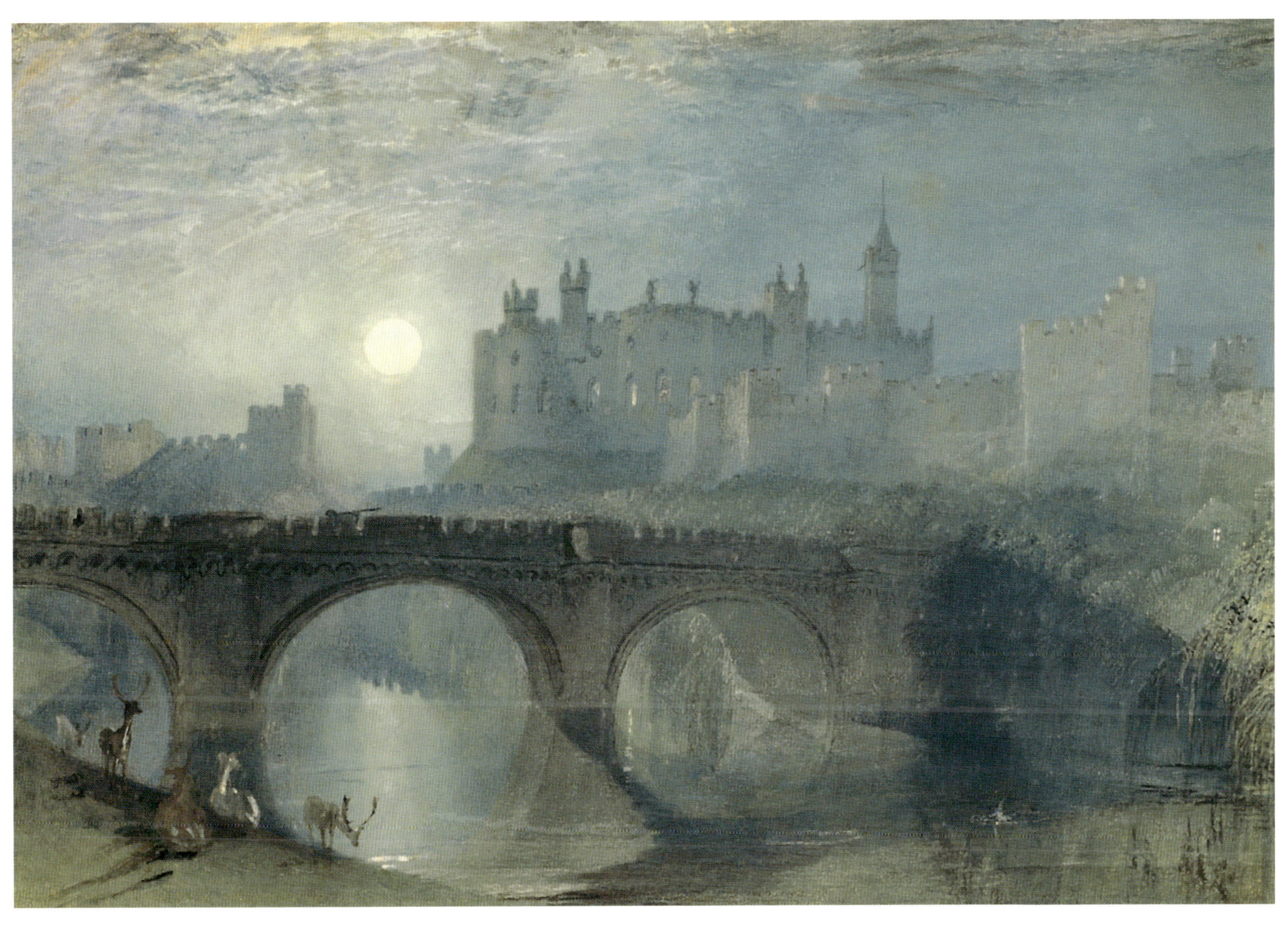

31. J.M.W. Turner

Great Britain 1775–1851
The Red Rigi 1842
watercolour, wash and gouache with some scratching out 30.5 x 45.8 cm
National Gallery of Victoria, Melbourne
Felton Bequest, 1947 1704-4

Turner had never made any drawings [watercolours] like these before, and never made any like them again … He is not showing his hand in these, but his heart.[1]

An inveterate traveller, Turner visited Switzerland on his first continental tour in 1802, during the short-lived Treaty of Amiens. He was greatly inspired by the sublime qualities of the alpine landscape, although he did not return until 1836. However during his later years he visited continental Europe regularly, travelling through Switzerland annually from 1841 to 1844. The resulting watercolours are acknowledged as some of his most important works; a final flourish in his extraordinary output.

In the late summer of 1841 Turner spent time in Lucerne, exploring its surrounding mountains, valleys and lakes. One of the best-known local features is the Rigi, a mountain comparatively small in height (1798 metres) but with a dominant presence to the east of the town across Lake Lucerne. Unlike the numerous tourists who ascended the Rigi to witness sunset or sunrise from the summit, Turner was captivated by the mountain rather than its view, and was preoccupied with capturing the transitory effects of light and atmospheric conditions in numerous colourful wash sketches.

On his return to London Turner presented his dealer, Thomas Griffith, with a new format for marketing his art, providing him with fifteen small sketches from which his patrons could make selections to be worked up into finished watercolours, together with four such completed 'specimens' to demonstrate the result. The four included two contrasting views of the Rigi, one now known as *The Blue Rigi*,[2] in which the looming mass is shadowed by the radiant dawn light emanating from behind it, and this work, *The Red Rigi*, in which the mountain's heights glow ethereally pink with the last rays of the setting sun. In both, Turner explored the reflections and refractions in the foreground water and the activity on the lake's surface, probably viewed from his hotel window. *The Red Rigi* was purchased by his Scottish friend and patron H.A.J. Munro of Novar, who acquired half the resulting ten watercolours, commissioning another dawn view, known as *The Dark Rigi*.[3] Turner's great advocate John Ruskin first saw *The Red Rigi* displayed at Griffith's salesroom and recalled 'such a piece of colour as had never come *my* way before': within a few years his father had acquired it from Munro.[4] In 1851 Ruskin senior wrote to his son in Venice informing him of Turner's death, saying that *The Red Rigi* 'fed and soothed me like a Dead March all this evening …'.[5]

In 2007 the three finished Rigi watercolours were united for the first time, exhibited at Tate Britain, along with their sample sketches, additional studies and paintings based around Lucerne. Varying noticeably from their original sketches, the watercolours demonstrate the remarkable level of sophistication to which Turner had raised the medium. Skilfully combining stippling, hatching, scratching back to create highlights, washes and gouache, and with incomparable colouristic ability, Turner evokes a luminous grandeur to the Swiss vista that he studied with such contemplation.

Alisa Bunbury

1. John Ruskin in E.T. Cook and A. Wedderburn (eds), *The works of John Ruskin*, vol. xiii, London: George Allen, 1904, p. 484.
2. Collection of the Tate Britain.
3. Private collection, United Kingdom.
4. John Ruskin in *Ruskin on pictures: volume 1, Turner at the National Gallery and in Mr Ruskin's collection*, E.T. Cook (ed.), London: George Allen, 1902, p. 361.
5. John James Ruskin to John Ruskin, 21 December 1851, quoted in Ian Warrell, *Through Switzerland with Turner: Ruskin's first selection from the Turner Bequest*, London: Tate Gallery Publishing, 1995, p. 17.

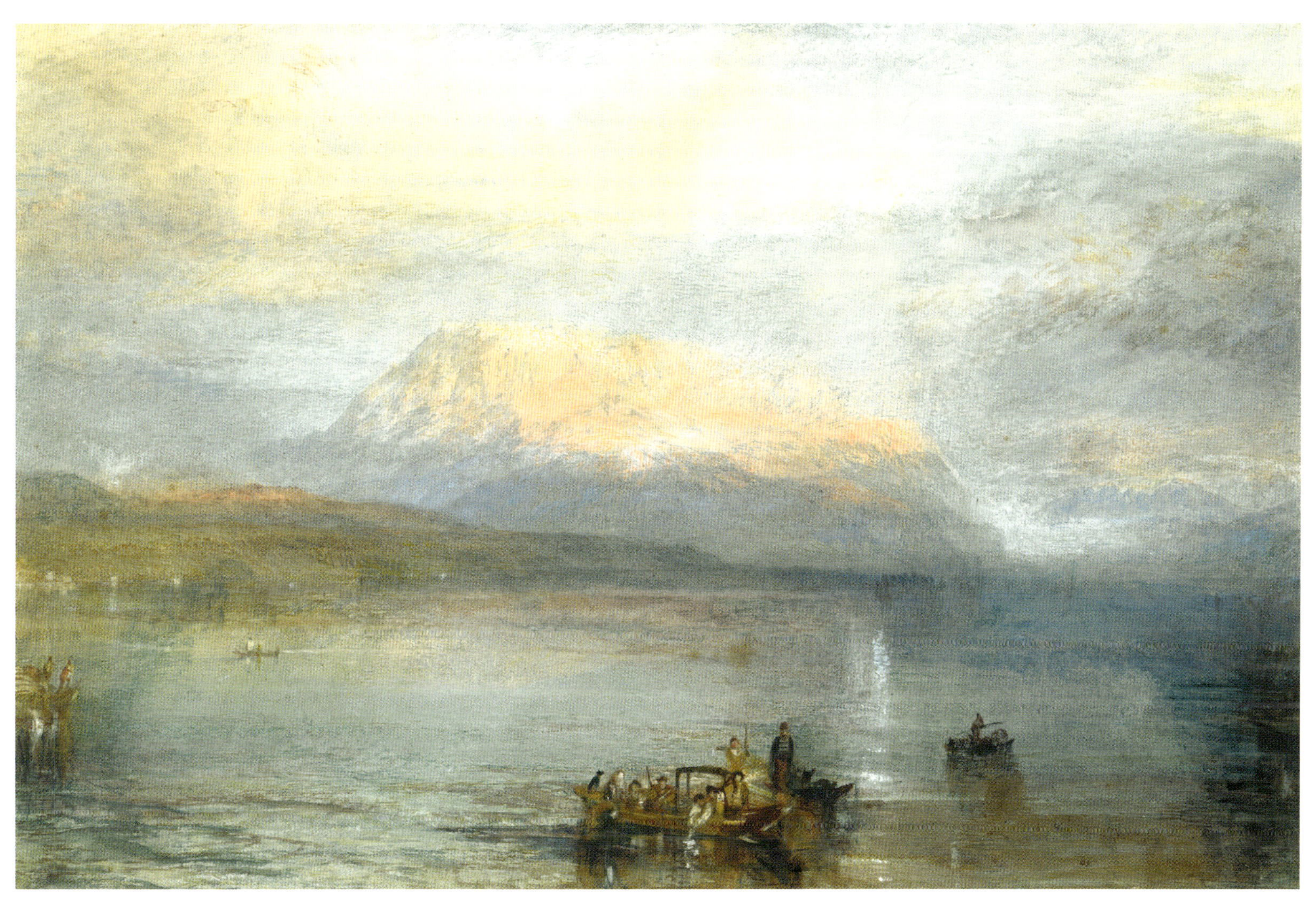

32. Samuel Palmer

Great Britain 1805–1881
Summer storm near Pulborough, Sussex c. 1851
watercolour and bodycolour on paper 51.5 x 72.0 cm
Art Gallery of South Australia, Adelaide
A.M. and A.R. Ragless Bequest Fund 1955

Palmer's landscapes are among the major achievements of the British genre in the first half of the nineteenth century. Though he was admired especially for his early intensely visionary landscapes, Palmer's later work is more conventional, showing greater concern both for naturalism and looking to the acknowledged seventeenth-century masters of landscape painting.

In *Summer storm near Pulborough, Sussex* black clouds have gathered, the wind has risen and driving rain is already falling, though there is a glimpse of distant sunshine. In the foreground a herdsman gestures to prevent his sheep stampeding off the road; his wife follows carrying a child on her back and beside her is an unhappy yet faithful dog. To the left, near a steadfast windmill and a ruined church, women scurry to retrieve their washing. At the edge of the darkness a horse-drawn wagon and a rider stoically proceed towards a farmhouse visible beyond the mill. Within the darkness, sunlight illuminates the travellers, the roadside stream and bridge. The streaming skirts of the woman, the flapping washing, flitting birds, waving trees and mounting clouds emphasise the force of wind and rain. In this way the artist builds and weaves tension and drama into his landscape.

Palmer's low-lying composition with its domineering clouds owes much to seventeenth-century Dutch realism, which was a growing influence in the development of British landscape in the first half of the nineteenth century. Turner, Glover and Palmer himself, all of them loyal to the Italian landscape tradition, also relied on Dutch models for naturalistic depiction of weather. In its naturalism and weather effects, however, Palmer's painting also owes much to Constable's realism. *Summer storm near Pulborough, Sussex* is not only a study of weather. It is has religious resonances, pilgrims with their flock of sheep, possibly heading into a deluge.

Palmer began his training in watercolour painting at the age of thirteen. While still in his teens, he met the landscape and portrait painter Linnell (cat. 20) who introduced him to the prints of Albrecht Dürer and Lucas van Leyden and, in 1824, to the ageing visionary William Blake. Palmer was deeply religious and he began to paint small, almost biblical, dreams of a pastoral paradise. He became the leader of a group of young artists known as the 'The Ancients' who were devoted to the Blake's work.[1] Palmer, even more than his fellow Ancients, deliberately turned his back on nineteenth-century progress. In 1837 Palmer married Linnell's daughter Hannah and the couple embarked on what was to become a very influential two-year stay in Italy, where the artist fell under the spell of the past Roman landscape painters Gaspard Dughet, Nicolas Poussin, Salvator Rosa and, above all, Claude Lorrain. The influence of those masters, and of Italian scenery, was to remain with him for the rest of his life, filtered through the Romanticism of his great contemporary, Turner.[2]

Ron Radford

1. For a catalogue of works produced by Palmer and the Ancients, see Raymond Lister, *Samuel Palmer and 'The Ancients'*, Cambridge: Fitzwilliam Museum & Cambridge University Press, 1984.
2. Ron Radford, *Island to empire: 300 years of British art 1550–1850*, Adelaide: Art Gallery of South Australia, 2005, pp. 268–71.

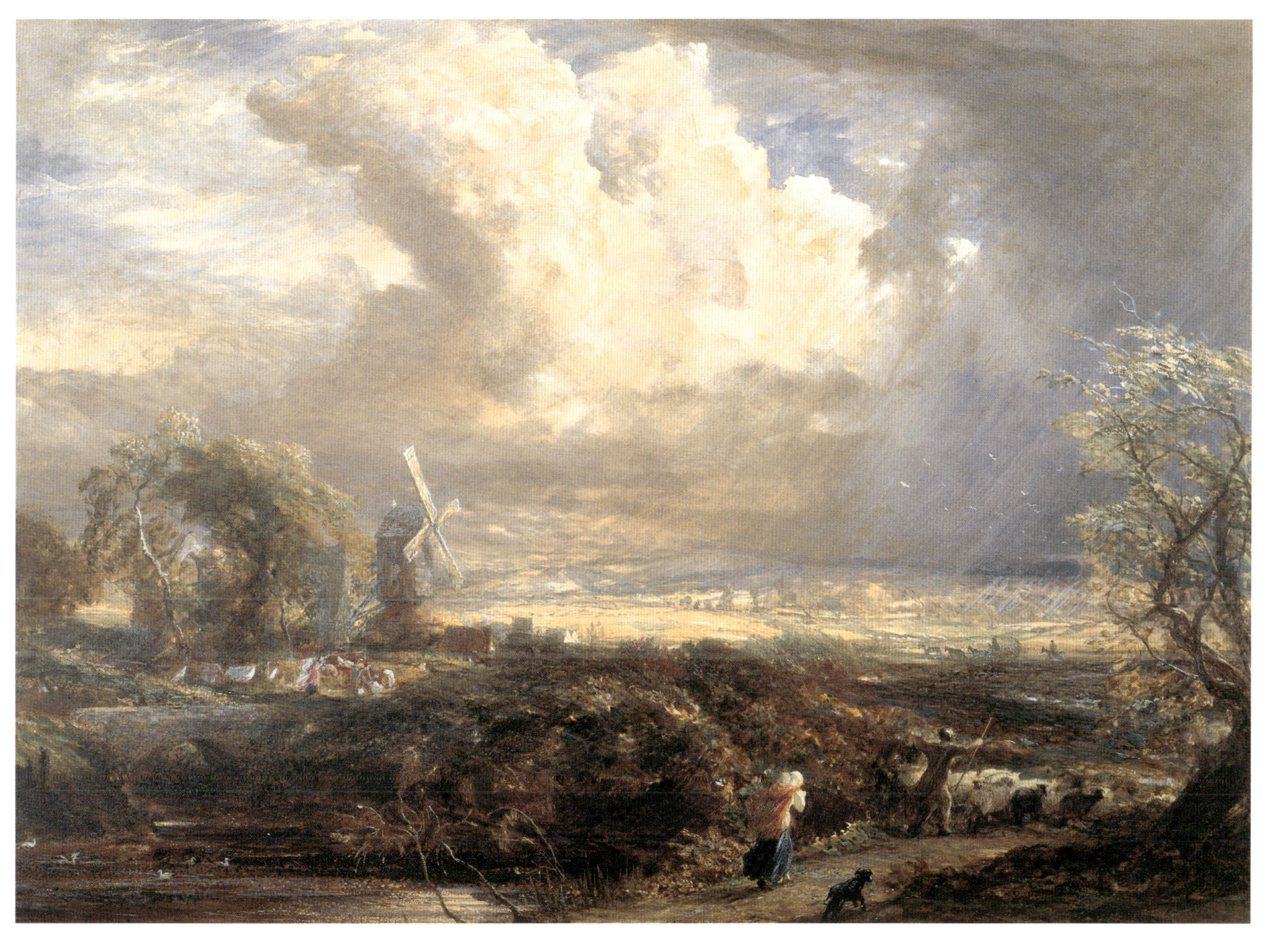

33. Samuel Palmer

Great Britain 1805–1881
Landscape with watermill c. 1855
also known as ***Landscape with mill***
watercolour, bodycolour with gum and black chalk
37.4 x 52.0 cm
Art Gallery of New South Wales, Sydney
Purchased 1953 9010

Throughout his career Palmer regularly visited both the National Gallery, London, and the Dulwich Picture Gallery. Until their rift, he was often accompanied by his mentor and father-in-law, John Linnell (cat. 20). During these many excursions, Palmer studied seventeenth-century European paintings, and their influence on his later style is evident in *Landscape with watermill*.

Claude Lorrain was among the artists whom Palmer most admired. Like Claude, Palmer preferred to paint pastoral and rural landscape scenes rather than uninhabited panoramas. Palmer's work focused on the inhabited English landscape, including small towns and hamlets, with people working in fields, and cattle or flocks of sheep. The Dutch landscape tradition also influenced him, particularly the paintings of Salomon van Ruisdael, with their delicate but craggy trees, billowy skies and rustic houses with streams.

Although a confirmed landscape painter, Palmer often included figures in his paintings. He described them as an 'adjunct' to the landscape itself, feeling that they should be shown moving, to create the illusion of a story being told.[1] *Landscape with watermill* is a fine example of Palmer's penchant for this, with the figures serving a dual purpose. First, they are a conscious artistic device to direct the eye around the painting – Palmer was fond of using *staffage* in the form of animals or humans, often in the foreground, to lead the viewer into the work. Hence a woman, wearing bright blue and red clothing and carrying a basket, draws the eye to the central focus point of the painting, the watermill.

Second, they were part of the artist's Protestant Christian sensibility regarding the use of land. Many of his landscapes show people working the land, reminding the viewers of God's gift to humans and their obligations to harness it. Palmer wrote that '[l]andscape is of little value, but as it hints or expresses the haunts or doings of man … Take away its churches, where for centuries the pure word of God has been read to the poor … and you have a frightful kind of paradise left – a Paradise without God'.[2]

Clustered in the centre of this painting, Palmer depicts a group of rustic houses and a watermill. A symbol of domesticity, mills for grinding grain had been a common sight in every English village. Yet, by the mid-nineteenth century, the industrialisation of Europe was in full swing. Many of the local mills no longer served an important role in the communities. Small villages, too, were disappearing, swallowed up by larger urban centres. However, despite – or because of – this urbanisation and the decline of quintessential rural English lifestyle, there was still an eager audience for works in the vein of *Landscape with watermill*.

Although based in London, from the 1840s onward Palmer travelled on summer sketching trips to Devon and Cornwall. From this time he adapted his style to reduce the warm colours in his palette. Here, Palmer has muted his emotion-filled earlier work in favour of subdued tones, which seemed to appeal more to the art market of Victorian England. In this instance Palmer reduces the warmth of the landscape by using a purple–blue wash.

Simeran Maxwell

1. Samuel Palmer, c. 1846, quoted in James Sellars, *Samuel Palmer*, New York: St Martin's Press, 1974, p. 110.
2. Samuel Palmer, quoted in Colin Harrison, *Samuel Palmer*, Oxford: Ashmolean Museum, 1997, p. 18.

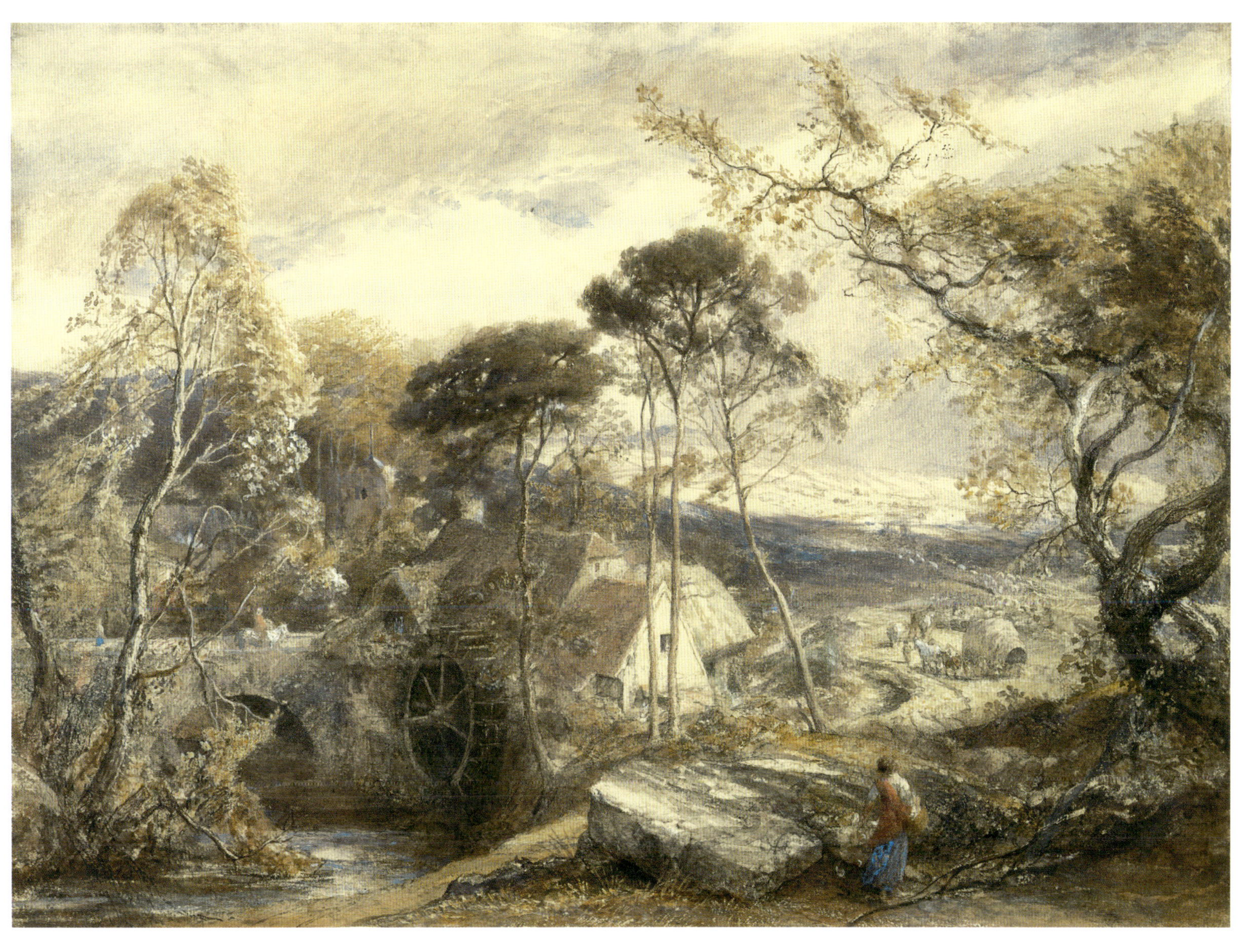

34. Conrad Martens

Great Britain 1801 – Australia 1878
View of Sydney from Neutral Bay c. 1857
watercolour, gouache, pencil, varnish on cardboard sheet 45.1 x 65.2 cm
National Gallery of Australia, Canberra
Purchased 1975 1975.58

When Martens arrived in Sydney from London in 1835, he had no plans to stay, but would become the first long-term, resident professional artist in New South Wales, living here until his death in 1878. Trained in Britain by Copley Fielding in the art of landscape painting in watercolour, Martens was greatly influenced by Turner (cat. 30), Claude Lorrain and Nicolas Poussin and also took on the ideas of the Picturesque and Romantic Sublime from Thomas Girtin (cat. 1), Francis Danby and David Cox. He was a great reader too, and espoused the teachings of Joshua Reynolds and John Burnet.[1]

From 1833 to 1834 Martens was artist on the H.M.S. *Beagle*. Here, in the company of the expedition's scientists and naval officers, he was introduced to the conventions of science. Through his friendship with Charles Darwin, Martens developed a keen eye for detail, and Captain FitzRoy, the ship's commander, shared his remarkable understanding of meteorological phenomena. By the time he settled in Australia, Martens had merged study of topography with his previous learning, creating atmospheric landscapes which earned him the foremost position in landscape art in New South Wales over the next forty years.

Martens had been resident in Australia almost twenty-five years when he painted *View of Sydney from Neutral Bay*. From the familiar he has created an idealised landscape in full Romantic grandeur. The vantage point for this magnificent vista is probably near what is now Wycombe Road, only a short distance from St Leonard's, where Martens had lived since 1844, and from where he had painted many times before. Over the years he witnessed the transformation of the fledgling settlement across the harbour into a burgeoning city, and in many ways his composition is a narrative for civilisation of the landscape.

In the foreground is virgin bush, yet Aboriginals, often present in Martens's earlier landscapes, are no longer present. There is, however, the same attention to detail in the dark, untouched foreground landscape – in the strata of the sandstone headland, and the eucalypts and groundcover. As we move through the foreground, sunlight falls upon a clearing on the right, with a track leading to a small settlement on the shore of Neutral Bay. Here rooftops and chimneys of two grand residences nestle amongst dense bushland. Across the water from Careening Cove and Kirribilli Point is the city of Sydney. All the trappings of a bustling port and prosperous new metropolis are evident, with church spires, government buildings, windmills and residential development stretching into the distant horizon. On the water, clusters of schooners symbolise the city's mercantile status.

The dark, foreboding storm clouds overhead owe much to FitzRoy. They predominate the background space and are clearly of the Romantic Sublime. With all the theatrics of nature, the looming clouds roll back and dazzling sunlight inexplicably streams down on just two buildings: the recently finished Fort Denison, protecting the waters of Port Jackson, and Government House, symbol of good governance and the most prominent building on Bennelong Point.[2] It is a classic Turneresque moment: an idealised landscape created in Australia in the British landscape tradition. But it could be anywhere.

Anne McDonald

1. See Conrad Martens, 'A lecture upon landscape painting', in Bernard Smith (ed.), *Documents on art and taste in Australia: the colonial period 1770–1940*, Melbourne: Oxford University Press, 1975, pp. 96–111.
2. Government House was described in 1842 by the correspondent for the *Sydney Herald* as one 'of the many beautifully picturesque scenes in the vicinity of Sydney'. See Rollo Gillespie, *Viceregal quarters*, Sydney: Angus & Robertson, 1975, p. 112.

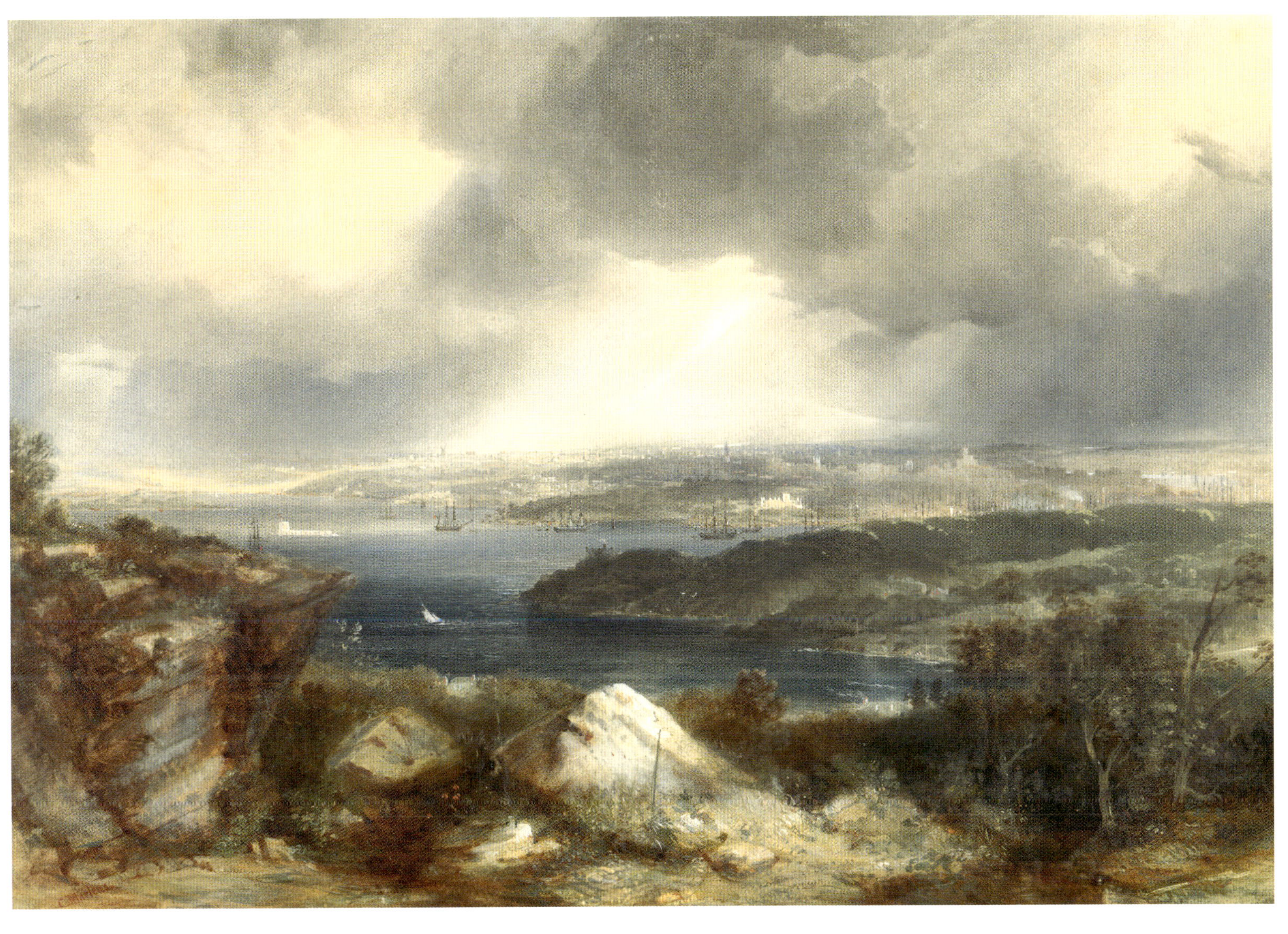

35. Carl Gustav Carus

Germany 1789–1869
Wanderer on the mountaintop [***Wanderer auf Bergeshöh***] 1818
also known as ***Pilgrim's rest*** [***Die Ruhe des Pilgers***]
oil on canvas 43.2 x 33.7 cm
Saint Louis Art Museum, Missouri
Museum Shop Fund 323:1991

Carus was a physician, scientist and naturalist, as well as a painter. Although he was never a professional artist, he is remembered as a theoretician of landscape painting whose publication, *Nine letters on landscape painting, written in the years 1815–1824*, is considered an important document of early nineteenth-century German Romanticism. These philosophic writings address the inherent bond between art and nature (or science) as epitomised in landscape painting. Carus's artistic theories, like his paintings, are very much inspired by the landscape paintings of his friend and mentor Caspar David Friedrich, the renowned Romantic artist (cat. 37).

In *Wanderer on the mountaintop* Carus adopted one of the basic formulations of Romantic art, used frequently by Friedrich (fig. 13, p. 19). A solitary figure, seen from the back, is centrally positioned within a majestic landscape, looking off towards a sea of clouds as though contemplating the infinite expanse. Here, the viewer is encouraged to identify with the pilgrim's communion with nature, which serves as a source for spiritual inspiration. His identity is constructed externally by raiment and symbols – plain gown and hat, cockle shell, and staff – and internally by his rapt contemplation of the infinite.

The painting is related to another by Friedrich from circa 1818, *Wanderer overlooking the sea of fog* (fig. 13, p. 19), which also features a traveller on top of a rocky outcrop gazing out at the vast universe before him.[1] Carus may have had this painting in mind when he wrote in the second letter of his *Nine letters on landscape painting*:[2]

> Climb to the topmost mountain peak, gaze out across long chains of hills, and observe the rivers in their courses and all the magnificence that offers itself to your eye – what feeling takes hold of you? There is a silent reverence within you; you lose yourself in infinite space; silently, your whole being is purified and cleansed; your ego disappears. You are nothing; God is everything.[3]

Carus frequently chose the same motifs as Friedrich, and the work of these artists is often close in spirit and construction. There is also a symbolic quality to their landscape paintings; both include elements like the winding footpath, representing life, and mountains or rocks indicative of strong religious faith. Carus's paintings, however, are distinguished by their remarkable level of detail. A man of science by profession, Carus's interest in art began as the desire to illustrate his own botanical studies. It was his belief in the observation of science or nature as the basis for understanding the world and the divine which ultimately led Carus to use art – landscape painting in particular – as a means to express his philosophical and spiritual ideas.

Emmeline Erikson

1. Collection of the Hamburger Kunsthalle.
2. Joseph Leo Koerner, *Caspar David Friedrich and the subject of landscape*, New Haven: Yale University Press, 1990, p. 194.
3. Carl Gustav Carus, *Nine letters on landscape painting, written in the years 1815–1824*, trans. David Britt, Los Angeles: Getty Research Institute, 2002, p. 87.

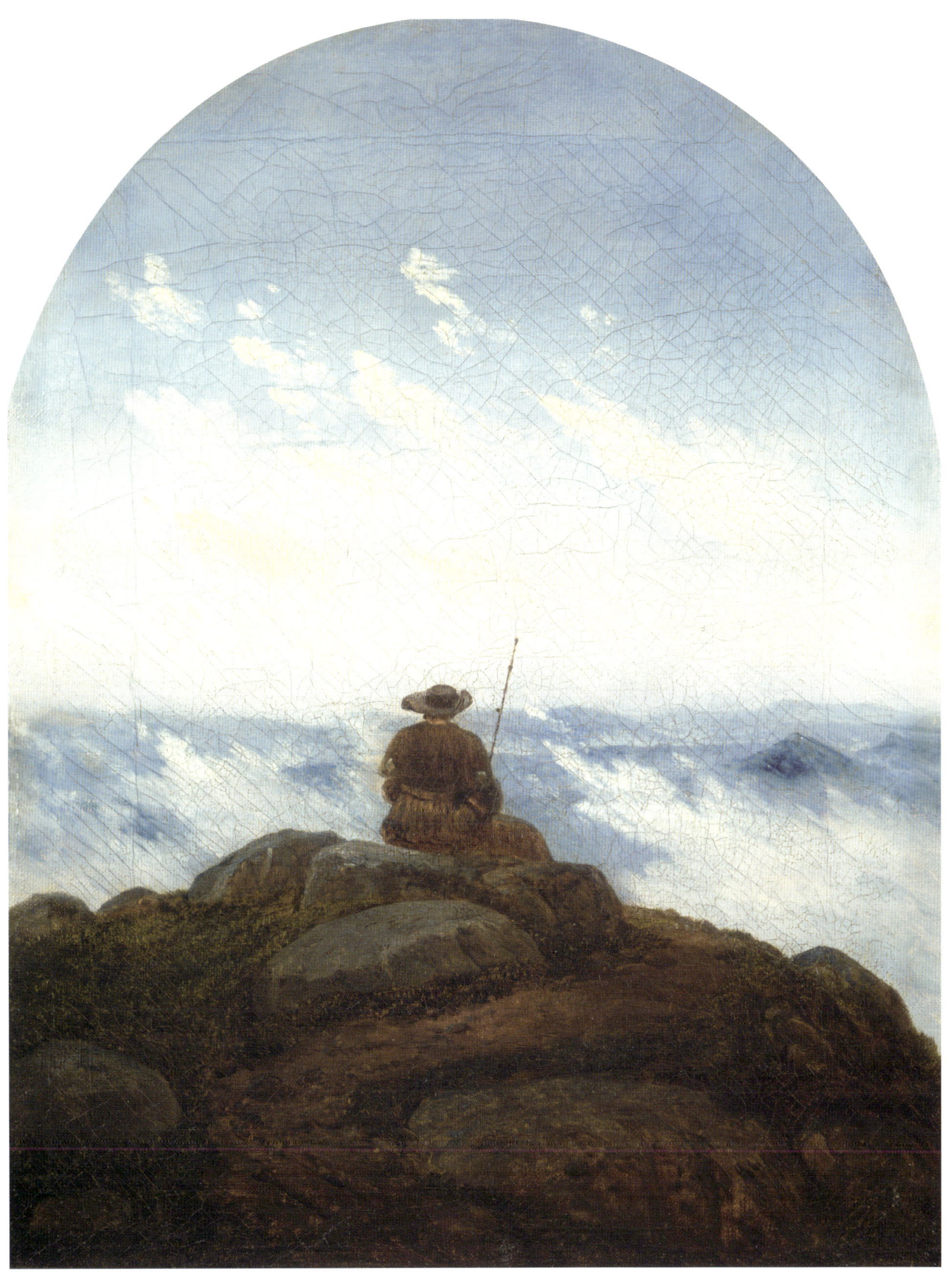

36. Caspar David Friedrich

Germany 1774–1840
Easter morning [***Ostermorgen***] 1833
oil on canvas 43.7 x 34.4 cm
Museo Thyssen-Bornemisza, Madrid

'Three women walk stiffly towards the cemetery very early in the morning.'[1] Wegener's description exactly captures the undertone of Friedrich's *Easter morning*; the words summarised a long acquaintance with the work, which was in Wegener's own collection.

The artist selected empirical facts according to the meanings they held out. His works reveal a sensibility that is contemplative even when excited, tuned to realising the grandeur of humanity through communing with nature (cat. 37). In those respects Friedrich's Romanticism resembled English Romanticism – that of the painter J.M.W. Turner and the poet William Wordsworth, for example. However, his perception was directed to a specific symbolism, a sensuous iconography of the soul, by which the cultural tradition of the north had long distinguished itself from the rest of Europe.

Typically, Friedrich's paintings include figures. Without them *Easter morning* would be a moonlit landscape, symmetrically organised and expressive of natural order; whereas the appearance of three women on the road imbues the scene with human and religious meaning. The three women have their backs turned to the viewer, walking away. One is clothed in black mourning. Her younger companions are the mirror image of one another – a repetition that has the effect of a rite. Similarly, the symmetry of the road with its flanking trees and the horizontal layering of hills between the bare foreground and tall sky define a composition that is fixed and ritualistic. Within that portentous composition the travellers on the ridge of the road are wedged under the horizon line: in fact it almost clips their heads, therefore encouraging their passage down the hill to the cemetery. The fog acts as a veil, hence one cannot say definitively that the objects in the distance are graves and graveyard poplar trees, although the title of the painting, *Easter morning*, suggests they would be.

The composition, even without the aid of the title, enforces a theme of between-ness, prelude, death, and anticipation: the road leads to the graveyard; the slope goes down to it; the older woman has younger companions; the light is between dusk and dawn; and the bare trees are in bud, indicating the transition from winter to spring. One notices, too, that an extensive craquelure of lines in the foggy penumbra of light around the moon mysteriously echoes the lacy pattern of tree branches.

The title *Easter morning* confirms what the picture's 'natural' organisation seems already to imply. The forces so quietly suggested are of death and regeneration. Three women of the 1830s (they could be of any time) are going to the graves of their loved ones. Their journey repeats that of the three Marys who visited Christ's grave early on the first Easter morning. In the context of this ritual, some upturned blocks of dressed stone beside the road in the left foreground may symbolise Christ risen from the grave. The women walk 'stiffly' and with trepidation towards death. Nature ushers them forward, and also pushes on with the cycle of life: rebirth after death and light after darkness.

Mary Eagle

1. William Wegener, 1859, quoted by Mar Borobia, at the museum's website, viewed January 2008, museothyssen.org/thyssen_ing/coleccion/obras_ficha_texto958.html.

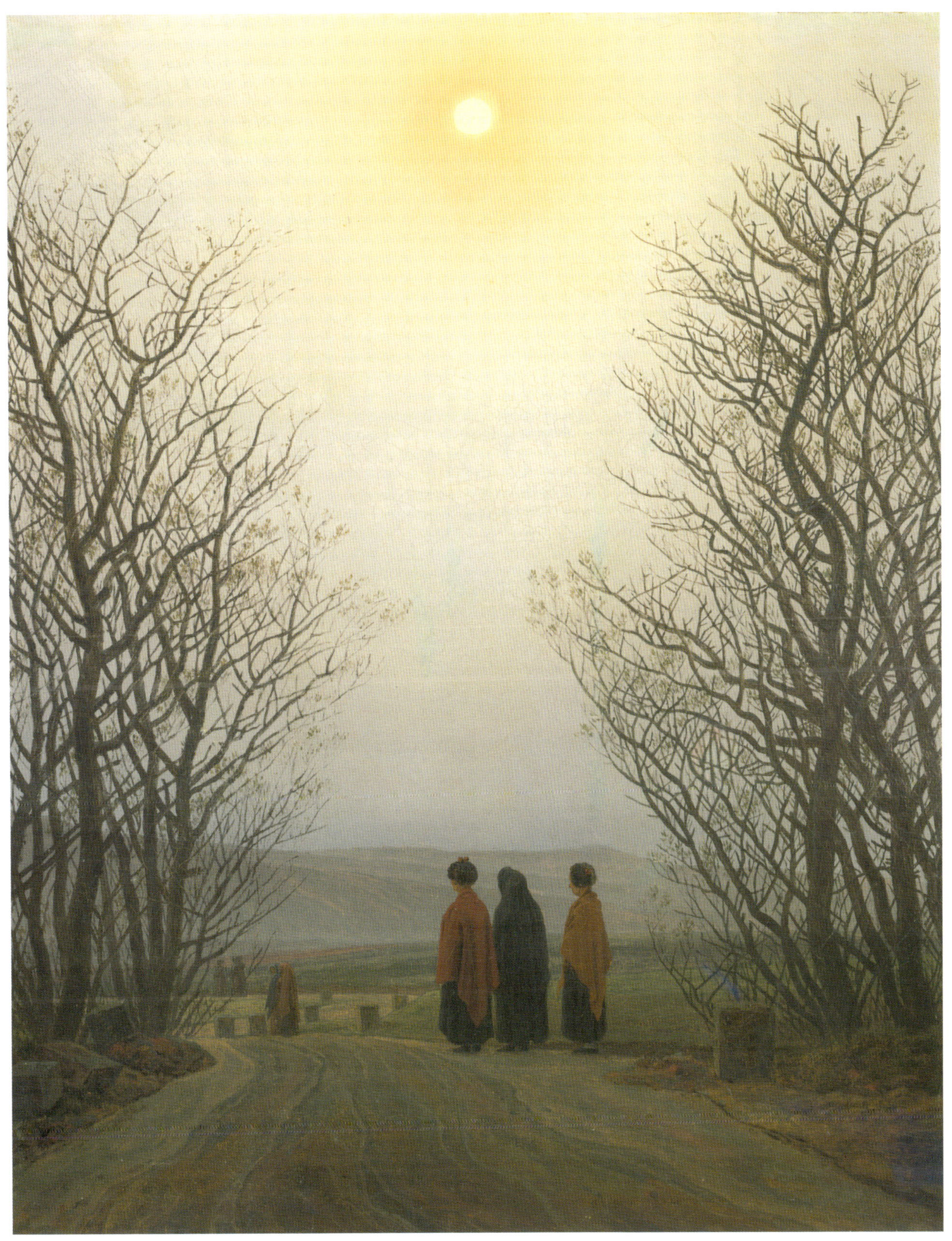

37. Caspar David Friedrich

Germany 1774–1840
Two men observing the moon
[*Zwei Männer in Betrachtung des Mondes*] 1830s
oil on canvas 35.0 x 44.5 cm
Galerie Hans, Hamburg

Two men on a hillside, standing on a stony outcrop, look at the crescent moon shining in a luminous sky. Framed between a strong, sinuous oak and an angular, spiky pine, the younger man leans on his companion's shoulder, as though overcome by beauty. These are not detached scientific observers scrutinising a lunar phenomenon, but witnesses of God's ever-surprising Nature. Instead of that scientific examination of natural phenomena so characteristic of German learning at the time, Friedrich's painting is a parable of Christianity and paganism. The oak, used for heathen rituals, is dying; the evergreen pine, a symbol of Christianity, lives. The men are protected underneath its branches.

Friedrich painted several versions of this scene, similar in composition although varying in character. The earliest known dates from 1819, another of a man and woman was made c. 1824, and at least two more were painted about 1830.[1] Friedrich's friend Dahl refers to later versions by the artist and others in a letter of 26 September 1840, at the time he donated the 1819 painting to the Dresden Gemäldegalerie in memory of Friedrich:

> This picture, full of sentiment and the quietness of nature, was painted by Friedrich in 1819 and he gave it to me in exchange for one of my own works. Friedrich had to copy it several times, but he did not approve of this, hence others copied it as well.[2]

While there is some disagreement about this version, close examination reveals Friedrich's blue underdrawing, a generous execution, and liberal and unique application of colour.[3] The characteristic freedom of the artist's hand can be seen here, with the silhouette of a dead branch on the right, jutting from a large rock – a pagan dolmen – which seems to buttress the old oak tree. A sawn stump on the left testifies to human life cut short while new vegetation, representing a growing Christianity, appears in a line of young pines on the right.

Friedrich's earlier works often show a lone hero in the landscape. A pair of figures now becomes part of the artist's repertoire, to symbolise friendship. They wear German national dress; the cloak and hat signalled opposition to the French invasions under Napoleon, and they were still popular signs of dissent against later reactionary German governments under Metternich. The men have been identified as Friedrich, leaning on a walking stick, and his pupil, August Heinrich (1794–1822), who died of consumption. It is touching the way the younger leans upon the older man, rather than the conventional reverse.

Friedrich captures the temporary and evanescent effects of this expedition to watch the moon and Venus, a strange phenomenon counterpoising the effects of light and darkness. The moon-filled sky is pale and glowing, denying blackness as the moon's natural element. The material world is dark, outlined against the eerie heavens.

Christine Dixon

1. The 1819 painting is in the Galerie Neue Meister, Dresden. A version made c. 1824, depicting the artist and his wife Caroline is in the National Galerie, Berlin. A c. 1830 version is in the Metropolitan Museum of Art, New York; this 1830s version is held in the Galerie Hans, Hamburg.
2. Letter to the Dresden Gemäldegalerie, Sächsische Hauptarchiv, cited in Helmut Börsch-Supan and Karl Wilhelm Jähnig, *Caspar David Friedrich: Gemälde, Druckgraphik und bildmässige Zeichnungen*, Munich: Prestel, 1973, p. 216, note 34.
3. Because of its spontaneity and breadth of handling, and original variations on the other versions, this painting is unlikely to be a copy by another artist. Copyists are notoriously careful in their imitation, and all too accurate in their replication. This version is attributed to Friedrich by Werner Sumowski 1969, 1971, 1975 and by Jens Christian Jensen 1999, refuting Helmut Börsch-Supan and Karl Wilhelm Jähnig 1973, who attribute it to a copyist, perhaps Julius Leypold.

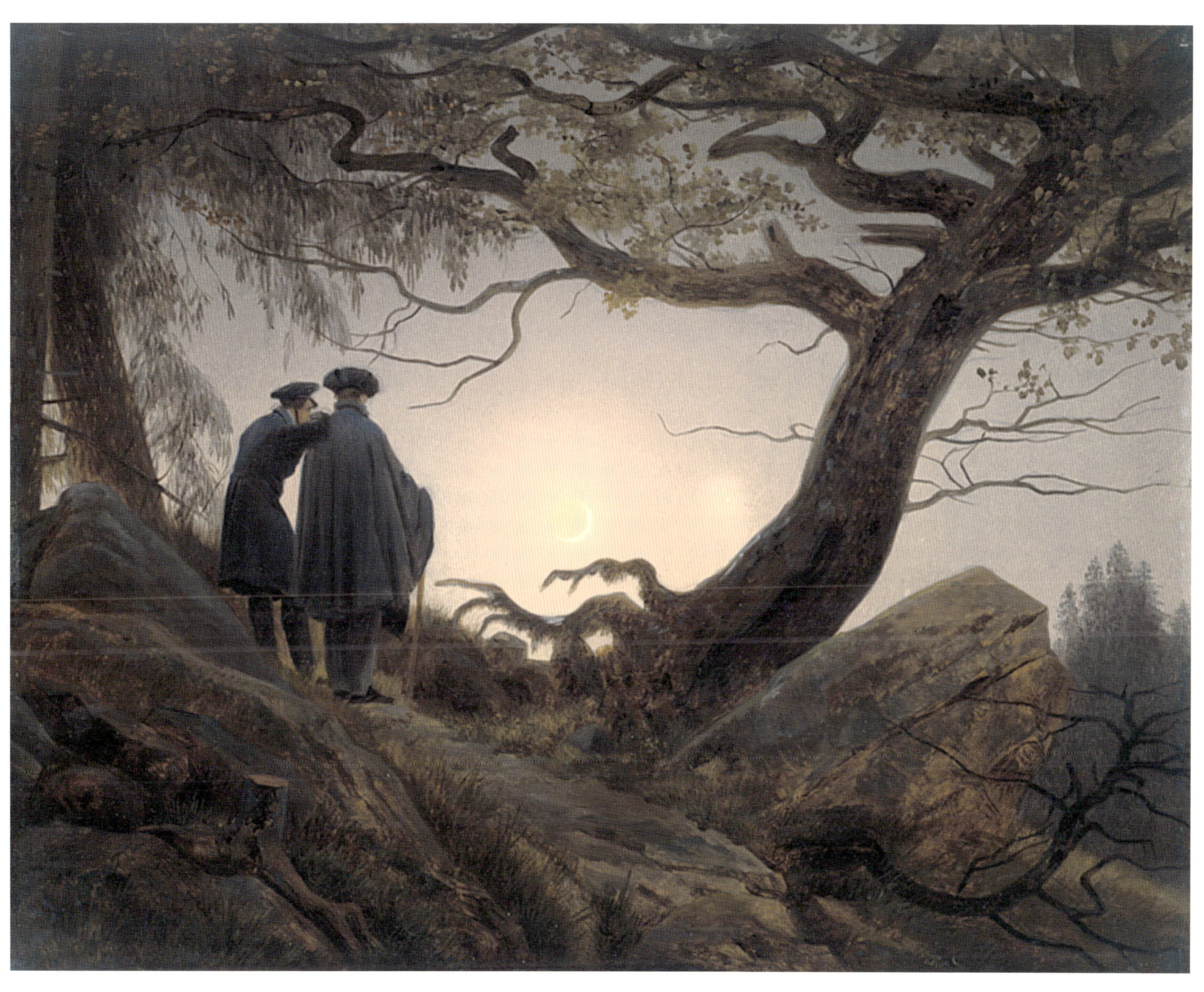

38. Johan Christian Dahl

Norway 1788 – Germany 1857
Dresden in moonlight [***Mondschein Dresden***] 1843
oil on canvas 66.7 x 101.2 cm
Bergen Kunstmuseum
The Rasmus Meyer Collection RMS.M.90[1]

In Dahl's nocturnal view of Dresden we see the familiar profile of the Saxon town on the Elbe river. The artist paints a panoramic view from the old town, by the August Bridge, silhouetting its most important buildings: the steeple of the Hofkirche, the castle tower (Hausmannsturm) and the large dome of the Frauenkirche. In the foreground the bank of the Elbe is populated with small figures. A shepherd and his sheep, a woman, boats and horses depict life along the river, providing a contrast in scale to the vast landscape. The scene is lit by a full moon, partly hidden by clouds to add a little drama, which generously showers the townscape with a silvery blue light. Moonlight and smoke from the city's many chimneys blend, creating a hazy atmosphere that obscures the architectural details of the buildings. The moon's glow is mirrored in the calm water of the river, its brilliant reflection providing a second source of light in the painting.

Dahl was a Romantic painter and, like Caspar David Friedrich, his neighbour in Dresden, transformed the landscape from a mere registration of natural formations to a rendering of Nature's Creation by the force of God. This was achieved by idealising the landscape, making it mysterious, with sky and light playing vital parts. The Romantics painted landscapes that were simultaneously frightening and attractive. Upon beholding it, the viewer should be in awe of God's Creation and compelled to contemplate his or her own existence.

Wild landscapes that incorporate figures in the foreground – their backs turned to the beholder – focus on humans' insignificance in contrast to the infinite space surrounding them. At the same time, these paintings, many of them nocturnal scenes, also focus on the beholder's inner space, one's soul. In art history the moonlit landscape has a rich symbolic tradition. Lunacy, loneliness, love and death, sleeping and dreaming, disaster and the macabre have all been connected to the moon.

Moonlight scenes are frequent in Dahl's oeuvre. The first was a view of Esrom Lake in Denmark, painted in 1814 during his period at the Academy of Copenhagen.[2] It was almost certainly inspired by his study of the Dutch Baroque masters in the Royal Danish art collection. The last was a moonlit Elbe painted in 1857, the year of his death.[3] Almost every year between 1814 and 1857, Dahl painted nocturnal landscapes, with the moon as an active source of light, making the landscape potent with mystery. They also presented him with an aesthetic challenge, particularly how to render the colour of night. Living in Dresden, Dahl often painted riverscapes of the Elbe, a view he experienced every day. He also painted nocturnal landscapes on his travels to Denmark, Norway, Italy and other parts of Germany. Altogether we know of nearly fifty paintings by Dahl where the light of the moon casts its magic over the landscape.

Knut Ormhaug

1. In 1844 the painting was bought by King Christian VIII of Denmark. It was later sold to a Norwegian owner, Johan Løken, from whom Rasmus Meyer bought the painting in 1907.
2. Marie Lødrup Bang, *Johan Christian Dahl, 1788–1857: life and works*, vol. 2, Oslo: Norwegian University Press, 1987, cat. 61, p. 49.
3. Bang, cat. 1169, p. 346.

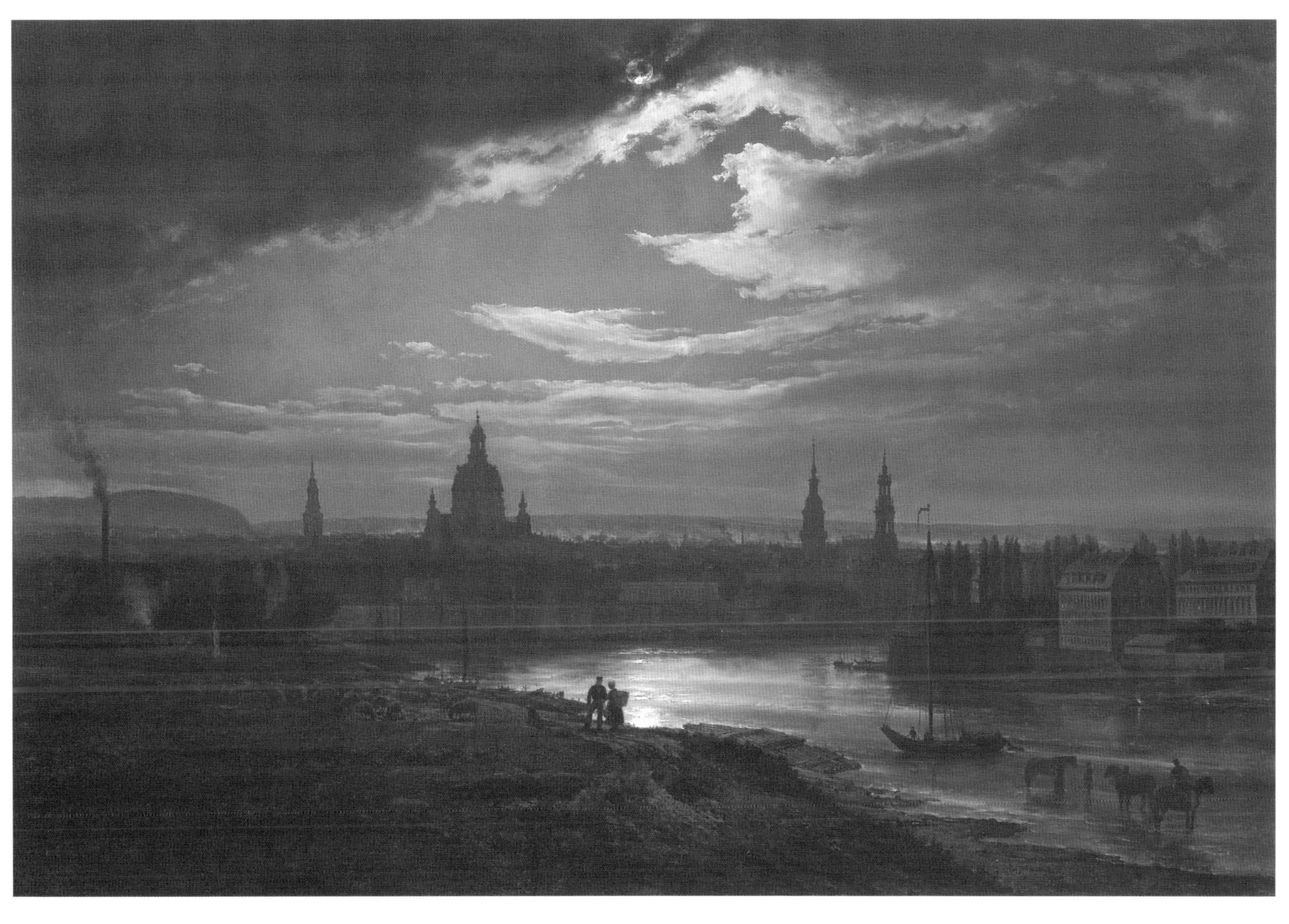

39. John Glover

Great Britain 1767 – Australia 1849
A corrobery of natives in Mills Plains 1832
oil on canvas on board 56.5 x 71.4 cm
Art Gallery of South Australia, Adelaide
Morgan Thomas Bequest Fund 1951

When Glover arrived in Hobart in 1831, the thirty-year conflict between the Tasmanian Aborigines and the European settlers was nearing an end. During this time George Augustus Robinson – the appointed Protector of Aborigines – had been relocating the majority of two hundred Indigenous people to Flinders Island. Only two months before he left Hobart for his new property of Patterdale in northern Tasmania, Glover made two group portraits showing twenty-six members of the Big River and Oyster Bay Aboriginal tribes before their transfer to Flinders Island. They became the subject of a number of significant paintings. Painted in 1832, the year of his move to Patterdale, *A corrobery of natives in Mills Plains* is Glover's finest and probably earliest Aboriginal subject. Although the artist's sketchbook contains a corroboree drawing for this landscape, he could not possibly have seen such an event on his property. As there were probably no Aborigines left in the area and certainly not enough to engage in a corroboree, the gathering is painted from his memory as well as his Hobart sketches.

Of the artist's numerous Aboriginal landscapes this is his first and his most moving and haunting, with its revelations of Glover's sympathy for the departed Tasmanian Aborigines. Here he depicts an imagined re-creation of a corroboree within a romantic setting. The giant native tree, silhouetted against the sky, is bent and dying as the sun sinks, and so becomes a metaphor for the fate of the ancient race. Eight dancing and standing men holding spears, five seated women, two children and what appears to be an infant are gathered beneath the towering eucalypt. Dwarfed beneath the gum they appear almost to be ghosts of a former civilisation. Although Glover has taken possession of the land, it is not without some sense of guilt. And certainly, the theme of dispossession haunted Glover for the rest of his life as he re-created at least twenty such landscapes with Aborigines.

Glover's Patterdale paintings are ultimately based on the landscape devices of Claude Lorrain, Gaspard Dughet and, particularly, Jacob van Ruisdael. But in *A corrobery of natives in Mills Plains* the mysterious and ominous mood of the painting emulates the wildly romantic landscapes of Salvator Rosa and his depictions of wind-blasted trees and *banditti* (Italian outlaws). Finally the dusky and lurid sky echoes the highly romantic evening landscapes of Glover's fellow countryman Joseph Wright of Derby.

Though this is probably the first oil painting depicting Tasmanian Aborigines, Glover's artistic forerunners in New South Wales had already painted night corroborees. Given the demise of the eighteenth-century concept of the 'noble savage' – which presented native people in light-filled arcadian paradises – it is not surprising that these images placed Indigenous peoples in a more ominous night light. Dances and ceremonies were presented as curious and heathenish while Indigenous people were represented as something to be feared and civilised by Christianity. Even so, the European settler's envy is also expressed at their apparently happy and non-materialistic life. *A corrobery of natives in Mills Plains* can be seen as Glover's valediction to a dying race. Traditions of European landscape art, romantic notions of the noble savage and his own Christian confidence in the face of paganism, enrich his melancholy testimony to the passing of a lively Aboriginal civilisation.

Ron Radford

Adapted from Ron Radford and Jane Hylton, *Australian colonial art: 1800–1900*, Adelaide: Art Gallery of South Australia, 1995, pp. 68–70.

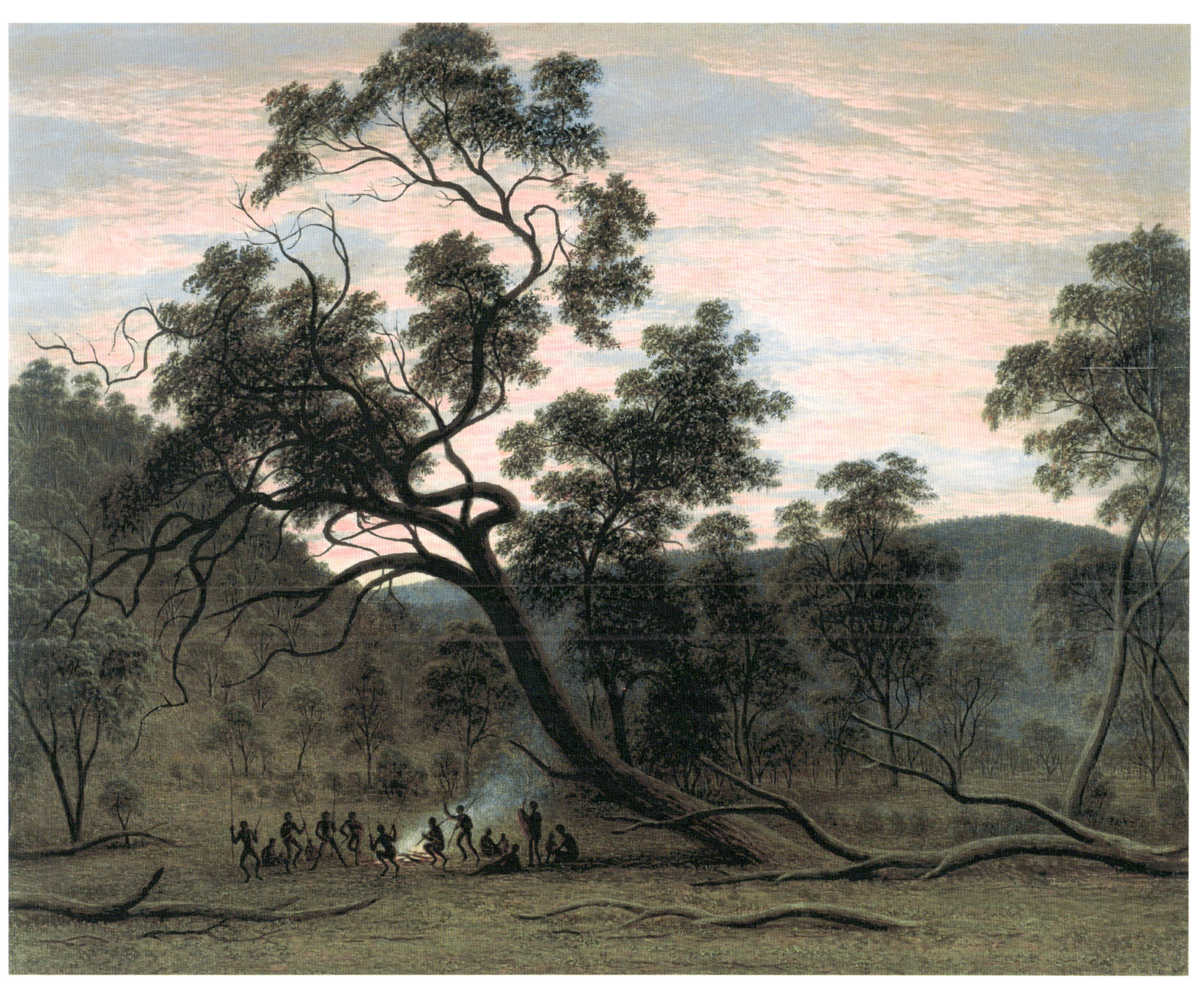

40. Eugene von Guérard

Austria 1811 – Great Britain 1901
worked in Australia 1852–81
Stony Rises, Lake Corangamite 1857
alternative title ***An Australian sunset***
oil on canvas 71.2 x 86.4 cm
Art Gallery of South Australia, Adelaide
Purchased with the assistance of the Utah Foundation
through the Art Gallery of South Australia Foundation 1981

When von Guérard first exhibited this, his most dramatically symbolic and poetic painting, at the Victorian Society of Fine Arts in December 1857 its title was *Stony Rises, Lake Corangamite*. The geological phenomenon of undulating rocky land lies between Camperdown and Colac in Western Victoria. A more appropriate title – supplied when the work was illustrated on the cover of the November 1857 issue of *News Letter of Australasia* – was the non-specific *An Australian sunset*. Although von Guérard was concerned with accurately recording geography, he was also interested in Romantic associations. Here one searches in vain for the site that could have been used for this painting. Although the artist takes pains to detail the topography and vegetation of the area, these features are exaggerated and altered for symbolic and poetic purposes. In this apparently naturalistic landscape of a specific place and time, von Guérard suggests the poignant moment in an Aboriginal Eden prior to the impact of European settlement. In April 1857 the artist visited the Stony Rises, possibly once a sacred area for the Indigenous inhabitants. At this time there were only sixteen survivors of the local Colac people, all of whom worked on local sheep or cattle stations.

In this painting, the rocky land around the Stony Rises acts as a dramatic setting for a valedictory gesture to the Aboriginal race, a gloomy monument to their displacement. The artist deliberately shows the people in the conditions of their immediate and uninterrupted past. At first glance the imagery conjures up safe and bountiful arcadian seclusion. Native trees and boulders form a protective wall, and an abundance of food is evoked by images of freshly caught wallaby and running water. Placed centrally in the immediate foreground is a single jubilant child, who welcomes his father's return from a successful hunt. He can be seen as the future of the race.

But is this really a scene of well-being? The glorious sunset has not produced an atmosphere of warm optimism. Rather the mood is brooding and melancholic: the camp is cast in shadow. Wisps of smoke, visible on the plains below, act as reminders of European encroachment. Carefully depicted flora, including what is most likely a prickly blackberry amongst native grasses in the left foreground, symbolise colonial intrusion into the haven. Even the native blackwood trees are evocative of Italian cypresses: these trees of European graveyards are traditionally associated with death. The tallest native tree is dying, and only the last rays of the sinking sun can be seen in the centre of the composition.

Von Guérard masterfully combines influences from Italian and northern European landscape traditions alongside nineteenth-century Romantic ideas. The Claudean tradition is evoked in the Classically balanced composition, a structured landscape that hints at Greek or Roman ruins, the figures at home in their environment like Arcadian shepherds, a dissolving vista and the tranquil mood and warm twilit sky. Seventeenth-century Dutch influences are manifested in a sombre, melancholic and dark, brooding mood, meticulous rendering of detail and the symbolic dying tree. Finally, the dark Gothic shapes silhouetted against the lurid sky remind us of the religious realms conjured by the great German Romantic Friedrich, of whose work von Guérard was certainly aware.

Ron Radford

Content for this essay is drawn from the author's previous essays. See Ron Radford 'Eden before the White Serpent' in D. Thomas (ed.), *Creating Australia: 200 years of art 1788–1988*, Sydney: International Cultural Corporation of Australia, 1988, pp. 80–1; and Ron Radford and Jane Hylton, *Australian colonial art: 1800–1900*, Adelaide: Art Gallery of South Australia, 1995, pp. 98–100.

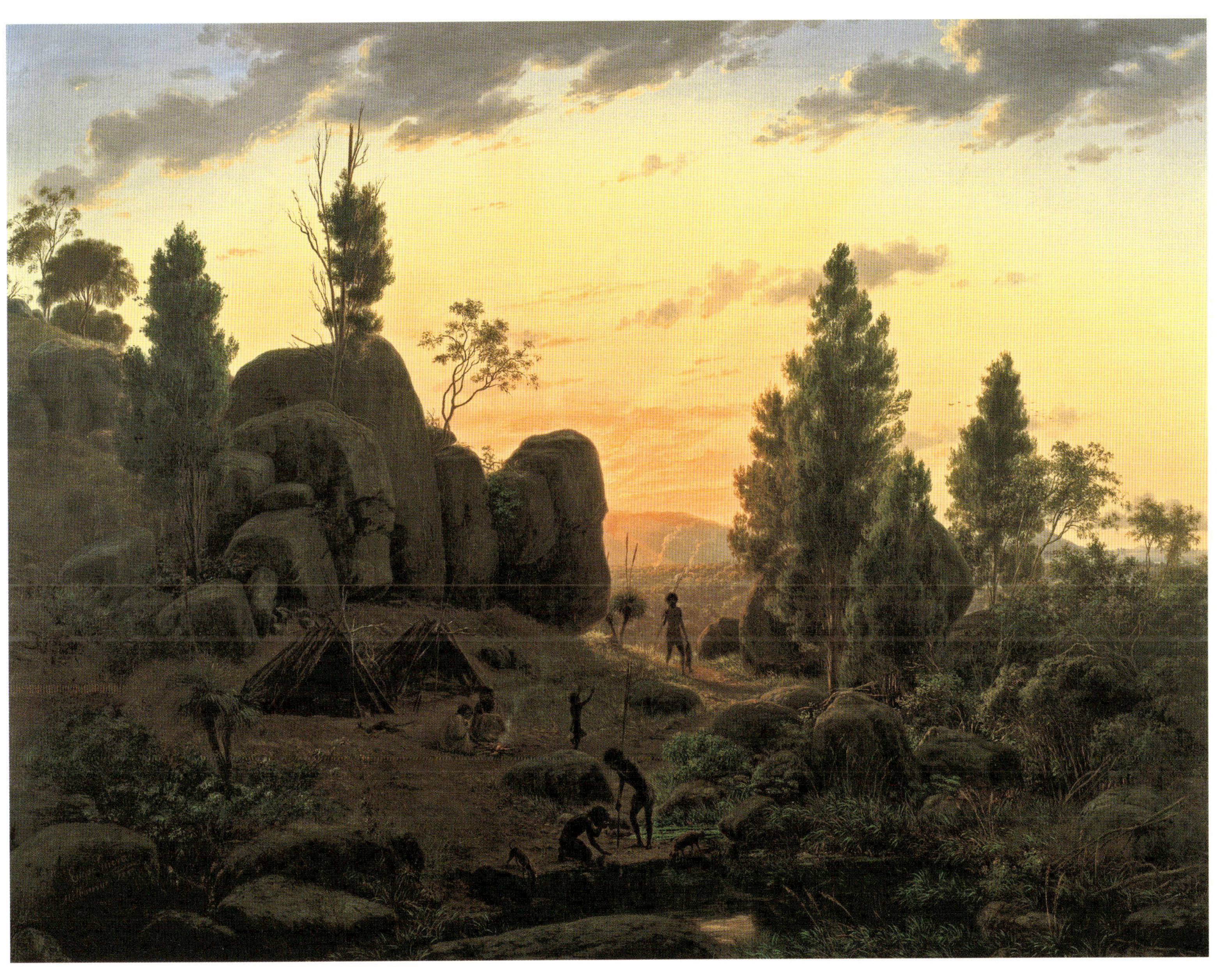

41. Eugene von Guérard

Austria 1811 – Great Britain 1901
worked in Australia 1852–81
North-east view from the northern top of Mount Kosciusko 1863
oil on canvas 66.5 x 116.8 cm
National Gallery of Australia, Canberra
Purchased 1973 1973.645

The *Australian Sketcher* of November 1873 shows von Guérard's grand Kosciusko painting displayed at the Vienna Exhibition with other contributions from the Australian colonies. It and another of the artist's paintings, *Cape Woolamai* 1872, are surrounded by photographs and maps, produce, flora and fauna, as well as a case of mineral samples and other specimens of interest.[1] There is some irony here. Von Guérard detailed the lichen on rocks in *North-east view from the northern top of Mount Kosciusko* – most noticeably on the platform on which the cloaked figure stands – but other parts are less convincing.

When von Guérard arrived in Australia in 1852 he was already an established artist, having trained in Rome and Düsseldorf. He had probably seen works by Friedrich; Carus's published writings also circulated widely during the 1830s and 1840s, the periods of von Guérard's study at the Staatliche Kunstakademie. In his new southern homeland the artist familiarised himself with native flora by sketching in the Melbourne Botanical Gardens, exactly the close observation of nature promoted by Carus. Von Guérard's works are an intriguing mix of topographical accuracy and German traditions of the Sublime: we find a range of protagonists throughout his oeuvre, figures often tiny, seen at an angle or with their backs to the picture plane. As Bruce puts it, von Guérard thus synthesises active, intelligent observation with a 'predominance of feeling over reasoning'.[2]

In 1862 von Guérard joined an expedition to the Australian Alps. Led by the Bavarian scientist Georg von Neumayer, the expedition was commissioned by the Government of Victoria, part of an international project to measure the Earth's magnetic fields. As well as a geophysicist and an artist, the party comprised Neumayer's assistant, two guides and his dog Hector – all of whom are immortalised in the painting. Von Guérard made a number of sketches during the course of the expedition. In Melbourne the following year he produced *North-east view from the northern top of Mount Kosciusko.*[3] It is a major painting, regarded as one of his finest artistically, and most accurate topographically.

In *North-east view from the northern top of Mount Kosciusko* areas of the foreground and the mound of large boulders at right are particularly perplexing. Indeed as Bonyhady tells, the rocks were introduced by von Guérard to emphasise human insignificance. They serve to provide a link between foreground, the distant mountains and the sky, that records the passage from heavy rain to bright sunshine.[4] Most importantly, in aesthetic terms, the rocks echo those on the peaks at the centre of the composition, gloriously patterned by the snow that has melted to reveal the grassy slopes underneath.

Mount Kosciusko, an anglicised spelling, was named by the explorer Count Paul Strzelecki in 1840 after the Polish-Lithuanian general Tadeusz Kociuszko.[5] The peak was subsequently discovered to be slightly lower than its neighbour, Mount Townsend – although in order that Mount Kosciuszko retain the distinction of the highest mountain in Australia, the names were reversed.

Lucina Ward

1. The *Australian Sketcher* engraving is reproduced in Candice Bruce, *Eugene von Guérard 1811–1901: a German romantic in the Antipodes*, Martinborough: Alister Taylor, 1982, p. 41; the present whereabouts of *Cape Woolamai* 1872 is not known.
2. Bruce, p. 8.
3. Studies held Mitchell and Dixson collections, State Library of NSW; the canvas is inscribed 'Mt Kosciusko/ 19 Nov. 1862/ Eug. von Guerard', the date of the expedition.
4. Tim Bonyhady, *Australian colonial paintings in the Australian National Gallery*, Canberra: Australian National Gallery, 1986, pp. 188–98, 192–3.
5. In 1997 the Geographical Names Board of NSW adopted the spelling 'Kosciuszko'; Australian pronunciation differs vastly from the Polish.

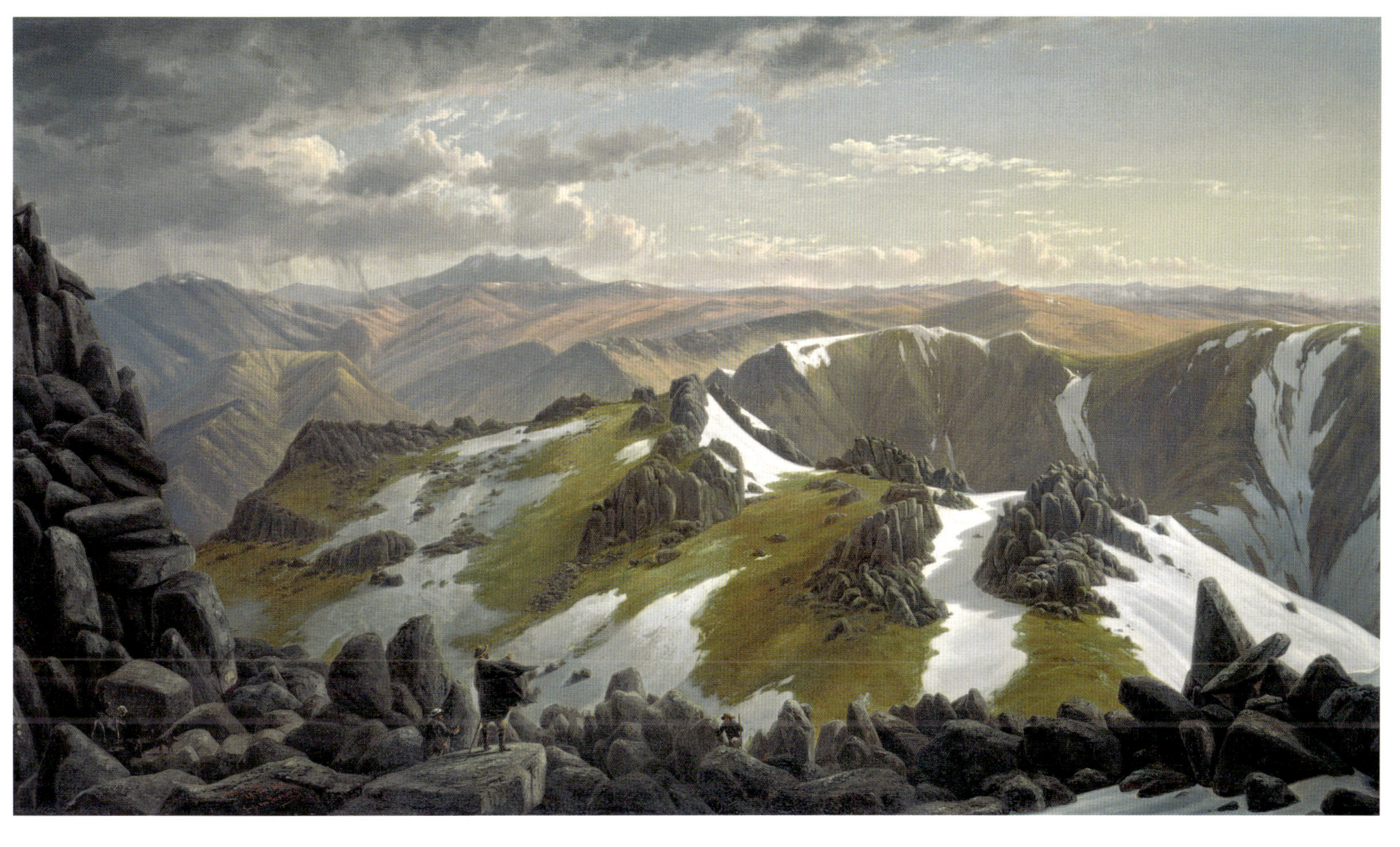

42. Johan Christian Dahl

Norway 1788 – Germany 1857
***Eruption of Vesuvius* [*Ausbruch des Vesuvs*]** 1823
oil on canvas 58.7 x 72.7 cm
Collection of Asbjorn R. Lunde, New York

… this amazing mountain continues to exhibit such various scenes of sublimity and beauty at exactly the distance one would chuse to observe it from; a distance which almost admits examination, and certainly excludes immediate fear … columns of flame, high as the mountain's self, shoot from its crater into the clear atmosphere with a loud and violent noise … a thick cloud, charged heavily with electric matter, passing over, met the fiery explosion …
Hester Thrale, 1789[1]

Mount Vesuvius was especially active in the late eighteenth and for most of the nineteenth century.[2] This fact, along with a growing awareness of the natural sciences in this period, meant the volcano attracted a great deal of interest. Indeed images of Vesuvius in various states of activity, as well as other scenes of uncontrollable nature – avalanches, storms, fires – became synonymous with the Sublime and with Romantic art. In the 1770s the English artist Joseph Wright of Derby, Frenchman Pierre-Jacques Volaire and German Jacob Philipp Hackert all produced views of Vesuvius, establishing the conventions for subsequent images. They presented the erupting volcano as a spectacle by moonlight, rivers of lava observed by tiny frock-coated gentlemen, juxtaposed against the built environment or surrounded by calm harbours. The paintings produced by later Romantic artists tended, on the other hand, to portray the volcano with as much precision and more emotion.

In 1818, Dahl, Bergen-born and Copenhagen-trained, set out for an extensive study tour of the continent – although he didn't make it very far. Travelling via Poland and then Berlin, he settled in Dresden where, apart from his 1820–21 sojourns to Italy and frequent trips back to Norway, he remained for the rest of his life. Dahl witnessed some of the 1820 eruptions while in Naples; he sketched Vesuvius on the spot, subsequently producing many paintings based on these experiences. Dahl shares this fantastic composition with his friend and compatriot, the Viennese painter Josef Rebell.[3] In both paintings, the profusion of colour, audacity of the scene and its sheer extremes – the gleam of the bright moonlit sky, the glow of molten lava tumbling into the sea, the treacherous waves set against perilous rocks – convey 'not a sense of fear but a sort of ecstasy'.[4]

Much of the fascination of *Eruption of Vesuvius* is a result of the combination of the opposing elements of fire and water. Usually a stormy sea such as this would be enough in itself to engender a sense of awe. Here it is pitted against a volcano, which shoots flames into the sky, fills the sky with black smoke and scatters fiery girandoles far and wide. The debris even reaches a stone monument adorned with a cross, on the rocky shore opposite – dangerously close to where we are standing! On the right-hand side, soot merges with the silhouetted coast. The moon ventures through the darkened clouds, just enough to cast light on the foreboding scene below. This is Sublime Nature. We feel the power of Vesuvius and anticipate its destructive forces.

Lucina Ward

1. Herbert Barrows (ed.), *Observations and reflections: made in the course of a journey through France, Italy and Germany by Hester Lynch Piozzi*, Ann Arbor: The University of Michigan Press, 1967, pp. 223–4.
2. There were six major eruptions in the 1700s and a further eight next century: in 1822, 1834 and 1839; two each in the 1850s and 1860s; and again in 1872.
3. It is not known if Dahl's is a copy after Rebell, or whether the two artists worked together in Italy. Rebell's *The eruption of Vesuvius at night* 1822 is in the Liechtenstein Museum, Vienna.
4. Johann Kräftner, *Liechtenstein Museum Vienna: Neoclassicism and Biedermeier*, Munich and New York: Prestel, Vienna: Liechtenstein Museum, 2004, p. 118.

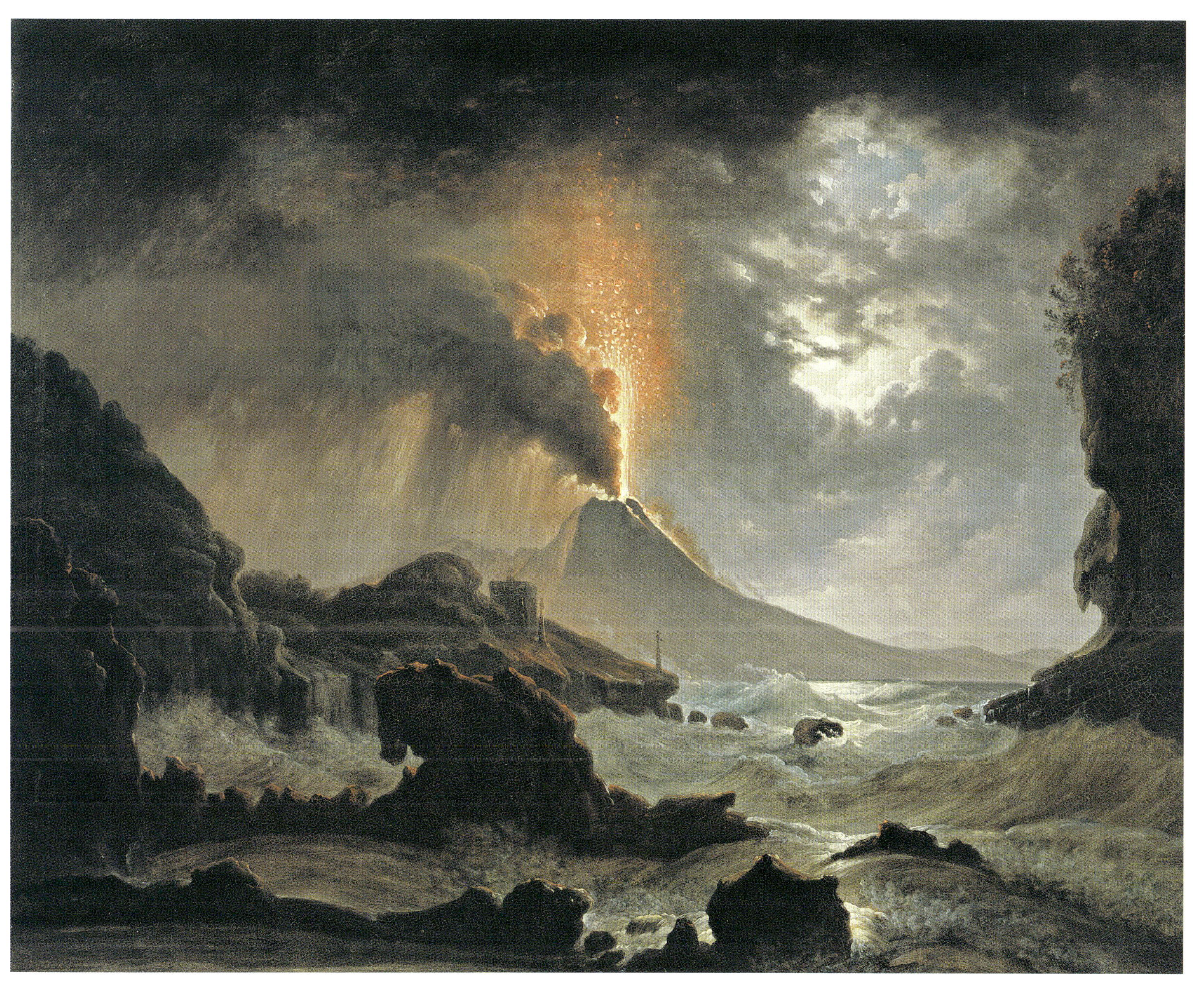

43. Johan Christian Dahl

Norway 1788 – Germany 1857
Vesuvius in eruption [***Vesuv i utbrud***] 1821
oil on canvas 61.0 x 87.5 cm
Bergen Kunstmuseum
Rasmus Meyer Collection RMS.M65

Being volcano-mad was madder than being picture-mad. Perhaps the sun had gone to his head, or the fabled laxity of the south. Then the passion was quickly rationalised as a scientific interest, and also an aesthetic one, for the eruption of a volcano could be called, stretching the term, beautiful. There was nothing odd in his evenings with guests invited to view the spectacle from the terrace of his country villa ... What was odd was that he wanted to be even closer.
Susan Sontag[1]

In 1820 Prince Christian Frederik – later King Christian VIII of Denmark – invited Dahl to join him in Naples. Between August 1820 and February 1821 the artist stayed at the prince's villa, making frequent excursions to Naples and surrounding districts. Dahl, who was born in Bergen (then part of Denmark) and first apprenticed to a house painter, studied at the Copenhagen Academy of Art under the influential Neo-Classicist Christoffer Wilhelm Eckersberg. His Romantic outlook was shaped by his experience of the collections in the Danish capital, and of Dresden, where he subsequently settled (cat. 38). Like many other painters, Dahl travelled to Italy to work in the extremes of southern light, to gather source material for his paintings, and to solicit patronage – particularly from the large number of British and continental tourists who desired images of their Grand Tour.

On 20 December 1820 Vesuvius began to erupt. Dahl climbed the volcano, observing the spectacle by daylight and in the evening. The following day he started a sketch, returning a few days later. He again visited Vesuvius towards the end of January when the eruption had ceased.[2] Dahl's subsequent paintings of Vesuvius became extremely popular and he painted many variants. This version, showing three visitors to the volcano's rim accompanied by a guide with donkeys, is the best known and exists in at least seven sizes. As Bang points out, these *staffage* figures are not the conventional tourists of earlier *vedute* paintings, who gesticulate at a safe distance from the awesome sight, but serious men contemplating the natural phenomenon, impossibly close to the glowing lava.[3] Silhouetted against a dramatic red backdrop, the people are minute compared to this awesome example of God's work. The fiery drama at the centre of the composition is set against a grand vista. Beyond the volcano we glimpse ships anchored in the calm waters and the sprawling city of Naples below.

Another painting of Vesuvius (cat. 42) shows the scene from a different vantage point. This emphasises two interrelated and symbiotic approaches in Romanticism: notions of the Sublime and the impact of careful observations taken 'in the field'. Through the artist's own authentic experience, we feel the frisson and heat of being there, at the edge of the smouldering volcano. After his return to Dresden in July 1821, Dahl's oeuvre is increasingly dominated by Norwegian subjects; they develop the combination of emotion, naturalism and specificity found in *Vesuvius in eruption*.

Lucina Ward

1. *The volcano lover*, London: Vintage, 1993, p. 25.
2. From the artist's diary entries, in Marie Lødrup Bang, *Johan Christian Dahl, 1788–1857: life and works*, Oslo: Norwegian University Press, 1987, vol. 2, p. 110, see also vol. 1, pp. 52–3.
3. Bang, vol. 1, p. 63.

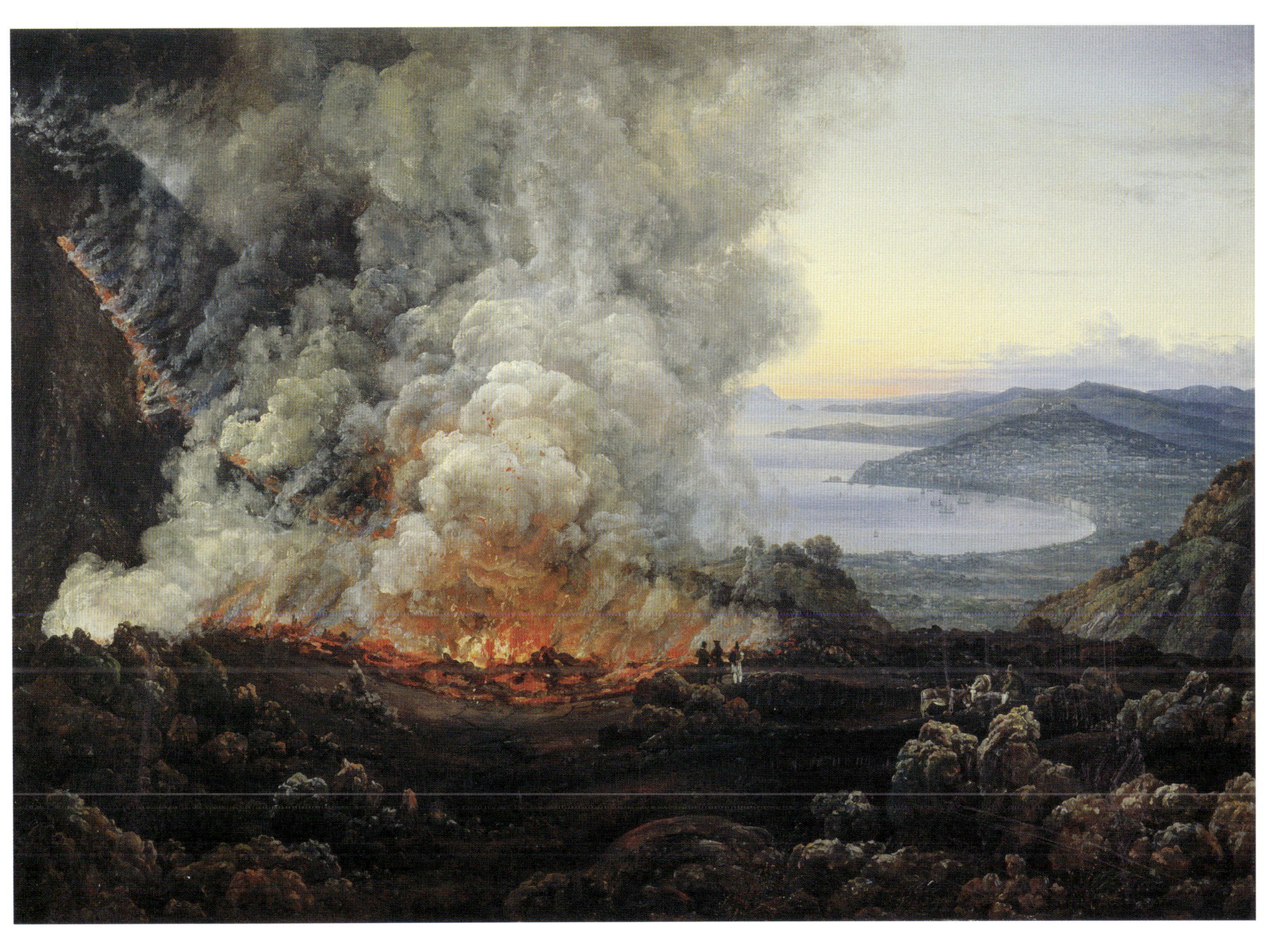

44. J.M.W. Turner

Great Britain 1775–1851
Waves breaking against the wind c. 1840
oil on canvas 60.4 x 95.0 cm
Tate Britain
Accepted by the British nation as part of the Turner Bequest 1856
N02881

By the early 1830s Turner was a regular visitor to the seaside town of Margate, on the eastern tip of the county of Kent, about seventy miles downriver from London. Turner's first introduction to Margate came in the 1790s, when the place was essentially just a small fishing town, but it had since become a bustling resort that Londoners could reach effortlessly by steamboat in half a day. The geographic setting is remarkable, benefiting from a magnificently open prospect over the sea to the north and east, which allegedly induced Turner to claim that the skies in this area were among the loveliest in Europe. In addition to this natural prospect, the attractions of Margate were somewhat unorthodox for Turner, stemming from his clandestine relationship with Sophia Caroline Booth (1798–1875), a young widow, who was initially his landlady and subsequently his mistress and muse.

From the windows of Mrs Booth's lodging-house, near the harbour quay, Turner was able to watch the arrival and departure of the London steamers, a couple of which formed the subject of a painting he displayed at the Royal Academy in 1840 *Rockets and blue lights (close at hand) to warn steamboats of shoal water.*[1] The basic composition of that work was anticipated by a study, *Waves breaking on a lee shore* c. 1840, which is a pair to the work exhibited here.[2] The studies focus on the shore on either side of Margate harbour; in this case looking back from the west to the light tower at the end of the protective outer wall, which is created as a dull silhouette by the later application of a lighter area of whitish grey paint around it. As in even his earliest depictions of the sea, Turner sought to give his painted representation dramatic textures that replicate, and seemingly act as a substitute for, the movement of water.

Both of the Margate studies are painted with such expressive vigour that it has generally been assumed they may have been direct observations of the rolling sea, capturing the surge of the waves as they splay upwards into flying crests, before crashing on the beach. Though Turner evidently did make *plein air* studies in pencil and watercolour at Margate, the impracticalities of working in oils, while witnessing such fast-changing weather conditions, make it unlikely that this picture would have been painted in the same way. This makes the apparent spontaneity and directness of his images all the more impressive, especially his vivid attempts to provide an impression of the sea in motion, at a time before the introduction of photography enabled artists greater opportunity to dissect the underlying principles of movement more precisely.[3]

Ian Warrell

1. Martin Butlin and Evelyn Joll, *The paintings of J.M.W. Turner*, rev. edn, New Haven and London: Yale University Press, 1984, cat. 387; collection of Sterling and Francine Clark Art Institute, Williamstown.
2. Butlin and Joll, cat. 458, collection of the Tate; Ian Warrell (ed.), *J.M.W. Turner*, Washington: National Gallery of Art, 2007, cat. 133, where re-dated from c. 1835 to c. 1840.
3. For a more qualified appraisal of Turner's depictions of the sea, see Christiana Payne, *Where the sea meets the land. Artists on the coast in nineteenth-century Britain*, Bristol: Sansom & Co., 2007, p. 49, notes 31, 60.

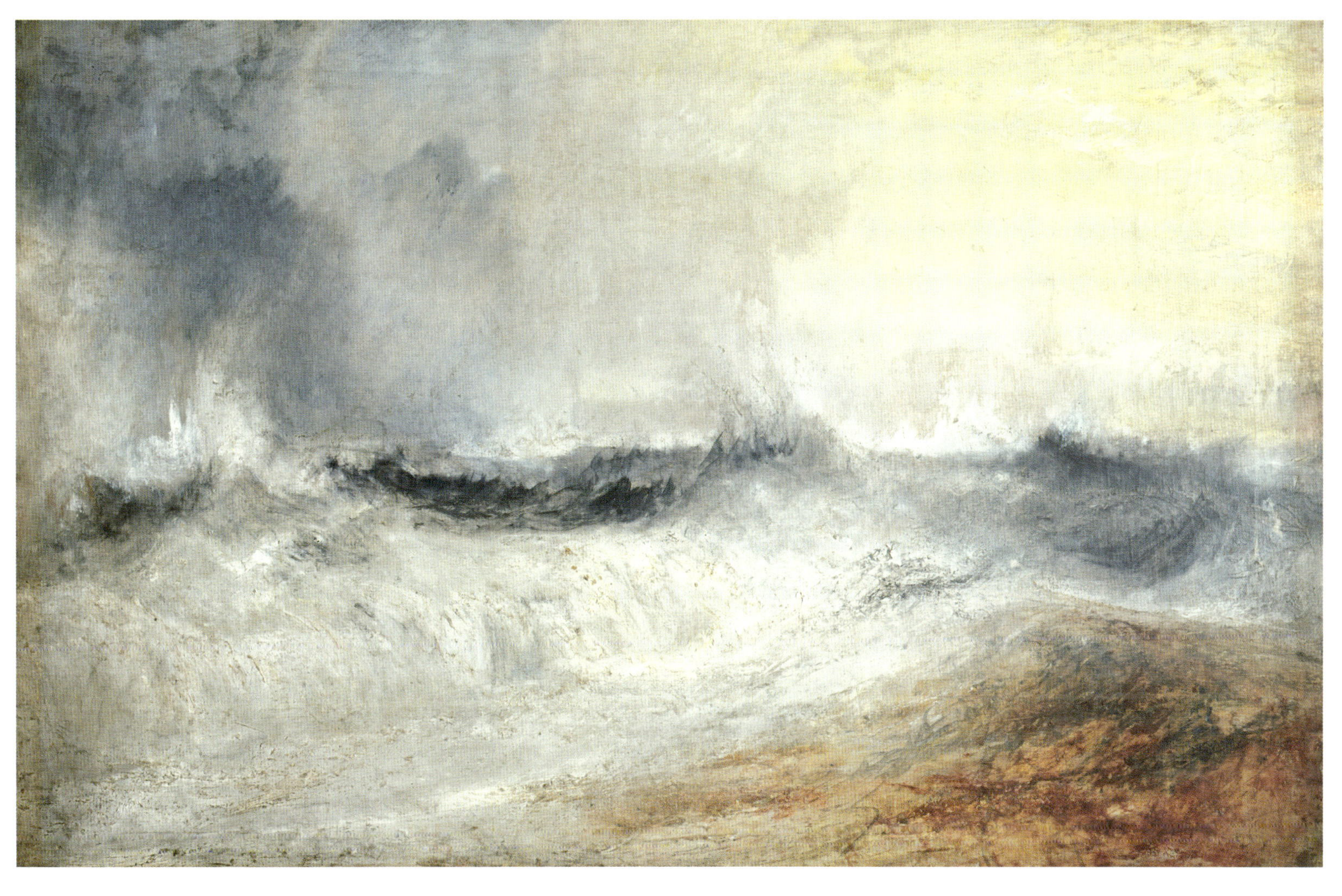

45. J.M.W. Turner

Great Britain 1775–1851
Stormy sea with blazing wreck c. 1835–40
oil on canvas 99.4 x 141.6 cm
Tate Britain
Accepted by the British nation as part of the Turner Bequest 1856
N04658

The sea, described by the artist as 'power supreme', is the subject of nearly one-third of Turner's paintings. From his early *Fisherman at sea* 1796 to *Snowstorm: steam boat off a harbour's mouth making signals in shallow water, and going by the lead. The author was in this storm on the night the Ariel left Harwick* 1842, Turner recorded the sea in all its moods.[1] Occasionally he combined the two elements of fire and water, as if to emphasise further the pitiful, puny nature of humans set against the forces of Nature. From his early influences, including Joseph Vernet, Joseph Wright of Derby and Dutch marine painting, Turner's oeuvre is now synonymous with the Sublime: vast, awe-inspiring spaces, often obscured or with irregular elements, invoking the terror of the unknown.

Marine painting as a genre emerged from ships and their symbolism in religious art, as well as secular depictions of important naval vessels, battles, explorations and other nautical events as part of commemorative paintings and print culture.[2] The rise of landscape as an independent pictorial genre also contributed to the importance of coastal scenes and seascapes. The Romantics built on Dutch marine traditions but developed their paintings to concentrate more on the sea and sky; the drama of swelling waves and building clouds became their subject. Turner takes this one step further. In his paintings, sea and sky are vehicles to explore emotional conditions, and a demonstration of the nature of paint itself.

In *Stormy sea with blazing wreck* Turner tilted the picture plane so that shore and water consume half the canvas. The painting verges on monochrome. The foreground is indistinct, the horizon uncertain. A blazing wreck on which the composition hinges is surrounded, almost subsumed by the oppressively dark and overpowering sea. The ship's skeletal remains, trailing a plume of white smoke, are framed by ominous orange-tinged clouds. Turner uses oranges and yellows liberally, colours not typical of seascapes.

In setting this scene at night, something he rarely did, Turner emphasises the true horror of the circumstances. Once we have allowed our eyes to adjust, and only then, do figures emerge from eerie yellow areas at left, and we recognise the sails of the ship on the horizon. Perhaps the people on the shore are wreckers, and their deception has lured the ship onto the rocks.[3] Butlin and Joll suggest that *Stormy sea with blazing wreck* may have a companion piece in the form of *Yacht approaching the coast* c. 1840–45.[4] This pairing provides two possible endings for a maritime voyage. In an age of air travel and wars fought by remote-control missiles, it is easy for us to forget the terror of the unknown that confronted earlier sea voyagers.

Lucina Ward

---

1. Both collection of the Tate.
2. Marie Lødrup Bang, *Johan Christian Dahl, 1788–1857: life and works*, Oslo: Norwegian University Press, 1987, vol. 1, p. 151.
3. See also *Wreckers: coast of Northumberland, with a steamboat assisting a ship off shore* 1834, Paul Mellon Collection, Yale Center for British Art.
4. Collection of the Tate Britain.

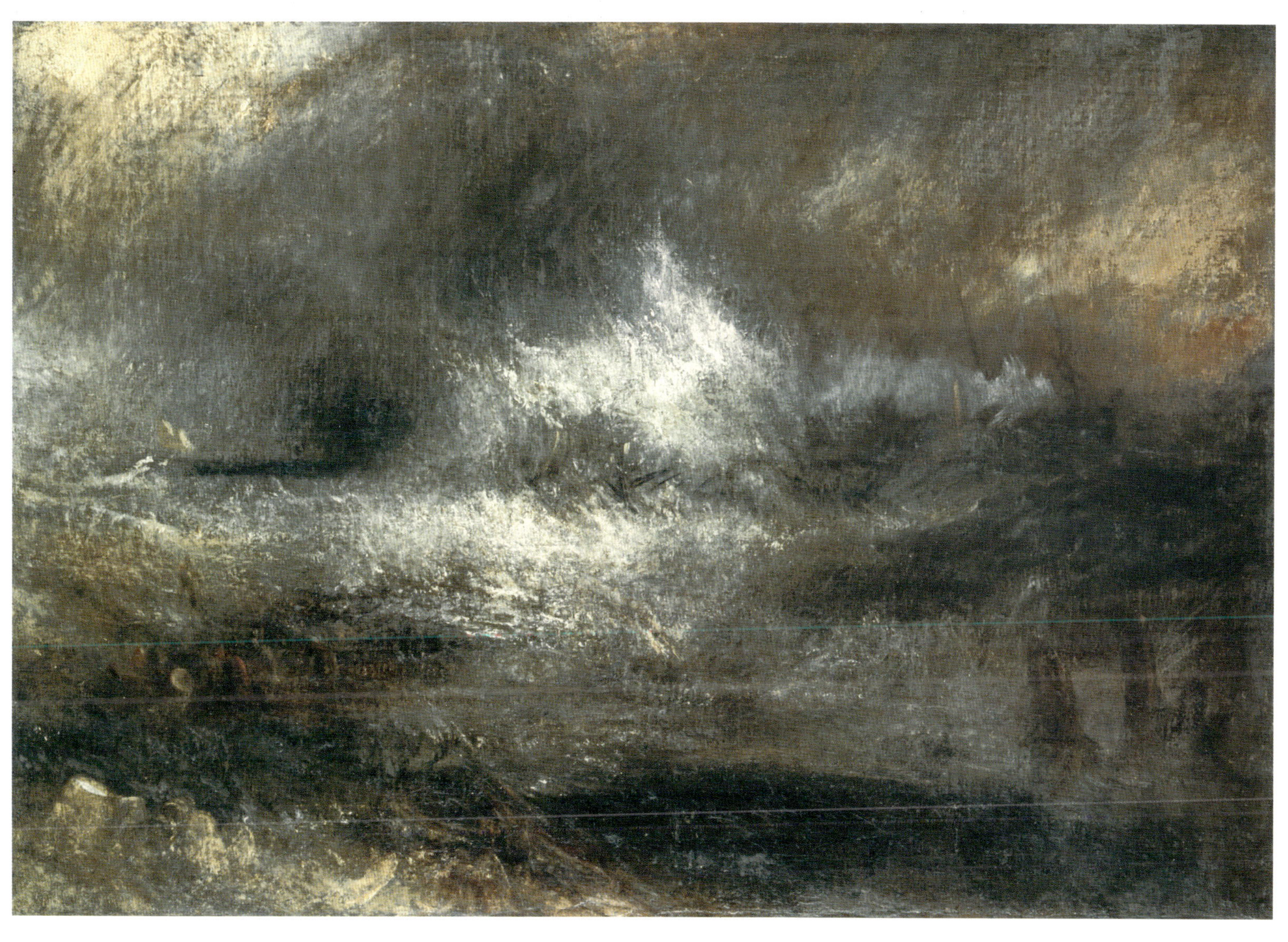

46. J.M.W. Turner

Great Britain 1775–1851
A mountain scene, Val d'Aosta c. 1841–45
oil on canvas 91.5 x 122.0 cm
National Gallery of Victoria, Melbourne
Purchased with the assistance of a special grant from the Government of Victoria and donations from Associated Securities Limited, the Commonwealth Government (through the Australia Council), the National Gallery Society of Victoria, the National Art Collections Fund (Great Britain), The Potter Foundation and other organisations, the Myer family and the people of Victoria 1973 E2-1973

This canvas was not exhibited during Turner's lifetime, and remained almost unknown until it came to light, sensationally, in the early 1970s.[1] It is one of the few 'unfinished' works that somehow left Turner's studio instead of becoming part of his bequest. These revelatory works were only discovered at the end of the nineteenth-century. They preserve the indistinct state in which the artist submitted his canvases to Royal Academy exhibitions: the process of development is here arrested, but the image would have been magically transformed by Turner's addition of form and detail during the 'Varnishing Days' prior to the public opening.

The scene depicted has always been associated with the Alps, and its traditional title is *A mountain scene, Val d'Aosta*. Turner had visited the Aosta valley, on the Italian side of Mont Blanc, during his first continental tour in 1802, and again travelled through the area in 1836. There he produced a group of atmospheric watercolours that are far from formulaic in their response to the setting.[2] He afterwards drew on these for an oil painting exhibited at the Royal Academy in 1837: *Snow-storm, avalanche and inundation – a scene in the upper part of the Val d'Aouste, Piedmont*.[3] It was presumably an awareness of that work that encouraged the first known owner of this later canvas to make the topographical link with his own painting.

Turner's renewed interest in alpine subject matter culminated in the annual tours he made of Switzerland between 1841 and 1844, and the series of unsurpassed late watercolours, including *The Red Rigi* (cat. 31). It is now also clear that Turner embarked on a small group of Swiss oil paintings during this later period.[4] In terms of its handling of paint, and its suggestion of solid and aerial forms, this painting has far more in common with these final Swiss works, and has rightly been dated to the 1840s. Nevertheless, over the last thirty years, some scholars have been inclined to associate the work with a group of about ten pictures in which Turner reworked some of his *Liber studiorum* designs, linking it with the published mezzotint of *Ben Arthur, Scotland* 1819.[5] More persuasively, however, in 2000 Hill proposed instead a link with the series of watercolour sketches Turner made of the Rhine falls at Schaffhausen in 1841.[6] The viewpoint is closest to a study in the Courtauld Institute of Art.[7] It looks across and down into the falls, where the certainties of the foreground give way to the turbulence and impenetrable spray churned up by the water, before it drops away to the right. Turner had depicted the Rhine falls in both 1806 and c. 1831–32, and his watercolours of 1841 indicate that he continued to find it a captivating motif.[8] So it is probable that he was returning to it again in this painting, but that he abandoned work once he had laid down the underlying structure. What we see was perhaps sufficient for his own eyes, even if the taste of the time would have required that he add more concrete information.

Ian Warrell

1. Martin Butlin, 'A newly-discovered masterpiece by J. M. W. Turner', *Art Bulletin of Victoria*, Melbourne: National Gallery of Victoria, 1975, pp. 2–10.
2. David Hill, *Joseph Mallord William Turner. Le Mont-Blanc et la Vallée d'Aoste*, exhibition catalogue, Aosta: Museo Archeologico Regionale, 2000.
3. Martin Butlin and Evelyn Joll, *The paintings of J.M.W. Turner*, New Haven: Yale University Press, 1984, cat. 371; collection of the Art Institute of Chicago.
4. Ian Warrell, 'Turner's late Swiss watercolours – and oils' in *Exploring late Turner*, exhibition catalogue, New York: Salander-O'Reilly Galleries, 1999, pp. 139–52.
5. Plate 69 in the *Liber* sequence; see Gillian Forrester, *Turner's 'Drawing book': The Liber studiorum*, London: Tate Publishing, 1996, p. 131.
6. Numbers 1460–69, in Andrew Wilton, *The life and work of J.M.W. Turner*, London: Academy Editions, 1979; see Hill p. 258.
7. Wilton, no. 1462.
8. *Fall of the Rhine at Schaffhausen*, exh. 1806, collection of the Museum of Fine Art, Boston; *Falls of the Rhine at Schaffhausen*, c. 1831–32, collection of the Birmingham Museums and Art Gallery.

47. Eugene von Guérard

Austria 1811 – Great Britain 1901
worked in Australia 1852–81
Bush fire between Mt Elephant and Timboon 1857 1859
oil on canvas on board 34.8 x 56.3 cm
Ballarat Fine Art Gallery
Gift of Lady Currie in memory of her husband the late Sir Alan Currie 1948

Von Guérard spent almost three decades in Australia, and painted more than 150 views and yet only three of his Australian canvases depict disasters.[1] Given the Romantic outlook imbibed in his Düsseldorf Academy training in the 1830s, it seems that calamitous natural events were not to von Guérard's taste. The Sublime had two sides: extremes of heightened emotion versus the realms of philosophy. The latter included the pictorial exposition of spiritual and scientific enquiry. Because von Guérard might not have witnessed any volcanic eruptions, floods or earthquakes, he could not paint them. But he did see this bushfire, as inscribed on the stretcher are the pencilled words: 'E. v. Guérard taken on the spot'.

The canvas of *Bush fire between Mt Elephant and Timboon 1857* is divided horizontally in the ratio of two parts darkened bush to three parts sky. A line of separation between Earth and the heavens is marked in spectacular fashion by yellow flames racing along the edge of the world. Reddened plumes of smoke billow out across the sky, while the full moon sheds a faint crepuscular light onto trees and ground. A long lake reflects the blaze, showing the opposing, but ill-matched, powers of water and fire. Barely discernable in the centre, galloping up through the bushland, come two figures on horseback, followed by a man on foot. While their urgency is apparent, they seem to be running towards the fire, rather than escaping from it.

The painting was executed in von Guérard's studio in Melbourne two years after the event, certainly based on the artist's sketches as well as his visual recollections. Two drawings of the bushfire have been identified, one in a sketchbook, the other made in pen, ink and watercolour.[2] The oil was exhibited in Geelong in 1869 under the title *Bush fire, taken on the spot from Meningoort, in March, 1857; locality, between Cloven Hill and Timboon, now Camperdown*.[3] Such details of personal experience, the exact place and time, all point to the artist's need to confirm the authenticity of his composition.

Von Guérard's acute scrutiny of the bushfire's unique effects is evident in the way he portrays a haze of smoke and cloud obscuring the clear sky. The fire and its smoke appear about to engulf the moon completely, as strong winds whip the bushfire across the horizon. As this moonlit natural phenomenon is so extraordinary, the normal palette of landscape painting cannot apply: there are no greens or blues here, nor any silvery nocturnal hues. Instead, the overpowering effects of black and red, which seem strangely modern in their simplicity, give intensity to the painting.

Christine Dixon

1. Enumerated as this bushfire scene and two shipwrecks, in Candice Bruce, Edward Comstock and Frank McDonald, *Eugene von Guérard 1811–1901: a German Romantic in the Antipodes*, Martinborough: Alister Taylor, 1982, p. 25.
2. Both collection of Dixson Galleries, Sydney, DGB16, vol. 5, folio 18, and DGD24, cited Bruce et al., p. 205.
3. The current title is inscribed on the back of the canvas.

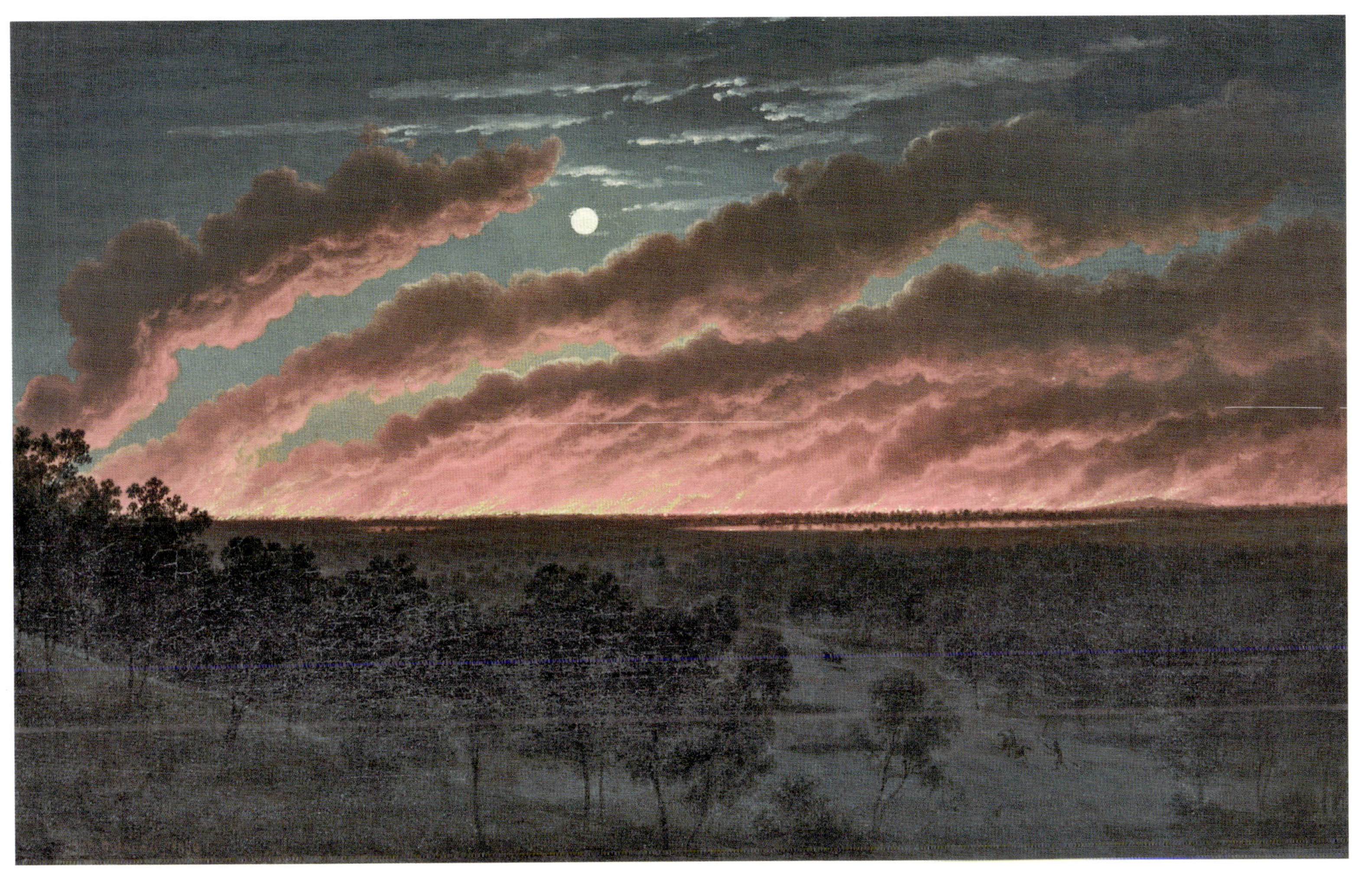

48. Isaac Walter Jenner

Great Britain 1836 – Australia 1902
Cape Chudleigh, Coast of Labrador 1893, reworked 1895
oil on canvas on composition board 76.5 x 126.9 cm
Queensland Art Gallery, Brisbane
Gift of the artist 1895 1:0014

A large, ambitious scene of arctic exploration, imagined fifty years after the event and half a world away, seems an unlikely Australian project. Jenner, a self-taught English immigrant painter, tried to establish a cultivated artistic climate in Queensland at the end of the nineteenth century. Such grand history paintings, employing all the stratagems of the Sublime, would make the artist's reputation unassailable, he thought, as well as serving another purpose, that of elevating public taste.

His subject was Sir John Franklin's doomed expedition of 1845, to find the fabled Northwest Passage between the Atlantic and Pacific Oceans. The venture fascinated the public, writers, and the press for decades; the British government, prodded by Lady Franklin, sent thirty-two expeditions to find the vanished explorers, Swinburne wrote a long poem in 1860, and Jules Verne published two novels inspired by the topic in the 1870s. Reports of cannibalism among survivors kept the story alive and scandalous.

Jenner remembered arctic scenery and details from a journey taken in his youth. He sailed in the early 1850s, he said, on 'a voyage to Lapland, Nova Zembla and Spitzbergen'.[1] At the age of eighteen in 1855, Jenner joined the Royal Navy for a decade, then retired to his birthplace, Brighton, to become an artist. Unhappy with his prospects as a marine and genre painter there, he emigrated with his large family to Brisbane in 1863. En route he witnessed the effects of Krakatoa's eruption, another instance of Nature's grand and sublime spectacles.

For his modern history painting *Cape Chudleigh, Coast of Labrador*, Jenner painted icebergs in Labrador, populated by hundreds of great auks – large, penguin-like birds, hunted to extinction in the 1840s. The whole is lit by a full moon under a cloudy sky. Apart from icy white and blue for freezing water, sea and sky, atmosphere and rocks are rendered in smoky brown and grey, with red reflected from the ship on fire behind an iceberg.[2]

The ghostly theatre of Franklin's fatal voyage is accentuated by Jenner's spectral depiction of translucent ice, a disappearing mountain and bizarre spectating birds, scattered like the ill-fated crew through the sea and absent land. Jenner's invisible hero, Franklin, was linked closely to colonial Australia's brief history: he accompanied Matthew Flinders on the *Investigator*'s initial circumnavigation of the continent in 1801–04, and served as Governor of Tasmania from 1836 to 1843.

Nonetheless, the artist's extravagant vision of the voyage was profoundly unfashionable. The extremes of the Sublime, especially delight in terror and heightened emotions, had dissipated their effect by the end of the century, while unsuccessful English explorers no longer caught the imagination of poets and engravers. European aesthetic manners and themes were replaced in Australia by the local and immediate paintings of the Heidelberg school.[3] Jenner was triply unfortunate, in that his subject and style were no longer appreciated, and any audience was sparse. Nonetheless, he ensured some posterity by reworking and donating this large canvas to the infant Queensland National Art Gallery upon its opening in 1895.

Christine Dixon

1. Margaret Maynard, 'Jenner, Isaac Walter (1837–1902)', *Australian Dictionary of Biography*, online edition, viewed November 2007, adb.online.anu.edu.au.
2. Gavin Fry, Bronwyn Mahoney, Bettina MacAulay, *Isaac Walter Jenner*, Sydney: Beagle Press, 1994, p. 34.
3. See Glen R. Cooke, Catalogue worksheet for Acc. number 1:0014, Queensland Art Gallery, ms.

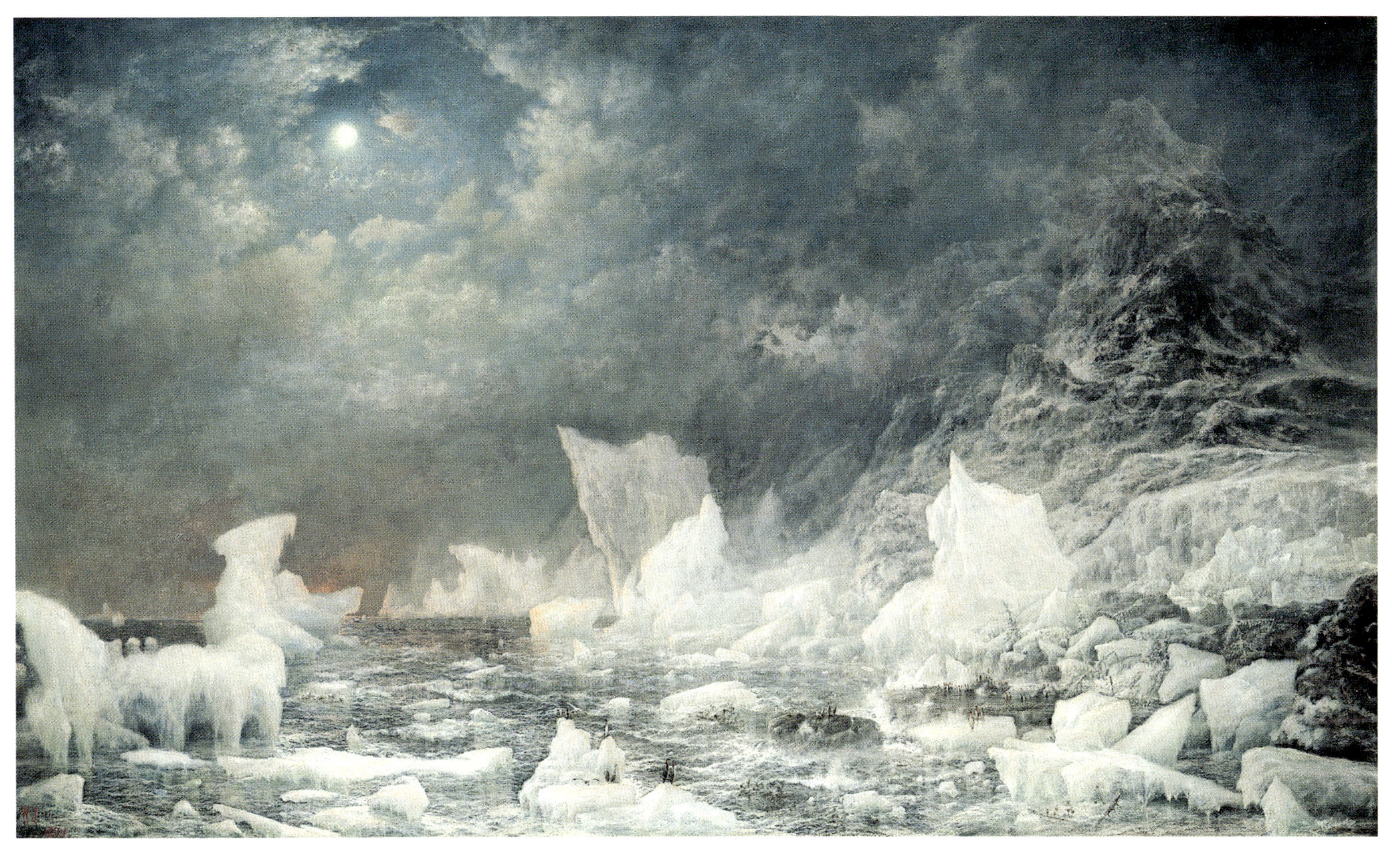

49. W.C. Piguenit

Australia 1836–1914
The flood in the Darling 1890 1895
oil on canvas 122.5 x 199.3 cm
Art Gallery of New South Wales, Sydney
Purchased 1895 6105

The 1890 flood of the Darling River was the subject of intense media coverage. It brought the harsh nature of the Australian climate into sharp focus, prompting Piguenit to travel to western New South Wales to witness firsthand the effects of the deluge on the surrounding countryside. The artist produced several sketches during this visit and these formed the basis of *The flood in the Darling 1890*, completed in 1895. The work, which is regarded as the pinnacle of Piguenit's artistic achievement, was bought for the collection of the Art Gallery of New South Wales following its appearance in the Art Society of New South Wales exhibition in 1895.[1]

Though it took no human lives, the flood had a devastating effect on farmlands and brought the agricultural boom to a decisive end. The impact of the disaster was far-reaching, and the challenges of living at the mercy of Australia's climactic extremes were brought home. Piguenit created *The flood in the Darling 1890* five years afterward, and it has been suggested that the work be read as a history painting.[2] This reading is supported by the work's monumental scale and its depiction of a momentous event that in 1895 was still fresh in the public imagination.

The image that Piguenit presents in the work is one of both desolation and awe; a portrait of the elemental forces of Nature and their astonishing power. The devastated land is devoid of life but for a small cluster of water birds. The flood stretches without break to the low horizon, where the glint of the sun's reflection on the unending waters indicates the extent of the disaster.

This silver sheet acts as a mirror to the painting's dramatic focus: the sky. Here heavy storm clouds give way to bursts of clear, bright sunshine, imbuing the work with a luminous glow. This radiance creates a sense of stillness and serenity that is at odds with the reality of the flood itself. The contrasting use of light in the fore- and background gives the landscape real emotional tension and leads one to the conclusion that it is more 'skyscape' than landscape.

The flood in the Darling 1890 is an ambivalent work which celebrates the harshness and unpredictability of Australia's natural environment, while recoiling from it.

Emilie Owens

1. Andrew Sayers in Elizabeth Johns et al., *New worlds from old: 19th century Australian and American landscapes*, Canberra: National Gallery of Australia, 1998, p. 185.
2. Tim Bonyhady in 'A brush with landscape: part one', 16 August 2007, radio transcript, ABC Radio National Sunday Special Program, viewed 31 October 2007, abc.net.au/arts/headspace/rn/special/brush/brush1.htm.

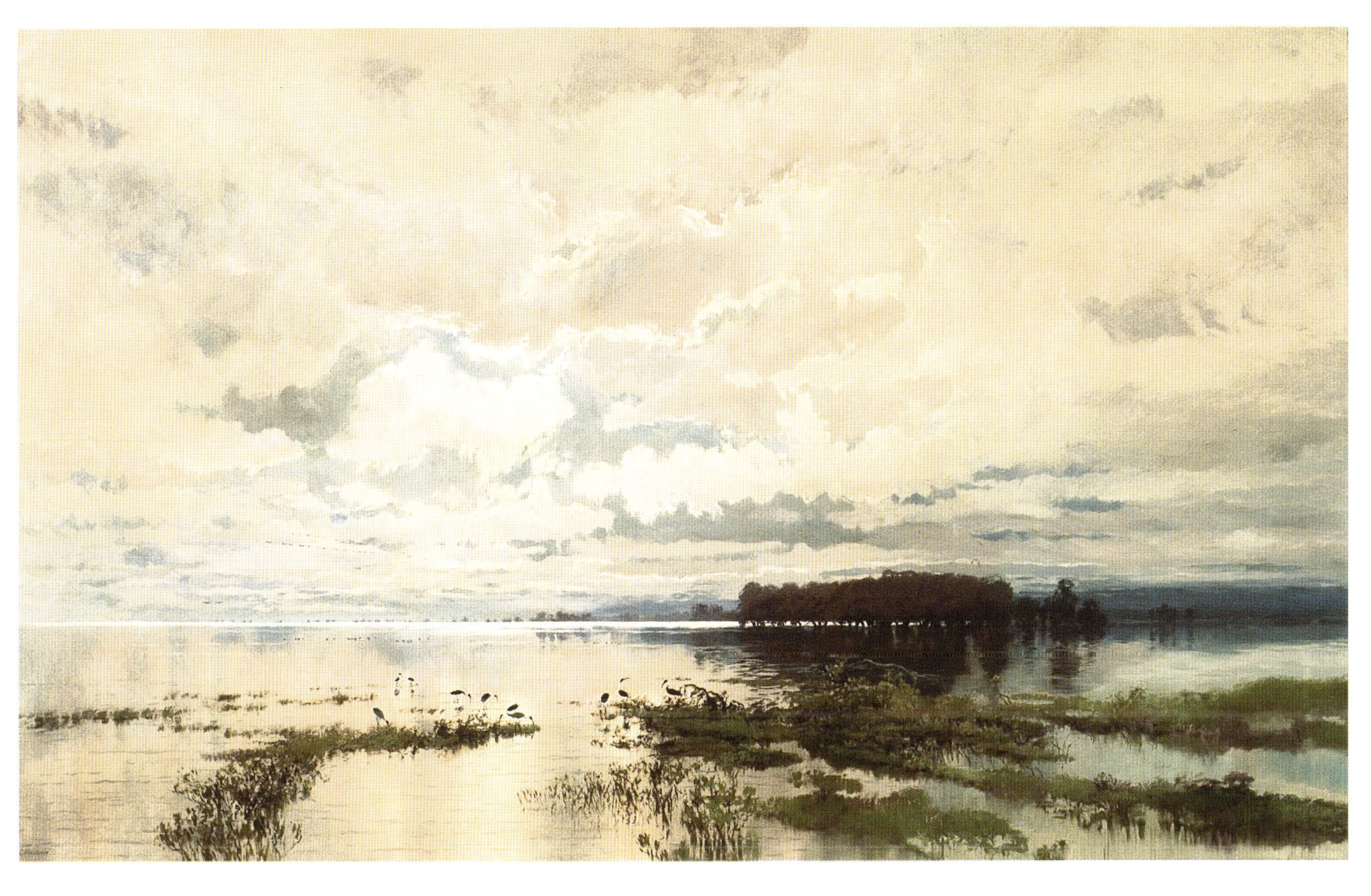

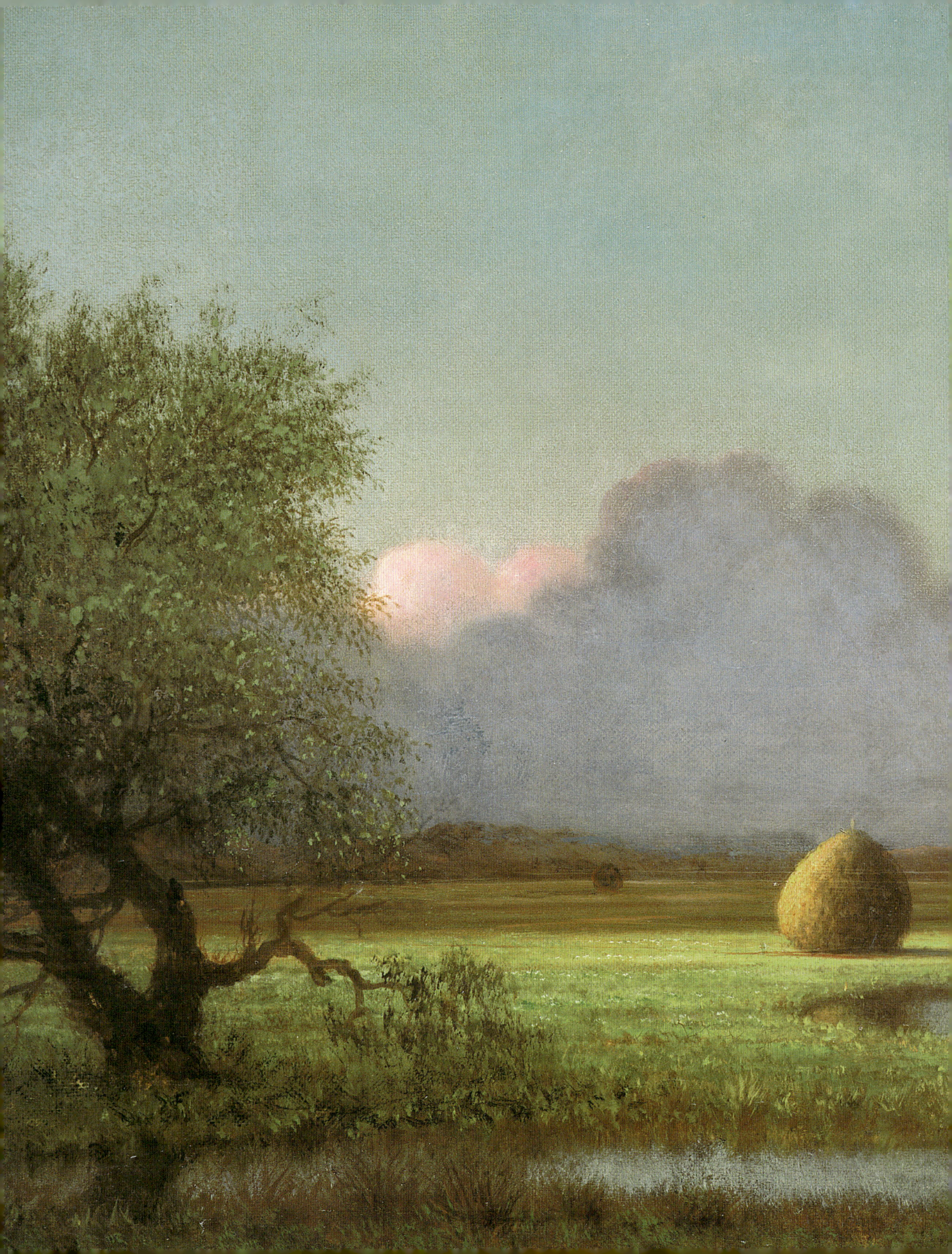

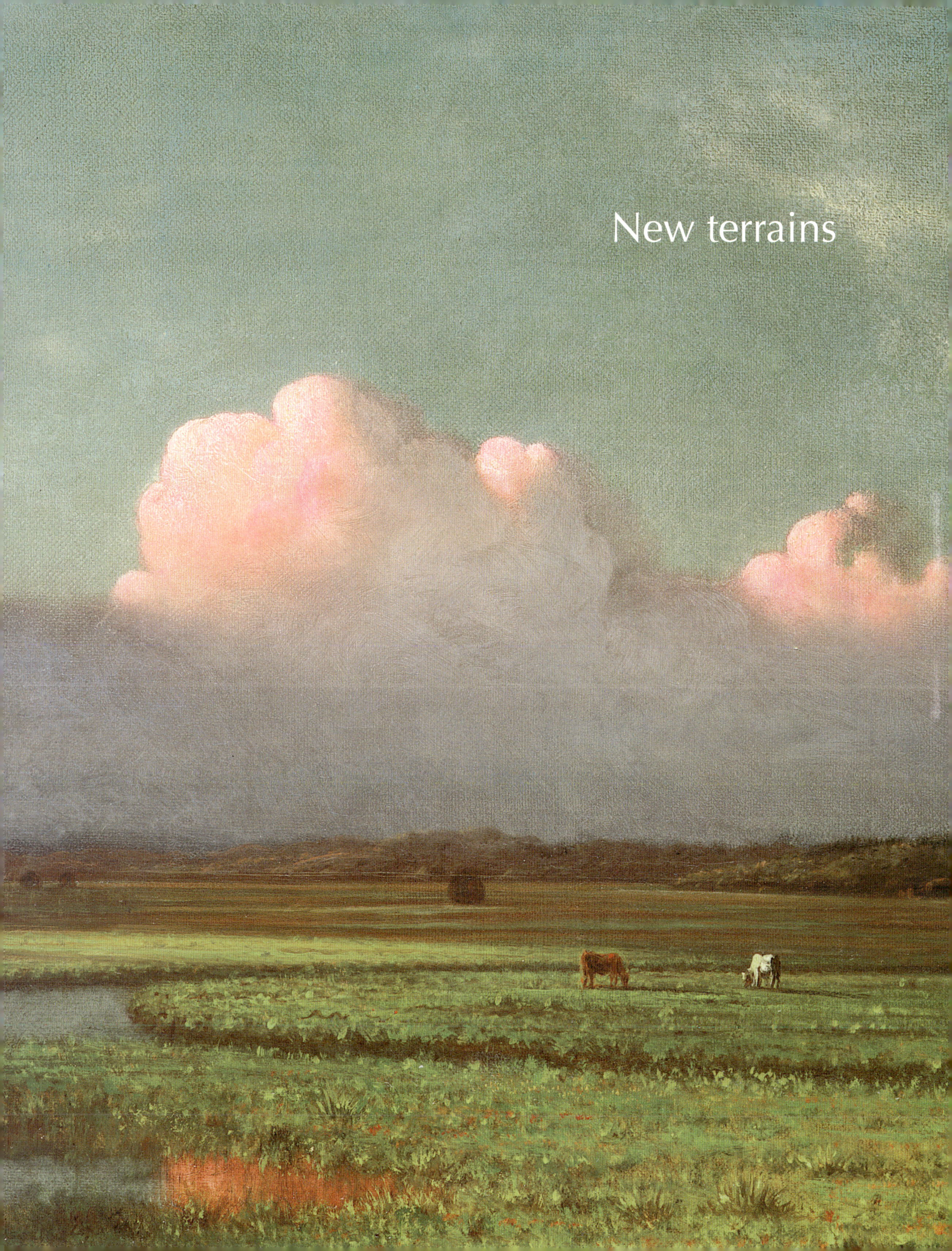

New terrains

50. William Westall

Great Britain 1781–1850
View of Sir Edward Pellew's Group, Gulph of Carpentaria 1802 1811
oil on canvas 88.0 x 100.0 cm
Ministry of Defence Art Collection, London

The scene is idyllic; abundant cabbage-tree palms sway on the beach as sea fowls soar above Pellew's Group of Islands in the Gulf of Carpentaria. In December 1802 the *Investigator*, under the command of Captain Matthew Flinders, sailed into the Gulf, continuing its arduous circumnavigation of Australia. Aboard the sloop was the young artist William Westall, who produced a wide range of sketches during his Australian voyage (see fig. 7, p. 7). Upon his return to England the Admiralty commissioned nine oil paintings of New Holland, including *View of Sir Edward Pellew's Group, Gulph of Carpentaria 1802.*

Art historians such as Bernard Smith have recognised that this is an innovative and remarkable painting.[1] It is notable both for its heightened sense of light and the well-defined horizontal lines, delicately intersected by palms. In standard Picturesque paintings the foreground is dark and brooding, receding to a light background, usually with one tall feature, such as a tree or a mountain, placed at the side to frame the composition. By placing the palms in the centre of a sun-drenched vista, Westall negates this customary sense of recession and avoids neatly enclosing the scene; instead it is left open, clear and light.

Painted nearly a decade after he was in the Gulf, Westall has made significant alterations to the original pencil sketch.[2] Most obvious is the addition of the *mia-mia*, a small shelter under which are housed *rangga*, sacred objects. In his account of the voyage, Flinders mentions 'a small monument' made up of 'two cylindrical pieces of stone', as well as nutmeg 'growing upon a large spreading bush' and 'a pretty kind of duck', all incorporated into Westall's work.[3]

For the artist, the 'monument' and other additions are useful because they give the painting that variety and interest demanded of Picturesque landscapes. Westall was clearly aware of Picturesque formulas when he made the changes to his original rough sketches. While in Australia scientific accuracy was Westall's priority, in London the paintings were intended to win him artistic acclaim. According to theorists such as William Gilpin, the Picturesque should stimulate the imagination to reverie or admiration, and must include a variety of elements. Westall believed the real Australia contained none of these fundamentals: he was scathing in his description of the 'barren' coastline, writing that his New Holland subjects could neither 'afford pleasure from exhibiting the face of a beautiful country, nor curiosity from their singularity'.[4] It was therefore incumbent upon him to use his artistic skills to compensate for the dull landscape by making improvements and adjustments.

View of Sir Edward Pellew's Group, Gulph of Carpentaria 1802 is an intriguing work. Westall has conformed to the Picturesque, adding the obligatory variety and interest, while also demonstrating how a new aesthetic can evolve in a new land.

Elisabeth Findlay

---

1. Bernard Smith, *European vision and the South Pacific*, 2nd edn, Sydney: Harper and Row, 1985, p. 196.
2. Collection of the National Library of Australia, Canberra.
3. Matthew Flinders, *A voyage to Terra Australis*, London: G. & W. Nicol, Vol II, 1814, entry for 25 December 1802.
4. Letter from William Westall to Sir Joseph Banks, 31 January 1804, Banks Papers CY3008/171-6, State Library of New South Wales, Sydney.

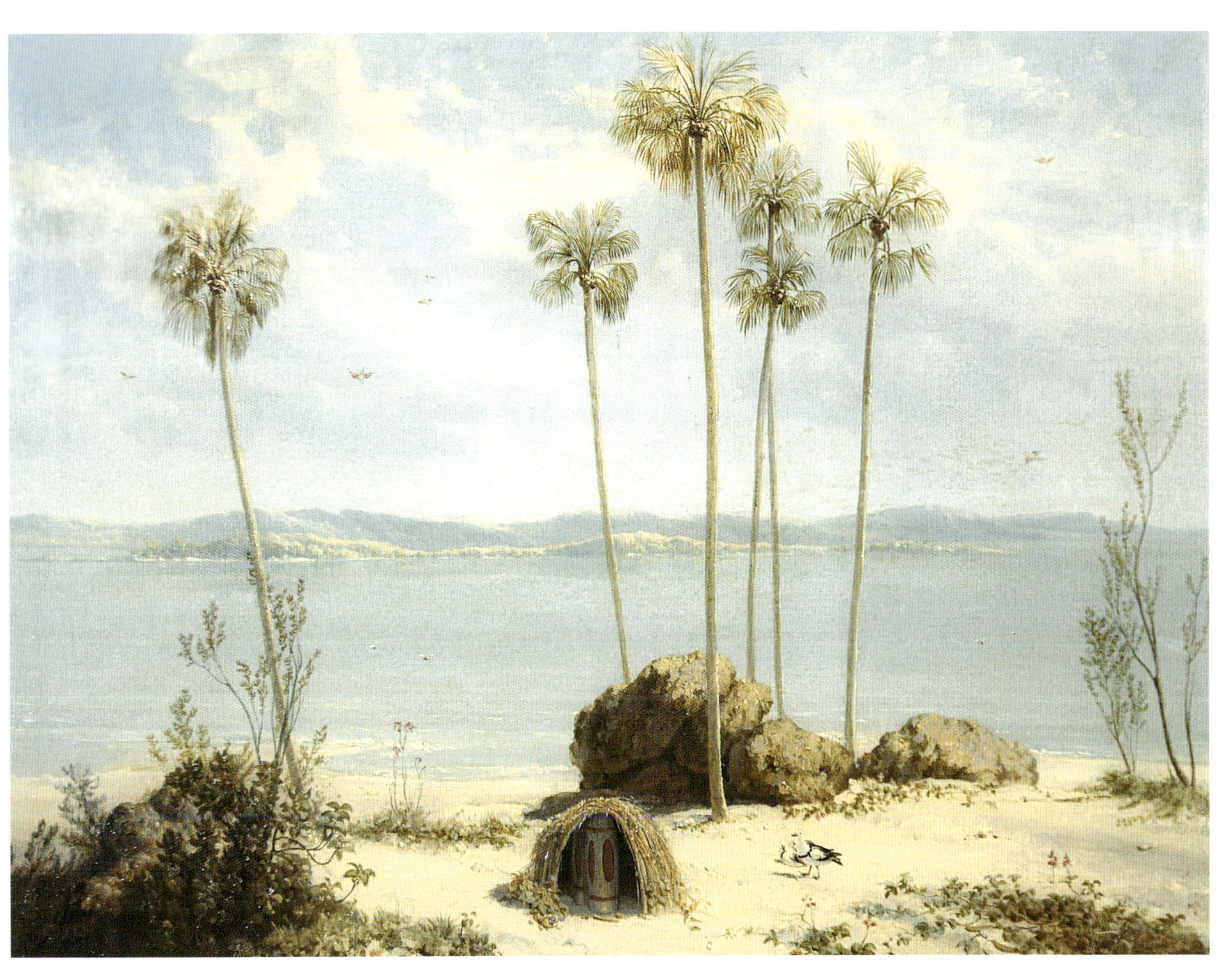

51. Thomas Cole

Great Britain 1801 – United States of America 1848
Peace at sunset (evening in the White Mountains) c. 1827
oil on canvas 69.0 x 82.0 cm
M.H. de Young Memorial Museum, Fine Arts Museums of San Francisco
M.H. de Young Art Trust Fund 46.13

The painter of American scenery has indeed privileges superior to any other; all nature is here new to Art. No Tivoli's, Terni's, mount Blanc's, Plinlimmons, hackneyed and worn by the daily pencils of hundreds, but virgin forests, lakes & waterfalls feast his eye with new delights, fill his portfolio … because they had been preserved untouched from the time of creation for his heaven-favoured pencil.
Thomas Cole's journal entry, 6 July 1835[1]

When he died in 1848 at the age of forty-seven, Cole was at the height of his fame. Known for allegorical and mystical paintings, he was the model for America's Hudson River School, especially for his only student, Church (cat. 55). Cole spent his youth in industrialised Lancashire in north-west England, arriving in the United States with his family in 1818. His early works combine stylistic elements of Claude and Salvator Rosa, representing the ideal of beauty and notions of the Picturesque, respectively. Cole's paintings are unique for their ability to persuade viewers that they have been catapulted into the American wilderness. Indeed, the slightly elevated viewpoint in many of his works makes us feel as though we are seeing wilderness for the first time.

Religion and landscape are inextricably intertwined in Cole's oeuvre. Like the Romantics before and Victorians after him, he believed that art should instruct, that a 'moral, religious or poetic effect be produced on the mind'.[2] Cole's artistic development coincided with, and in turn his art contributed to, a growing nationalistic interest in American scenery. Baigell explains:

> … to simplify brutally, the American landscape, no longer the howling wilderness of the Puritans, was considered the prime symbol of the American nation as well as a revelation of God's handiwork.[3]

Cole first visited the White Mountains in 1827 and this trip, as well as those to the Catskills, Adirondack Mountains and the Maine coast, made him a pioneer of landscape tourism.[4] Rugged and picturesque, the White Mountains of New England are part of the Appalachian system, which extends into southern Canada. In New Hampshire and western Maine especially, the mountains are much visited by nearby inhabitants of Boston and New York City.

Cole's description of American scenery and landscape is, conveniently, free from human presence. In *Peace at sunset (evening in the White Mountains)* the obligatory explorer is replaced by a lone deer and several birds. He renders the scruffy underbrush and jagged rocks in great detail. The stumps and blackened, bare branches – testament to nature's great destructive powers – symbolise the cycles of life and, to emphasis this, Cole sets a tree rich with new growth at the centre. Trees were also regarded as stand-ins for picturesque ruins. In this way the trunks at either side of the painting, leaning into the composition, may be imagined as the remains of a Gothic arch. The 'peace' of the title probably refers to an idealised period before the wilderness becomes frontier and the land is taken over for lumber and settlements, signalled by the coming storm.

Lucina Ward

1. Marshall Tymn (ed.), *Thomas Cole: the collected essays and prose sketches*, St Paul: John Colet Press, 1980, p. 131; and quoted in William H. Truettner and Alan Wallach (eds), *Thomas Cole: landscape into history*, New Haven: Yale University Press, Washington: National Museum of American Art, Smithsonian Institution, 1994, p. 51.
2. From Cole's unpublished essays, 'Notes on art', 1829, and 'Influence of the plastic arts', 1840, cited in Matthew Baigell, *Thomas Cole*, New York: Watson-Guptill Publications, 1981, p. 10.
3. Baigell, p. 10.
4. Cole was encouraged to explore the White Mountains, and had his itinerary prepared for him by his patron Daniel Wadsworth. The 1827 trip, another of the following year with the Boston artist Henry Cheever Pratt, as well as his 1839 tour with Asher B. Durand, provided Cole with material for a large number of paintings. See, for example, 'Thomas Cole: landscape and the course of Empire', in Truettner and Wallach, pp. 23–111, p. 51.

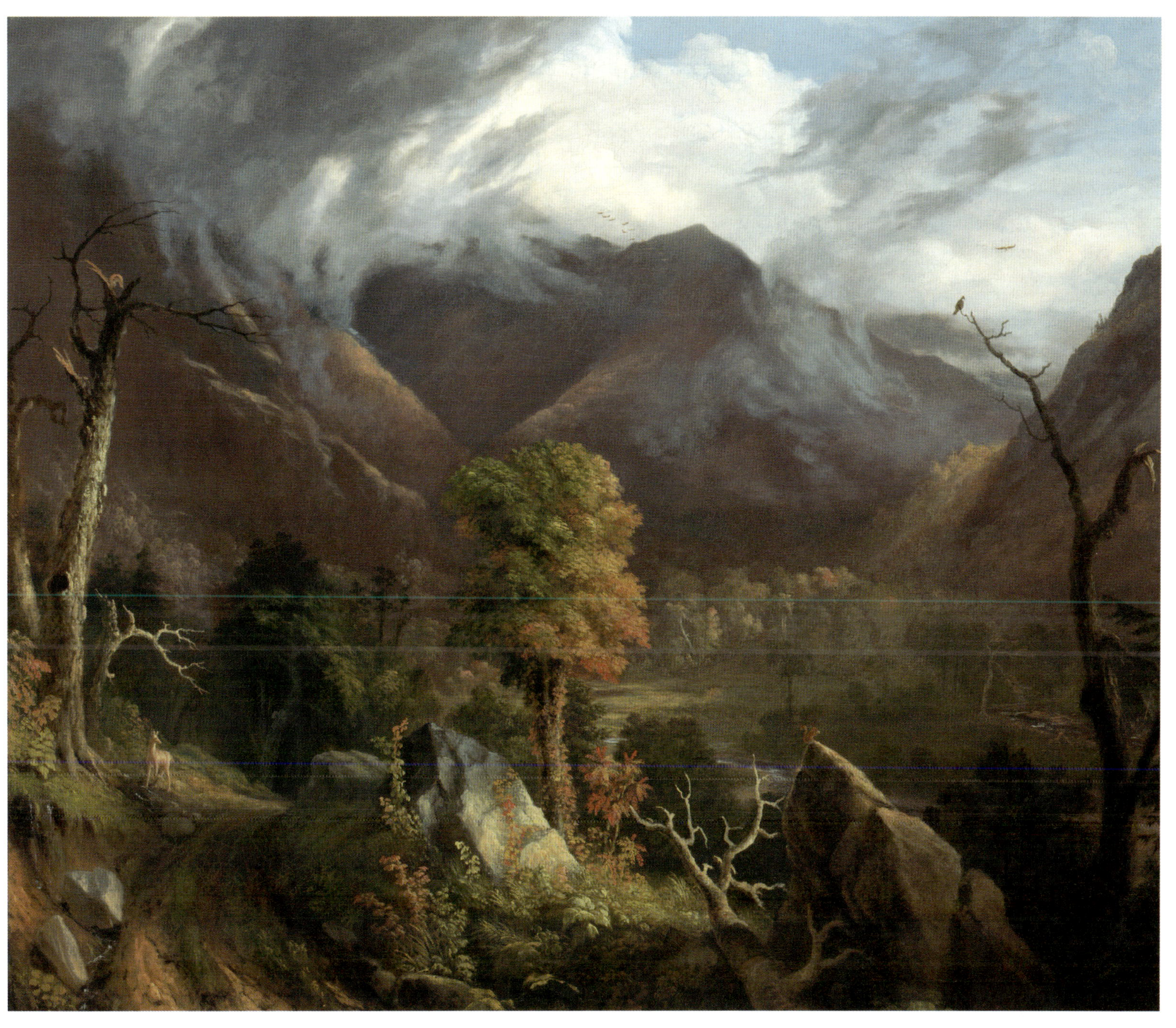

52. John Glover

Great Britain 1767 – Australia 1849
View of Mills Plains, Van Diemen's Land c. 1833
oil on canvas 76.2 x 114.6 cm
Art Gallery of South Australia, Adelaide
Morgan Thomas Bequest Fund 1951

View of Mills Plains, Van Diemen's Land signifies a breakthrough in Australian colonial landscape painting, as the country's first truly faithful Australian landscape.

Excited by the prospect 'of finding a new Beautiful World – new landscapes, new trees new flowers new Animals Birds …' in 1830 Glover cast off his successful English career and emigrated to Van Diemen's Land.[1] By March 1832 he had settled into his own microcosmic 'new Beautiful World' – his working agricultural and pastoral farm Patterdale, on Mills Plains near the northern Tasmanian town of Deddington, about forty kilometres south-east of Launceston. It was to become the artist's home for seventeen years, until his death in 1849.

View of Mills Plains, Van Diemen's Land was one of the first of several scenes of his beloved property painted by Glover from different vantage points during the 1830s. It was almost certainly among the more than sixty Australian subjects he sent to London to be exhibited in 1835. This distant rear view of his farm looks north-east into a low range of hills, and is painted from the lightly wooded wide valley that led south-west to the boundary of his neighbour, Mr Pitcairne. Blanketed in afternoon shadow, the tranquil scene is enlivened in the middle distance by the fall of soft, illuminating light which reveals in miniature detail the very nucleus of the artist's world: his recently built two-storey stone house, purpose-built studio/'exhibition room', farm dwellings and his paling-fenced 'first garden'. This ambient view of rural domesticity demonstrates seventeenth-century Dutch accents. However, Glover's accurate rendering of the form and colour of the Australian environment makes the work, and many of those soon to follow, the most significant of his entire European and Australian oeuvre, and the finest landscapes of the early colonial period.

After his arrival in Van Diemen's Land, Glover astutely observed 'a remarkable peculiarity in the Trees in this Country; however numerous, they rarely prevent your tracing through them the whole distant Country'.[2] He played with the distinctive permeability of eucalyptus tree foliage within his compositions and, arguably for the first time in his career, relinquished trees from their primary role as 'framing' devices, by spreading them from the edges horizontally across the middle ground of his Australian landscapes. And while, spiritually, *View of Mills Plains, Van Diemen's Land* represents a sense of belonging, visually it celebrates the magnificence of the Australian eucalyptus tree. Positioned here in the central foreground, with its arched, regal canopy forming the apex of the composition, Glover pioneers the elevation of the tree as a subject in its own right.

The delicate organic patterning of the gum's majestic canopy, backlit by the high-keyed sky, resonates like a beautiful Eastern religious architectural *jali*, or perforated screen. Separated from the Old World, and worshipping all that surrounded him in his 'new Beautiful World', Glover created a fresh vision by painting from the inside looking out.

Tracey Lock-Weir

1. Letter from Glover to Sir Thomas Phillipps, 15 January 1830, ms. Phillipps-Robinson, b.124 f 92, Bodleian Library, Oxford, cited in David Hansen, *John Glover and the Colonial Picturesque*, Hobart: Tasmanian Museum and Art Gallery and Art Exhibitions Australia, 2003, p. 86.
2. *A catalogue of sixty eight pictures descriptive of the scenery and customs of the inhabitants of Van Dieman's Land, together with views in England, Italy, &c. painted by John Glover, Esq. Now exhibiting, at 106, New Bond Street* [*sic.*], London, E. Morgan, 1835, note on no. 36, Launceston and the River Tamar (cat. 68), cited in Hansen, p. 98.

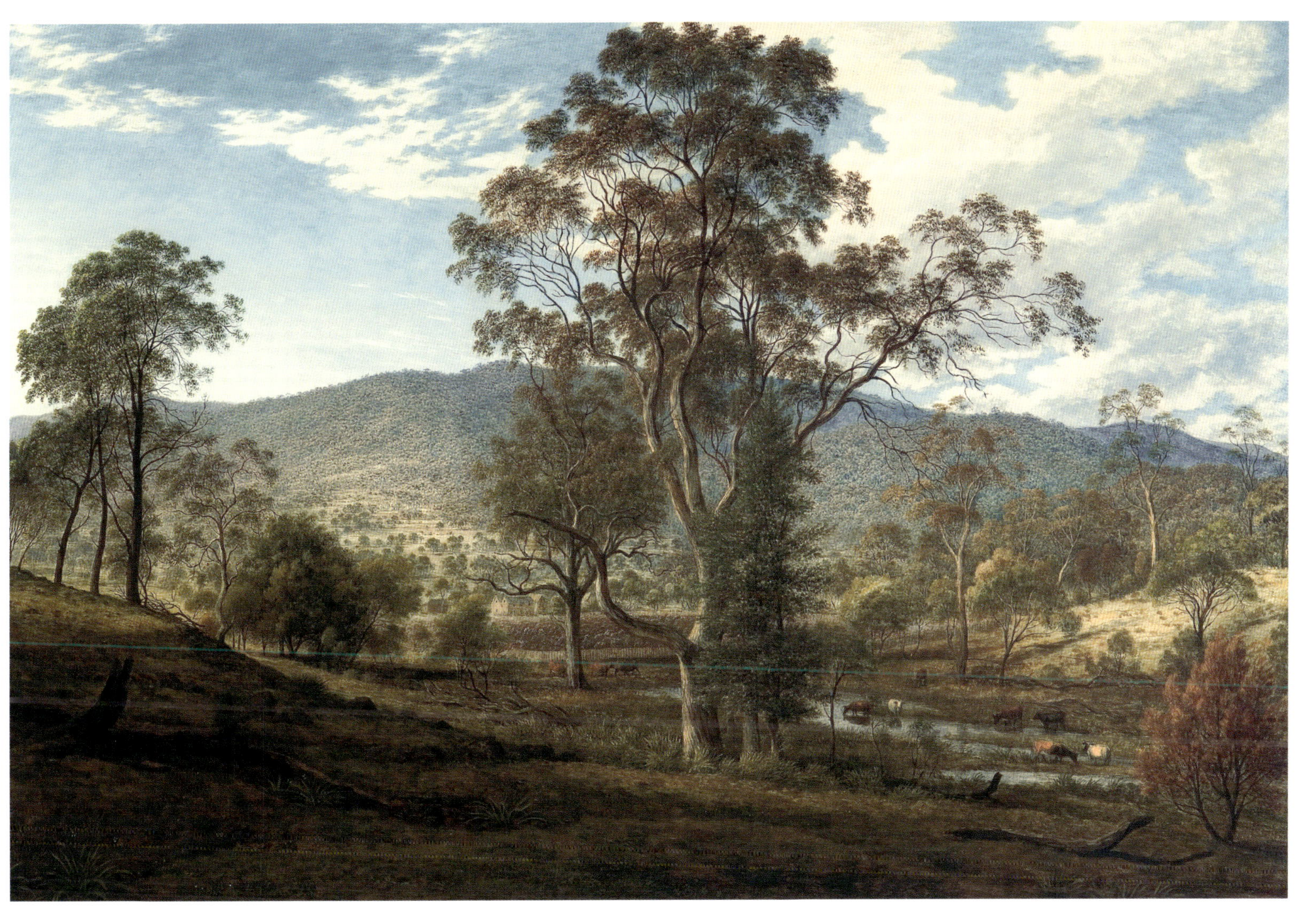

53. John Glover

Great Britain 1767 – Australia 1849
'Cawood', on the Ouse River 1838
oil on canvas 75.5 x 114.0 cm
Tasmanian Museum and Art Gallery, Hobart
Presented by Mrs George C. Nicholas in memory of her husband, 1935

Glover is undoubtedly Australia's most important colonial artist before 1850 and one of the most significant landscape artists of his generation working outside Europe. After a successful career in England, he arrived in Van Diemen's Land (now Tasmania) on 18 February 1831, the day of his sixty-fourth birthday. Reinvigorated by his new location he created fresh imagery, views of the land suffused with light.

'Cawood', on the Ouse River is one of Glover's magical late landscapes in which he looked down on the scene from above and created a panoramic vista. The sky is luminescent, the tree-spotted hills drenched in warm sunlight, and the light radiating over the landforms and glistening on the trees makes it appear a 'blessed place', a pastoral arcadia. Glover showed Australia as a place of plenty, a land of sheep and cattle (and a few wallabies). In doing so, he overlooked any hardships which he – and other settlers – experienced in developing their land.

Here, unlike so many of his British and early Australian landscapes, he rejected a Claudean viewpoint with trees framing the composition and instead conveyed the wide-open space of his new country. He depicted an open foreground with the arced edge marked by a line of eucalypts and acacias and shows the plains and rolling hills beyond as an extensive expanse. These trees have a leafy transparency, typical of Australian eucalypts, in contrast to the dense mass of English foliage. He turned from a darker palette to a lighter one of pinks, oranges, pale greens and blues.

Glover based this portrait of a rural property on a preliminary drawing of 1837–38 in which he depicted numerous tree stumps in the foreground. These indicate the landowner's vigorous program of clearing native vegetation, and also suggest the triumph of order over the unruly antipodean bush. Glover hinted at the threat of untamed nature by showing the extensive walls and fences which protected the owners and their livestock from bushrangers and the wild.

Cawood is located on the River Ouse in the Derwent Valley in southern central Tasmania, eighty-eight kilometres north-west of Hobart. The property belonged to Thomas Frederick Marzetti, an Englishman of Italian extraction, who was granted a thousand acres shortly after his arrival in Van Diemen's Land in May 1824. He named his property after the town of Cawood on the River Ouse in Yorkshire. According to David Burn, the colonial playwright who lived in the area in the 1840s, Marzetti's Cawood became known, amongst other things, for the 'unbounded hospitality of its proprietor'.[1] Marzetti, however, subsequently found himself in financial difficulties and was forced to sell Cawood in 1844.

When Glover visited the property in the late 1830s it was well established with a large Georgian-style family homestead, numerous outbuildings as well as a dovecote or fowl house and beehives. He portrayed the homestead with extensive outbuildings, together with the cattle grazing in one paddock, a shepherd with his dogs and a flock of sheep in another and the suggestion of haymaking closer to the house. He presented Cawood as a highly productive and thriving property, a monument to hard work and labour – and to God's bounty.

Anne Gray

1. *Cawood farm cottage*, viewed November 2007, cawoodfarmcottage.bigpondhosting.com.

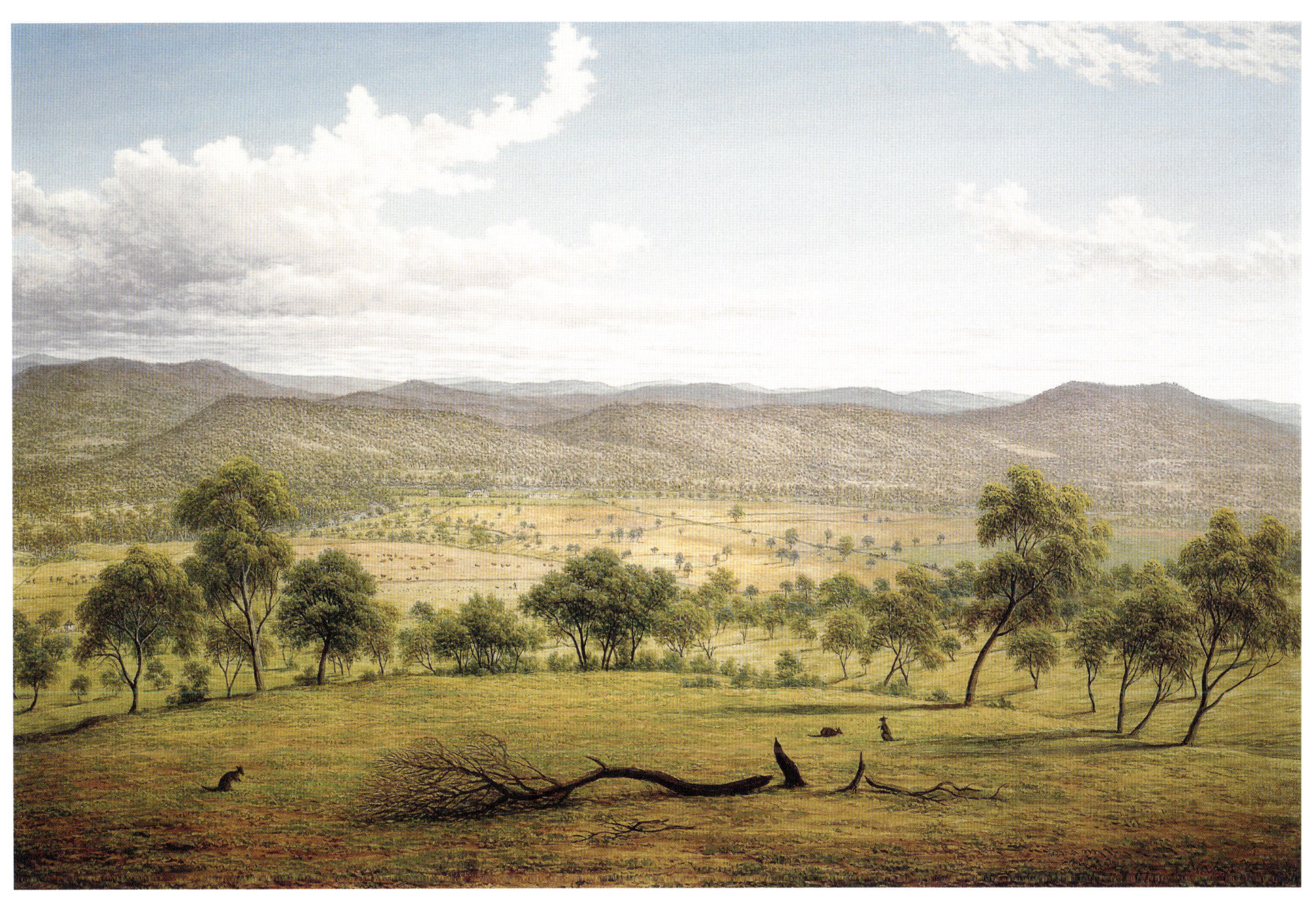

54. Alexandre Calame

Switzerland 1810 – France 1864
Torrent in the Alps [***Torrent des Alpes***] 1849
oil on canvas 57.8 x 76.0 cm
Collection of Asbjorn R. Lunde, New York
 Photograph: Michael Agee

A torrent of icy water breaks through age-old rocks in the Swiss mountains. Each summer the river wears away its stony bed, in a perennial race of melting alpine snow. The artist depicts the scene as a horizontal layering of elements: sky above, mountains and trees across the centre, water and rocks in the foreground. All seem moderate in size until you notice two human figures on the left. They are tiny in comparison with the rest of God's handiwork: Calame shared that Romantic vision of Nature as a manifestation of divine creation, with moral lessons to be offered on the brevity of human life.

The man and woman in *Torrent in the Alps* are examples of *staffage*, a pictorial device used to provide a measure of scale, or to add interest for the viewer. Here, he stands while she sits, two walkers in the mountains briefly pausing to observe the scene. Like the viewer of the painting, they already know how to appreciate those elements that make up the beauty of landscape. By the middle of the 1800s this pictorial convention was secure, although the subject of wild scenery had little art-historical foundation until Salvator Rosa painted his 'savage' landscapes in seventeenth-century Italy.

Calame, little known now, was one of the most famous and successful artists of his day, primarily because his mountain scenes caught the public's imagination due to their naturalistic fidelity and drama. The Swiss Alps, their beauty barely articulated by painters or poets until the eighteenth century, became an extremely popular subject, especially in the benign mood shown in *Torrent in the Alps*. Calame also portrayed extremes of weather: storms and blizzards figure large in his pictorial vocabulary. Despite many drawings made *en plein air*, his paintings exemplify the picturesque manner of composition, that is, coherent combinations of differing motifs. Patrons who commissioned a painting could choose which elements they wanted to him to include. Andrés lists some in the artist's repertoire: 'streams, torrents, lakes, glaciers, rocks, waterfalls, steep slopes, cliffs, peaks, firs, beeches, stumps, wind, storms, snow, sunrises and sunsets …'[1]

Torrent in the Alps was painted a year after the signing of a new Swiss constitution. It settled the brief civil war of 1847 between Protestant and Catholic cantons, in which the Helvetian Federation was confirmed and the Jesuit order banned. While the painting seems to contain no overt political meaning, Calame, a devout Protestant, is nonetheless recognisably Swiss. He frequented lake and alpine areas honoured in Switzerland's history, especially Brunnen and Lake Lucerne.[2]

Calame influenced New World painters such as Nicholas Chevalier and Albert Bierstadt, both of whom lived in Switzerland in the 1840s and 1850s. Chevalier (cat. 57) studied in Lausanne from 1845 to 1850, and certainly knew Calame's work. The German-born American Bierstadt (cat. 61) worked in Germany, Austria and Switzerland in the 1850s. His first success took place in New York with a Swiss subject, *Lake Lucerne* 1858.[3] Bierstadt admired Calame, although we do not know whether they met. The artists exhibit traits in common: painstaking observation, meticulous brushwork, sparkling highlights, and awe at Nature's might.

Christine Dixon

1. Alberto de Andrés, *Alpine views: Alexandre Calame and the Swiss landscape*, Williamstown: Sterling and Francine Clark Art Institute, 2006, p. 25.
2. De Andres pp. 11–12.
3. Collection of the National Gallery of Art, Washington.

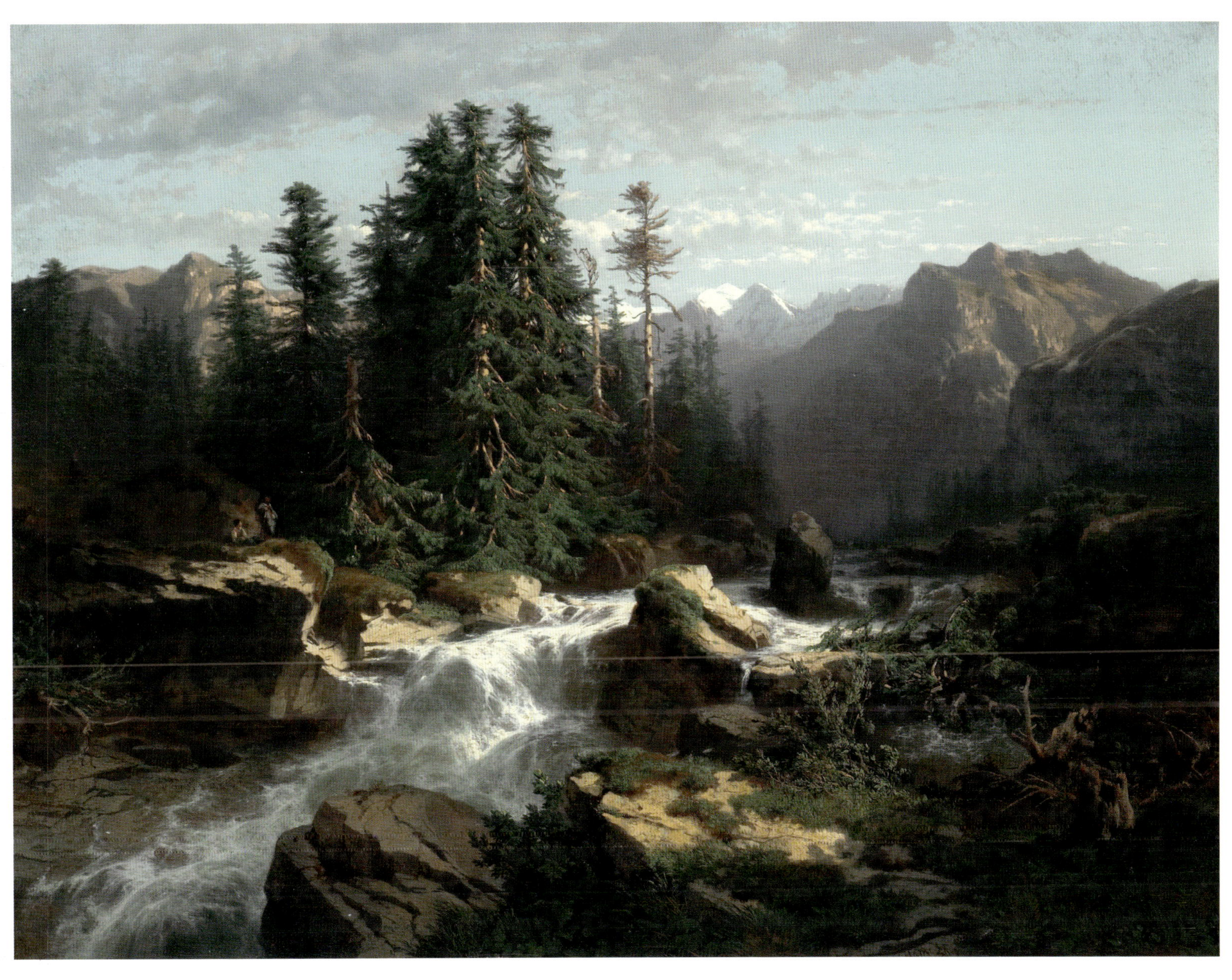

55. Frederic Church

United States of America 1826–1900
South American landscape 1856
oil on canvas 59.5 x 92.0 cm
Collection Carmen Thyssen-Bornemisza

This is a devotional image, paying homage to science, Nature and God. Huge in its pictorial implications, the painting is nonetheless modest in size. *South American landscape* is one of the 'prototype' South American subjects the thirty-year-old Church composed before embarking on his magisterial *Heart of the Andes* 1859, which lifted him to first place among American artists.

In *South American landscape* Church responds to the renowned geographer Alexander Humboldt who identified the Andes as best portraying the separate ecologies that together made the global geography. Humboldt's theory stemmed from an expedition to South America from 1799–1804, when he and his companions travelled from tropical jungle at sea level to mountains with permanent snow. Charles Darwin, travelling to South America thirty years later – with Humboldt's writings in hand – found evidence that a parallel to Humboldt's adaptive ecologies existed in biology. Church, visiting Colombia and Ecuador in 1853, deliberately set out to capture in art Humboldt's geography of the cosmos.

Looking at the painting, it soon becomes apparent that this is not a landscape taken from one place. Rather, it is an assemblage of unlikely points of view which combine to overwhelming effect. Judged by photographic realism, the scene is frankly impossible; yet it is precisely because the painting lacks a governing perspective that the artist is able to suggest a scale that is measureless. Church's concept is therefore unlike the panoramic landscapes by von Guérard, Bierstadt and Daubigny, which show the scope of a scene from a single vantage point (cat. 41, 61, 68, 73).

Church painted for an audience whose aesthetic embraced the idea that the path to inspiration was through education. Within this approach, *South American landscape* expresses two types of 'truth'. One is the truth of inspired imagination; another is the minutiae of description. Knowledgeable viewers in the mid-nineteenth century used opera glasses to study the details incorporated into the picture from Church's many field drawings. Failing a handy magnifying glass, we still view the image as a composite of separate parts, each with its own scale and perspective.

Multiple possibilities offer themselves. Following the path of light from a bridge and waterfall gleaming in the chasm on the left, the eye is led vertically to a church poised on the peak of a mountain. The dark, sheer rugged country between those signs of human habitation conveys a subliminal message that the eye may travel where a human body cannot. Another kind of separation is implied on the other side, where a figure strolls towards us along a sun-striped path. A giant in comparison to the trees flanking the path, the figure is likewise strangely dissociated from the scene by a nonchalant disregard for what it portends. Behind is a tumescent mountain capped with snow, hazed and ruddy-coloured below, where it rises from a labyrinth of impassable mountains and bottomless clefts. This scene cannot conform to practicable travel, even tourism to the exotic: it is visionary.

The urgency of Church's vision of natural ecology is relevant again in our time. The canvas suggests vast natural rhythms of an ongoing natural evolution on a scale that stretches human faith and imagination. Disjunctive landscape forms and abrupt conjunctions of tones and colours enforce incredible combinations, whereby a tropical palm is cheek-by-cheek with eternal snow. The idea of order seems interchangeable with cosmic disorder.

Mary Eagle

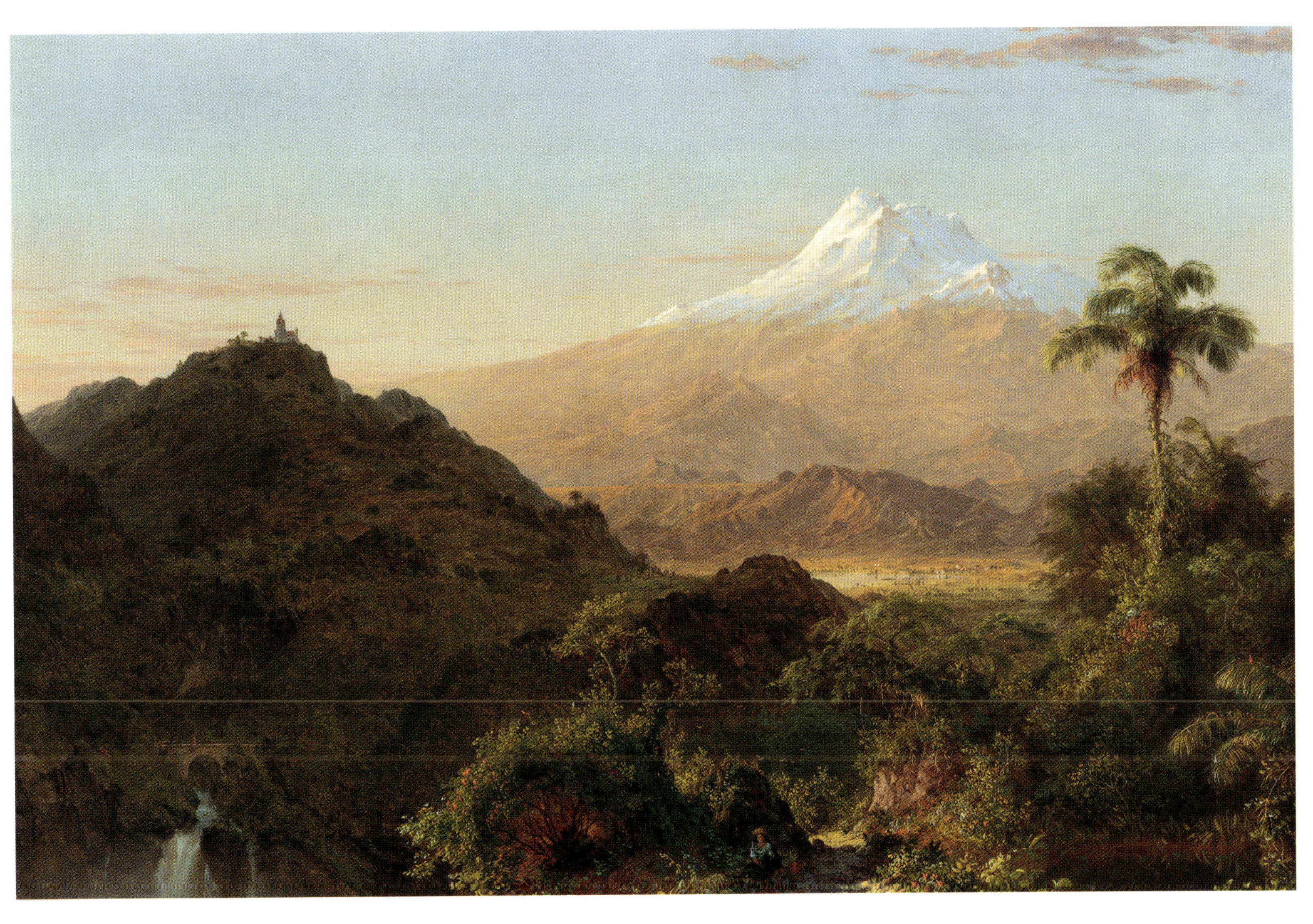

56. William Bell Scott

Great Britain 1811–1890
Ailsa Craig 1860
oil on canvas 32.5 x 48.9 cm
Yale Center for British Art, New Haven
Paul Mellon Collection, USA B1976.7.151

Situated off the southwest coast of Scotland, the pyramid-shaped island of Ailsa Craig lies at the entrance to the Firth of Clyde. The artist–poet Scott took this curious landmark as the centrepiece of his painting of the Ayrshire coastline, with the Isle of Arran and Kintyre Peninsular on the horizon. Executed with an almost preternatural clarity and attention to detail, *Ailsa Craig* epitomises the mid-century Pre-Raphaelite landscape and that movement's clarion call to 'go to nature in all singleness of heart … rejecting nothing, selecting nothing and scorning nothing'.[1]

An intimate of D.G. Rossetti, Scott was familiar with Pre-Raphaelite ideals. Parallels exist between his landscapes and those of William Holman Hunt, which also depicted sunlit scenes of sheep at pasture with views of a 'glittering sea' beyond.[2] Scott did not, however, prescribe to the Pre-Raphaelite practice of painting outdoors directly from the object, and promoted instead his own regimen of sketching from nature. In his *Autobiographical notes* he declared:

> I have always believed the best unofficial education for an artist is daily sketching … If he in this way records … every beautiful feature or form he observes, not only in … active human life, but also in vegetation or among the lower animals, he will be real and natural in expressing whatever he invents … [F]or designing, for thinking pictorially, the vital habit necessary is observing and recording … the multitudinous aspects of nature.[3]

In *Ailsa Craig* Scott carefully records the evidence of human life (drystone walls and steam ship) as well as the local vegetation and 'lower animals' (yellow flag, Scotch thistles and blackfaced sheep) within a harmonious light-filled composition that is both true to nature and resolved in design and intent. He artfully weaves the various patterns within his composition – the trail of the steamer through the waves, the sheep paths on the hills, and the spring trickling through the strata of rocks – to suggest the more fundamental journey of natural creation through time.

Alongside these deeper ruminations, the painting of *Ailsa Craig* held great personal significance for the artist, for the island could be seen from the battlements of Penkill Castle, the home of Scott's 'dear' friend, Alice Boyd.[4] Scott first visited this ancient fortified house, situated on a promontory above the beautiful Glen of Penwhapple, in the summer of 1860, and was soon inspired to paint some 'delightful landscape subjects'.[5] Scott had produced few such works before this period, and later acknowledged the site's catalytic role:

> The glen below the house was most interesting to me, and revived my ancient landscape proclivities. Every summer for nearly ten years I painted there. The 'friendship at first sight' [with Boyd] was confirmed.[6]

The sun-drenched view of *Ailsa Craig*, executed during that first visit, could thus be seen as much as a metaphor of Scott's new-found personal happiness, as a reflection of his professional fascination with the rugged scenery.[7]

Alison Inglis

1 John Ruskin, in *Modern painters*, vol. 1, 1843, quoted in Allen Staley, Christopher Newall et al., *Pre-Raphaelite vision: truth to nature*, London: Tate Publishing, 2004, p. 25.

2. See Allen Staley, *The Pre-Raphaelite landscape*, 2nd edn, New Haven: Yale University Press, 2001, p. 122; Alison Smith in Staley and Newall, 2004, pp. 36, 52; Malcolm Warner and Julia Marciari Alexander, *This other Eden, paintings from the Yale Center for British Art*, New Haven: Yale University Press, 1998, p. 160.

3. William Minto (ed.), *Autobiographical notes of the life of William Bell Scott*, 2 vols, London: Osgood, McIlvaine & Co., 1892, vol. 2, pp. 43–4.

4. For Scott's relationship with Alice Boyd, see W.E. Fredeman, 'The Letters of Pictor Ignotus: William Bell Scott's correspondence with Alice Boyd, 1859–1884', *Bulletin of the John Rylands University Library of Manchester*, vol. 58, 1975–76, pp. 66–78.

5. Minto, vol. 2, p. 59.

6. Minto, vol. 2, pp. 75–6.

7. Jane Vickers identified *Ailsa Craig and Arran: a summer day by the sea, July 1860* as one of Scott's landscapes in James Leathart's collection, increasing the parallels between Holman Hunt and Scott; see *Pre-Raphaelites: painters and patrons in the north east*, Newcastle upon Tyne: Tyne and Wear Museum Service, 1989, p. 103.

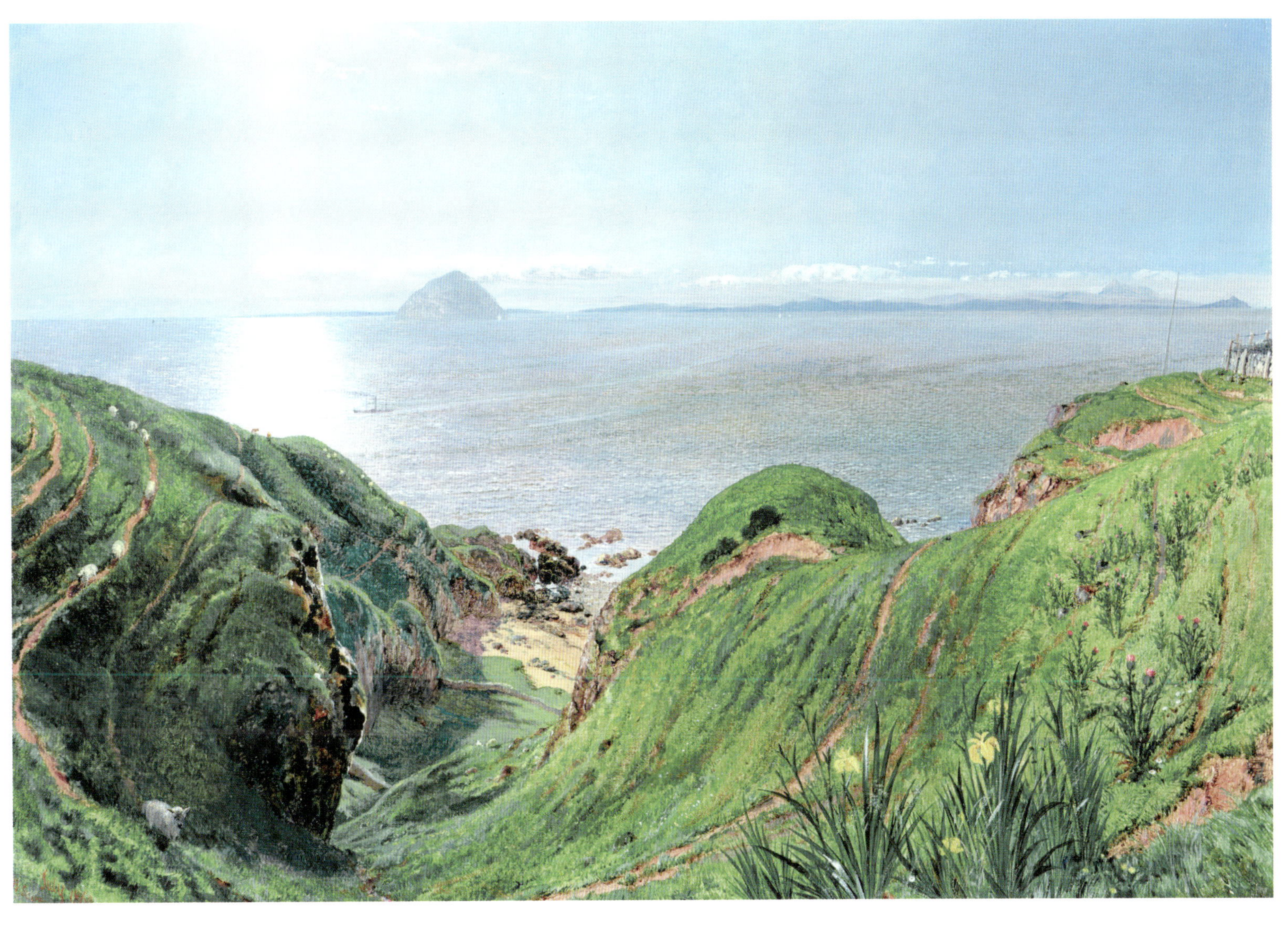

57. Nicholas Chevalier

Russia 1828 – Great Britain 1902
worked in Australia 1854–69
Mount Arapiles and the Mitre Rock 1863
oil on canvas 77.5 x 120.6 cm
National Gallery of Australia, Canberra
Gift of Dr Joseph Brown AO OBE 1979 1979.2344

Chevalier arrived in Australia on Christmas Day 1854, during the gold rush. He spent the next fifteen years in Australia and New Zealand, where the cosmopolitan artist executed landscapes in that grand tradition he had learned in Europe. Born in St Petersburg of a Russian mother and Swiss father, he studied painting in Lausanne at the Musée Arlaud under Jean Samson Guignard, and later architecture in Munich. He then worked for the lithographer W.H.L. Gruner in London – useful experience later when he made his living as a newspaper and magazine illustrator and cartoonist, notably for Melbourne *Punch*. However, Chevalier's ambitions lay in high art and, with his father's help, he studied watercolour painting in Rome in 1853–54.

Chevalier first visited Mount Arapiles, thirty kilometres west of Horsham in the Wimmera district of north-western Victoria, in May 1862.[1] He and von Guérard (cat. 41) accompanied the Bavarian scientist Georg von Neumayer on his official expedition, a magnetic survey of the colony. Such collaborations were common at the time, part of the Humboldtian ambition to describe the world. The commanding presence of Mount Arapiles was first documented by a European, the explorer Major Thomas Mitchell, in 1836. He inscribed a name with Spanish military associations on the Australian map, replacing Djurite, used by the local Djurid Balug people.[2] The striking Mitre Rock was named for its likeness to a Christian bishop's headdress.

By the time Chevalier visited the area, the mountain and nearby monolith were part of a station owned by Alexander Wilson. He or his brother Charles commissioned the painting, which was exhibited in Melbourne in 1864 to high praise. In *Mount Arapiles and the Mitre Rock* the artist attempted to portray the might of nature compared with puny human presence. This was an important theme of the Sublime, the aesthetic doctrine pondering the awe-inspiring, indifferent and immeasurable vastness of Creation. Picturesque elements such as cattle – animals new to the ancient continent – are insignificant in the foreground, while the surveyors' camp is all but obscured under the trees. Neumayer wrote in his report that on 5 June 1862 the party 'enjoyed a magnificent view of the setting sun'.[3] This inspired Chevalier, who contrasted the enduring granite of the rocks with evanescent light effects. The artist seems overwhelmed by the large – and lurid – Australian sky, which dominates the painting.

Despite its Romantic subject matter – spectacular rock formations and a magnificent sunset – the painting stands within a conservative naturalist tradition. Carefully delineated details are combined with a highly finished surface, perhaps revealing the artist's primary aim to be topographical accuracy, the visual description of a geological marvel. His technique reveals the artist's training in watercolour, while his seemingly exact transcription of a dazzling coloured sky limits any larger imaginative project. The evening sun's light reflects from Mount Arapiles on the left and from the water below: Chevalier reins in more emotional or poetic associations.

Christine Dixon

1. See Tim Bonyhady, *Australian colonial paintings in the Australian National Gallery*, Canberra: Australian National Gallery, 1986, pp. 40–5.
2. He named Arapiles after the Spanish mountains where Wellington, the British commander, defeated the French army at the battle of Salamanca in 1812. Mitchell fought there, a part of the long struggle of the Napoleonic Wars.
3. *Results of the magnetic survey of the colony of Victoria executed during the years 1858–64*, Mannheim: Schneider, 1869, p. 54, quoted in Bonyhady, p. 41.

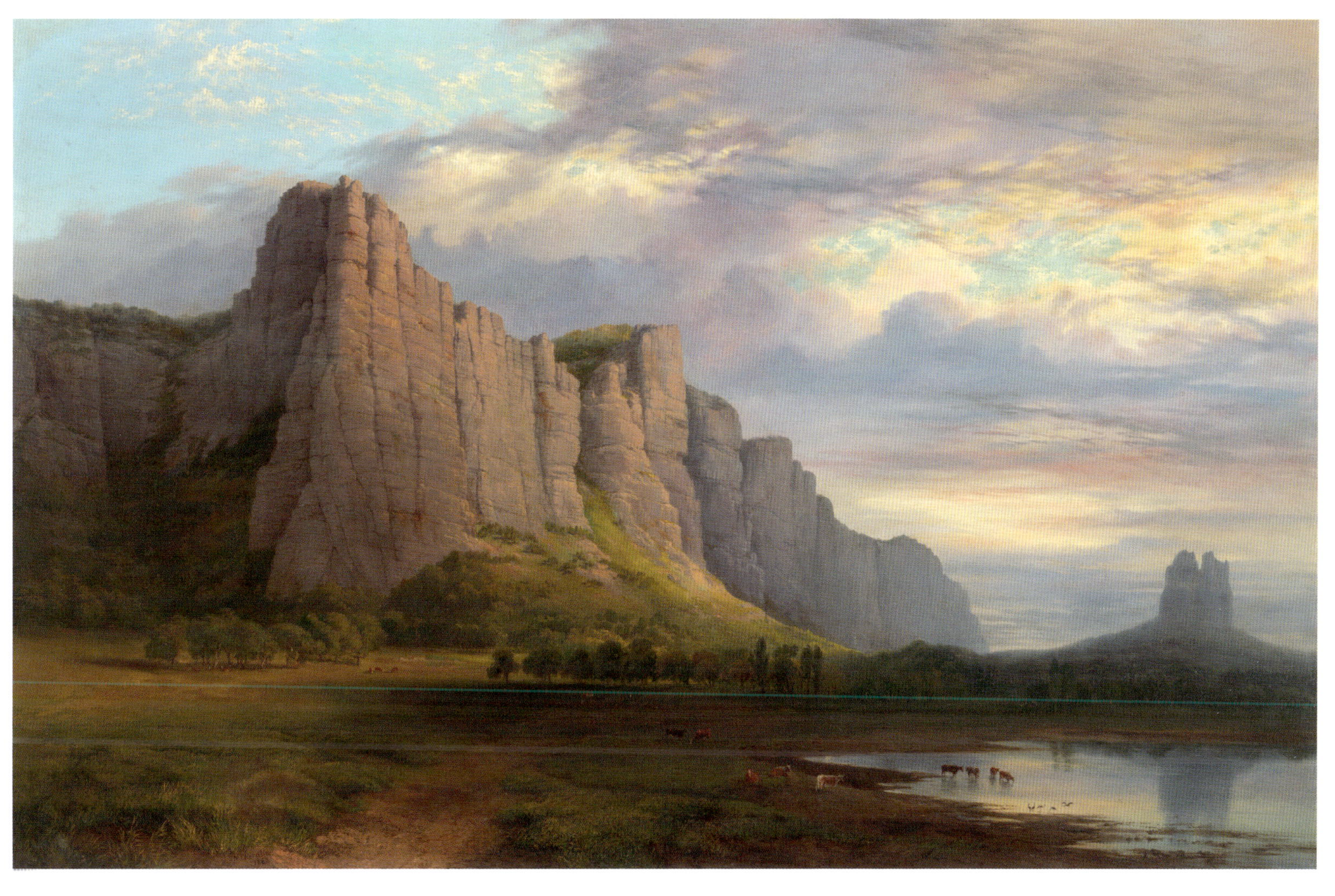

58. Eugene von Guérard

Austria 1811 – Great Britain 1901
worked in Australia 1852–1881
Milford Sound, New Zealand 1877–79
also known as ***Milford Sound with Pembroke Peak and Bowen Falls on the west coast of the Middle Island, New Zealand***
oil on canvas 99.2 x 176.0 cm
Art Gallery of New South Wales, Sydney
Purchased 1970 OA1.1970

Von Guérard sailed into Milford Sound on the SS Otago on the evening of Monday 24 January 1876. The passengers on the eagerly anticipated four-and-a-half day voyage from Melbourne were not disappointed. Myriad waterfalls dashed down the steep sides of the granite peaks, following recent rain, and the clouds lifted to reveal Mitre Peak and Mt Pembroke – their towering forms reflected in the mirror-like surface of the fiord.

The Otago dropped anchor by Bowen Falls at 7 pm. Von Guérard 'at once had himself conveyed to an island' where he executed sketches, and three drawings documented with notes on colour and vegetation, before the midsummer sun finally set.[1] From his chosen viewpoint he developed a panoramic composition of a series of pyramidal forms that stretch across the canvas, rising above the line of the water and reflected in it. Through the power and austerity of the composition, von Guérard communicates the monumental scale and geological age of the dark, angular rocky peaks, the depths of the fiord and the haunting silence of the Sound. His own personal experience is registered in the vignette of tiny figures seen disembarking from their rowboat. Their exhilaration at finding themselves in a place described by a journalist on the Otago as 'unsurpassed, if equalled, by any cynosure of beauty on the earth's surface', is palpable.[2]

The intensity of von Guérard's response to Milford Sound was informed by his scientific interest in its geology and vegetation.[3] Contemporary reviewers, such as the writer for the *Argus*, who referred to 'the steamer, floating like a child's toy at the foot of one of the "awful cliffs"', responded to Milford Sound in terms of the British Sublime.[4] The Sublime played a part in von Guérard's vision, but a more revealing context for understanding his portrayal of the subject is the scientific and specifically geological direction taken by German landscape painting in the early nineteenth century. Carus (cat. 35), in his *Nine letters on landscape painting*, argued for a new type of landscape art, one that revealed the history of the Earth's formation through a scientifically accurate portrayal of its geology. In *Milford Sound* von Guérard observed and portrayed the hard, erosion-resistant character of the granite, gneiss and diorite rock formations and the vertical ridges of their foliated geological structure. The glacier at the top of Mt Pembroke – a flash of white in a predominantly dark composition – is a reminder of the glacial activity that shaped this landscape over six million years ago.

Von Guérard's New Zealand journey was the last of his many expeditions in the southern hemisphere. The two major works from this trip, *Milford Sound* and *Lake Wakatipu with Mount Earnslaw, Middle Island, New Zealand* 1877–79, were immediately acclaimed by contemporary reviewers.[5] *Milford Sound* was exhibited at the Exposition Universelle de Paris in 1878, and won a 'First degree of Merit Special for Landscape Painting' at the Sydney International Exhibition in 1879.

Ruth Pullin

1. 'The Otago's Trip to Milford Sound', *Otago Witness*, Issue 1262, 5 February 1876, p. 7.
2. *Otago Witness*, p. 7.
3. Von Guérard's scientific accuracy is also evident in his portrayal of the plants found at Milford Sound. It is probable that the feathery flowered grasses in the foreground are the species *richardii*, a member of the *Cortaderia* genus. It is known by the Maori as *toe toe*. My thanks to Richard Neville, Conservation Botanist, Royal Botanic Gardens, Melbourne, for identifying this plant species.
4. *Argus* (Melbourne), 2 January 1877, p. 4.
5. Collection of the Auckland Art Gallery Toi o Tamaki.

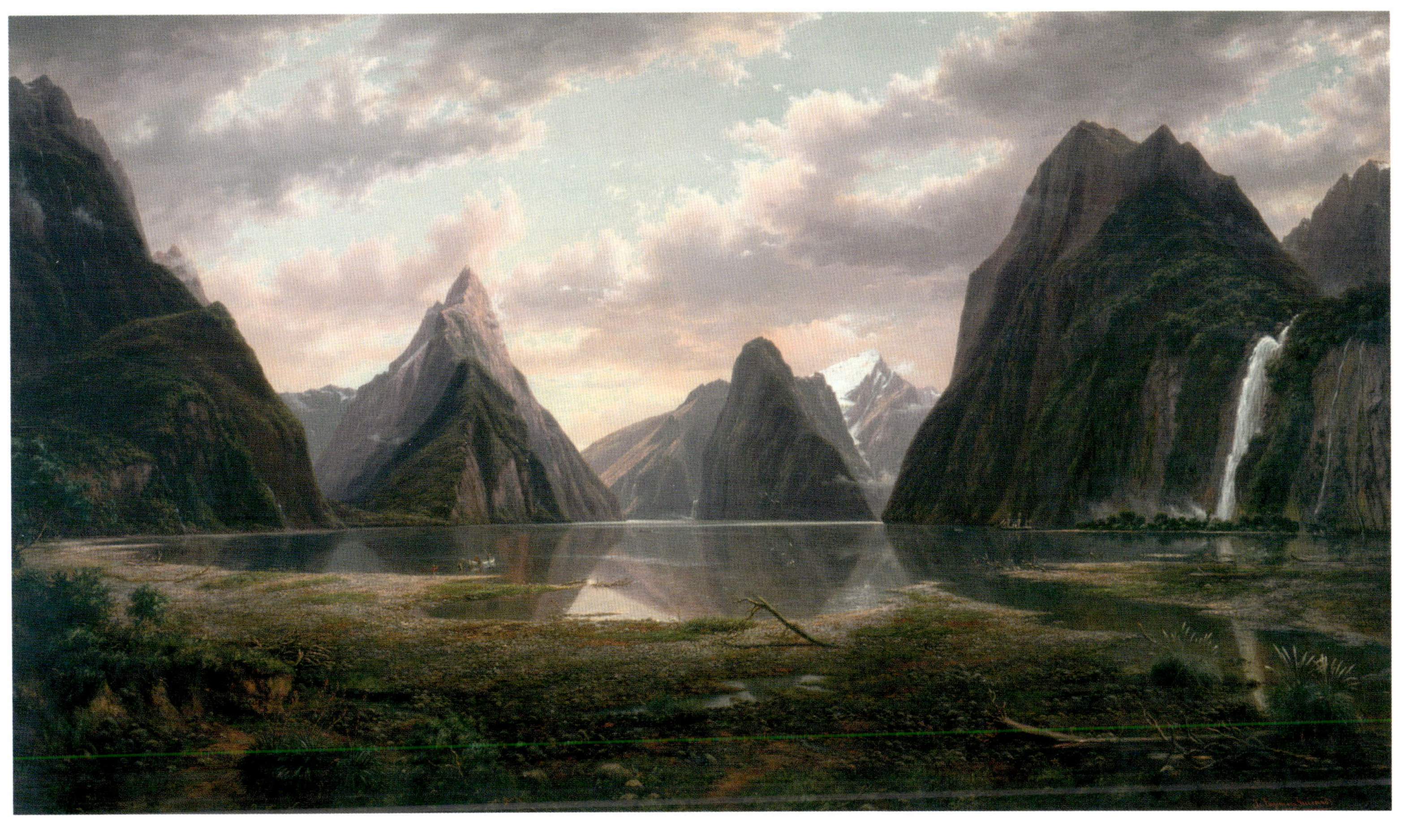

59. Martin Johnson Heade

United States of America 1819–1904
Sunlight and shadow, the Newbury Marshes c. 1871–75
oil on canvas 30.5 x 67.3 cm
National Gallery of Art, Washington
John Wilmerding Collection
Image courtesy of the Board of Trustees, National Gallery of Art, Washington

Three bands make up the painting: a blue sky, pink and grey clouds, the green meadow. A tree at left frames the composition, the central haystack provides a point of focus, a few animals add extra interest, and some exquisite reflections persuade us of the artist's painterly skills. If we were to follow the thin, flat bayou meandering through the marshland, where would it take us? The distant hills have none of the grandeur or drama expected of landscapes at this period. Even the hand of the artist seems peculiarly absent. We are left with a haystack at the centre of the painting which, on closer examination, is a rather strangely shaped mound. Where, exactly, are we?

Marshlands – at the mouth of the Parker River in Ipswich, Massachusetts, or Hoboken in New Jersey, or Southport, Connecticut – held a great fascination for Heade; he produced more than a hundred paintings of the subject. These canvases have various descriptive titles: passing or approaching storms, sudden shower, after the rain, sunrise, sun breaking through, after the rain. Our attention is drawn to the natural forces and meteorological phenomena that shape these environments. Clearly, it was the changing atmospheric conditions and variations in light that attracted the artist. Is this what fascinates us still?

Heade began painting salt marshes in about 1858 and continued to paint them for more than four decades, in pairs, thematic groups, or as long series. He worked on marshland subjects intermittently, alternating them with Romantic mountain, tropical, southern or northern landscapes.[1] At times, for variety, Heade included duck hunters or their hutches, hayricks or covered haystacks in his marsh scenes – he even created still-life paintings of marsh canvases propped up on trestles.[2] Despite all these variants, even with *staffage*, the best of Heade's paintings are characterised by a mysterious emptiness.

Just as a marsh is a transitional zone between land and water, Heade's Luminist paintings sit slightly apart from those of the Hudson River School. Like many of his contemporaries, Heade travelled widely: in his early twenties he spent two years in Rome, travelled in Brazil from 1863 to 1864 and his life in the United States was peripatetic. *Sunlight and shadow, the Newbury Marshes* encapsulates both major European aesthetic traditions: idyllic, light-filled scenes or intense, northern specificity. Looking at Heade's marsh paintings, those who value stillness may be think of Friedrich's *The Great Preserve* c. 1832 (fig. 15, p. 25). Conditions of light in both paintings – twilight in Friedrich's, the combination of sunlight and shadow in Heade's – liberate colour from naturalism, contributing an intriguing violet tinge to each scene. Both artists use unnatural colour palettes, and only a few motifs. But like composers, they obtain seemingly endless variations from these notes. In *Sunlight and shadow, the Newbury Marshes*, Heade makes the ordinary exotic. Lurid colours give the painting a hallucinatory quality, the solitary haystack takes on mystical power, and the deceptive simplicity of the scene makes it seem hyper-real. Here the Sublime verges on the transcendental.

Lucina Ward

1. Heade and Church were close friends – Church passed his studio, in a 10th St New York, to Heade – and Church also encouraged his interest in South America (see cat. 55).
2. See *Gremlin in Studio II* c. 1871–75, Wadsworth Atheneum, Hartford; for this and others, see Theodore E. Stebbins et al., *The life and work of Martin Johnson Heade: a critical analysis and catalogue raisonné*, New Haven: Yale University Press, 2000.

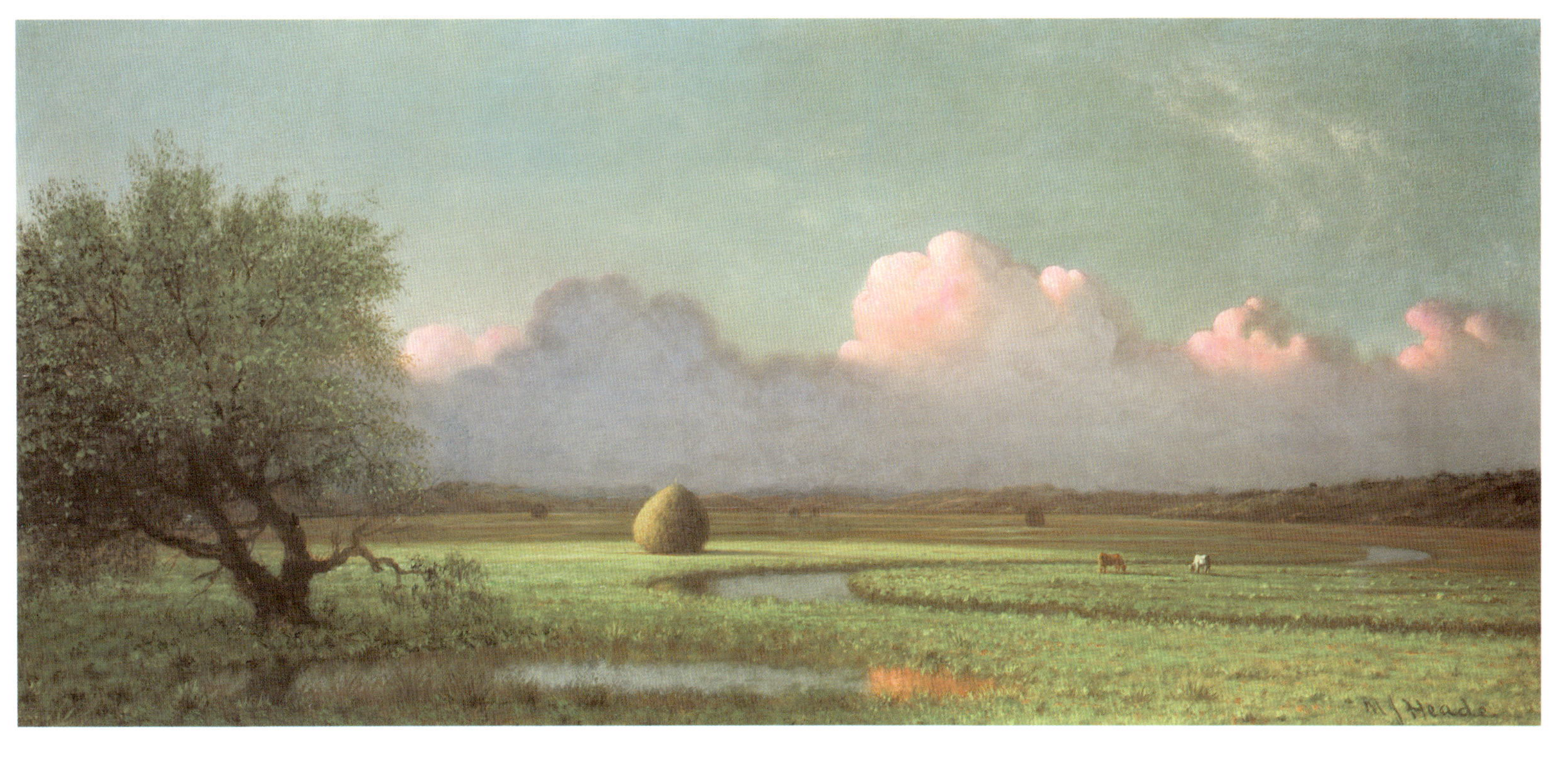

60. Thomas Moran

Great Britain 1837 – United States of America 1926
Hot springs of the Yellowstone 1872
oil on canvas 41.1 x 76.2 cm
Los Angeles County Museum of Art, California
Gift of Herbert M. and Beverly Gelfand M.84.198

The panoramic majesty and epic, scenic *terribilità* of America's West still defy description. Numerous commentators have remarked upon how the catastrophic American Civil War of 1861 to 1865 encouraged the damaged nation to look to the largely unexplored West as an unspoiled site of hope and renewal, where a new national identity could be cultivated. In the late 1860s the miracle of Yellowstone, a volcanic wonderland spread across Wyoming and Montana, remained shrouded in mystery, tales of its geothermal surreality disregarded as superstitious fabrications.

In 1871 Ferdinand Hayden allowed Moran to accompany his federally funded scientific expedition to Yellowstone as a guest. Recognising the inadequacy of words and scientific data alone to document this extraordinary region, Hayden also employed the photographer William Henry Jackson to record Yellowstone's myriad wonders. Moran's trip was funded privately by the publisher of *Scribner's Monthly* magazine and the financier of the Northern Pacific Railroad, who both sought to profit from the nation's interest in unlocking the secrets of this strange and daunting wilderness. Collectively, Hayden's official report on the region's immense natural resources, Jackson's photographs and Moran's confrontingly beautiful watercolours, were to influence the 1872 US Congress to preserve Yellowstone by declaring it the nation's first national park – indeed, the first in the world.

Time has cemented Moran's achievements as an artist working directly in tandem with the concerns of a ground-breaking voyage of geographic discovery and documentation. For Moran, the experience of visiting Yellowstone was utterly transforming. As he wrote to Hayden:

> I have always held that the Grandest, Most Beautiful, or Wonderful in Nature, would, in capable hands, make the grandest, most beautiful or wonderful pictures, and that the business of a great painter should be the representation of great scenes in Nature. All the characteristics attach to the Yellowstone region.[1]

One of the most distinctive features of Yellowstone is the Mammoth Hot Springs, which one member of Hayden's party in 1871 described as:

> one of the grandest sights imaginable. Before us rose about 600 feet a mass of white sediment arranged in separate terraces looking like a vast frozen cascade. Each one of the terraces has a number of hot springs, while in beautiful basins (formed of the deposit) – some of them white, others red, others of a delicate pink tint – rising one above the other were innumerable pools of water, some hot, others warm and still others cold.[2]

Moran's *Hot springs of the Yellowstone* skilfully combines naturalistic observation and painterly interpretation, framing visionary scene within a consciously artful composition. This otherworldly scene reflects Moran's accord with Ruskin's view that mountains are nature's cathedrals, and that painters could find aesthetic revelation through the patient observation of natural phenomena – the sublime truths of geology, botany and climatic atmosphere.[3]

The graceful arc of Moran's rainbow pays homage to Turner and the Romantic tradition.[4] It also functions as Moran's assertion of the unique and divinely created beauty of this startling volcanic region which, in earlier times, was described by the few trappers who saw it as a kind of hell on earth. A contemporary newspaper reported on how Moran himself had likened Yellowstone to: 'a country bespattered with rainbows. It seemed unreally strange, like a dream-land, and he could hardly believe at times that he was not in a dream instead of an exploring expedition'.[5]

Ted Gott

1. Letter of 11 March 1872; cited in Joni Louise Kinsey, *Thomas Moran and the surveying of the American West*, Washington: Smithsonian Institution, 1992, p. 65.
2. Albert Peale's diary, 21 July 1871; quoted in Joni Louise Kinsey, *Thomas Moran's West. Chromolithography, high art and popular taste*, Kansas: Jocelyn Art Museum and University Press of Kansas, 2006, pp. 86–8.
3. William H. Truettner, '"Scenes of majesty and enduring interest": Thomas Moran goes West', *The Art Bulletin*, vol. 58, no. 2, June 1976, pp. 241–59.
4. Trained in Philadelphia in printmaking and publishing, Moran was encouraged to study Turner. In 1862 he travelled to London to view and copy his works.
5. 'A picture gallery of the Yellowstone', *Newark Daily Advertiser*, 6 October 1871, quoted in Nancy K. Anderson, *Thomas Moran*, Washington: National Gallery of Art, 1997, p. 52.

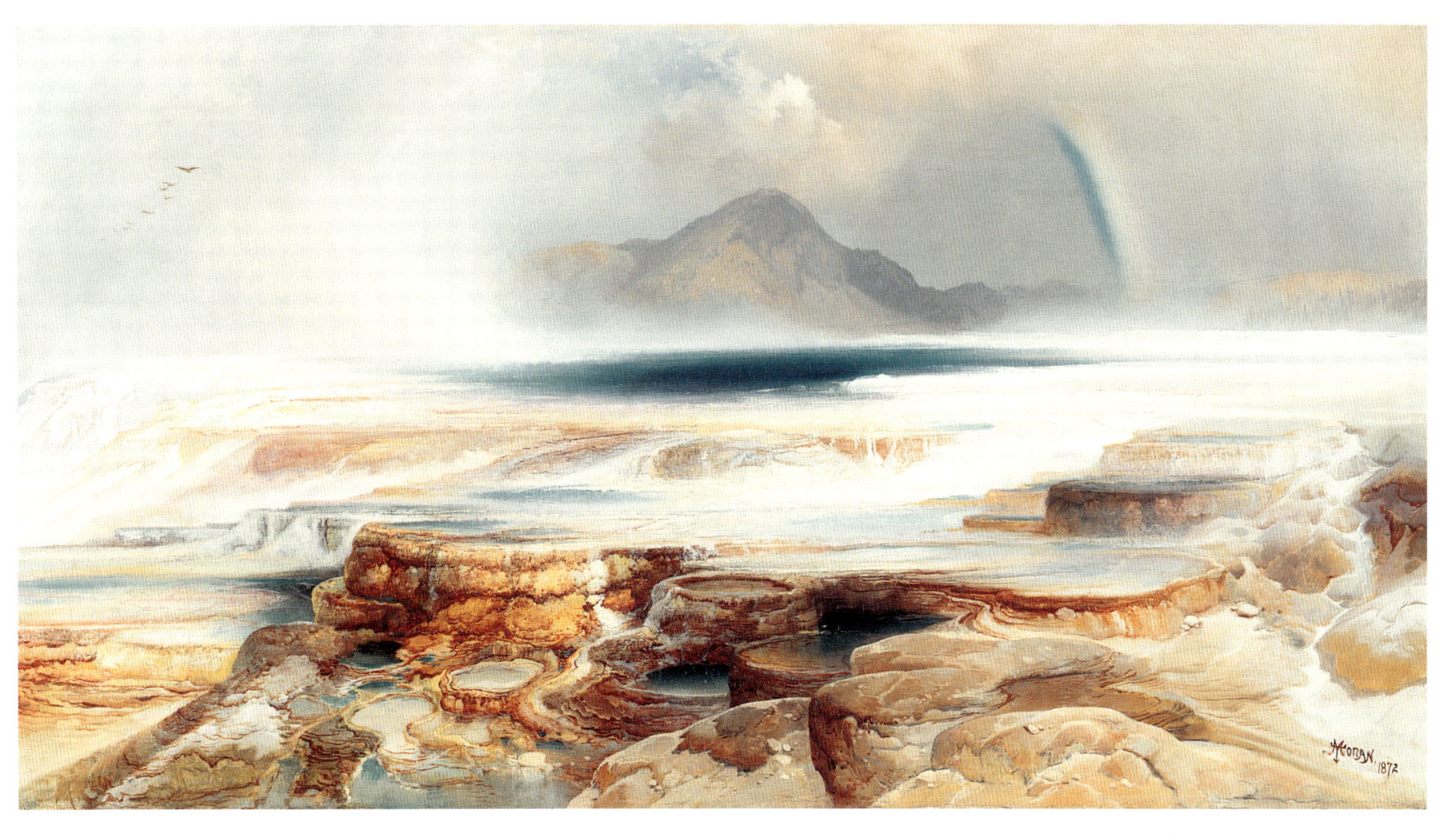

61. Albert Bierstadt

Germany 1830 – United States of America 1902
Cathedral Rocks, Yosemite Valley c. 1872
Gates of the Yosemite c. 1882
oil on paper on canvas each 35.6 x 50.8 cm
Smithsonian American Art Museum, Washington
Bequest of Marvin J. and Shirley F. Sonosky
in memory of Harryette Cohn 2006.1.1-2

For Bierstadt, the landscape of the American West represented a very real, lived experience, and was a vehicle for evoking personal and contemplative ideas. The German-born, American-raised artist delighted in capturing reflective qualities of crystal-clear lakes, snow-tipped craggy mountains and the inherent power of torrential waterfalls. He was interested in conveying the awe-inspiring beauty of the landscape and the atmospheric effects of nature.

Bierstadt painted *Cathedral Rocks, Yosemite Valley* and *Gates of the Yosemite*, almost ten years apart, for a growing American market eager to own images of the 'frontier' landscapes unique to the United States. Since the late 1850s artists, writers, scientists and photographers had been drawn to the Yosemite region in the state of California, an area which quickly became known for its spectacular topography. Following his return from study and travel in Europe, Bierstadt first travelled to the 'frontier West' in 1859, and to the Yosemite Valley in 1863. On return to the east he began to produce monumental images of real and imagined sites, constructed from drawings, sketches and photographs. The artist entered a period of critical favour and commercial success. In an entrepreneurial fashion Bierstadt responded by painting smaller works for the local market. Paintings such as these were uplifting reminders of the magnificent promise of the American continent at a time when large numbers of Europeans were relocating to the United States, during and after the turmoil of the American Civil War (1861–65).

In both works we are drawn into the scene through a body of water flanked by woodlands. *Cathedral Rocks, Yosemite Valley* is the more contemplative of the two: a still body of water reflects the trees which surround the lake. Careful geometric balance of this composition accentuates the dramatic vertical drop and sheer size of the granite cliffs. The precipice is counterbalanced by opposing horizontal masses of water and sky. The clearing at the water's edge possibly indicates human-made tracks, created by an increase of tourists to the area when the transcontinental railroad was completed in 1869. Beyond the dense woods, Bierstadt depicts the imposing Cathedral Rocks, his treatment of the painted surface revealing elements of detail within the landmass. Like the apex of a town cathedral, the presence of these rocks distinguishes the surrounding landscape.

In *Gates of the Yosemite* the scoop of the imposing cliffs emphasises the feeling of looking into a distant valley. On the banks of the bubbling river Bierstadt shows wildflowers growing in the meadows. The low water levels and bright light of the painting indicate this could be a summer scene. In the water, a felled tree is eroded by the tide, suggesting the cycles of nature and regeneration.

Through his presentation of largely unfamiliar, grand and beautiful lands, Bierstadt's images of the American West helped to define a national sense of place in the second half of the nineteenth century. At the Smithsonian American Art Museum in the national capital, these two works are usually displayed in a gallery alongside finely crafted mahogany furniture, decorative arts and still-life paintings from the period – objects which celebrate the bounty and promise of the American land.

Beatrice Gralton

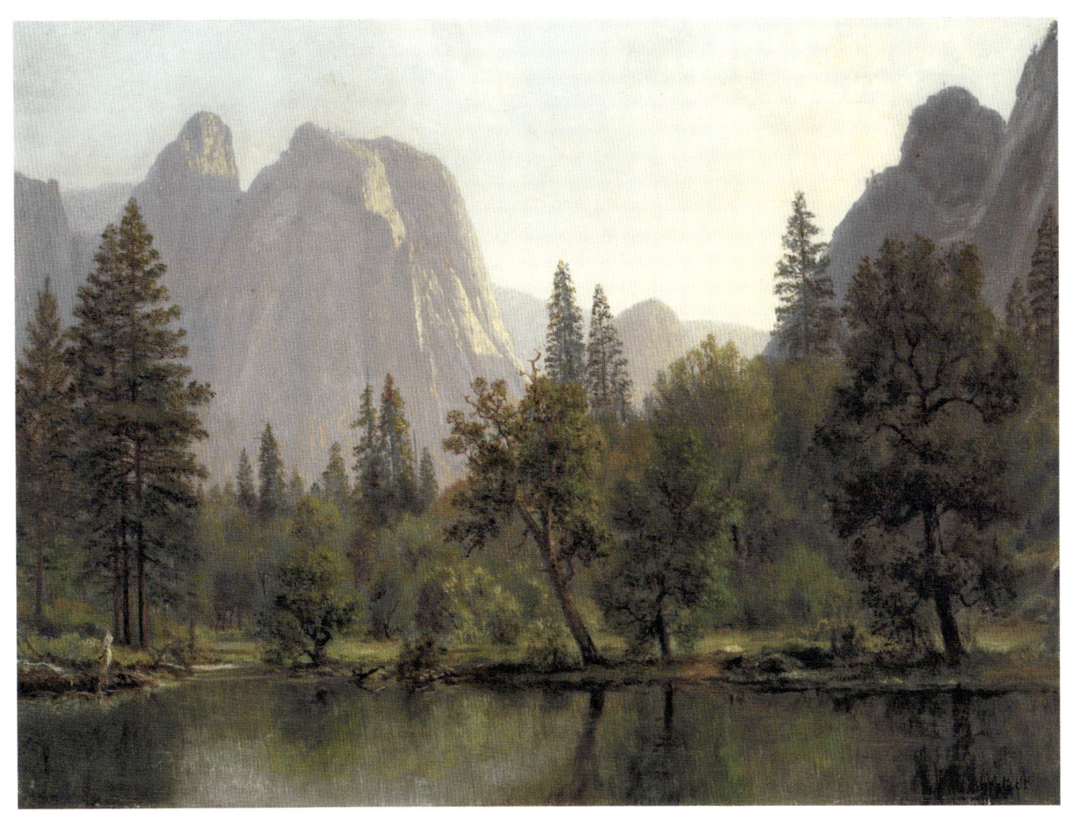

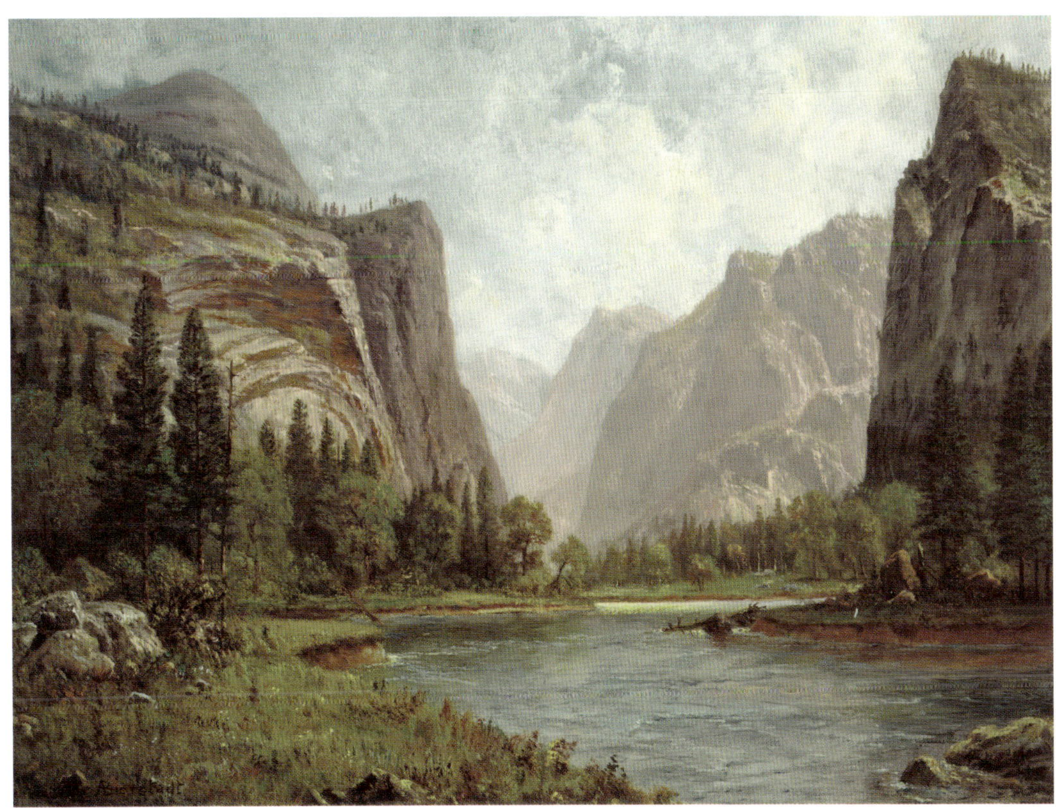

62. Ivan Shishkin

Russia 1832–1898
***A sandy coastline* [*Peschaniy bereg*]** 1879
oil on canvas 134.6 x 83.8 cm
French & Company, New York

Russian painters invented a new, heroic art of landscape in the second half of the nineteenth century. Shishkin demonstrates some of its elements in *A sandy coastline*: the painting holds an implied moral narrative with nationalist overtones. A few giant but slender pines inhabit the shoreline, their roots gripping into uncertain soil. Waves lap up the beach, unceasing tides which will eventually undermine the trees. Darkest sky lurks behind them, threatening an impending storm and, perhaps, oncoming night. Other trees still stand upon firmer ground in the grass, although many have been felled, hauled away for timber. Bright, intense light glares onto the sand and off the silhouetted trunks. This is nature's drama, which twists the largest tree away from the viewer, while it withstands the continuous assault of wind and water.

Shishkin was a highly-accomplished painter, who trained in the Classical fine art academies of Moscow and St Petersburg from 1852 to 1860. He then studied in Munich, Prague and Düsseldorf from 1862 to 1865, absorbing naturalistic tenets from the German schools. He was a founding member of the famous artists' group the Wanderers, who began to depict the vastness of Russia's lands in the 1870s. These reformist painters rejected the artificiality of contemporary pictorial themes, instead commenting on contemporary social ills while developing the first Russian interest in their own surroundings, looking at the bleak beauty of their plains, steppes and mountains. In 1879 Shishkin travelled in the Crimea from May to September, so that he could 'make *plein-air* studies in accordance with his fascination for working outdoors'.[1] *A sandy coastline* was exhibited in the *7th Wanderers' exhibition* in St Petersburg in 1879, the year it was painted.

Forests became Shishkin's major subject. His compositions are based on direct observation instead of that compilation of elements that underpins Classical and Picturesque landscapes. His works are also marked by extraordinary attention to detail, seen here in such elements as a tangle of debris washed up on the sand. He combined such realistic renderings with larger poetic truths. *A sandy coastline* sets up many qualities for us to ponder: light and dark, sunshine and shadows, strength and fragility, enduring time and a fleeting moment.

Christine Dixon

1. Notes on the painting by David Jackson, ms, French & Company.

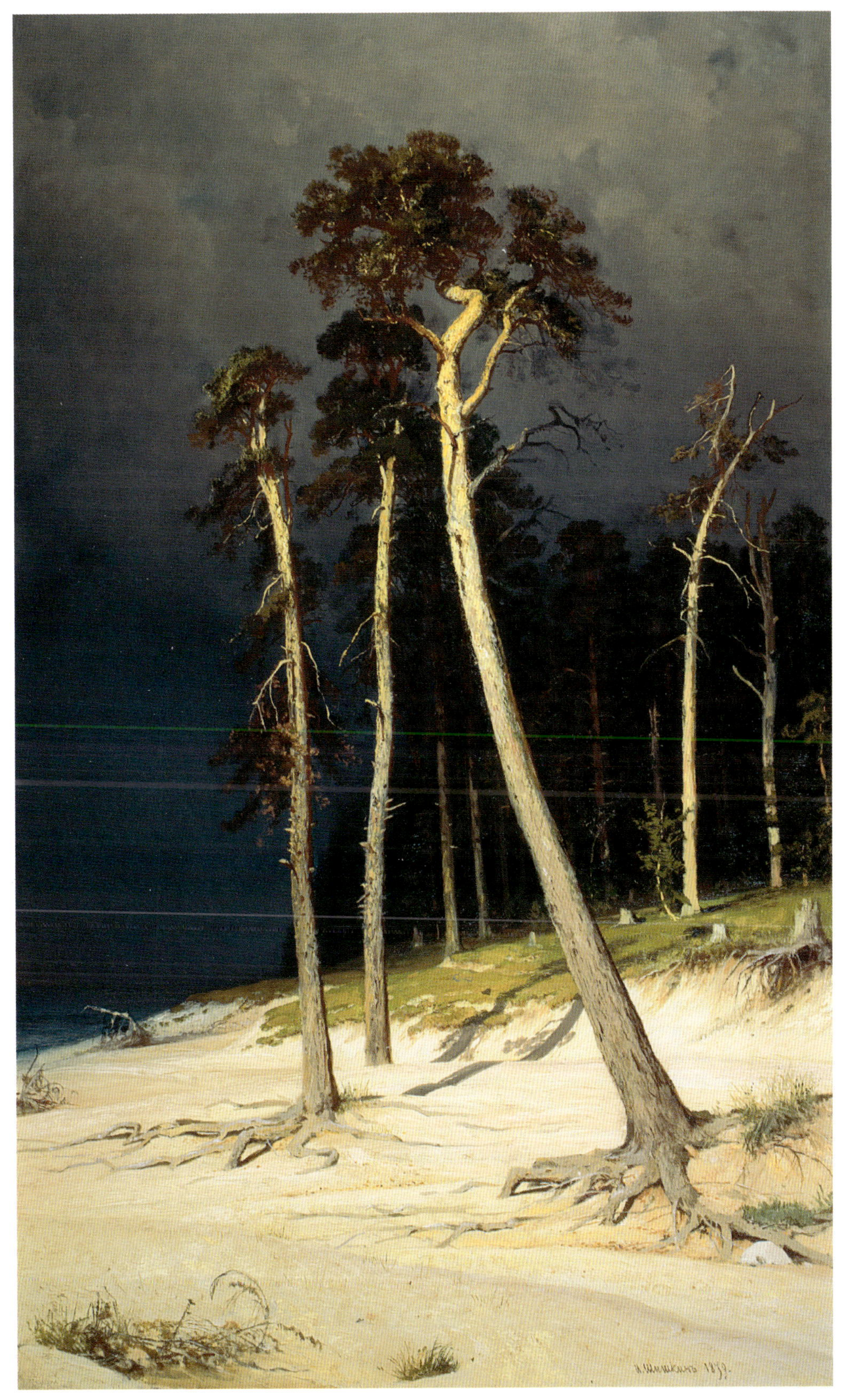

63. Arthur Streeton

Australia 1867–1943
'Fire's on' 1891
also known as ***'Fire's on!' (Lapstone Tunnel)***
oil on canvas 183.8 x 122.5 cm
Art Gallery of New South Wales, Sydney
Purchased 1893 832

It is astonishing to think that Streeton was only twenty-four years old when he painted *'Fire's on'*, a work that remains one of the great icons of Australian landscape painting. When Streeton wrote to his friend Frederick McCubbin (1855–1917) about the work he was undertaking in the Blue Mountains, his excitement and ambition were palpable. It was the quintessentially Australian landscape and light that inspired him: 'the vast hill of bright sandstone' crowned by bush and the 'deep blue azure heaven'.[1] Streeton was also taken with the fact that this landscape was the location of one of the engineering feats of the late nineteenth century, the construction of the 'Zig Zag' railway line across the Great Dividing Range and a new tunnel that would make this part of the country more accessible.

Towards the end of 1891 Streeton spent three months at Glenbrook in the Blue Mountains undertaking numerous sketches and watercolours. By the time he came to paint *'Fire's on'*, he had familiarised himself with the terrain and was following the development of the railway tunnel with interest. In Streeton's letter to Roberts in December 1891 he conveyed a tension between his enthusiastic response to the landscape and the dangers involved in the work being undertaken.

> I arrive at my cutting, 'the fatal cutting', and inwardly rejoice at the prosperous warmth all glowing before me as I descend and re-ascend the opposite side up to my shady, shelving, sandstone rock, perched high up … 12 o'clock … and now I hear 'Fire, fire's on', from the gang close by … BOOM! and then rumbling of rock, the navvy under the rock with me, and watching says, 'Man killed'.[2]

On the one hand the scale of the landscape and the historic activity of constructing the railway may be seen as an expression of a heroic, nationalistic viewpoint. Yet *'Fire's on'* is a complex work, far removed from picturesque or pristine views of the land or people triumphing against the odds. Instead Streeton conveys a clear-eyed view of the pell-mell local scrub and the precarious rocks, dead tree-trunks and random scatter of stones on the steep hillside. On the right, it is as though a layer of earth has been peeled back by human progress to reveal the dazzling white sandstone, ochre soil and gaping mouth of the tunnel. Above the tunnel, delicately drawn figures are dwarfed by the environment, dissolving into its heat haze, while the figures below reveal the perilous nature of their endeavour.

Compared with depictions of similar subjects on the theme of human labour in the landscape, it is notable that in *'Fire's on'* people are not the main focus. Instead the human drama is enmeshed with the towering, implacable presence of the land. Ultimately it is Streeton's passionate feeling for the environment as a whole and the heat and light of an Australian summer, conveyed through expressive brushwork, a daring compositional structure and intense, luminous colour, that would be an inspiration for generations of Australian painters to follow.

Deborah Hart

1. Letter published in R.H. Croll, *Smike to Bulldog: letters from Sir Arthur Streeton to Tom Roberts*, Sydney: Ure Smith, 1946, pp. 20–3.
2. Letter published in R.H. Croll, *Tom Roberts: father of Australian landscape painting*, Melbourne: Robertson & Mullens, 1935, pp. 187–9.

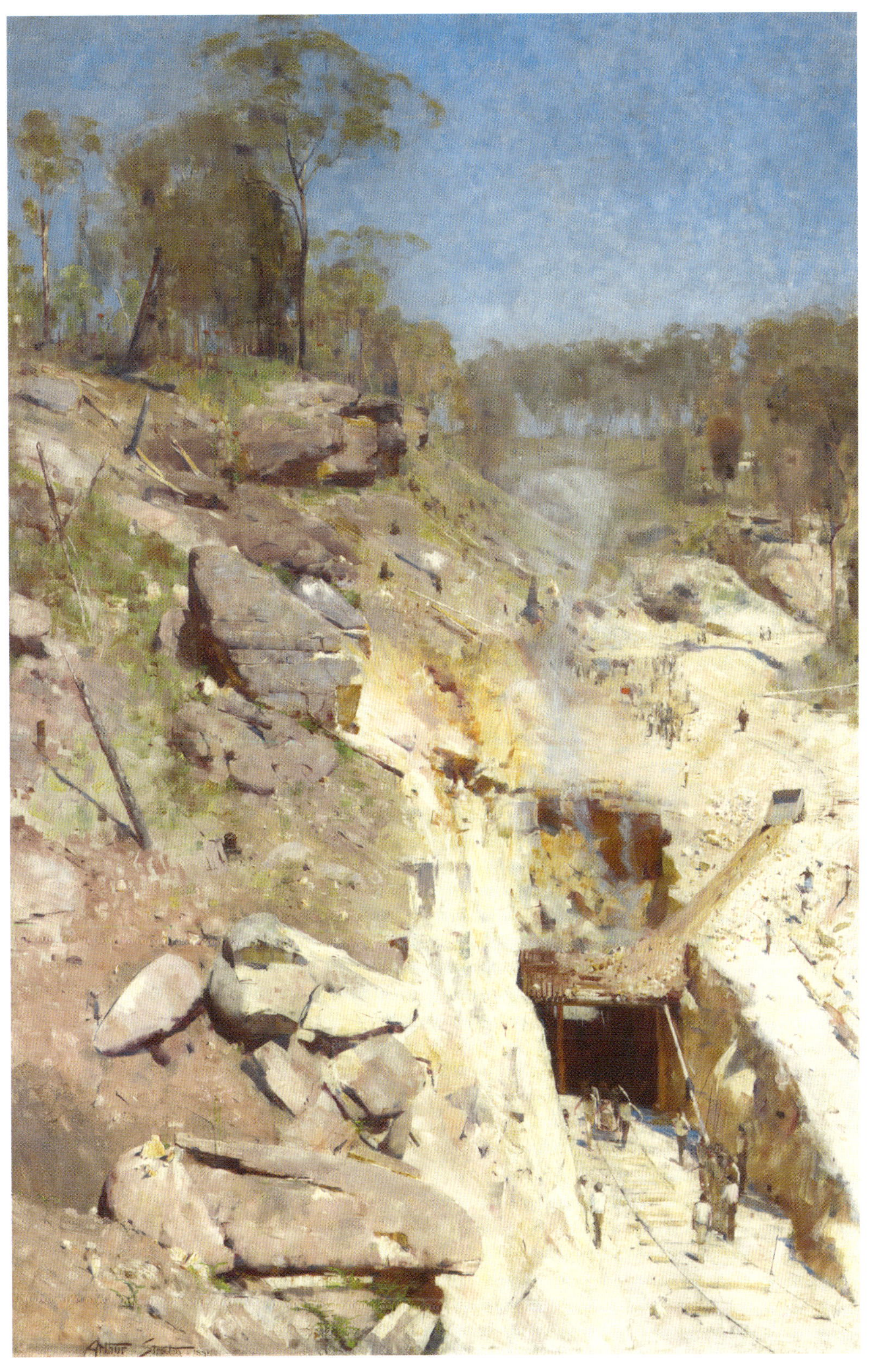

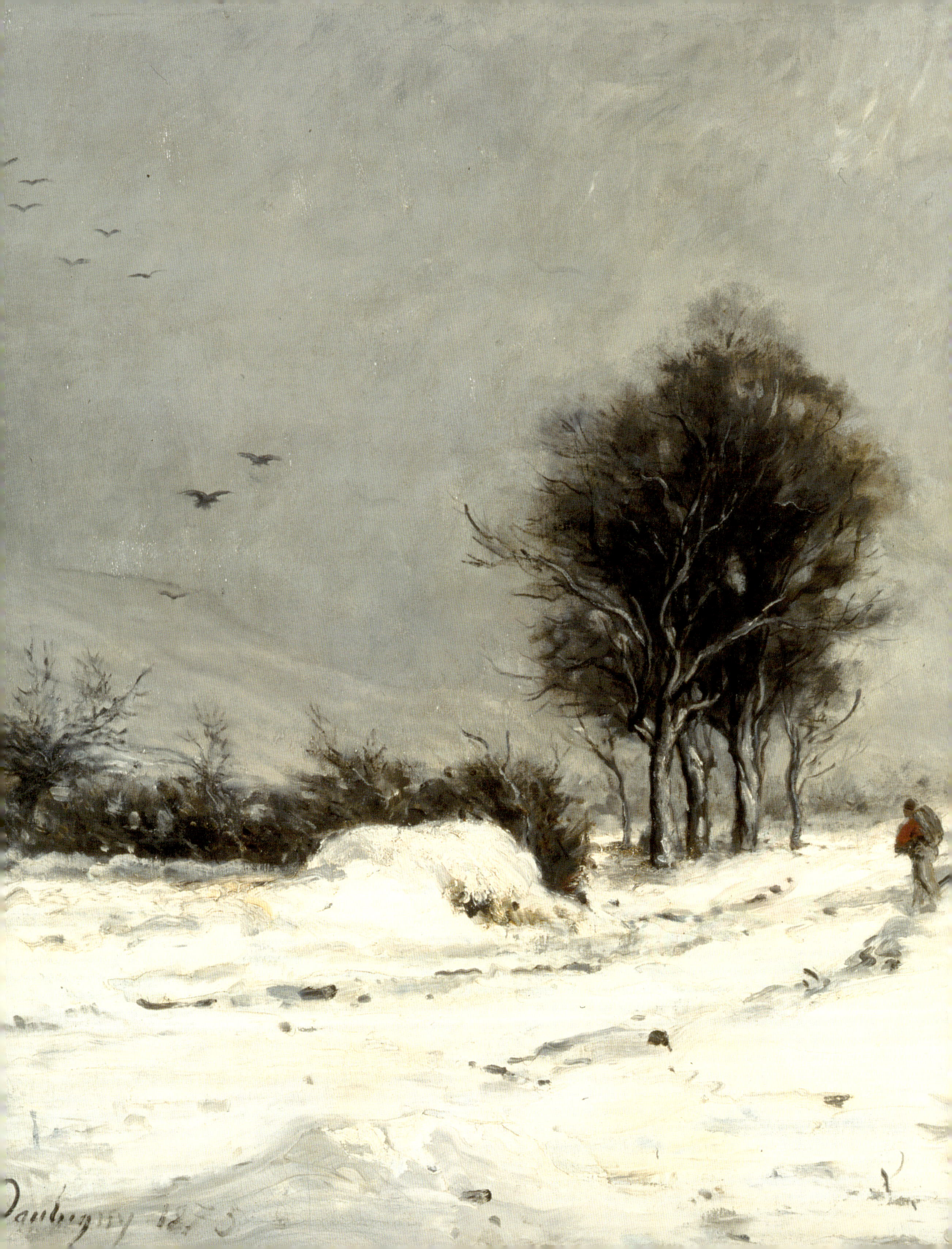

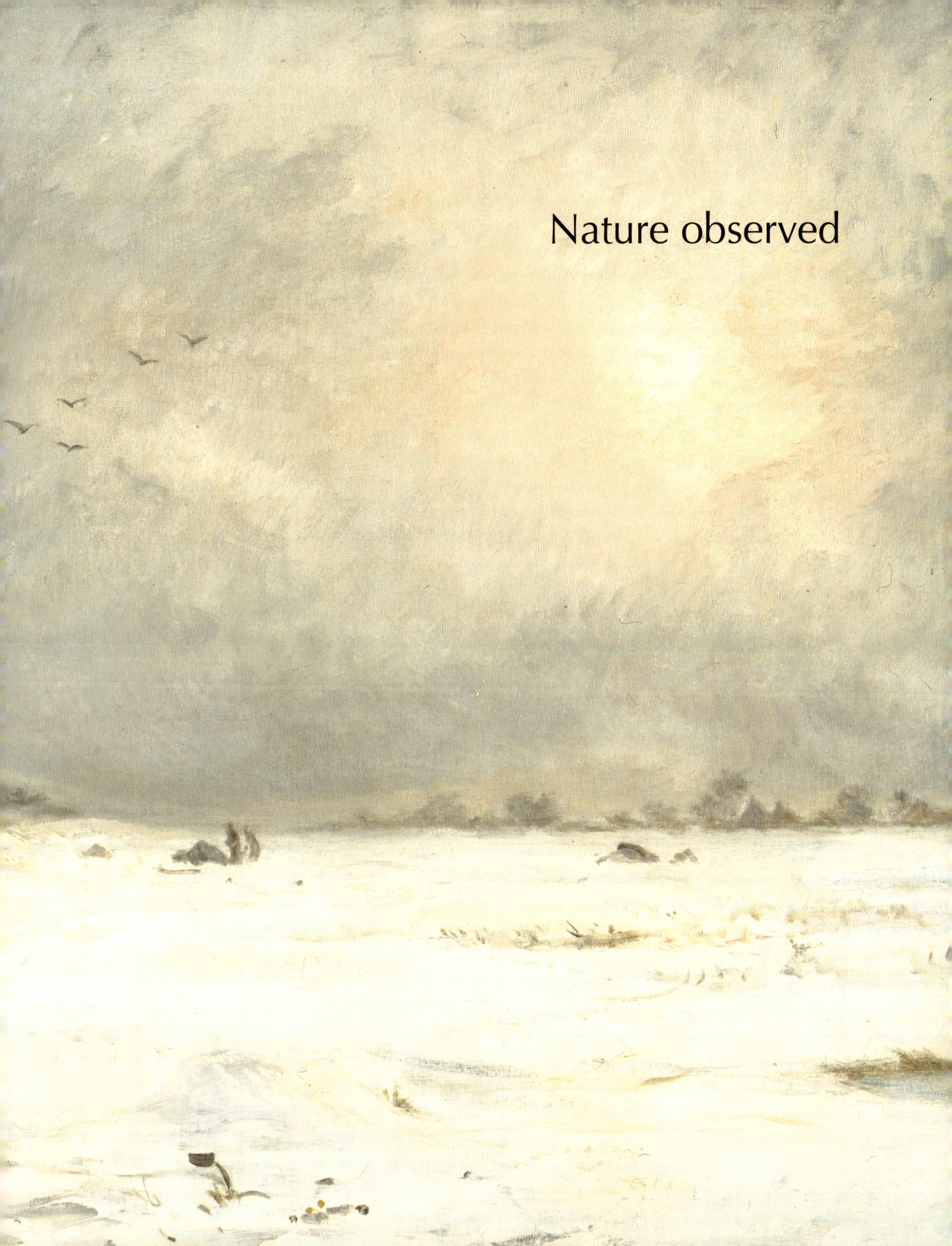

Nature observed

64. Wilhelm von Kobell

Germany 1766–1853?
A country lane [***Ein Feldweg***] c. 1821
oil over pencil on paper 21.5 x 30.8 cm
Hamburger Kunsthalle, Hamburg

Feldweg can be translated as 'country lane', or more literally as 'path through the fields', implying natural or cultivated lands. Kobell makes manifest the material world of dirt pathways, lush grazing and a hot summer day. Thus he communicates the sensory pleasures of experiencing nature in an everyday setting.

The artist here scrutinises a small, undramatic feature of some unremarkable countryside around Munich. The intensity of his gaze, an unusual viewpoint, and reduced palette, reveal Kobell at his observant best. The painting is built of three horizontal bands: an upper sky of brilliant summer blue, a green copse of trees and bushes in the centre and, below, filling half the composition, a grassy hillside riven by light ochre earthen paths. While the subject is a country lane, the humans and animals who made it are absent. Their presence is clear, however: various tracks were beaten into being by rabbits or sheep perhaps, larger ones made by people passing through, and by drovers or wagons.

A high horizon line places the artist below the scene. Usually, a landscape painter looks across a vista, or down onto a contained subject. Here we look up the little hill, a rise really, as do those who will walk up it. The minimal range of colours – brown, green, blue – concentrates the viewer's attention on the spareness, the lack of glamour, on which Kobell insists. This is a study of the real world, albeit a tiny piece of it. The artist attempts an objectivity unusual in German art at the time, totally unlike Caspar David Friedrich's religious apotheoses of Nature in Dresden, or Philipp Otto Runge's Romantic fancies in Hamburg.

Before the unification of Germany in the 1860s, artists gathered around the city seats of royal or episcopal courts. Kobell, a third-generation artist trained in Mannheim, left for the Bavarian capital Munich in 1790. He was professor of landscape painting at the Academy of Fine Arts there from 1814 to 1826. He travelled to Paris in 1809–10 and to Rome in 1818, where he encountered the Nazarene painters. They were a group of Austrian and German artists noted for their search for religious and artistic sincerity, often demonstrated by allegiance to close observation of nature and a crisp, linear style. Originally famous for large battle scenes, Kobell wanted to widen his reputation, and began to paint human encounters in rural settings. Later he returned to the inspiration of his youth, Dutch landscape painting of the seventeenth century, and produced genre subjects of peasants and farm animals. *A country lane* is notable for its sincerity and fidelity to observed nature.

Christine Dixon

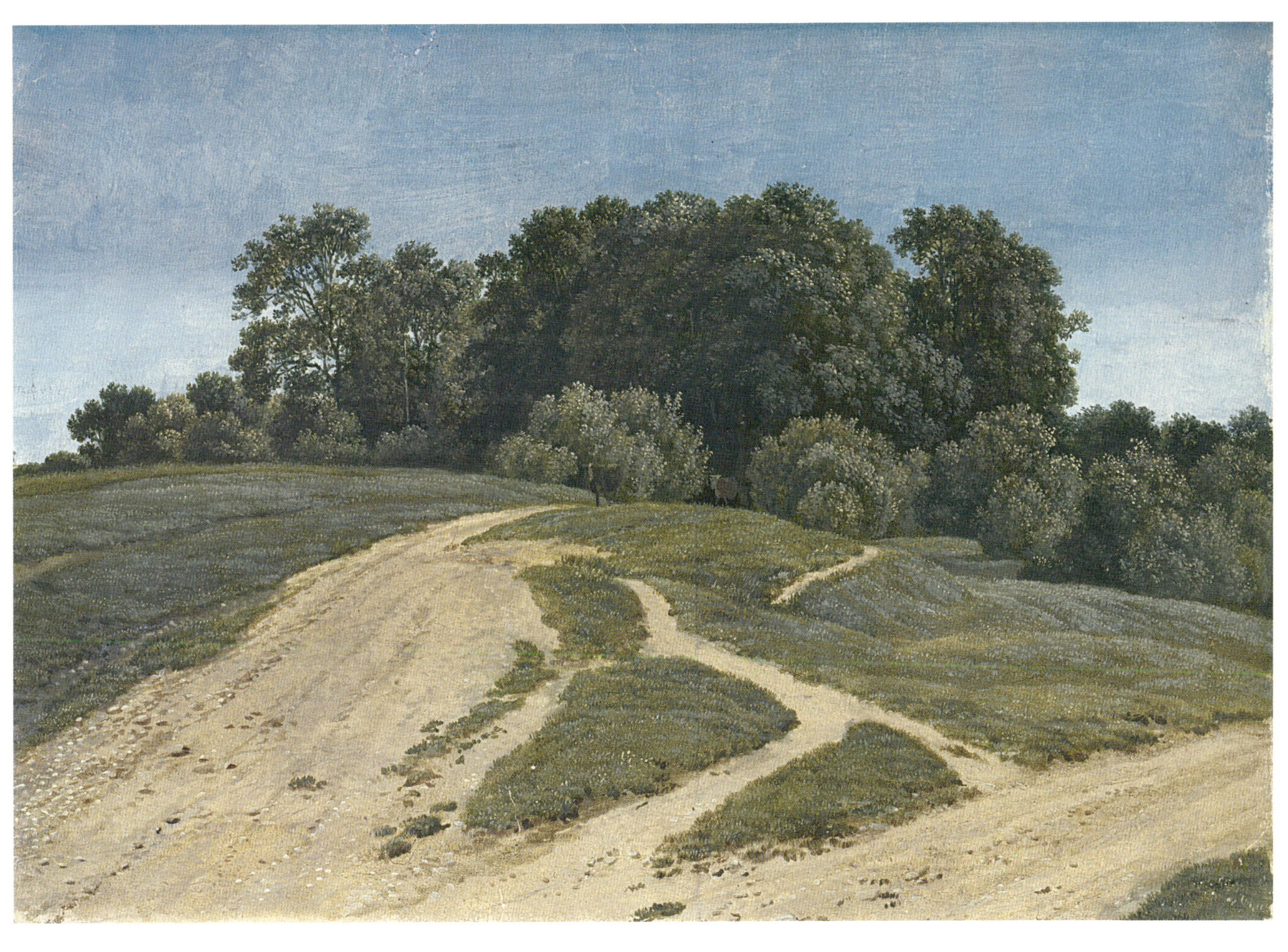

65. Camille Corot

France 1796–1875
Bridge on the Saône River at Mâcon 1834
also known as ***Village on the riverbank*** [***Le village au bord de la rivière***]
oil on paper on canvas 25.0 x 33.6 cm
National Gallery of Art, Washington
Ailsa Mellon Bruce Collection 1970.17.22
Image courtesy of the Board of Trustees, National Gallery of Art, Washington

Corot was modest and chaste. He never married, in company was nearly always overlooked, the Salon 'treated him rudely,' and the only painting by him to enter the Luxembourg Museum was 'bought almost accidentally by the state in 1851'.[1] Yet the great Charles Baudelaire was one of many who admired the qualities of simplicity and sureness in Corot's art and personality – traits that were at the opposite extreme to Baudelaire's flamboyance. Corot, he wrote, exerted complete control over his compositions, guaranteeing that every element would be well seen, well observed, well understood and well imagined.[2]

In *Bridge on the Saône River at Mâcon* the paint has been laid on directly and unaffectedly. This gives the small work a deceptive look of Impressionism. With their festive and casual appearance, Impressionist paintings were to make a holiday of looking. But Corot's washerwomen on the river bank are not Monet's or Manet's holidaymakers lolling about and enjoying the sun. Likewise, Corot in front of nature seems a disciplinarian rather than a sensualist.

The date 1834 is not at all early for an outdoor sketch – which this possibly is – yet it does seem early for such a masterly exercise in facing down nature for the sake of form.

Nature has here been translated by rule and measure, scale and calculation. One takes pleasure in the composition of four symmetrical rectangles and repeated arcs, the enveloping, sand-coloured light and well-managed paint textures. Selective accents of shape, tone and texture stand out by virtue of their difference. Paint strokes that seem spontaneous are, in fact, controlled. The ground from mid-way has been fastened down in solid, creamy earth colours. Above and to the sides, the semi-transparent blues and greens of sky, foliage and water vaporise against the underlying earth colours. Rough against smooth, a small area of mottled dabs describes shallow water near the bank and, on the other side of the picture, striations of green paint across the grain of the support ruffle the foliage as if simulating a breeze.

Visual sensation had a place when it suited Corot's purpose. In memorable early paintings he downplayed the figurative subject through using lively visual effects. The light in a canvas featuring a woman prone on the grass goes past her to a glowing clay bank in the middle distance.[3] The gleaming but otherwise meaningless lump of wet clay takes centre stage, successfully eclipsing the woman. In another work a man on horseback rides away from us; the eye is captured less by the figure, painted grey against grey, than by the sunlight jolting on the uneven bridle path this side of the figure.[4] A remarkable landscape sketch is captured by a shapeless black shadow that leaps across the sunburnt fields.[5] The irresolution between sketchiness and precise form in *Bridge on the Saône River at Mâcon* has the same liberating effect, what Corot's detractors called lack of finish and Baudelaire his 'awkwardness'. Where lesser artists finished off a work of art, the end for Corot was to open it.

Mary Eagle

1. Charles Rosen and Henri Zerner, *Romanticism and Realism: the mythology of nineteenth century art*, London: Faber, 1984, p. 230.
2. Charles Baudelaire, 'The Salon of 1845', trans. Jonathan Mayne, *Art in Paris 1845–1862: salons and other exhibitions reviewed by Charles Baudelaire*, London: Phaidon, 1965, p. 24.
3. *The Forest of Fontainebleau*, 1834, National Gallery of Art, Washington – The Chester Dale Collection.
4. *A View Near Volterra* 1838, National Gallery of Art, Washington – The Chester Dale Collection.
5. *Le Petit Chaville, near Ville-d'Avra* c. 1823, The Ashmolean Museum of Art and Archaeology – Bequeathed by Frank Hindley Smith, 1939.

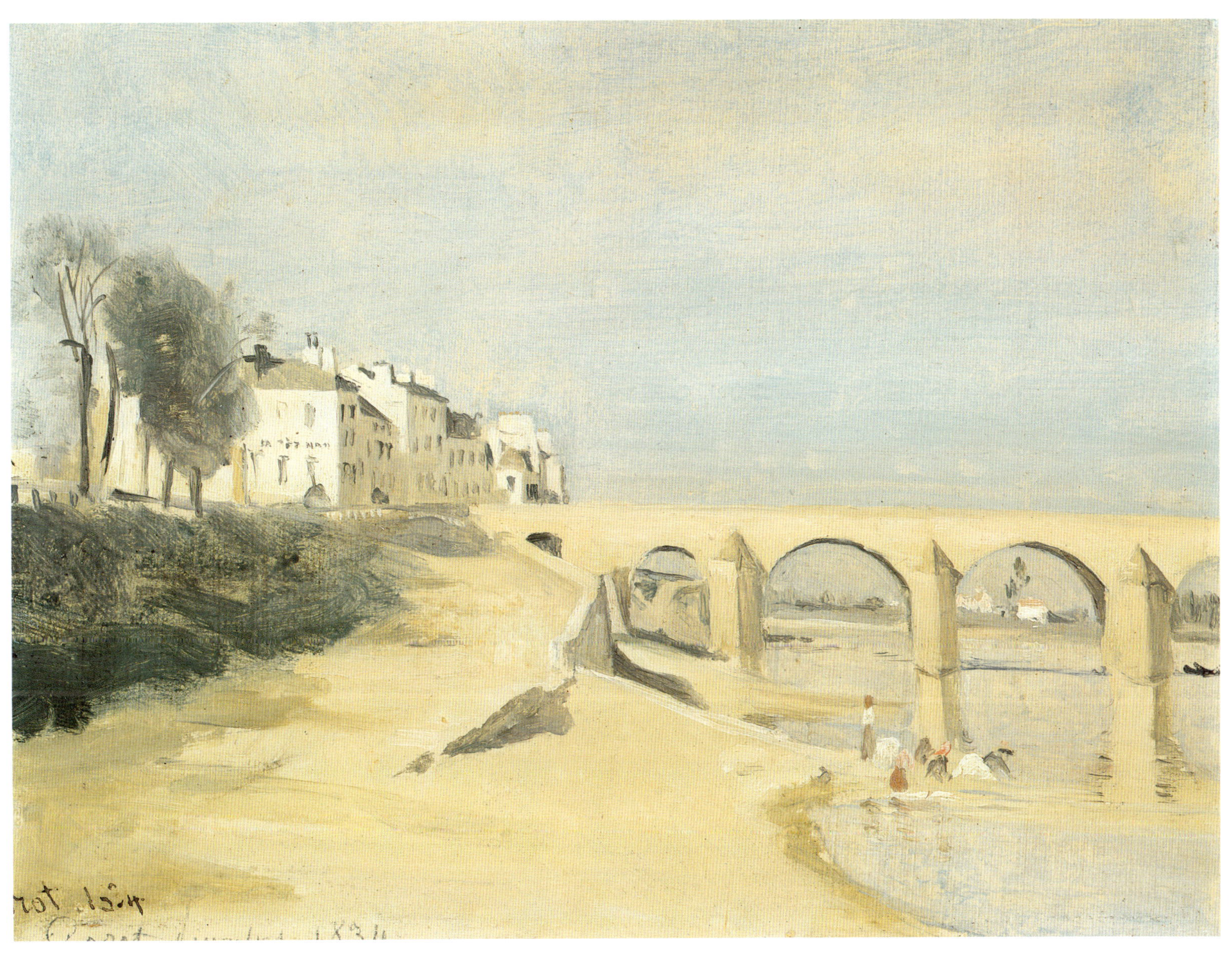

66. Camille Corot

France 1796–1875
Lake Geneva 1839?
also known as ***Geneva: view of part of the town***
[***Genève. Vue d'une partie de la ville***]
oil on canvas 26.0 x 35.2 cm
Philadelphia Museum of Art, Philadelphia
John G. Johnson Collection 1917 cat. 925

He is a rare and exceptional genius and the father of modern landscape painting. Whether they know it or not, there is not one landscape painter who does not proceed from him.
Delacroix 1861[1]

For so modest a man, Corot's reputation and influence were extraordinary. His work is little-known today outside France, but throughout the nineteenth century such severe critics as Baudelaire declared, of his contribution to the 1845 Salon: 'At the head of the modern school of landscape stands M. Corot'. In 1897 Monet said: 'There is only one master here – Corot. Compared to him, the rest of us are nothing, absolutely nothing!'[2]

After his first journey to Italy in 1825, where he remained until 1828, it seems inevitable that Corot would return to that source of light and Classical inspiration. He travelled from Italy to Paris via Geneva in 1834, revisiting the city in 1842, and then six times more in the 1850s. *Lake Geneva* is made of the smoothest possible brushstrokes, in the most subtle tonal cadences. It is painted in a very high key, with a simple palette. Corot uses subdued but glowing hues of light blue for the sky, the water and the mountain; the stone pale yellow and the leaves are very green. The sky reflects its blue into the limpid waters of the lake, while faint ripples disturb its glassy surface. There are two darker notes: a black boat in the centre of the composition, and black–brown tree-trunks on the right.

Most of nature is contained inside the limits of human construction. Expanses of air, water and vegetation contrast with the severe blonde geometries of a stone embankment and the town, composed of square houses with their triangular roofs. Even the gently rocking boat at the centre of the composition implies humans' use of nature for their purposes, transport, fishing for food or pleasure. Only the darker mountains behind Geneva, and the sky above, hint at nature unconfined.

When did Corot paint *Lake Geneva*? Originally regarded as a sketch from the artist's first encounter with Lake Geneva in 1834, its execution was then attached to his second visit in 1842.[3] Now the painting has been dated to 1839, created between visits and presumed to be a *souvenir*, a reworking from memory after his *plein-air* oil drawing on the spot. The artist's first biographer, Alfred Robaut, notes off-handedly that the boat was 'added later'.[4] That is, Corot rethought the composition and decided it needed a visually dramatic focal point. Formally and tonally, the black boat radically changes the painting, concentrating our attention onto the centre of this placid scene.

Christine Dixon

1. Quoted in John Goodrich, June 2004, review of *Early paintings of Corot* exhibition at Salander-O'Reilly Galleries, viewed December 2007, artcritical.com/goodrich/JGCorot.htm.
2. Quoted in Michael Pantazzi, Vincent Pomarède and Gary Tinterow, *Corot*, New York: Metropolitan Museum of Art, 1996, Baudelaire, p. xiv, note 6, p. xv, and Monet, p. xiv, note 1, p. xv.
3. *Paintings from Europe and the Americas in the Philadelphia Museum of Art*, Philadelphia: The Philadelphia Museum of Art, 1984, p. 125; Pantazzi et al., p. 136.
4. Pantazzi et al., p. 136, note 7, p. 137.

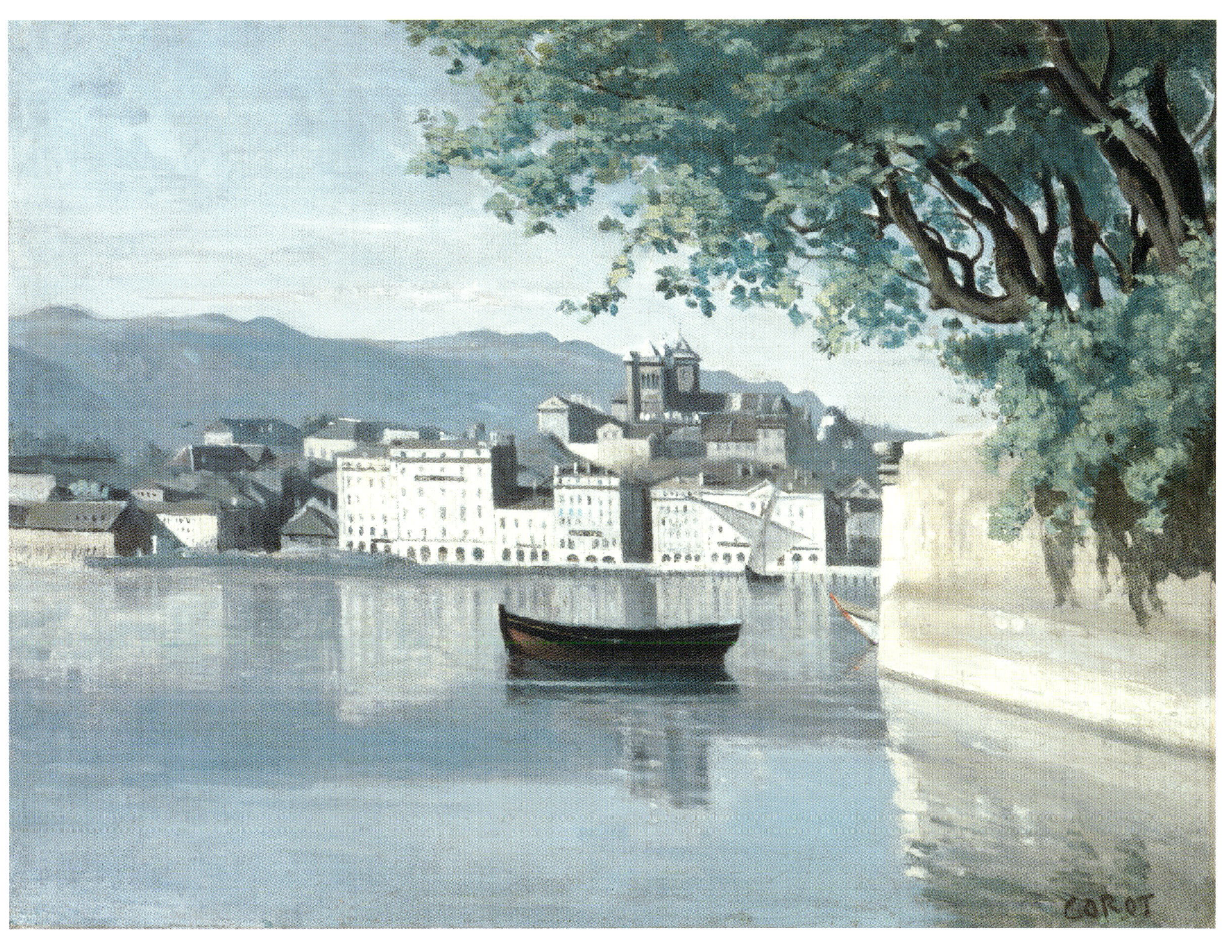
COROT

67. Théodore Rousseau

France 1812–1867
Under the birches, evening 1842–43 also known as
Under the beeches, evening [***Sous les hêtres le soir***] and
The priest [***Le curé***]
oil on wood panel 42.2 x 64.5 cm
Toledo Museum of Art, Ohio
Gift of Arthur J. Secor 1933.37

Rousseau began to paint *Under the birches, evening* in Berry in central France, at the lowest point of his official artistic career. After initial success at the Paris Salon from 1831 to 1835, all of his works were refused between 1836 and 1841. Discouraged, he then refrained from submitting works to the jury until after the 1848 Revolution, when the selection system was reformed. The artist then received an official commission, subsequent acceptance at the Salon, and honours from the state. In the early 1840s, however, when this painting was executed, Rousseau's dreams of winning the Prix de Rome were over; nonetheless he continued to paint, in his own way.

The atmosphere and charm of *Under the birches, evening* also characterise the artist's better-known sojourns in the Forest of Barbizon, a place identified with Rousseau for three decades. In summer he worked outdoors in a little hut made for him, painting studies and sketches that were then finished in his studio in Paris.[1] Most striking in the composition of *Under the birches, evening* is the theatrical presentation of a central clump of trees, birches bright with autumnal foliage and their unique black-and-white bark. The dark foreground is echoed by the steel blue–grey fading light of day, changing as night begins to fall. Light is concentrated upon a central oval, where a slight narrative interest is given by human presence in the form of the humble *curé*. No means of entry is provided to the viewer, however, no path, rising hill nor descent into a valley. The grove is presented as a visual fait accompli, a feature that struck the artist's eye full-on.

Rousseau's debt to seventeenth-century Dutch landscape is obvious in his division of the canvas into three horizontal bands, concentrating on the middle ground, and his stubborn portrayal of the unexceptional, anti-Romantic theme. Contemporary English masters – Constable, Bonington, Turner – awoke painters in France to the importance of exact depictions of changing conditions: light, atmosphere, times of day. For Rousseau, the lessons of past Dutch and present English art meant a continuing attachment to his own country and its unique landscapes. There is nowhere more satisfying to be than here, under these trees at this moment, and no finer artist than Rousseau to describe the scene for us.

Christine Dixon

1. *Théodore Rousseau 1812–1867*, Paris: Réunion des musée nationaux, 1967, cat. 22, p. 35.

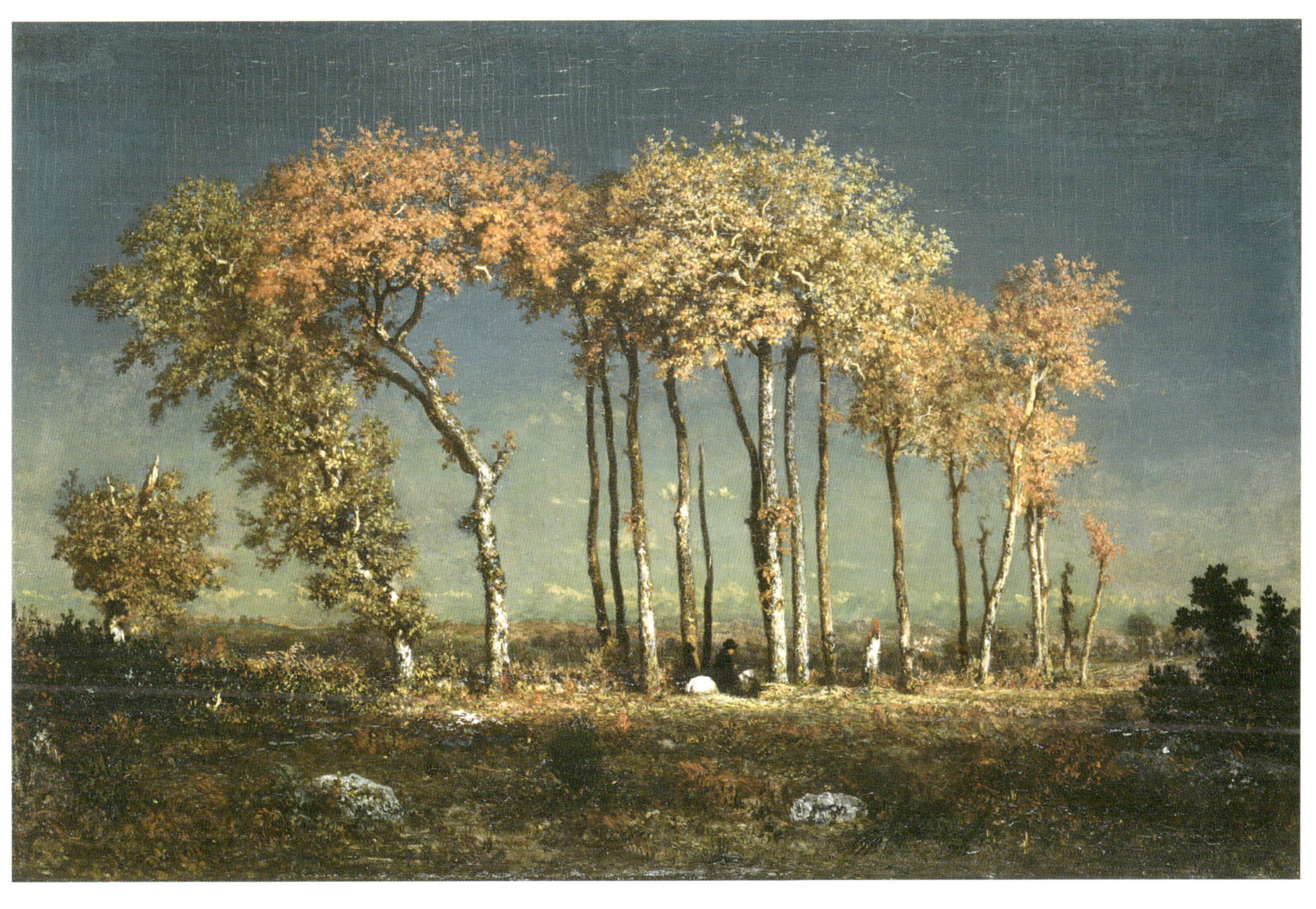

68. Charles Daubigny

France 1817–1878
***Banks of the Seine* [*Rive de la Seine*]** 1855
also known as ***Les Iles Vierges à Bezons***
oil on canvas 35.3 x 54.0 cm
Art Gallery of South Australia, Adelaide
Morgan Thomas Bequest Fund 1950

In 1817, when Daubigny was born, landscape became a legitimate academic genre in France. Its acceptance, however, depended upon artists' submission to strict Neo-Classical codes governing technique, composition and narrative content. In the space of one generation though, its very *raison d'être* was to be redefined by Daubigny and his contemporaries, Théodore Rousseau (cat. 67), Narcisse Diaz de La Peña and Jean-François Millet. Inspired by the dazzling example of Constable, they eagerly sought out the woods of Barbizon and Fontainebleau to transcribe nature *en plein air* and to read aloud Constable's notes on painting in their resting moments.

Throughout his career Daubigny's single subject was nature, captured in all its fleeting and complex interactions of light, air, foliage and water. His response to direct visual experience was often more immediate than that of his colleagues, and his compositions less formally composed. In order to preserve the spontaneity of his paintings, he eschewed the convention of 'finishing' his studies indoors and in this – perhaps more than any other painter – set a crucial precedent for the Impressionists.

Daubigny also stood apart in his preference for the scenery along the Seine and Oise rivers. The commune of Bezons where *Banks of the Seine* was painted lies ten kilometres north-west of Paris. The artist depicted its environs many times between 1850 and 1868. It was a scene of Bezons which brought him his first marked success in 1852, and praise for his glowing colours, fluid atmosphere and modest motifs.[1] Its sketchy qualities nevertheless disturbed one admirer who wondered whether 'Mr Daubigny [was] afraid of ruining his work by finishing it?'[2] A decade later this perceived lack of finish was still a target of complaint with one critic lamenting that Daubigny 'who possesses such … a natural feeling, is contented with an *impression* … his pictures are no more than sketches, badly begun'.[3]

The low and central vantage point from which the present picture was composed suggests Daubigny was painting from a boat – presumably hired. In 1857 the artist acquired his own *péniche* called *Le Botin*, which he used as a floating studio and steered along the Seine and Oise, sometimes in the company of Corot.[4] The Isles Vierges, a group of small, uninhabited islands in the river at Bezons, are shown as clumps at either side of *Banks of the Seine*. It proved a highly popular motif, perhaps because it so happily recalled earlier images of the poplar-covered island at Ermenonville, burial place of the Enlightenment philosopher and nature-lover Jean-Jacques Rousseau. In the modern era of Baron Haussmann, Bezons came in its own way to symbolise a notion of unspoiled nature. In 1881 the place was described by Guy de Maupassant:

> At last … they crossed the Seine a second time, and the bridge was a delight. The river sparkled in the sun, and they had a feeling of quiet enjoyment, felt refreshed as they drank in the purer air that was not impregnated by the black smoke of factories nor by the miasma from the deposits of night soil. A man whom they met told them that the name of the place was Bézons.[5]

Sophie Matthiesson

1. *The Seine at Bezons* c. 1852, collection Musée d'Orsay, Paris.
2. 1852 Salon, Madeleine Fidell-Beaufort and Janine Bailly-Herzberg, *Daubigny: la vie et l'oeuvre*, Paris: Geoffroy-Dechaume, 1975, p. 45.
3. Théophile Gautier, *Abécédaire du Salon de 1861*, Paris: E. Dentu, 1861, p. 119.
4. *Le Bateau-atelier*, collection Louvre, Paris.
5. Guy de Maupassant, *A country excursion*, 1881, in *Sur l'eau and other Stories*, 1911, trans. Albert M.C. McMaster, A. Henderson and L. Quesada, Whitefish, Montana: Kessinger Publishing, 2004, p. 20.

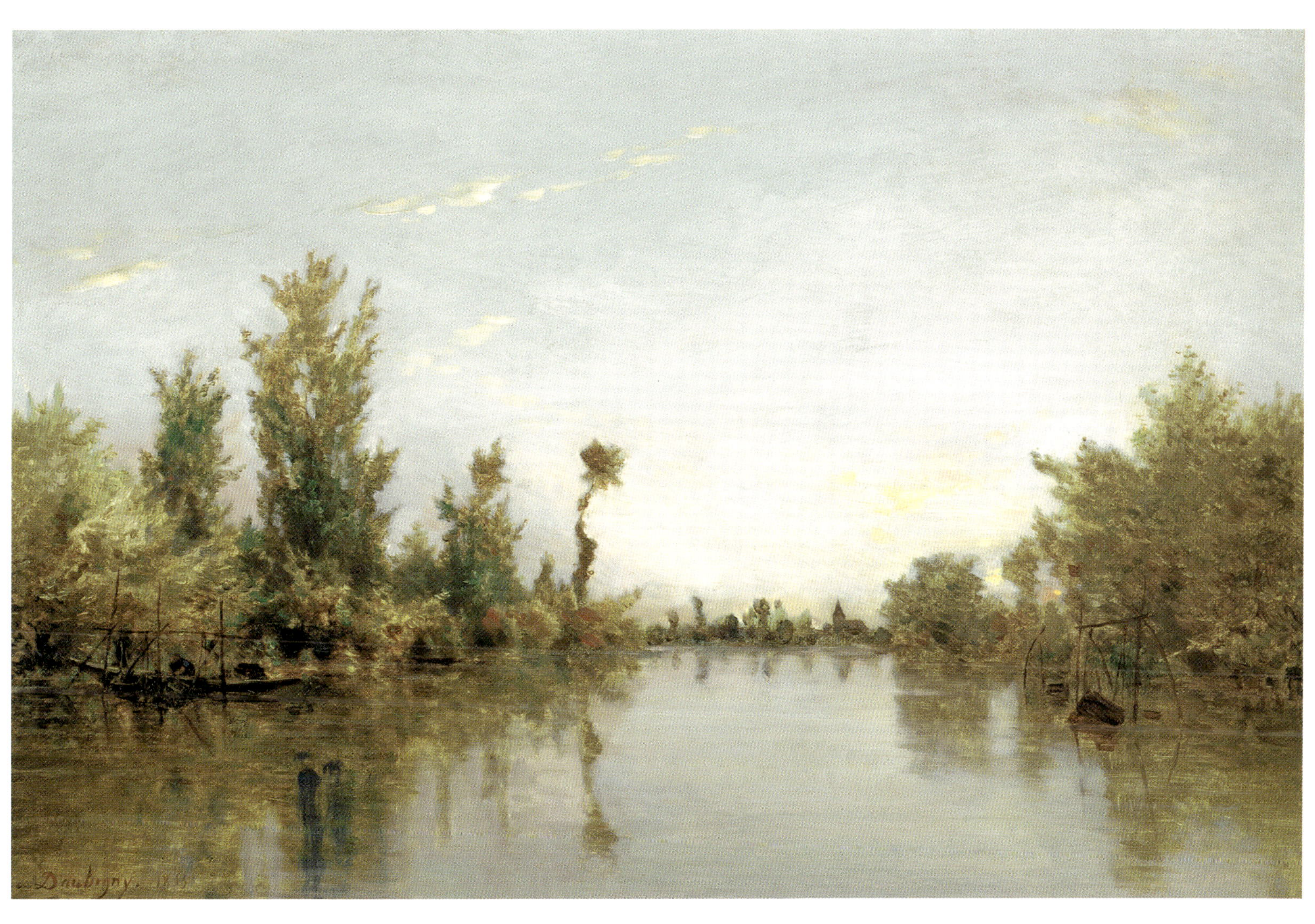
Daubigny.

69. Gustave Courbet

France 1819 – Switzerland 1877
Source of the Lison [***Source du Lison***] 1864
oil on canvas 91.0 x 73.0 cm
Galerie Paffrath, Düsseldorf

Although a genius, Courbet was certainly a magnet for trouble. No other artist in nineteenth-century France so often found himself surrounded by controversy, apart from Edouard Manet – although Manet extricated himself, while Courbet seemed constantly enmeshed in scandal and uproar. But he was also firmly connected to the best artists working in the middle decades of the century, from Corot to Whistler, and Cézanne to Monet – he was even the witness at Monet's wedding in 1870. Courbet remains the most radical painter of his time, while his work marks the rupture from Romanticism via Realism that produced modern art.

A deep attachment to his native region inspired Courbet throughout his life, and is demonstrated in his art. He knew the farms near Ornans, the town and its people, and gloried in the rugged beauty of the Jura mountains in his eastern province of Franche-Comté. The rivers of the Jura, the Loue and the Lison, their limestone cliffs, grottoes, waterfalls and vegetation, provided a never-ending subject for the artist.

In Paris, Courbet played the coarse peasant new to the city, but there was a serious purpose in his stout defence of regions against the centre. Throughout the century the French state tried to centralise all power to the capital and government institutions, artistically as well as politically, and Courbet was a rebel by conviction.

Most of his landscapes of the 1860s – made after the scandals of the Salon and before the catastrophic defeat of the Paris Commune, his imprisonment, and self-exile – concentrate on a limited, almost claustrophobic vocabulary of motifs. As well as enclosed forest scenes with deer and views of hunting, there are Courbet's *Source* paintings. Stone, water and darkness are enlivened by rushing currents, decorated with green moss, spring growth or autumn foliage. Apart from over-determined, psychoanalytic readings (grotto = wish for a return to the womb), the Jura works display broad and vigorous handling as well as local particularity based on *plein-air* observation.

In *Source of the Lison*, as in his other Jura landscapes, Courbet cuts off the sky or any conventional vista, and medium or long views. We are forced close to the rocky cliffs and mysterious cave, confronted with cold, green–brown water pouring from its geological origin, the rising of the river. Paint is mainly brown, with white, bright green and orange highlights. It is applied thickly, pushed around with palette knife and spatula, to accentuate the materiality of the subject. The canvas is vertical, and Courbet accentuates the height of the cliffs by forcing movement down the cliff-face and over the splashing waterfall. Cézanne's cubes, spheres and pyramids owe some of their genesis to Courbet's admiring yet brusque painterly treatment of his native landscape.

Christine Dixon

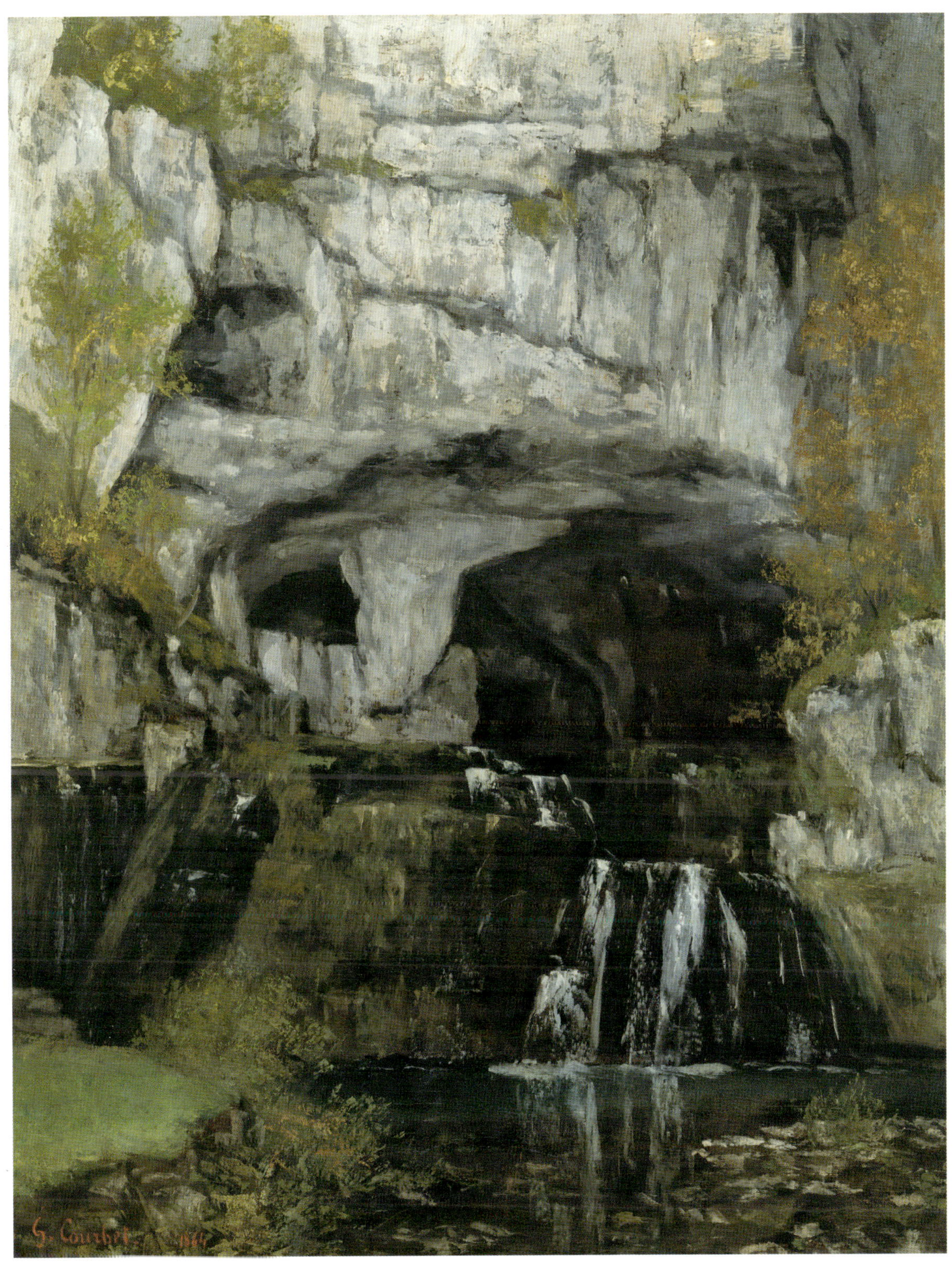
G. Courbet. 1864

70. Gustave Courbet

France 1819 – Switzerland 1877
Low tide, the beach at Trouville
[***La plage de Trouville à marée basse***] 1865
also known as ***Seascape: low tide, the beach at Trouville***
oil on canvas 46.4 x 61.0 cm
Kerry Stokes Collection, Perth

This attractive, modestly sized painting of beach, sea and sky is rendered in a palette limited to blue and white, creams and flesh-tones. By adopting a frontal viewpoint and low horizon, the artist makes the sky dominate. Filled with billowing clouds, the sky consumes almost two-thirds of the canvas; it is reflected by an outgoing tide and small pools of water. Without the small section of sandy ground in the distance, sky and sea would merge seamlessly. The paint in the foreground, applied with palette knife, contrasts with the more smoothly, carefully modulated clouds.

After a while our eyes fix on a pair of figures, described with just a few strokes of black paint: this lone walker and a dog stroll along the waterline. They provide a sense of scale and human interest for the scene. This almost minimalist rendering of marine and coastal atmospheric conditions could easily be a work by James McNeill Whistler, or even Constable. It is actually one of a group of canvases painted by Courbet at the town of Trouville, on the Normandy coast, at the end of the northern summer and the autumn of 1865.

Of the nearly forty paintings completed by Courbet in this three-month period, twenty-five are *paysages de mer* [landscapes of the sea].[1] As Eyerman points out, Courbet's term suggests his self-conscious innovation within the conventions of the landscape genre.[2] Working *en plein air*, he concentrated on portraying the mood of the beaches – he found the ocean and light conditions 'thrilling' – and the resulting paintings are devoid of narrative. There are no cues to suggest any specific locale. Rendered in a delicate range of blues, greys and soft pinks or violets or, indeed, orange, the basic structure of these seascapes is consistent: the sky dominates and only occasionally is the beach punctuated by rocks or small waves. At times Courbet includes small groups of figures or tiny boats on the horizon. Sometimes he adjusts his colour range to capture the sunset or a forthcoming storm. This kind of serial approach later adopted by Monet who, like Courbet and Whistler, was painting at Trouville at this time.

New railway lines linking Paris to the coast made Trouville part of the burgeoning resort culture that developed during the Second Empire, and gave a broad range of middle-class and wealthy patrons access to the seaside. Unlike Eugène Boudin, whose paintings of holidaymakers at the same site motivated Courbet, *Low tide, the beach at Trouville* merely hints at human presence. Indeed, Boudin's and Courbet's paintings might almost be 'before' and 'after' scenes: the fashionably dressed Parisian crowds having departed, the beach is deserted except for a local man and his canine companion. The artist was painting to sell, and claimed to have produced some of his seascapes in just two hours. In a letter to his friend and patron Alfred Bruyas in 1866, he records his joyful summer holiday at Trouville and the paintings he produced there: 'twenty-five autumn skies – each one more extraordinary and free than the last'.[3]

Lucina Ward

1. Courbet exhibited ten of the seascapes as *Marines diverses* in his 1867 show, but it is impossible to distinguish which paintings were included.
2. Charlotte Eyerman, *Courbet and the modern landscape*, Los Angeles: J. Paul Getty Museum, 2006, p. 104.
3. Petra ten-Doesschate Chu (ed.), *Letters of Gustave Courbet*, Chicago: University of Chicago Press, 1992, p. 273.

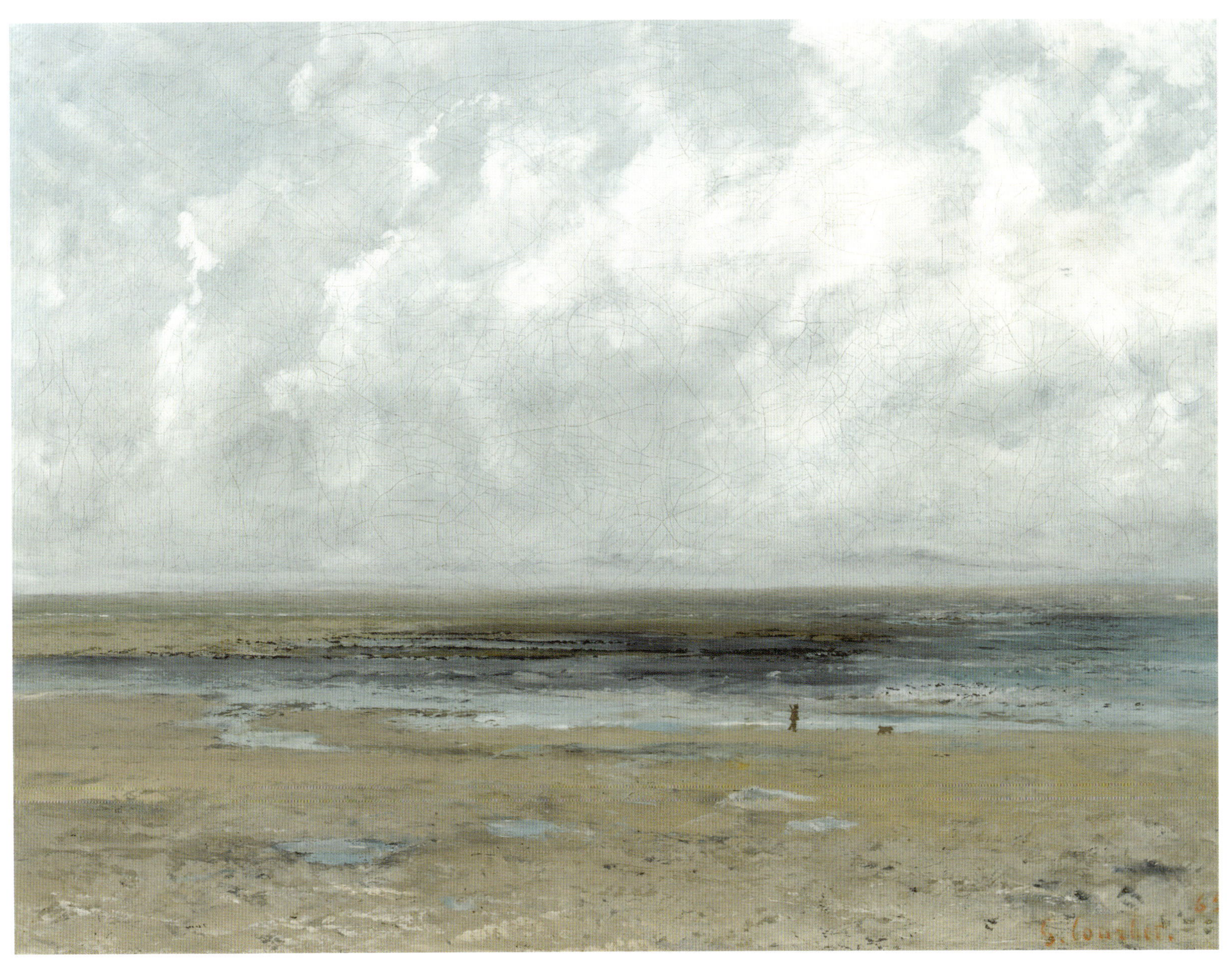

71. Gustave Courbet

France 1819 – Switzerland 1877
***The wave* [*La vague*]** c. 1872
oil on canvas 54.2 x 73.1 cm
National Gallery of Victoria, Melbourne
Felton Bequest, 1924 1309-3

The wave, part of a series of marine pictures by the French Realist painter Courbet, depicts a wave approaching a beach on a stormy day. The work was painted after 1872, when Courbet was living far away from the sea.[1] Nevertheless, it strongly relates to the artist's memory of visits he made to the Normandy coast in the 1860s. Courbet smears thick layers of paint across the canvas with a palette knife in a series of broken areas, emphasising the material quality of the pigment. The dark hues of the clouds and the heaving sea suggest stormy conditions, while the straining sails and tilting masts of the distant boast evince a strong wind. It is a powerful image of the elemental force of Nature, but also a work that draws attention to its own properties and therefore can be considered a work of early modernism.

Opinion is divided on the significance of Courbet's 'marines'. Herding finds political meanings in the later seascapes, arguing that the dissolving forms of Courbet's wave paintings are part of an argument in favour of social equality in which the sea stands as a metaphor for the people.[2] Wagner, disagreeing with this view, interprets the painterly dissolution and highly evident facture in Courbet's painting as appealing to the need of metropolitan, bourgeois viewers for a pleasing antidote to the turmoil of urban life.[3] Neither interpretation takes into account the important influence of French Romanticism on Courbet's appreciation of the sea.

Courbet was responding to French Romantic literature, such as Victor Hugo's novel *The toilers of the sea* of 1866, which revelled in the perilous situation of humanity before the untrammelled force of Nature. Although he preferred to let the natural motif speak for itself, what Courbet gleaned from Romanticism was the idea that nature cannot be easily tamed. Indeed, the critical reception of Courbet's sea pictures, including *The wave*, demonstrates that the artist refused to visually 'tame' the Normandy foreshore. He achieved this by defeating viewers' expectations about the representation of the sea. At its first Australian showing in 1924, for example, a critic for the *Argus* commented that: 'The wave, which is painted with the palette knife, is anything but liquid'.[4] Instead of a pleasing spectacle of a marine landscape, we are brought up short against this uncanny wave that seems to have been frozen in mid-swell or turned into a solid material completely foreign to the fluidity of water.

Although it is difficult to see *The wave* as an explicit argument for political equality, it did challenge prevailing, metropolitan models for understanding the sea. As Herding argues of Courbet's marine pictures, *The wave* demonstrates the artist's belief in 'the power of elemental nature to resist the exploitations of civilization'.[5] Drawing on the Romantic concept of the sea as an overwhelming natural force and physically intensifying it through his unique painting technique, in this work Courbet challenged the viewer's experience of the seashore as art.

Anthony White

1. Letter from Jean-Jacques Fernier to Sonia Dean, 1 March 1993, National Gallery of Victoria, Courbet file.
2. Klaus Herding, *Courbet: to venture independence*, New Haven: Yale University Press, 1991, p. 96.
3. Anne Wagner, 'Courbet's landscapes and their market', *Art History*, vol. 4, no. 4, December 1981, pp. 424–7.
4. 'Felton Bequest purchases: disappointing additions', *Argus*, 23 January 1924, p. 15.
5. Herding, p. 134.

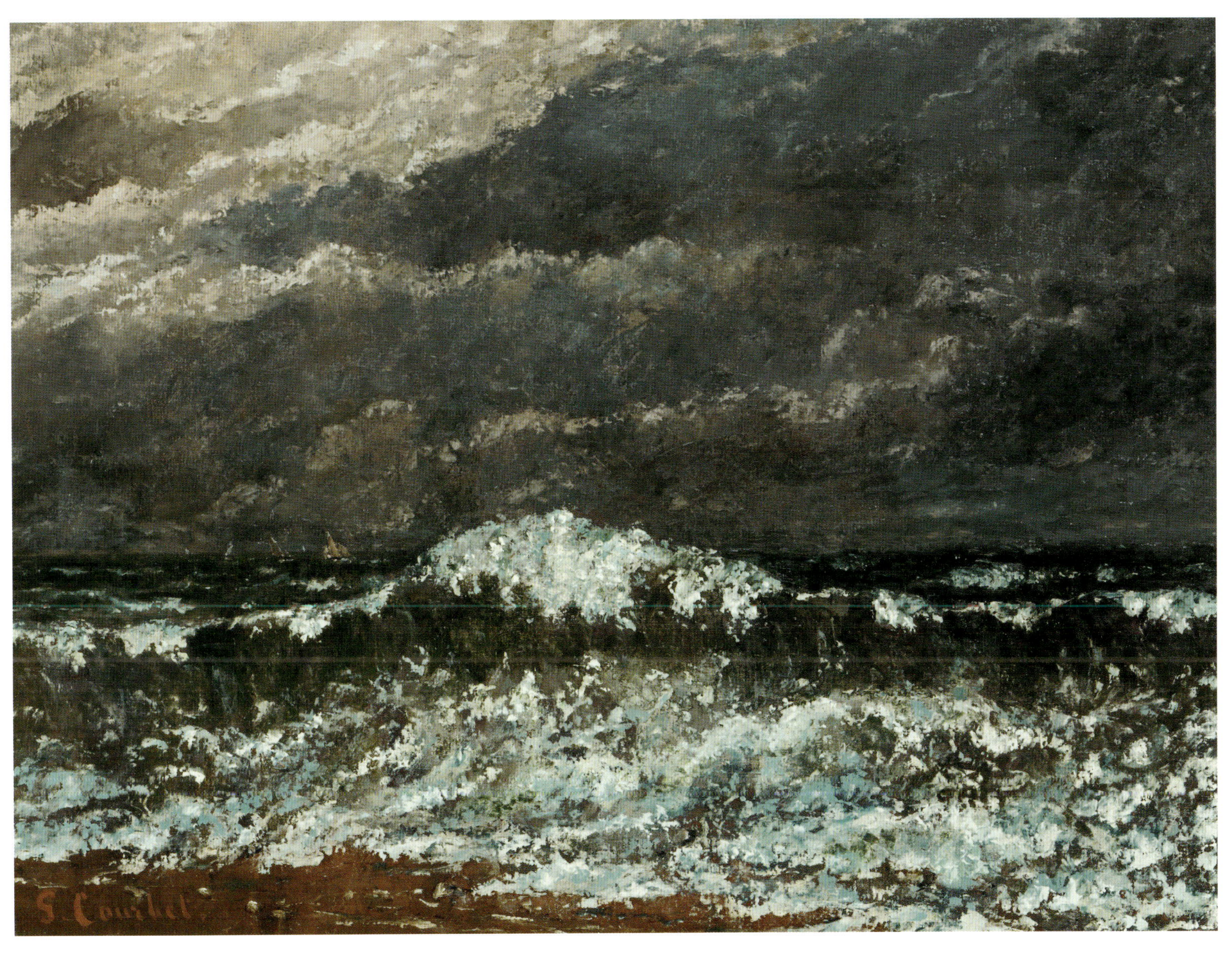
G. Courbet

72. Claude Monet

France 1840–1926
The Pointe de l'Ailly, low tide [***Pointe de l'Ailly, marée basse***] 1882
oil on canvas 60.0 x 100.0 cm
Kerry Stokes Collection, Perth

Monet's use of vivid yellows, blues and lilacs in *The Pointe de l'Ailly, low tide* seems almost poetically symbolic, reaching beyond topographical and climatic mimesis. By restricting his palette to three main colours, the artist emphasises the dramatic light conditions. Reflections of a foreboding sky, storm clouds and the dramatically eroded rocky point, all combine to confuse the recessional space. Structured diagonals of water's edge, bay and cliff make this a particularly lively composition. Finally, the eye settles on a tiny group of figures, bathing just offshore. Like Courbet's Trouville painting (cat. 70), we are prompted to speculate on the nature of this beach scene.

In February 1882, seeking new motifs for his art, Monet travelled to the coastal city of Dieppe in Normandy, for a two-month painting expedition. He soon left the urban noise of Dieppe for Pourville, a small fishing village five kilometres away – a spot popular with summer bathers. He described his happiness at finding this retreat in a letter to Alice Hoschedé:

> The countryside is beautiful, and I regret not coming here earlier, rather than wasting my time in Dieppe. You can't be closer to the sea than I am, right on the shingles, with the waves beating against the steps of the house.[1]

Monet worked hard at Pourville, taking numerous canvases out with him for each day's painting before a chosen vista, such as that in *The Pointe de l'Ailly*. He wrote reassuringly to his dealer, Paul Durand-Ruel, saying: 'I have found so many beautiful things to paint, that I am working away without a breather'.[2] To Alice he recounted a typical session:

> Yesterday I worked on eight studies, figuring that I would give each one an hour's worth. You can see that I'm not letting time waste, especially when one factors in my trek from one motif to another.[3]

In June 1882 Monet returned to Pourville with his extended family – his children, Alice Hoschedé and her children – for a working holiday, renting a house for the summer. Durand-Ruel also spent his vacation at Dieppe, creating what Herbert has termed a 'proximity that summer of dealer and artist [which] reflects common bourgeois patterns of vacationing, and also the market ties that bound one to the other'.[4] Despite the potentially distracting presence of his family, Monet continued to work steadily during his second stay: his two sojourns at Pourville yielded some 100 finished canvases in all. These paintings were later to sell extremely well, cementing his relationship with Durand-Ruel, but this later success was not immediately apparent to the artist. He lamented:

> I am more and more discouraged and disgusted by my work. In short, this has been a wasted season … Amidst all the paintings I've begun, I can't see a single good one.[5]

Those canvases that weather or temperament had prevented Monet from completing at Pourville were finished in the artist's studio during the subsequent months. It is difficult to determine whether *The Pointe de l'Ailly, low tide* was painted during the artist's first or second campaign. Like *Haystacks, midday* (cat. 89) and most of Monet's other major works, however, it is questionable whether any one painting would have been composed entirely on the beach or completed later, indoors, from memory and imagination.

Ted Gott

This is a revised version of the author's entry in Caroline Mathieu, Monique Nonne and Ted Gott, *The Impressionists: masterpieces from the Musée d'Orsay*, Melbourne: National Gallery of Victoria, 2004, pp. 70–1.

1. Monet, letter of 15 February 1882 in Daniel Wildenstein, *Claude Monet: biographie et catalogue raisonné*, Tome II, *1882–1886 Peintures*, Lausanne & Paris: La Bibliothèque des Arts, 1979, p. 214.
2. Monet, letter of 21 February 1882, in Wildenstein, p. 215.
3. Monet, letter of 7 April 1882, in Wildenstein, p. 218.
4. Robert L. Herbert, *Monet on the Normandy coast. Tourism and painting, 1867–1886*, New Haven: Yale University Press, 1994, p. 44.
5. Monet, letter of 26 September 1882, in Wildenstein, p. 220.

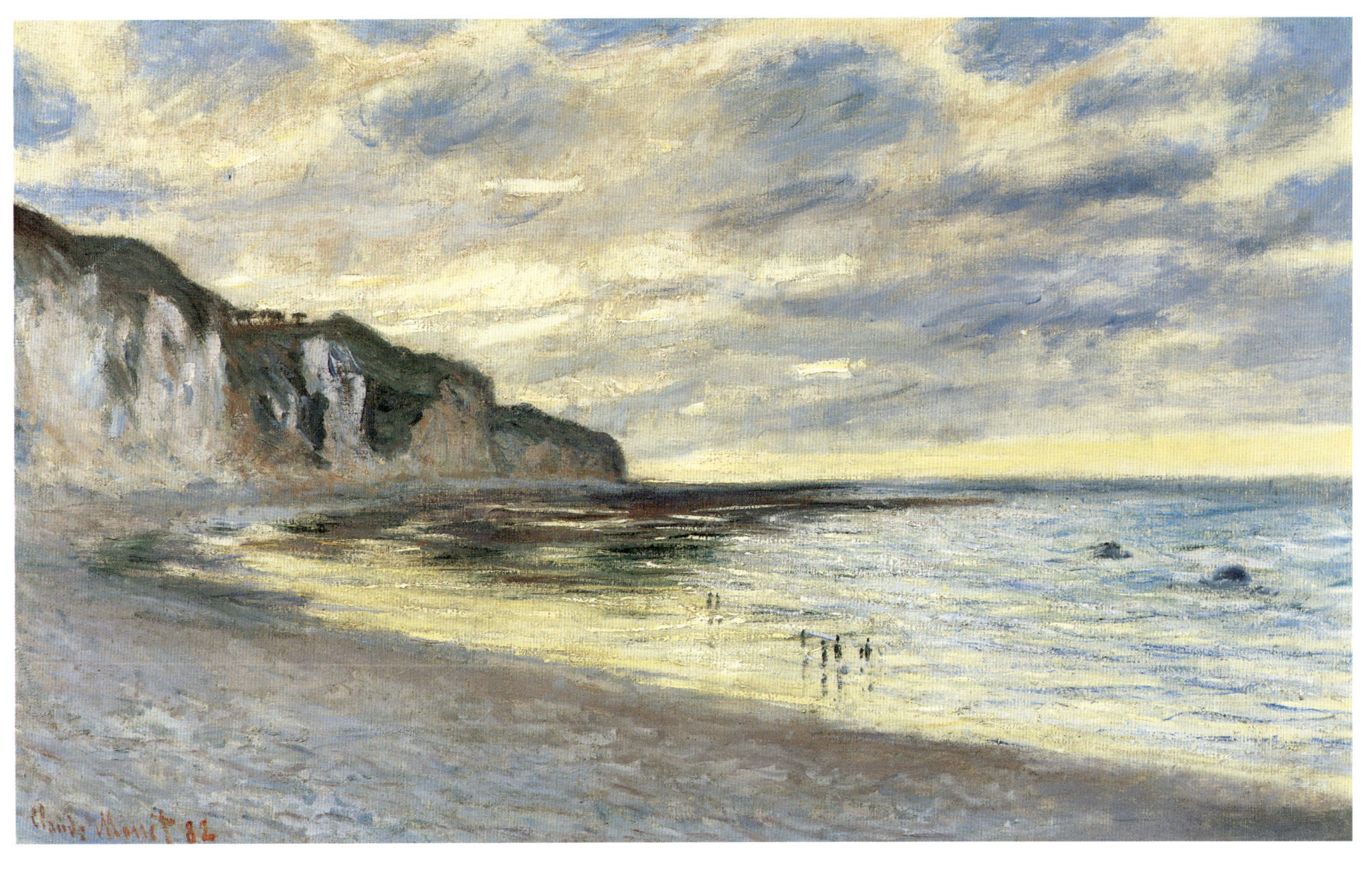

73. Charles Daubigny

France 1817–1878
A snow scene, Valmondois [***Neige près de Valmondais***] 1875
oil on canvas 88.7 x 153.3 cm
Art Gallery of Western Australia, Perth
1904.00 P2

A progressive artist, Daubigny had a significant impact on French landscape painting during the mid-nineteenth century, through his art and in his avid support of the Impressionists. He often painted out of doors and adopted an expressive approach to paint. He was interested in capturing the changing effects of light and atmosphere at a particular time of day. In his use of rapid, broken brushstrokes he helped break down the distinction between a finished painting and a sketch, but the more conservative artists and critics accused him of exhibiting what they considered to be only working sketches.

Coming from a family of painters, Daubigny adopted a traditional manner of working, but later altered his approach to paint spontaneous impressions directly from nature. His subjects include many riverside landscapes of northern France, as well as coastal views painted out of doors.

Daubigny spent much of his childhood at Valmondois, a village on the Oise river to the north-west of Paris. He first went there with his nurse when he was nine. He remained attached to this place, of which he had many happy childhood memories. Although his principal residence was in Paris, he regularly returned to Valmondois to paint.

In this bleak snow scene of a plain near Valmondois, Daubigny created a rural scene of quiet and repose, capturing the light and atmosphere of a grey day. He was interested in the play of whites and blacks, with his whites including touches of blue, pink, red and brown. His buttery paint, spread on thickly, conveys the heaviness of snow, in contrast with the more ethereal feathery strokes with which he depicted the tree, through which light and air can be seen. Daubigny painted the sky with thin layers of paint and the sun in thick impasto to evoke the effect of a wintery light viewed through layers of atmosphere. While creating a seemingly spontaneous impression, he carefully constructed the image, introducing a transition from the foreground to the distance through the winding track. He provided a splash of colour through the deep red jacket of the figure trudging down this path, a focus and point of human interest. The crows in the sky form a triangle as they move down to the tree and up and away from it.

Two years before he painted this work Daubigny exhibited a similar snow scene *Snow* [*La neige*][1] in the Paris Salon of 1873. It was severely criticised because of what the reviewers perceived as his rough execution and lack of finish. Max de Montifaut wrote that 'Mr Daubigny's *Snow* is a piece of plaster spread with a palette knife', while Duvergier de Hauranne suggested that the trees had been painted 'with a broom of birch twigs'.[2]

This atmospheric landscape, with its richly textured paint, suggests why Daubigny's work appealed to Impressionists such as Monet and Pissarro. Equally, it is a revelation of his highly personal vision, the way he painted images of everyday scenes in terms of tone, using lively, direct brushstrokes.

Anne Gray

1. Collection of the Musée d'Orsay, Paris.
2. 'Charles-Francois Daubigny Snow', Musée d'Orsay, viewed November 2007, musee-orsay.fr/en/collections/works-in-focus/painting/commentaire.

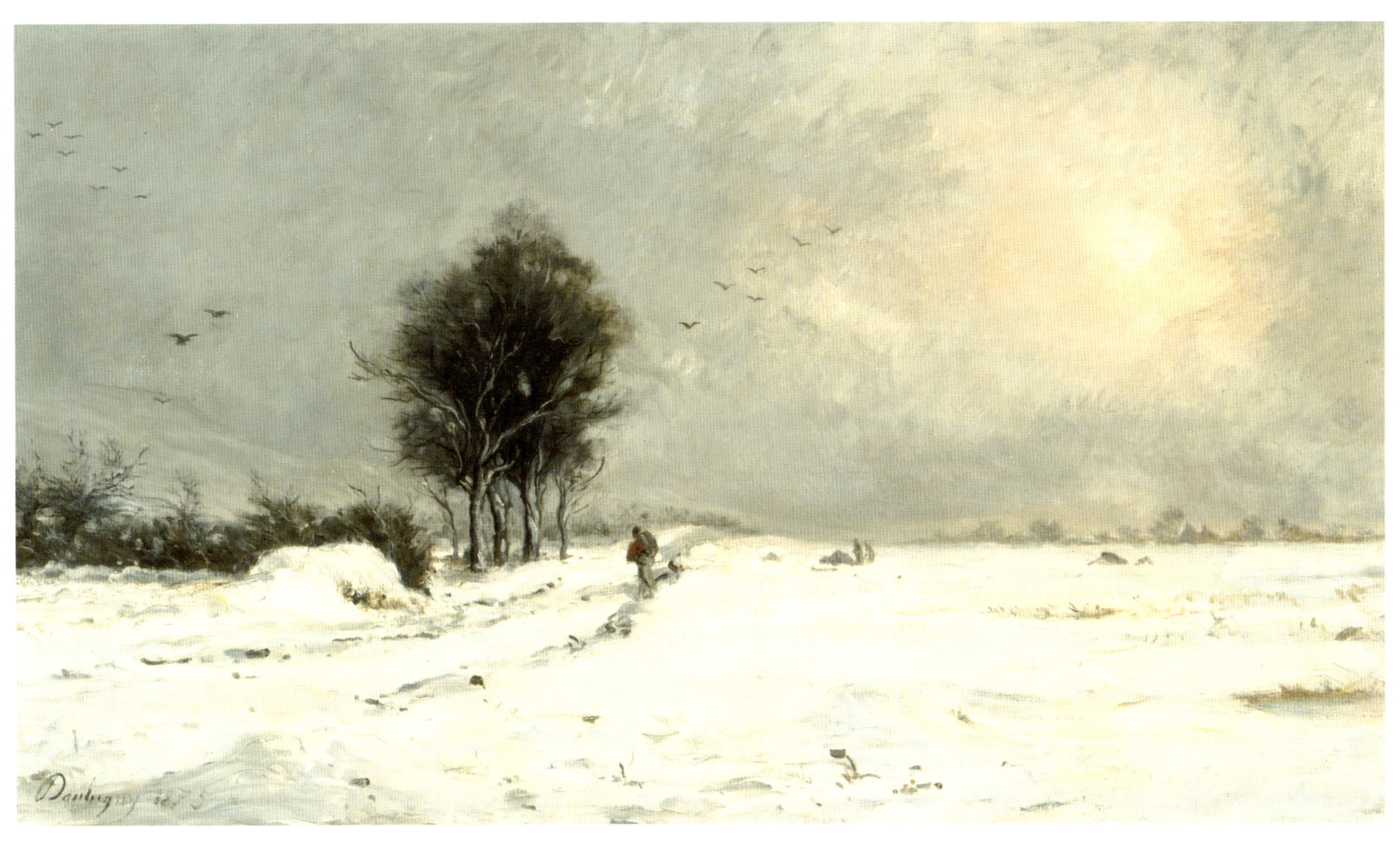

74. Jules Bastien-Lepage

France 1848–1884
Snow effect, Damvillers **[*Effet de neige, Damvillers*]** c. 1882
oil on canvas 43.0 x 53.0 cm
Fine Arts Museums of San Francisco, Palace of the Legion Of Honor
Museum Purchase, Grover A. Magnin Bequest Fund 2001.1.127

Nothing happens here, it seems. A field of snow is marked by some trees on the top, a road at the right, clouds, and the intimation of lightening on the horizon. A few vertical scratches indicate grass poking through a crust of snow. But what intensity of observation! The paint wiped around the hill makes the viewer think about the colour white, how it can be made yellow, grey or blue. The trees are nothing but black blobs marking edges, while snow-filled clouds animate the scene, pushed across the sky by winter wind.

In his short career, Bastien-Lepage was famous for naturalistic depictions of peasants, especially girls working in the fields; robust and alive, their figures dominate the scene.[1] His land was always under cultivation, sowing or harvest. Here the landscape is beyond human use, made fallow by the season, by the ruthless power of winter. For Bastien-Lepage, the fecundity of agriculture represented France recovering its pride and productivity after the disastrous military defeat by Prussia in 1870. In this work the small village of Damvillers is enshrouded in snow and ice, under a watery sky, but there is a hint of light and hope that prefigures a change of weather and, eventually, of season.

Because he was neither academician nor Impressionist, Bastien-Lepage has been neglected in the analysis of the culture wars that raged in the nineteenth century between conservatives and radicals. Even an apparently subjectless painting like *Snow effect, Damvillers* may seem progressive because it lacks detail, finish, incident and preferably a moral, all demanded by the Academy. But the artist's observations are not only of the moment, like Monet's *Haystacks, midday* (cat. 89). The hill is eternal, not simply created by the light in which it is observed: the effects may be fleeting, but the land remains, permanent and solid, underneath the snow.

Christine Dixon

1. See, for example, *Season of October: the potato gatherers* 1878 in the collection of the National Gallery of Vicitoria, Melbourne.

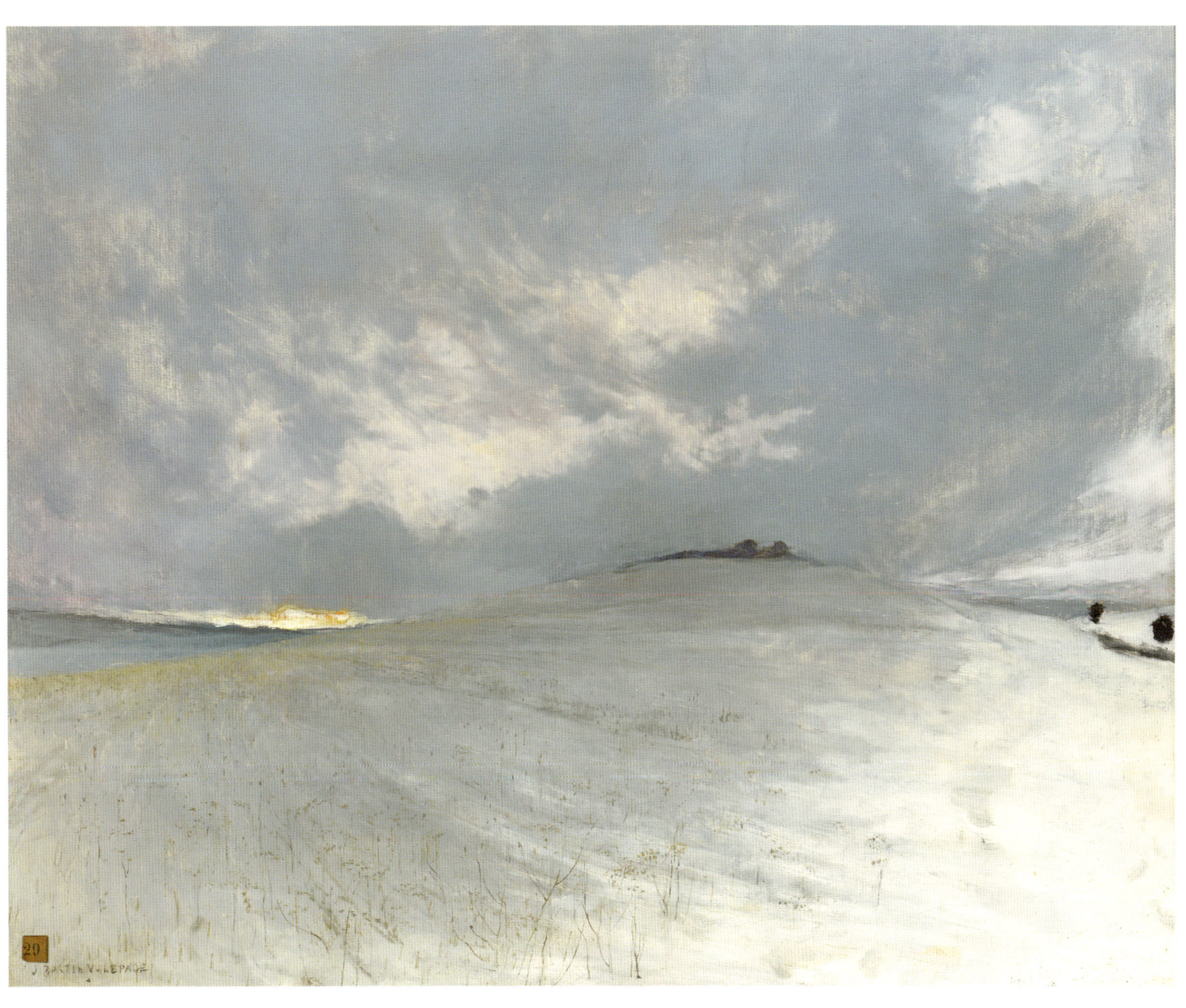

75. Claude Monet

France 1840–1926
Vétheuil 1879
oil on canvas 60.0 x 81.0 cm
National Gallery of Victoria, Melbourne
Felton Bequest, 1937 406-4

Vétheuil marks a turning point in the life and work of France's best-known Impressionist painter. After moving to the small village of Vétheuil in 1878, Monet ceased painting metropolitan scenes of Paris life, to concentrate entirely on depictions of the countryside. His landscapes became less inhabited and their locations more remote. Whereas the modernity of his work was previously conveyed both by his painting method and the depictions of urban life, industry and tourism, it would now rest almost exclusively on his innovations in technique.

The painting presents a broad expanse of the Seine river bank on a sunny day, with the village of Vétheuil in the background. Light pervades this picture. Monet has almost completely removed darker tones, giving it an all-over luminosity. The vivid hues create a powerful sense of brightness, particularly in the clouds, where the artist has juxtaposed yellow highlights and purple shadows, adding extra brilliance by pairing opposing colours. Applied in broad, quick strokes, the paint gives the appearance of rippling movement in the water and of the shifting patterns of summer clouds, while also drawing attention to the picture surface. By eliminating objects from the foreground of his picture – thereby removing a device used by more traditional landscape painters to provide a visual contrast with the far distance – Monet avoids creating a strong illusion of depth. He also divides the canvas into three horizontal bands, as defined by the lines of the river bank and those of the horizon line. The intense lighting, evident brushwork, refusal of spatial illusion and geometric division of the canvas all strongly distinguish Monet's work from the Classical and Picturesque traditions of earlier landscape.

Although the painting depicts the town of Vétheuil, signs of modern life, in the form of industry, boating parties or picnickers, are lacking. This sharply differentiates the work from Monet's previous landscapes. It is, to some degree, a reflection of the nature of Vétheuil itself, a small agrarian village without a tourist trade, which offered the Monet family relatively cheap accommodation at a time when the artist was struggling financially.[1] At the same time, the artist's choice of view deliberately avoids the many signs of industry on the Seine, including barges and washerwomen, which were clearly visible from other vantage points during that time at Vétheuil.[2] Monet has deliberately selected a perspective of the town which shows it motionless between the radiant sky above and the shimmering water beneath.

Monet's disavowal of industry and concentration on the bare essentials of the village, and the surrounding landscape to which it belongs, has been interpreted by McNamara as introducing a 'timeless, elegiac aspect'.[3] It was also a means whereby the artist removed incidental details from the work in order to concentrate, in a series with an essentially similar motif, on the fleeting impressions created by the changing weather and time of day.

Anthony White

1. Carla Rachman, *Monet*, London: Phaidon, 1997, p. 133.
2. Carole McNamara, 'Monet's Vétheuil paintings: site, subject and debacles', in *Monet at Vétheuil: the turning point*, Ann Arbor: The University of Michigan, 1998, p. 68.
3. McNamara p. 76.

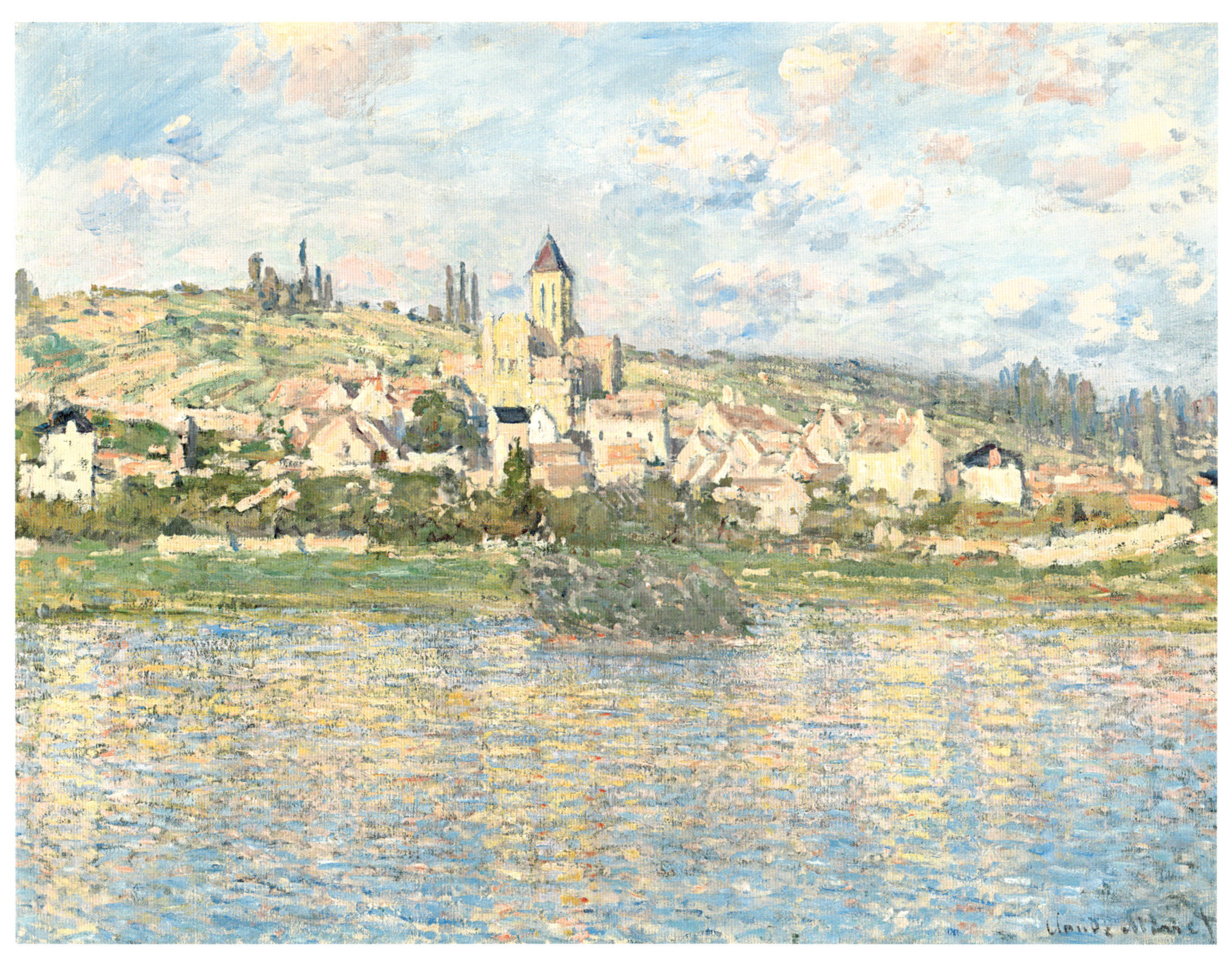

76. Tom Roberts

Great Britain 1856 – Australia 1931
Slumbering sea, Mentone 1887
oil on canvas 51.3 x 76.5 cm
National Gallery of Victoria, Melbourne
Purchased with the assistance of a special grant from the Government of Victoria 1979 A12-1980

Seated at the tiller, he cleaved the water with his oar and gazed tranquilly before him, filled with the desire to thus continue rowing forever over this velvet plain. On the sea, warm and generous impulses rose within him, filled his soul and in a measure purified it of the defilements of life. He enjoyed this effect and liked to feel himself better, out here, amid the waves and air where the thoughts and occupations of life lose their interest and life itself sinks into insignificance. In the night, the sound of its soft breathing is wafted over the slumbering sea, and this infinite murmur fills the soul with peace, checks all unworthy impulses and brings forth mighty dreams.
Maxim Gorky[1]

The story is summarised by the 'slumbering sea' of Roberts's title, plus the inscription 'Mentone', referring to a well-known beach resort.[2] In a tranquil scene the sea is calm and warm. Two boats rest on its stillness. The breeze is just sufficient to swell the sails of the outermost without ruffling the surface of the water. A party of holidaymakers have visited the secluded cove. With the exception of an alert dog and a small boy, the adults of the party appear dazed by radiant heat, sunlight and sand: one reviewer has described them as 'melting' into the scene.[3] On the gravel bank at one side of the picture sits a woman in a white dress. She looks across at the others – she may be about to stand up but seems fixed in place, eternally, languidly detached from the action at centre picture. There, at the water's edge, are the dog, the boy and a second woman in white. The woman leans forward to steady a sailboat, in readiness for the people to get out. They, however, make no move to stand and leave the boat.

The title of the painting, personifying the sea, influences the interpretation. Somnolent sea surrounds the two people at the far end of the boat. In the line of figures stretching across the composition, these two are outermost. Man and wife, or mother and widowed daughter, they sit, one within the arms of the other, dressed in the black and grey of mourning. Isolated at their end of the boat, cantilevered over the water and marked by death, they cling together in the hush of the slumbering sea.

The palette – creams, whites, warm ochres and grey blues, accented with thin black stripes and round touches of red – is reminiscent of Corot. Roberts and his friends studied closely the works of the French artist. The composition of reciprocal triangles and long horizontals crossed by small verticals has Corot's poise and correctness. But Roberts's description of a specific time and place distinguishes him from Corot. Neither was he a pure Impressionist. *Slumbering sea, Mentone* expresses the subjective overtones of a situation in contemporary life. The artist's interests in the symbolic qualities of weather and in spreading the influence of a mood over a scene of human activity are characteristic of the last decades of the century.

Mary Eagle

1. From the short story *Tchelkache*, translated for J.F. Taylor & Co., New York, 1902, in *Twenty-six and one and other stories*, viewed December 2007, en.wikisource.org/wiki/Tchelkache.
2. This essay owes much to Daniel Thomas, 'The Sunny South: Bayside Melbourne Life and Landscape, 1886–90', in Terence Lane, *Australian Impressionism*, Melbourne: National Gallery of Victoria, 2007, pp. 87–93.
3. Michael Fitzgerald, 'New Worlds', *Time*, 16 March 1998.

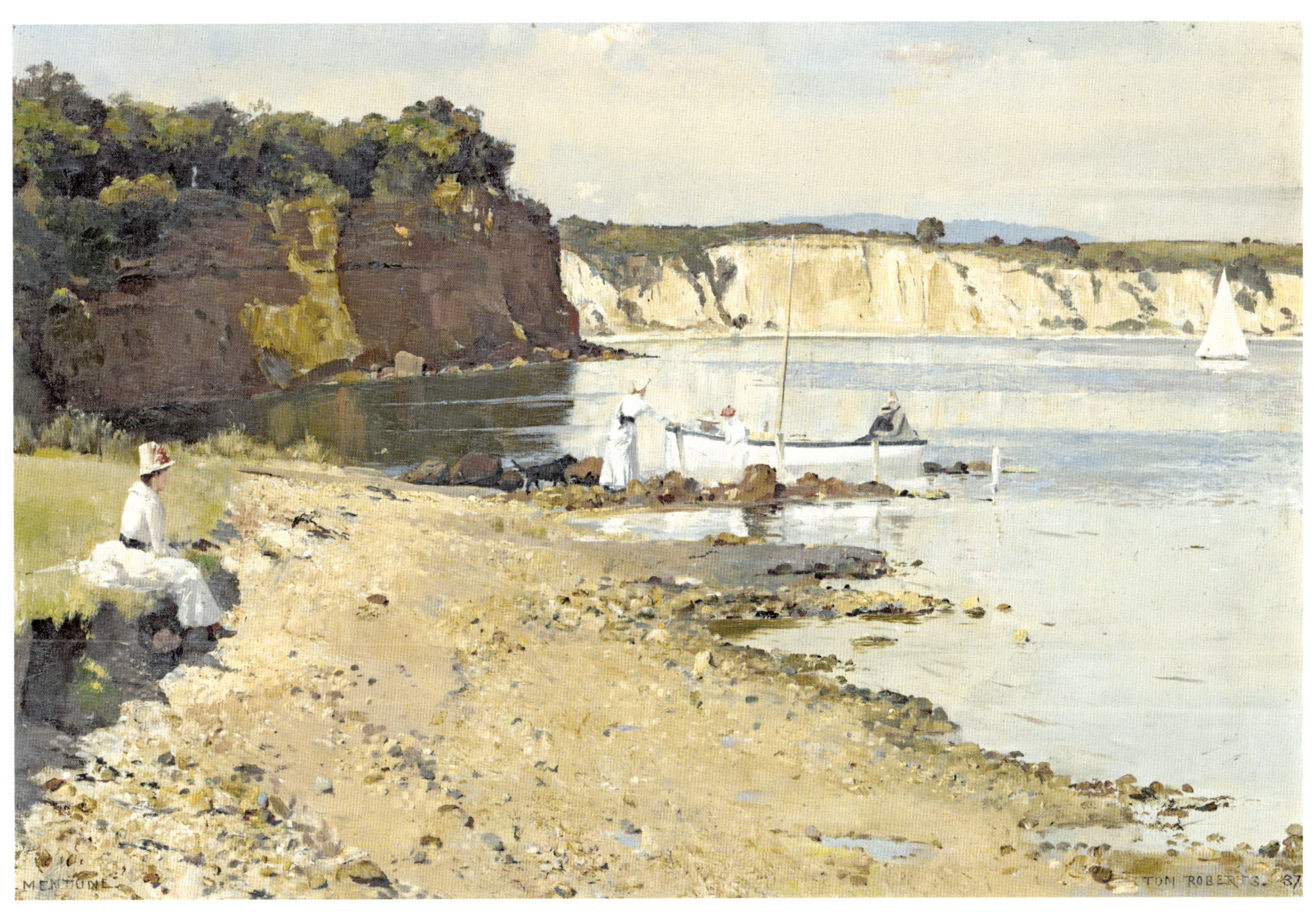
MENTONE
TOM ROBERTS. 87

77. Charles Conder

Great Britain 1868–1909
Australia 1884–1890
Bronte Beach 1888
oil on paper on cardboard 22.6 x 33 cm
National Gallery of Australia, Canberra
Purchased from Gallery admission charges 1982 NGA 1982.1670

Looking at *Bronte Beach*, we revel in a sense of lazy relaxation. The paint is not applied thickly to the canvas, so the work looks as if it were made entirely without exertion or force, and is instead the result of a simple moment of idle brushstrokes. In this way Conder creates a painting that seems to exist entirely for us, the viewers. It's as if we were there on the sand, opened our eyes briefly to observe the beach, and then languidly rolled back, eyes closed, yet with the image of the sun and waves still in our mind's eye.

Bronte Beach is a small, early work; it was painted by Conder, working alongside his friend Girolamo Nerli (1863–1926), on the Queen's Birthday holiday of 24 May 1888. Nerli imparted his own Macchiaioli influences and Impressionistic sensibilities to the young artist. The Macchiaioli, a group of Italian painters who painted out of doors, were renowned for their use of broad patches of high-keyed colour to create a sense of shade and light.

This way of working, combined with a range of other influences. sharpened Conder's ability to capture the fleeting nature of beauty. During his brief time in Australia the artist was well equipped to explore the pervading spaciousness of the landscape.

In *Bronte Beach* Conder's use of oil paint resembles watercolour, characterised by 'faded tints, transparent colours and fine outlines', as Eagle points out.[1] His Australian friends encouraged Conder to abandon this watercolour quality, which he found difficult. Later, in France, he manipulated oil paint in a way similar to his Impressionist contemporaries, finally convinced that this watercolour effect undermined his ability as an artist (cat. 94).

Conder had a series of mentors and teachers during his time in Australia, but no other had the impact of Tom Roberts, who Conder later described as his 'friend, philosopher, and guide'.[2] Despite their close connection, Roberts and Conder had distinctive styles. Roberts's *Slumbering sea, Mentone* 1887 (cat. 76) and this work share similar subjects but are very different in approach. The Mentone painting also depicts a lazy day at the seashore, although it lacks the idle, unaffected quality that Conder so beautifully describes with his supple brushstrokes and chalky palette. Roberts, trained at the Royal Academy in London, took a more academic approach, and his technical ability is evident. Conder's *Bronte Beach* is much more a brief encounter between board and paint, without Roberts's forethought and polish.

Bronte Beach was painted two years before and a world apart from Monet's *Haystacks, midday* (cat. 89), but they share some characteristics. The elusive quality of time is captured by both artists, in the movement of the sun and a tangible sense of light. Conder seems to share the Impressionist goal of capturing an instant, for beauty is transient and a moment passed will not be repeated.

Elizabeth Welden

1. Mary Eagle, *The oil paintings of Charles Conder in the National Gallery of Australia*, Canberra: National Gallery of Australia, 1997, p. 22.2
2. See Helen Topliss, 'Tom Roberts' in *Australian dictionary of biography online edition*, viewed October 2007, adb.online.anu.edu.au/biogs/A110419b.htm?hilite=roberts.

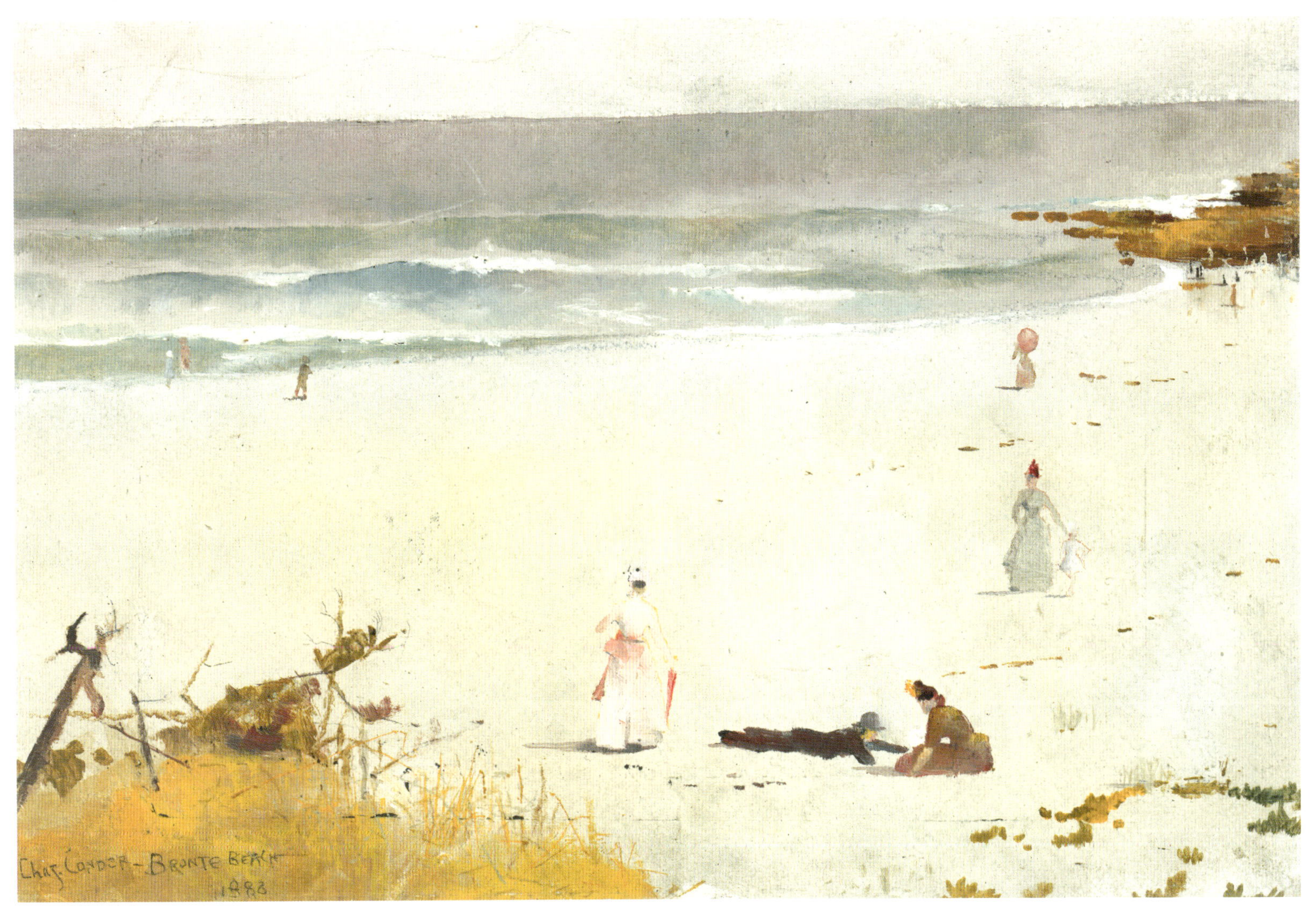
Chas. Conder – Bronte Beach
1888

78. Tom Roberts

Great Britain 1856 – Australia 1931
'Evening, when the quiet east flushes faintly at the sun's last look' 1887–88
oil on canvas 50.8 x 76.4 cm
National Gallery of Victoria, Melbourne
W.H. Short Bequest 1944 1375-4

Roberts's return to Melbourne in 1885, after four years' study in Europe, marked the end of his long artistic apprenticeship. By the age of twenty-nine he had developed a sophisticated eye and an exceptional technical facility that enabled him to capture the appearance of things. He was also a proselytiser and, back home, looked up his old friend Frederick McCubbin (1855–1917) and enthused him about the European style of *plein-air* painting. Together they established a weekend painting camp on Houston's Farm at Box Hill, some sixteen kilometres from the city. It was a primitive approximation to the artists' colonies of Europe and America, but quickly became a hub of the new painting in Melbourne. Many of the first great works of the Australian Impressionist movement were painted there, in or near the patch of remnant bushland on Gardiners Creek where the camp was located. Paintings such as McCubbin's *Lost*[1] and Roberts's own *A summer morning tiff*[2] and *Wood splitters*[3] captured the intimacy and patchy sunlight of the site.

Roberts's *'Evening, when the quiet east flushes faintly at the sun's last look'* was painted on the hillside above the camp and is more panoramic in format than the other early Box Hill views. It is also a nocturne – a type of twilight or evening subject that was still something of a novelty in late 1880s Melbourne. Streeton, who joined the group in 1887, recalled:

> We tried painting the sunset with somewhat conventional and melodramatic results. Roberts pointed to the evening sky in the east, and showed us the beauty of its subtle greys, and the delicate flush of the afterglow, when the shadow of the earth upon its atmosphere, resembling a curved band of cool grey, rises up, and succeeds the rosy warmth as the sun descends further below the western horizon. He was the first artist in Australia to notice it, and to point it out to the native-born.[4]

Roberts's painting skills enabled him to capture rapidly the topography of the valley of Gardiners Creek and the view to the Dandenongs. The facture is suggestive rather than descriptive, with a definite drift towards abstraction, particularly in the adjustments made in the studio to the foreground and other areas. Atmosphere was also important, and Roberts succeeded brilliantly in capturing *le moment crepusculaire*, the stillness of dusk. The only movement is a bird wheeling in from the left, and a waft of smoke rising from a field.

'Evening, when the quiet east flushes faintly at the sun's last look' is a national picture, in that its subtext is the claiming and clearing of the land, one of the great themes of nineteenth-century Australian life. As such, it demands a place on Roberts's list of national pictures, alongside such works as *Coming South*, *Allegro con brio: Bourke Street West*, *The sunny South* and *Shearing the rams*.[5] It is also his most poetic and elegiac landscape, Symbolist in its evocation of the slumbering land.

Terence Lane

---

1. Collection of the National Gallery of Victoria, Melbourne.
2. Collection of the Ballarat Fine Art Gallery, Victoria.
3. Collection of the Ballarat Fine Art Gallery.
4. *Argus* (Melbourne), 21 June 1932, p. 8.
5. All collection of National Gallery of Victoria, except *Allegro con brio: Bourke Street West* (cat. 82).

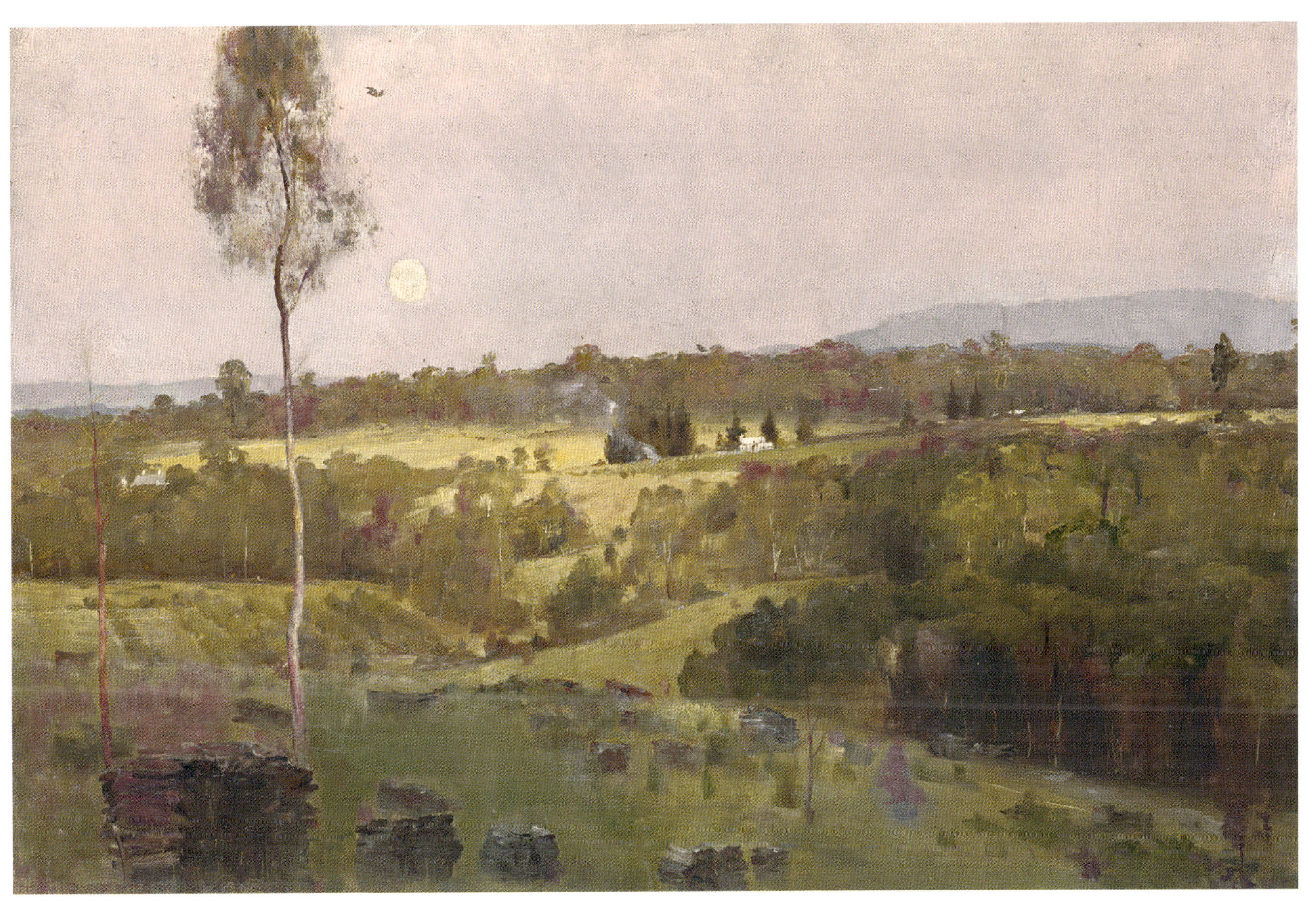

79. Arthur Streeton

Australia 1867–1943
Early summer – gorse in bloom 1888
oil on canvas 56.2 x 100.6 cm
Art Gallery of South Australia, Adelaide
Gift of Mrs Andrew Tennant through the Art Gallery of South Australia Foundation 1982

Streeton is famous for his Australian Impressionist pictures of blue skies and golden pastures. *Early summer – gorse in bloom* was his first masterpiece of this kind and one of his finest landscapes. The year 1888 was the centenary of European settlement in Australia and a significant year for the development of Australian Impressionism with its increasingly nationalistic agenda. But this painting is not self-consciously nationalistic, as his Australian landscapes would soon become. *Early summer – gorse in bloom* may have been his first major 'blue and gold' painting but the plant gorse, though sweet-scented, is after all an introduced weed and not a subject for national celebration. At first the painting appears disarmingly naturalistic, a glimpse of an ordinary paddock overrun with gorse. No trees frame the composition or produce a central focus. Nor is there a focus of a building, picturesque winding river or road, and no mountain vista, as seen often in Streeton's later landscapes. Rather this painting is a triumph of the non-subject.

Early summer – gorse in bloom was painted at Box Hill, probably in October when the yellow blooms begin to die in Victoria's countryside. The lower foreground records a snatch of half-dead gorse. Above it a culvert, fence and gravel cart-track follow the slope where two women can be seen disappearing into the distance. A young girl waits by the fence with a spray in her hand while another, possibly her sister, wanders down the track with her own blossoms, followed by a pet lamb. Have they come to meet their father home for lunch? Are they waiting for the postman? Whatever they are doing, they are merely *staffage* in the composition. It is the unusually high-keyed light and the gorse which are the real subjects of this Australian Impressionist picture.

Although the canvas looks as though it has been spontaneously painted on-site, much of the landscape is contrived, and has been carefully worked and re-worked in the studio. Streeton, for example, portrayed the golden gorse disappearing over the distant hillside, no mean feat, as yellow is a difficult colour to control in a landscape space where it jumps forward from the picture plane. He has succeeded by giving an illusion of the use of yellow in the distance where he has instead used – without compromising realism – a light, almost khaki, green which helps the gorse to recede over the curve of the hill.

At the time the painting was begun, the artist had just met Charles Conder who helped to open up the decorative possibilities of aestheticism and Asian art for Streeton. The blossom motif, high horizon line, grassy foreground, cut-off gorse at the bottom of the picture, and its exaggerated horizontal proportions are the devices and motifs of Japanese landscape screens, while the pink of the principal girl's stockings and hat, and the blue dress of the other child are deliberately placed to create a satisfying arrangement. The painting is the first in a new phase in Streeton's art, in which the decorative elements in landscape compositions would become increasingly self conscious.

Ron Radford

Adapted from Ron Radford and Jane Hylton, *Australian colonial art 1800–1900*, Adelaide, Art Gallery of South Australia, 1995, pp. 153–6.

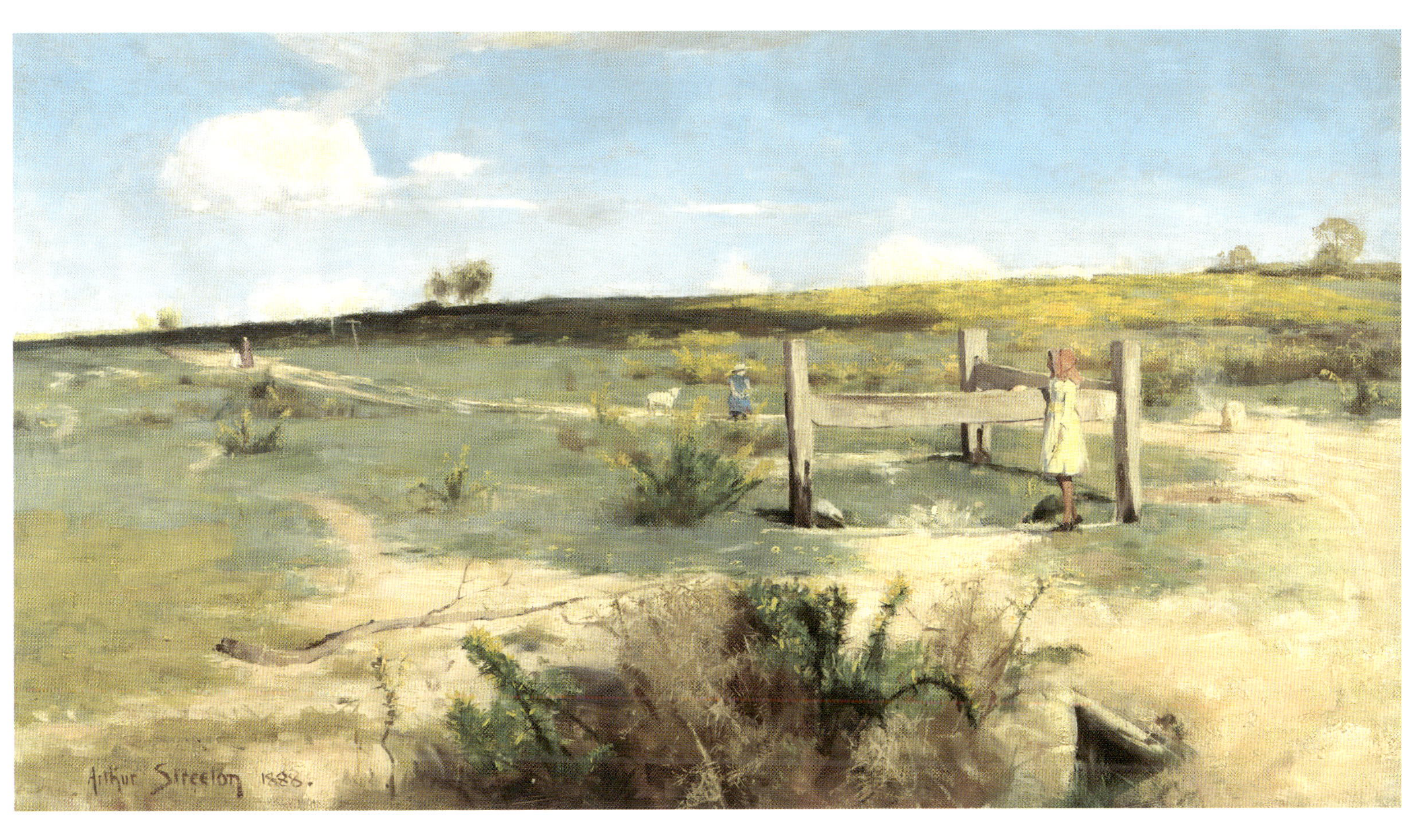
Arthur Streeton 1888.

80. Alfred Sisley

France 1839–1899
***A path at Les Sablons* [*Un sentier aux Sablons*]** 1883
oil on canvas 46.0 x 55.0 cm
National Gallery of Australia, Canberra
A Millennium Gift of Sara Lee Corporation 2000 NGA 2000.229

Sisley's lively, sketch-like painting is deceptive. It has the immediacy of an 'impression', the qualities of a moment captured in paint, and yet something is awry. Unlike Monet's carefully laboured 'envelope' of light in *Haystacks, midday* (cat. 89) and *Morning haze* (cat. 97) – or works produced by Seurat and Cézanne in the same decade (cat. 86 and 100) – Sisley's flurry of paint seems nervous in parts. There is an apparent contradiction between treatment and subject. In *A path at Les Sablons*, the artist offers a fleeting vision, a vignette of life in the country so ordinary we might deem it hardly worth remark.

Like Friedrich and Constable before him, Sisley's travel was local. Apart from several short trips to England, he limited his trips to a few regions on the outskirts of Paris: towns and small villages such as Louviennes, Marly-le-roi and Moret-sur-Loing. He came to know these places intimately, producing many paintings in which aspects of his environs are combined. Apart from a handful of portraits and still lifes, Sisley confined himself to rural landscapes. His subjects were not crowded city bars and cafés, parks, busy boulevards and railway stations, nor beach resorts and expeditions to the Normandy coast made by other Impressionists. These subjects did not appeal to him.

A path at Les Sablons presents a series of contrasts – of colours, of shapes and planes, of paint application. The pale ground is glimpsed through thinly scumbled paint. In parts, Sisley dragged his brush through still-wet colours. The energy of the central tree, with flicks making yellow leaves, and undulating limbs, is juxtaposed against three upright poplars. The solidity of mulberry-brown blocks of tiled roofs and white or tan chimneys is viewed against a veil of clouds and blue sky. At left we glimpse a carefully arranged, compartmentalised garden over the fence. The purples, greens, yellows and white of this enclosure are echoed in more casually rendered fruit trees and beehives at right. In the centre, a path meanders across an inexact triangle of green. Further up, as the oblique angle of the fence converges with the path, vertical forms merge with the foliage and side of the building.

In 1880 Sisley moved to the region of Seine-et-Marne, south-east of Paris, where he remained for the rest of his life. Brettell describes *A path at Les Sablons* as one of the few canvases painted at this time within the artist's studio, not out of doors.[1] Each pictorial component was established by Sisley in a rough pencil sketch.[2] Examined individually, the parts of *A path at Les Sablons* are relatively straightforward. But, as a whole, the scene becomes more problematic. What happens at the end of the path? According to landscape convention, it should lead the eye into the composition. Has Sisley employed a small number of colours, nuanced palette and tilting picture planes in order to undermine landscape conventions? Could this be a composite view? The painting remains a conundrum.

Lucina Ward

1. Richard R. Brettell, *An Impressionist legacy: the collection of Sara Lee Corporation*, 3rd edn, New York: Abbeville Press, 1990, pp. 112–13.
2. In a sketchbook now held in the Louvre, Paris; reproduced in Richard R. Brettell, *Monet to Moore: the millennium gift of Sara Lee Corporation*, New Haven: Yale University Press, 1999, p. 176.

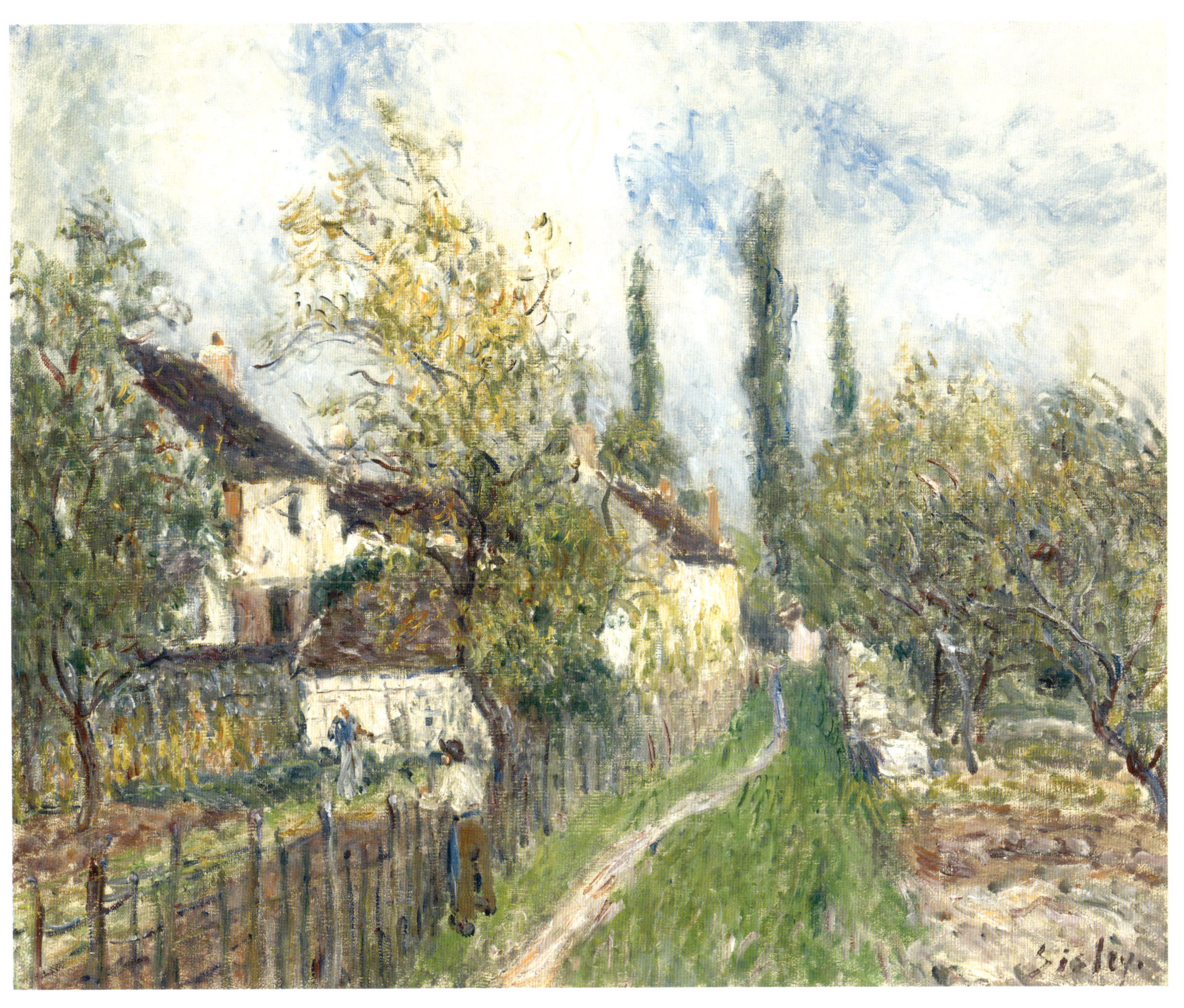
Sisley.

81. Paul Cézanne

France 1839–1906
The uphill road **[*La route montante*]** 1881
oil on canvas 61.4 x 74.3 cm
National Gallery of Victoria, Melbourne
Felton Bequest, 1938 543–4

I do not remember ever having seen Cézanne at the Nouvelle-Athenes; he was too rough and savage a creature, and appeared in Paris only rarely. We used to hear about him – he used to be met on the outskirts of Paris wandering about in his jack-boots ... His work may be described as anarchy in painting, as art in delirium.
George Moore[1]

While Moore's colourful description of Cézanne may exaggerate the wildness of one of the nineteenth century's most important painters, it suggests the radical nature of his art and the passion with which he undertook it.

By the late 1870s Cézanne's search for creative expression saw him reject the Impressionists, with whom he had previously exhibited, in his desire to find a stylistically new way of depicting nature. On 24 September 1879 the artist wrote to his childhood friend Emile Zola: 'I am still striving to discover my right way as a painter'.[2] This 'striving' is evident in *The uphill road*, a painting that can be considered transitional in Cézanne's career as he moved away from the Impressionist interest in capturing transitory effects, towards a more solid and structured approach to nature. He painted this work between May and October 1881, when staying in Pontoise near his friend and mentor Pissarro.[3]

The uphill road is one of a series that showed the small villages of the area set amongst their natural surroundings; a subject that attracted Cézanne less for its picturesque qualities than for the challenge of representing geometric relationships between the landscape and buildings. It appears, at first glance, to be a simple enough painting: a group of carefully articulated buildings with their distinctive grey roof tiles are separated from a grassy hill and country road by a low stone fence. The scene is given added complexity through a carefully conceived composition in which Cézanne divides the picture space into four bands, comprising sky, houses, grass and road.

Despite this formal arrangement the painting seems sketchy in parts, especially in the foreground where the grassed area is an almost undelineated block of light colour. The thinness of Cézanne's paint and his use of rapid diagonal brushstrokes, particularly in the sky, give the canvas a spontaneity that suggests it was not completed. This impression is reinforced by the fact that when he returned to Paris from Pontoise, Cézanne left *The uphill road* with Pissarro, and probably worked on it again many years later. That, even then, he still does not appear to have finished the painting, suggests the demanding temperament of an artist who was always searching for more complete ways to depict nature.

Isobel Crombie

Another version of this entry was published in *European masterpieces: six centuries of paintings from the National Gallery of Victoria, Australia*, Melbourne: National Gallery of Victoria, 2000, p. 162.

1. George Moore, *Reminiscences of the Impressionist painters*, Dublin: Maunsel, 1906, quoted in Jack Lindsay, *Cézanne: his life and art*, New York: Harper and Row, 1972, p. 207.
2. Letter LXV in John Rewald (ed.), *Paul Cézanne: letters*, trans. Marguerite Kay, London: Bruno Cassirer, 1941, pp. 139–40.
3. Birgit Schwarz, cat. 72, in Felix Bauman (ed.), *Cézanne: finished unfinished*, Ostfildern-Ruit: Hatje Cantz, 2000, p. 271.Victoria, 2000, p. 162.

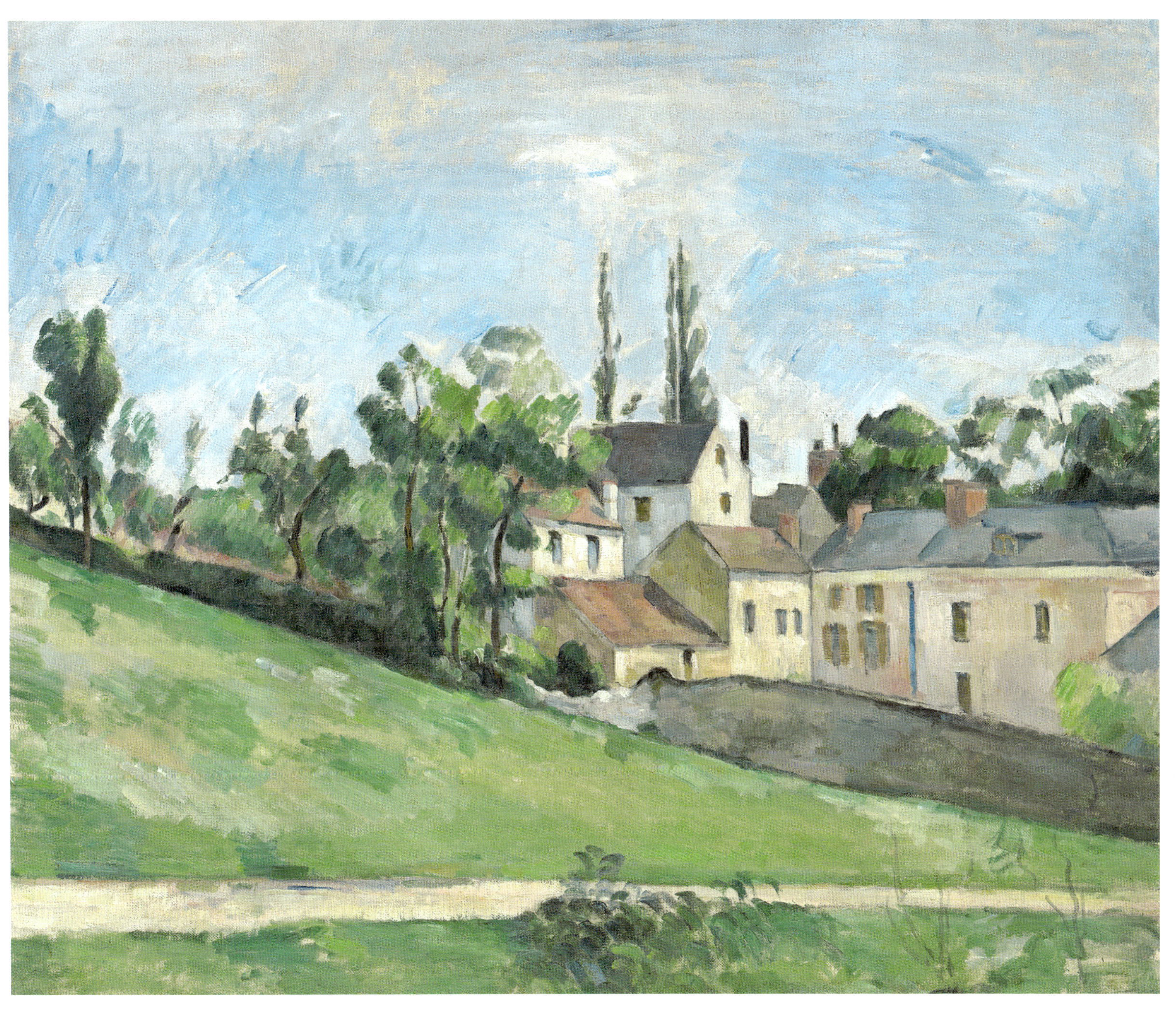

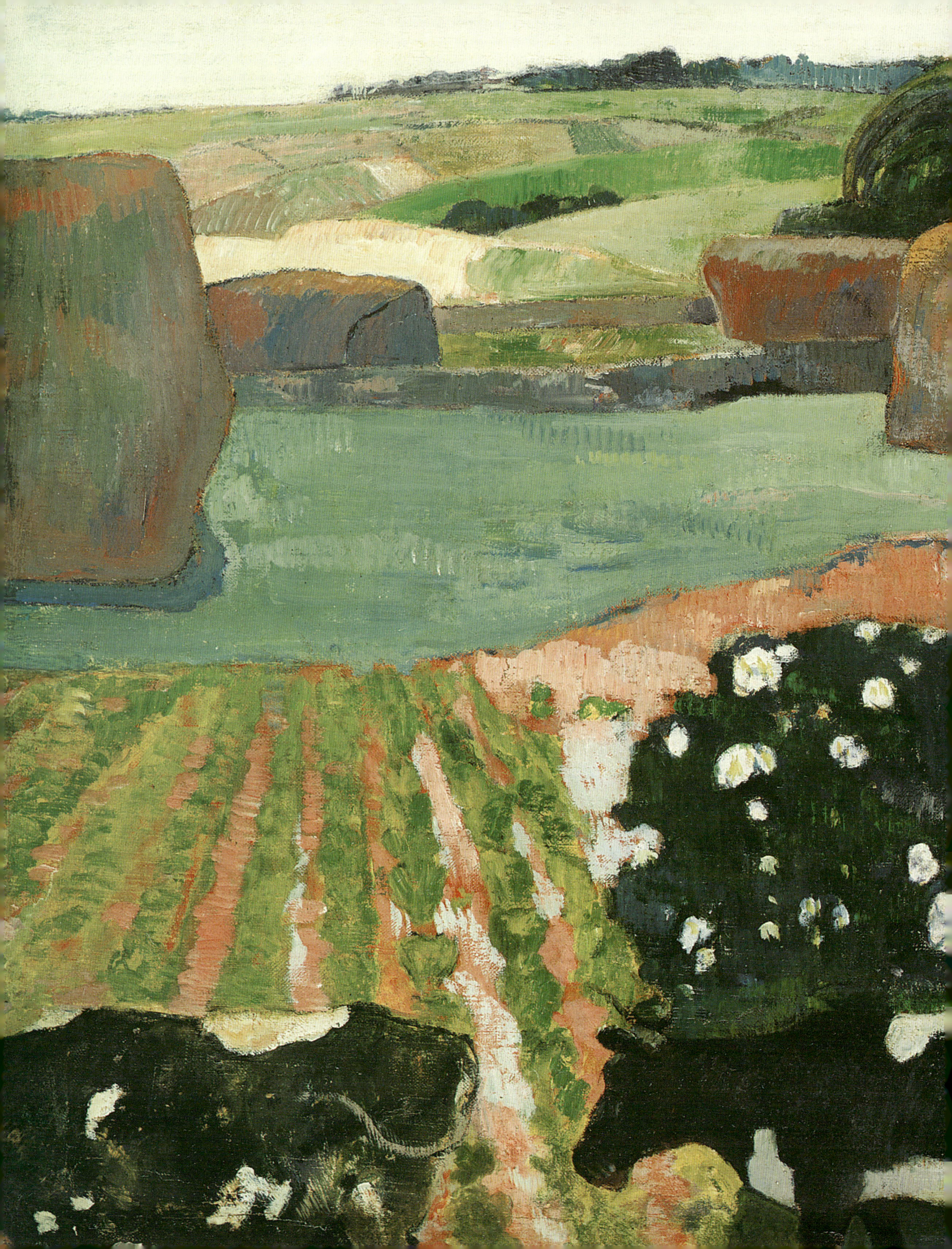

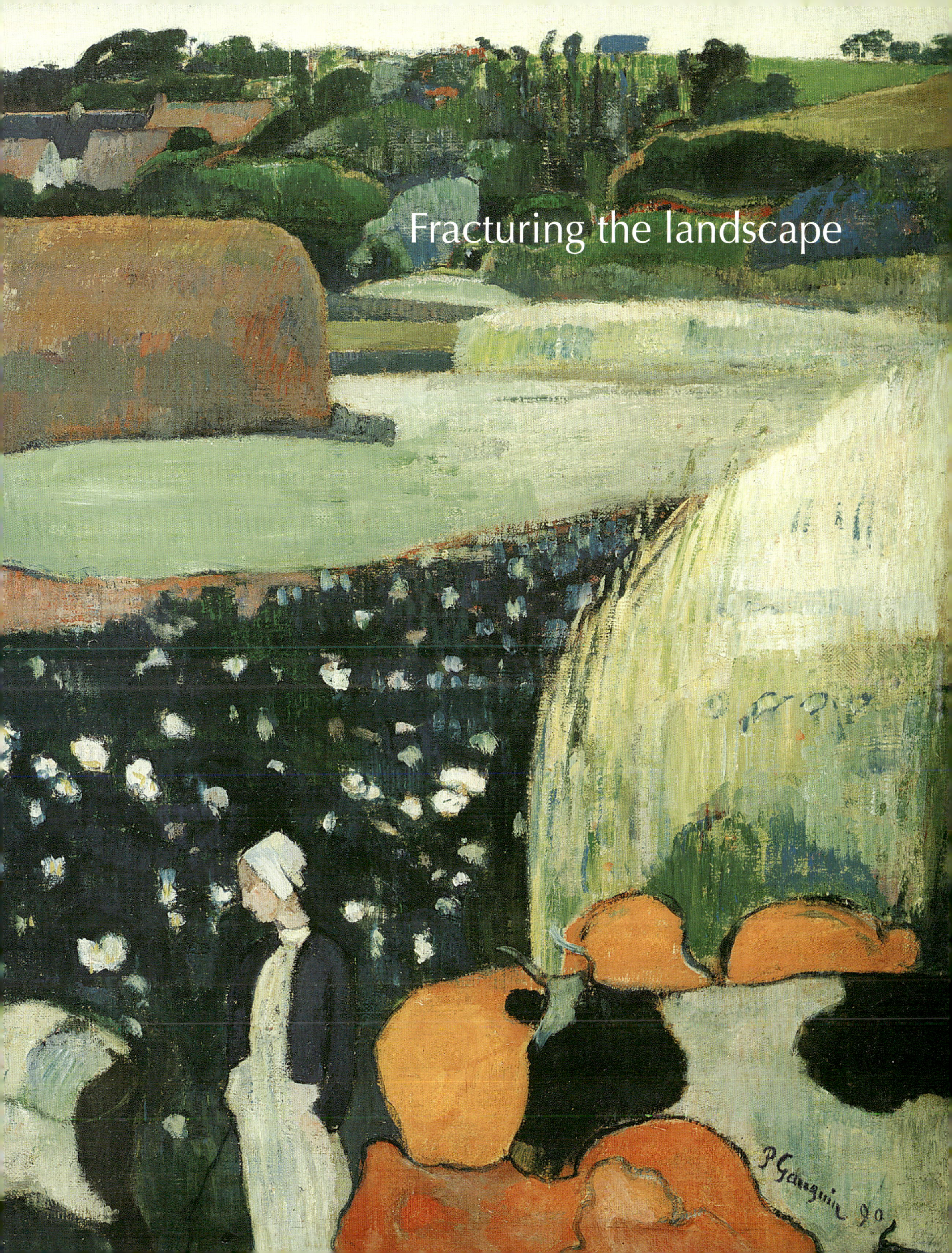

Fracturing the landscape

82. Tom Roberts

Great Britain 1856 – Australia 1931
Allegro con brio: Bourke Street west c. 1885–86, reworked 1890
oil on canvas on composition board 51.2 x 76.7 cm
National Library of Australia and National Gallery of Australia, Canberra
Purchased 1918

Like Pissarro, in his series of Boulevard Montmartre paintings (cat. 83), the Australian Roberts drew inspiration from Monet's *Boulevard des Capucines* 1873.[1] Although we cannot be certain whether, or when, Roberts saw Monet's painting, the affinities between the works are compelling.[2] Monet's, Roberts's and Pissaro's paintings all demonstrate a remarkable ability to capture the hustle and bustle of city life; they share an elevated viewpoint, reduced palette, and fractured brushstrokes. Moreover the three artists also embody a determination to embrace modernity: Paris after the Haussmann era, on the one hand, and the energy and excitement of 'marvellous Melbourne' on the other.

Allegro con brio: Bourke Street west is a lively composition, painted with spirit. The Italian part of the title is a musical term, a playing instruction meaning 'quickly, with brilliance'. It is one of a group of works painted by Roberts on his return to Australia from London in 1885. Back in Melbourne he resumed his friendship with Frederick McCubbin, then with Streeton and Conder: they regularly painted together at Box Hill, *en plein air*. The Heidelberg School painters, as they were known collectively, were interested in instantaneous effects, in experimenting with a range of short, broken brushstrokes. Because their works so effectively convey Australian conditions of heat and light, they are regarded as the first home-grown movement.

Allegro con brio: Bourke Street west is structured around one of the 'avenues' crossing Melbourne's central business district, at the intersection of Elizabeth and Bourke streets, on the Post Office corner. In the 1880s, as now, the west end of Bourke Steeet was a commercial zone. As McQueen points out, more than a third of the canvas is consumed by buildings.[3] Prominent signs announce businesses such as Booksellers Dunn & Collins, P. Philipson & Co. and John Danks. The smoke and haze in a clear blue sky, the contrast between the cream and tan exterior walls of the buildings with dark verandahs underneath, figures scurrying across the street or clustered in the shade, all make us aware of the uncomfortable heat. As if for emphasis, two carriages in the centre foreground seem to emerge from the dust. A row of cabs – cable trams were shortly to make horse-drawn vehicles redundant in much of the city – serves to highlight the recession of the street.

The word 'ICE' appears at the centre, on the side of a cart. At right is the *tricoleur* French flag; it sits almost at the same spot as a blossom-covered tree in the *Boulevard des Capucines*. Perhaps it is not too fanciful to imagine that Roberts left us some clues to his sources. *Allegro con brio: Bourke Street west* is a scene portrayed with much economy in parts, from grand, colonial-style buildings painted in blocks, to the squiggle of a tiny dog in a patch of sun at lower right. In his distinctly Australian portrait of a city that was one of the largest in the industrialised world at the time, Roberts was 'painting with fire'.

Lucina Ward

1. One version of Monet's *Boulevard des Capucines* was shown in the first Impressionist exhibition of 1874, the other at the Dowdeswell Gallery, London, in 1883. The paintings are in the Nelson-Atkins Museum of Art, Kansas City and the Pushkin Museum of Fine Arts, Moscow.
2. Although *Allegro con brio: Bourke Street west* is not dated, it is generally given to the years 1885–86, the revisions to 1890; Mary Eagle points out that Roberts sent four paintings to the 1886 Colonial and Indian Exhibition, London, but did not seem to have considered this work sufficiently resolved, or its perspective and drawing of an Academic standard, to include it; see Mary Eagle, *The oil paintings of Tom Roberts in the National Gallery of Australia*, Canberra: National Gallery of Australia, 1997, p. 28.
3. Humphrey McQueen, *Tom Roberts*, Sydney: Macmillan, 1996, see also 'Tom Roberts: Allegro con brio, Bourke Street west', viewed November 2007, home.alphalink.com.au/~loge27/roberts/roberts_allegro.htm.

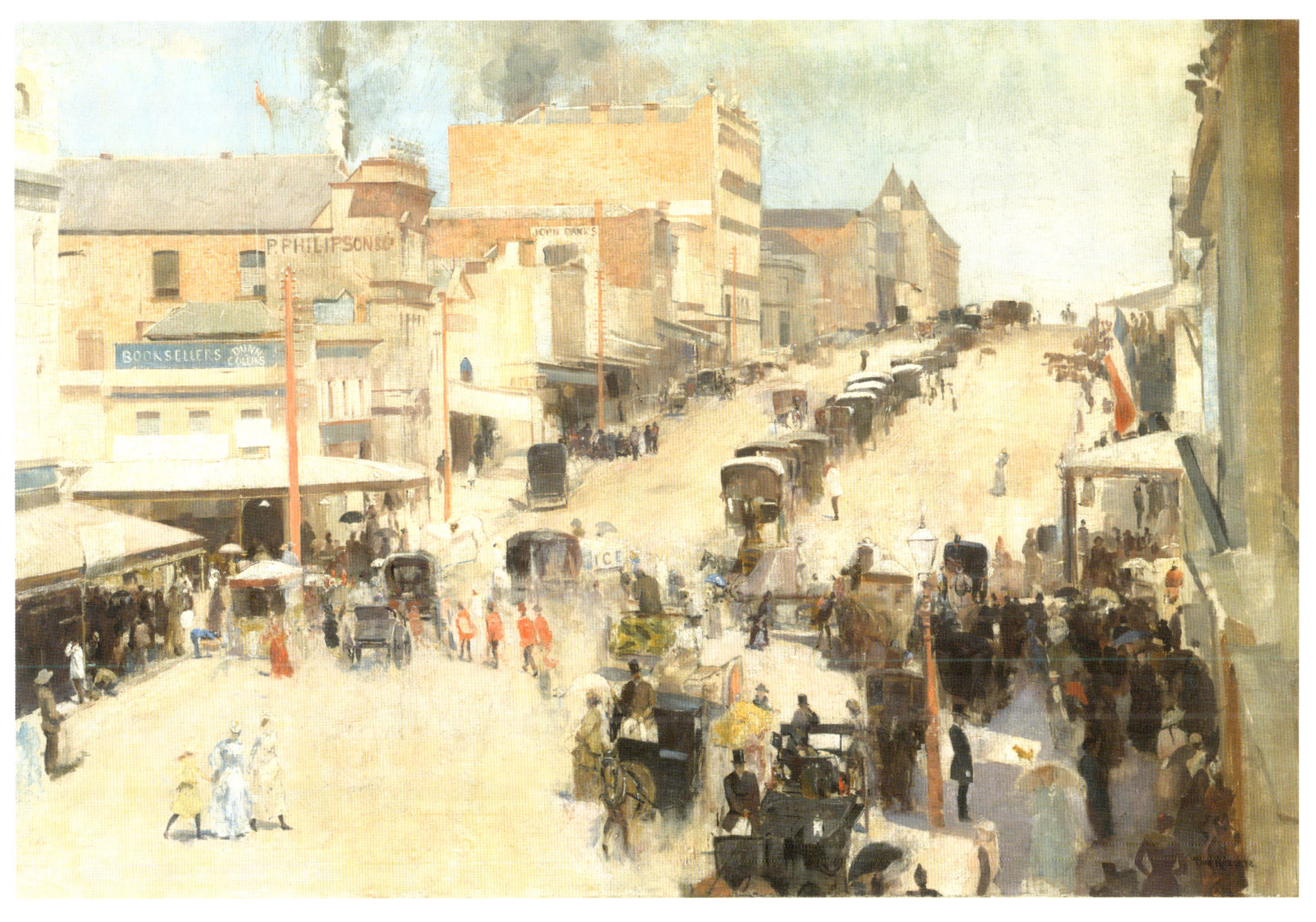
P. PHILIPSON &Co
JOHN DANKS
BOOKSELLERS
ICE

83. Camille Pissarro

Danish Virgin Islands 1830 – France 1903
Boulevard Montmartre, morning, cloudy weather
[***Boulevard Montmartre, matin temps gris***] 1897
oil on canvas 73.0 x 92.0 cm
National Gallery of Victoria, Melbourne
Felton Bequest, 1905 204.2

I have always loved the immense streets of Paris, shimmering in the sun, the crowds of all colours, those beautiful linear and aerial perspectives, those eccentric fashions, etc. But how to do it? To install oneself in the middle of the street is impossible in Paris.
Ludovic Piette, letter to Pissarro 1872[1]

Early in 1897 Pissarro began a series of paintings of the intersection of the boulevards Montmartre, Haussmann and des Italiens with the rues de Richelieu and Drouot. Between 10 February and 17 April he painted fourteen views looking east along the Boulevard Montmartre, and a further two towards the Boulevard des Italiens. From the 1860s Baron Haussmann's interventions transformed Paris. The narrow, winding streets of the medieval city – easily barricaded in the 1848 revolution – were destroyed. Approximately 150 kilometres of road were constructed, with long avenues, apartments of a standard height, public gardens, the Paris Opéra and other public buildings, new bridges, gas lamps, a new water supply and sewers, reinvented the city.

By the late 1880s Pissarro solved the conundrum suggested by his friend Piette: elevation. From a room in the Hôtel de Russie, on the corner of the Boulevard des Italiens and Rue Drouot, Pissarro looked down onto the new spaces of Paris. Although the artist and subsequent commentators are very particular about the locations of the Boulevard Montmartre series, the city's topography is not his subject. Rather it is the changing conditions of the streets themselves. Pissaro took several cues from Monet; the high viewpoint and bustling street recall his friend's painting *Boulevard des Capucines* 1873.[2] Both artists show the city's hustle and bustle – a scatter of people *à la japonaise*, the melange of dress and hats, pillar boxes and carriage wheels – channelled down the grand boulevard.

Boulevard Montmartre, morning, cloudy weather is an extraordinarily energetic painting. Pissarro's ink and wash drawing of 1897 shows the basic components of the fourteen canvasses, but in the paintings the vanishing point is higher.[3] This gives the scene greater vibrancy, and makes us feel as if we are leaning out into the street. The merging of the boulevards in the distance, fringed on either side by footpaths, street-level shops and regulation-height apartments, all serve to emphasise the high perspective. A forest of chimneys is echoed by spindly trees, which line the boulevard. The patchwork of shop windows at right seems to take on elements of the crowds. An 'imperial coach', the heads of passengers visible through the open roof, ferries people down the boulevard. The scene is rendered with a palette of great subtlety: greys, browns and whites accented with red and tiny amounts of green. Pissarro's fixed viewpoint meant that he recorded the ever-shifting configurations of crowds and traffic. At times the differences between the position of people in the street from one *Boulevard* painting to another is so slight that we could be looking at photographs of the same scene, taken only moments apart.

Lucina Ward

1. In Janine Bailly-Herzberg (ed.), *Mon cher Pissarro – Lettres de Ludovic Piette à Camille Pissarro*, Paris: Editions du Valhermeil, 1985, p.73.
2. Monet, either the version in Nelson-Atkins Museum of Art, Kansas City, or the painting in the Pushkin Museum of Fine Arts, Moscow.
3. *Carriages on the Boulevard Montmartre* 1897, private collection; see Karen Levitov and Richard Shiff, *Camille Pissarro: impressions of city and country*, New York: Jewish Museum, 2007, p.70.

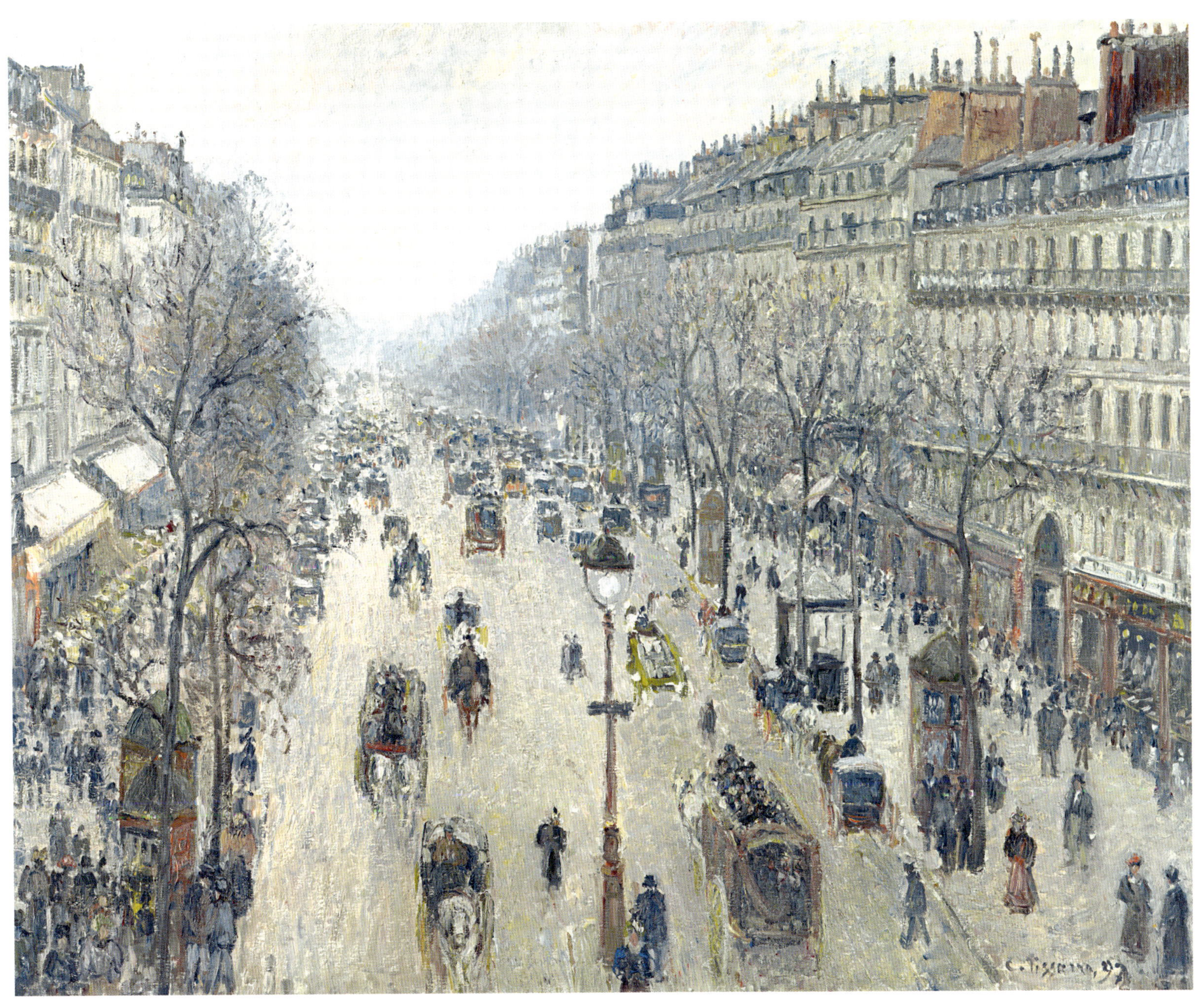

84. Paul Cézanne

France 1839–1906
Viaduct at l'Estaque [***Le viaduct à l'Estaque***] 1882
oil on canvas 45.1 x 53.6 cm
Allen Memorial Art Museum, Oberlin College, Ohio
R.T. Miller, Jr Fund and Mrs F.F. Prentiss Fund, 1950

L'Estaque, a fishing village on the French coast of the Mediterranean, was a place that Cézanne visited often in the 1870s and 1880s. Why, amongst more picturesque features such as blue sea and a pretty village of ochre stone and red tiles, did the artist address such a difficult and unappealing prospect as this? A viaduct is only an overland passage between more dramatic features – under mountains or cliffs, through a valley or over a river far below – and this bridge for the railway track has none of the elegantly classical appeal of Corot's Roman arches (cat. 65). Indeed, the viaduct is barely noticeable: it sits in the lowest band of the painting, the main horizontal of the composition. Perhaps it was, as always, simply because he could. The nature of beauty itself was changing as the century continued, from gentle to hard, from simple, lush and historic to complex, spare and modern. For Cézanne, eternal verities became mutable, and reality was filled with infinite possibilities.

During February and March 1882 Pierre-Auguste Renoir, a much more luscious painter than the austere Cézanne, paid a visit to his contemporary at l'Estaque while en route from Italy to Paris. They painted the same scene, but the two resulting landscapes could not differ more, considering they were executed side by side.[1] Johnson describes Cézanne's strategies on the canvas:

> The flatness of the effect, accentuated by repetition of the receding and advancing color and tone values may, on first impression, bear some resemblance to tapestry design; but this quality is denied by the special depth and volume and solidity of the forms which Cézanne achieves … He has piled the planes up vertically and has silhouetted distant hills instead of allowing them to dissolve in air and space.[2]

The contest between fact and fiction, which underlies landscape painting in the nineteenth century, is seen plainly here, in the choices that Cézanne makes. He understands that the horizontal railway lines below the cliffs undermine the vertical and diagonal slopes of the mountains. The dizzying stacks of rock, made of parallel hatched strokes of paint, communicate insecurity rather than the permanence of stone and mountains. The close-up, frontal encounter reinforces the dominance of the artist's view. It is the implied struggle between doubt and certainty that makes Cézanne so modern.

Christine Dixon

1. John Rewald, *The paintings of Paul Cézanne: a catalogue raisonné*, vol. 1, New York: Harry N. Abrams, 1996, cat. 441, p. 297; the other canvas is Renoir's *Crags at l'Estaque*, in the Museum of Fine Arts, Boston.
2. Ellen H. Johnson, 'Cézanne and a pine tree: *Viaduct at l'Estaque*, a footnote', *Allen Memorial Art Museum Bulletin*, vol. 21, no. 1, Fall, 1963, pp. 24–8, quoted in Rewald, p. 297.

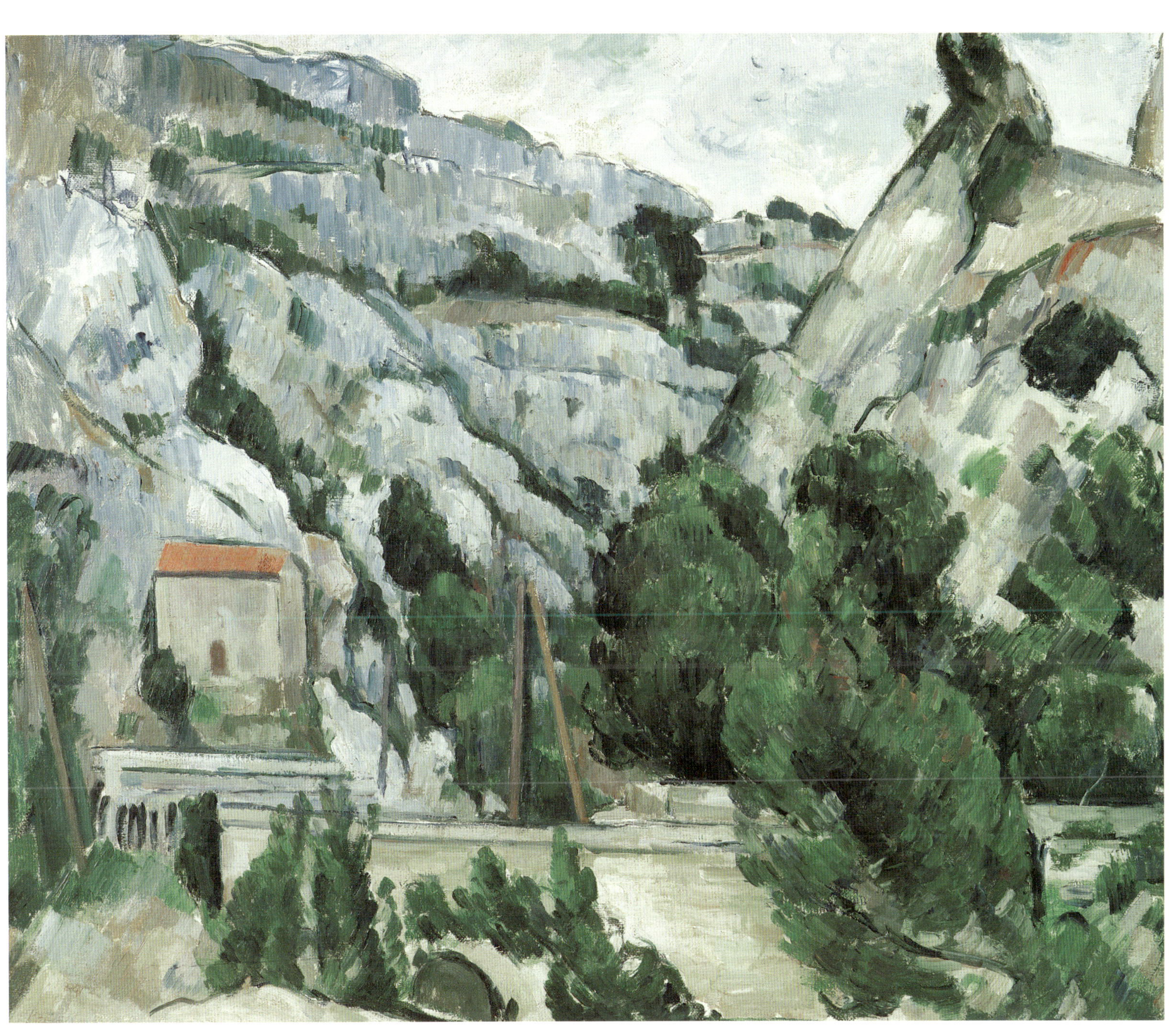

85. Georges Seurat

France 1859–1891
Study for ***Le Bec du Hoc, Grandcamp*** 1885
oil on panel 15.6 x 24.5 cm
National Gallery of Australia, Canberra
Purchased from proceeds of The Great Impressionists exhibition 1984
1984.1933

The immediacy of this painting links Seurat to the Impressionists. While such studies could capture a fragment in time, the artist was fascinated by the science of colour contrasts. His finished paintings show a precise use of Pointillism, his trademark style. *Study for Le Bec du Hoc, Grandcamp* reveals the approach Seurat used on the spot, quickly painting a scene that he would later manipulate in his studio.

Seurat's landscapes often emerged from his holidays. The artist visited Grandcamp after ten months' work on his famous, monumental *Sunday afternoon on the island of La Grande Jatte* 1884–86.[1] Nevertheless this small painting, made *en plein air*, was part of the artist's painstaking process for creating large paintings. A typical first-stage study, from it was created *Le Bec du Hoc, Grandcamp* 1885.[2] Seurat is focused almost entirely on the main subject, the Bec – 'nose' or 'nozzle' – of the Hoc, a distinctive feature of the Normandy coastline. The eye is reluctant to linger for long on other areas of the study.

Seurat's figurative works lead to thoughts of abstraction, but in landscape his dot-by-dot approach highlights the severity of Nature's beauty and structure. The study features small blocks of paint and unexpected colours that can only be seen on close inspection. The sea is rendered in a series of short horizontal strokes, in satisfying contrast with the grass, which he textured by cross-hatching greens, creams and pale pinks. The cliff-face has been painted in short strokes of blue, purple and orange, yet at a distance the area appears a deceptively natural brown. In his marine works Seurat is famous for simple scenes and stillness. Water, rocks and grass all benefit from his technique, as do sunsets, afternoon sun, and even a suggestion of wind.

Parts of the study appear in the completed painting, and others were altered or improved. For the final work Seurat omitted the brown rocks at the water's edge, and increased the amount of visible sky. Above the peak he inserted a small flock of birds. A tiny white sailing boat to the left of the cliff, almost imperceptible in the study, was later moved to the right and made more prominent. In the study the artist made a rough note to himself about the contrasts on the grassy cliff, which he then rendered in a more naturalistic form. The sea is choppy here, recorded in unsettling shades of green, but eventually the water became a blue–grey sheet, cut only by the white froth that appears on deep water from small waves. Overall, Seurat manipulates this study into a finished and peaceful scene to create *Le Bec du Hoc, Grandcamp*.

The study implies a paradox of subject and approach. Seurat chooses the majestic form of the Bec du Hoc as an example of unadorned nature at its purest and most powerful. Then he imposes his own perfectionist and exact Pointillism. Many artists followed his lead, but other Impressionists could not ultimately reconcile their style with his. Landscape was one of a number of subjects which Seurat altered for his own original use, to demonstrate personal aesthetic theories and to aid the progress of painting.

Kathleen Warden

1. Collection of the Art Institute of Chicago; John Russell, *Seurat*, London: Thames and Hudson, 1965, p. 170; William Innes Homer, *Seurat and the science of painting*, Cambridge Massachusetts: M.I.T. Press, 1964, p. 115.
2. Collection of the Tate Britain; on loan to the National Gallery, London.

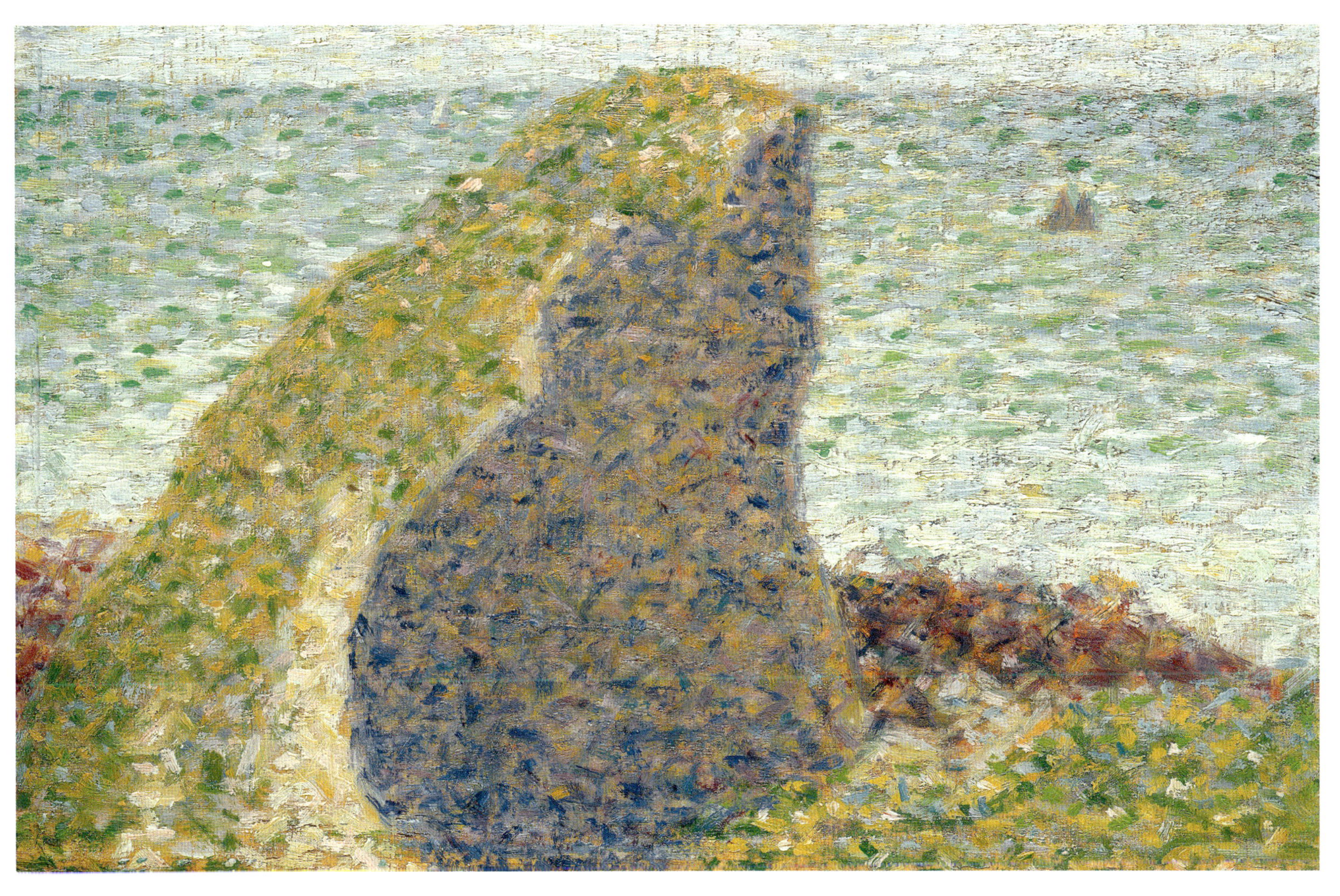

86. Georges Seurat

France 1859–1891
Lucerne, Saint-Denis [***La Luzerne, Saint-Denis***] 1885
also known as ***Field of alfalfa, Saint-Denis*** and ***Field of poppies***
oil on canvas 65.3 x 81.3 cm
National Gallery of Scotland, Edinburgh
Purchased with the aid of The Art Fund,
a Treasury Grant and the family of Roger Fry 1973 2423

Here we see a field of lucerne, the green crop infiltrated by red poppies. Along the skyline is strung a series of pale sheds and outbuildings under a silvery sky. In the distance is Saint-Denis, a suburb ten kilometres north of central Paris, which was industrialising rapidly in the last decades of the nineteenth century. The painting has a very high horizon line: Seurat depicts the plants as eighty per cent of the canvas. On the right against the sky is a small tree, and in the foreground a darker mass results from the shadow cast by a large tree behind the artist and the viewer.

The luscious intensity of Seurat's paintings is achieved by pure colour and his application of paint in small, organised strokes. The colour wheel was first elaborated by the chemist Chevreul in 1839, with red, blue and yellow being primary, and the mixtures violet, green and orange secondary colours. Each resulting hue can be lightened or darkened by white or black. Colour theory is based on the spectator's changing perceptions, each colour being affected by surrounding ones. Instead of pre-mixing paints, Divisionist or Neo-Impressionist artists like Seurat placed patches of pure colour alongside each other, so that the eye would blend them.

In *Lucerne, Saint-Denis* the bright green of the lucerne is produced by Seurat's short, straight strokes of blue and yellow, criss-crossed to produce the animated field. Joyous interruptions of red, white and pink occur when flowers emerge from the crop. The shade from the tree in the right front is produced by darker blue, with less yellow. Beyond the fence, paintstrokes become horizontal, calming the view and lightening in tone towards the distant horizon and sky.

Seurat employs these radical strategies to produce an all-over effect, so characteristic of art after the first Impressionist experiments in the 1860s and 1870s. There is no story to tell here, no incident to draw conclusions from, only the reproduction of visual effects as perceived by the artist. The nature of beauty has changed, as the painter makes new and different choices of subject and technique, so that the content and meaning of art are transformed.

Christine Dixon

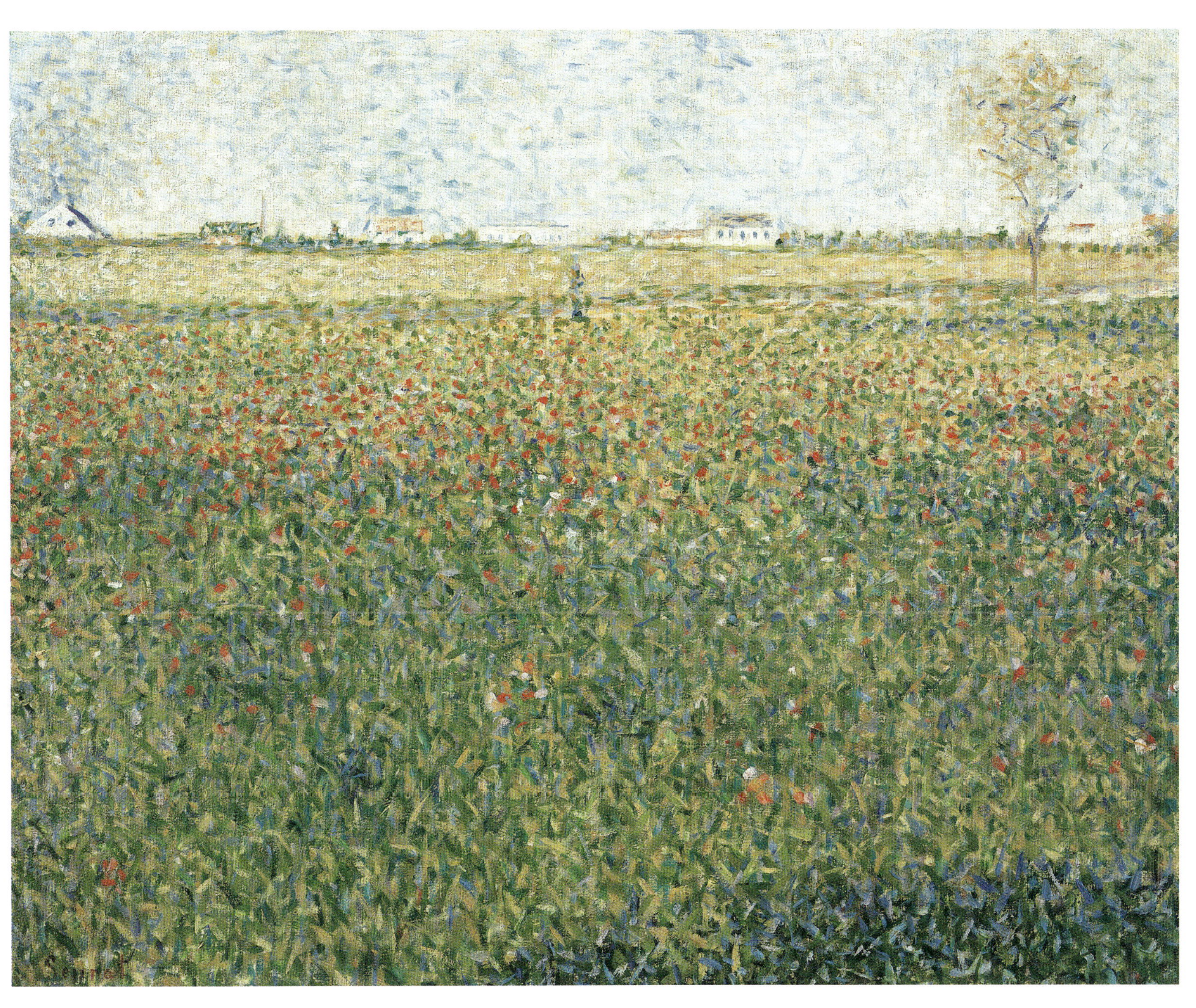

87. Paul Signac

France 1863–1935
Gasometers at Clichy [***Les gasomètres, Clichy***] 1886
oil on canvas 65.0 x 81.0 cm
National Gallery of Victoria, Melbourne
Felton Bequest, 1948 1817-4

Gasometers at Clichy was first exhibited in 1886 at 1 rue Laffitte, Paris, an elegantly appointed suite of five rooms above the chic Maison Dorée restaurant, in the eighth and last group showing of the Impressionists. Signac's friendship with Camille Pissarro, who he had met in 1885, led to his inclusion in this prestigious event. Pissarro, one of the show's principal organisers, was keen to add new blood to the original Impressionist group, in the form of younger artists building upon the founding principles of Impressionism. The Neo-Impressionist, or Divisionist painting, as it came to be known, of the young Seurat and Signac met some resistance from the older Impressionists however. As a result, the paintings by Signac, Seurat, Pissarro (who had himself adopted the Divisionist manner of painting in 1886) and his son Lucien were displayed together in a separate room of the exhibition.

Seurat's scientific theories of colour division abandoned the wet-on-wet application of harmonious tones favoured by Impressionism, in favour of placing strong, opposing blocks of colour side by side. These would blend optically to create light, it was argued, when the viewer stood at a certain distance. *Gasometers at Clichy* is one of the first works painted by Signac according to these Neo-Impressionist principles.

From the outset Signac's landscapes depicted semi-industrial subjects – a choice that followed naturally from his family's move to Asnières in 1880. It has been noted that large gas storage tanks, factories, cranes and chimney stacks that loomed up in close proximity to residential Asnières and the Quai de Clichy were motifs that Signac may have seen from the windows of his family home.[1] The unimposing urban scene depicted in *Gasometers at Clichy* was also only a short distance from the working-class leisure island of Grande-Jatte, the setting of Seurat's enormous and best-known canvas, *A Sunday afternoon on the Island of La Grande-Jatte*, also exhibited in the final Impressionist exhibition of 1886.[2]

The contradiction inherent in Signac's luminous depiction of a decidedly grubby subject was remarked upon by Fénéon, a firm supporter of the artist's work, in an influential review in *La Vogue*:

> Paul Signac is drawn to suburban landscapes, which he interprets in an individual and penetrating manner. The works that date from this very year are painted according to divisions of tone; they achieve a frenetic intensity of light: *Gasometers at Clichy* with its work pants and jackets drying on fence palings, its desolate peeling walls, its burned-brown grass and incandescent roofs beneath a blinding sky, gains momentum as the eye rises, and loses itself in an abyss of blinding blue.[3]

The removal of a discoloured varnish layer has recently restored this painting's pigments to their original blaze of light and colour.[4]

The dazzling effect of Signac's Neo-Impressionist palette received a mixed reception overall in the Parisian press of the day. Although Christophe wrote enthusiastically of the artist's 'gay, sun-filled, raw, intense' manner, Hermel was to complain of how Signac's 'raw coloration tires and angers the eye, while his violet tones exasperate it'.[5]

Signac's paintings of industrial views are equated with his support of Anarchist and socialist politics. The subversive nature of his urban landscapes lies in the manner in which they depict the polluted locales of working-class outer Paris, seldom visited by wealthy Parisian socialites.

Ted Gott

1. Marina Ferretti-Bocquillon et al., *Signac 1863–1935*, Paris: Réunion des musées nationaux, 2001, p. 154.
2. Art Institute of Chicago. For a comprehensive study, see Robert L. Herbert, *Seurat and the making of La Grande Jatte*, Chicago: Art Institute of Chicago, 2004.
3. Félix Fénéon, 'Les Impressionnistes', *La Vogue*, 13–20 June 1886.
4. *Gasometers at Clichy* was cleaned by the NGV's conservator Michael Varcoe-Cocks in late 2007, to startling effect.
5. Jules Christophe, 'Chronique: Rue Lafitte, no. 1', *Journal des Artistes*, 13 June 1886; Maurice Hermel, 'L'Exposition de peinture de la rue Laffitte', *La France Libre*, 28 May 1886.

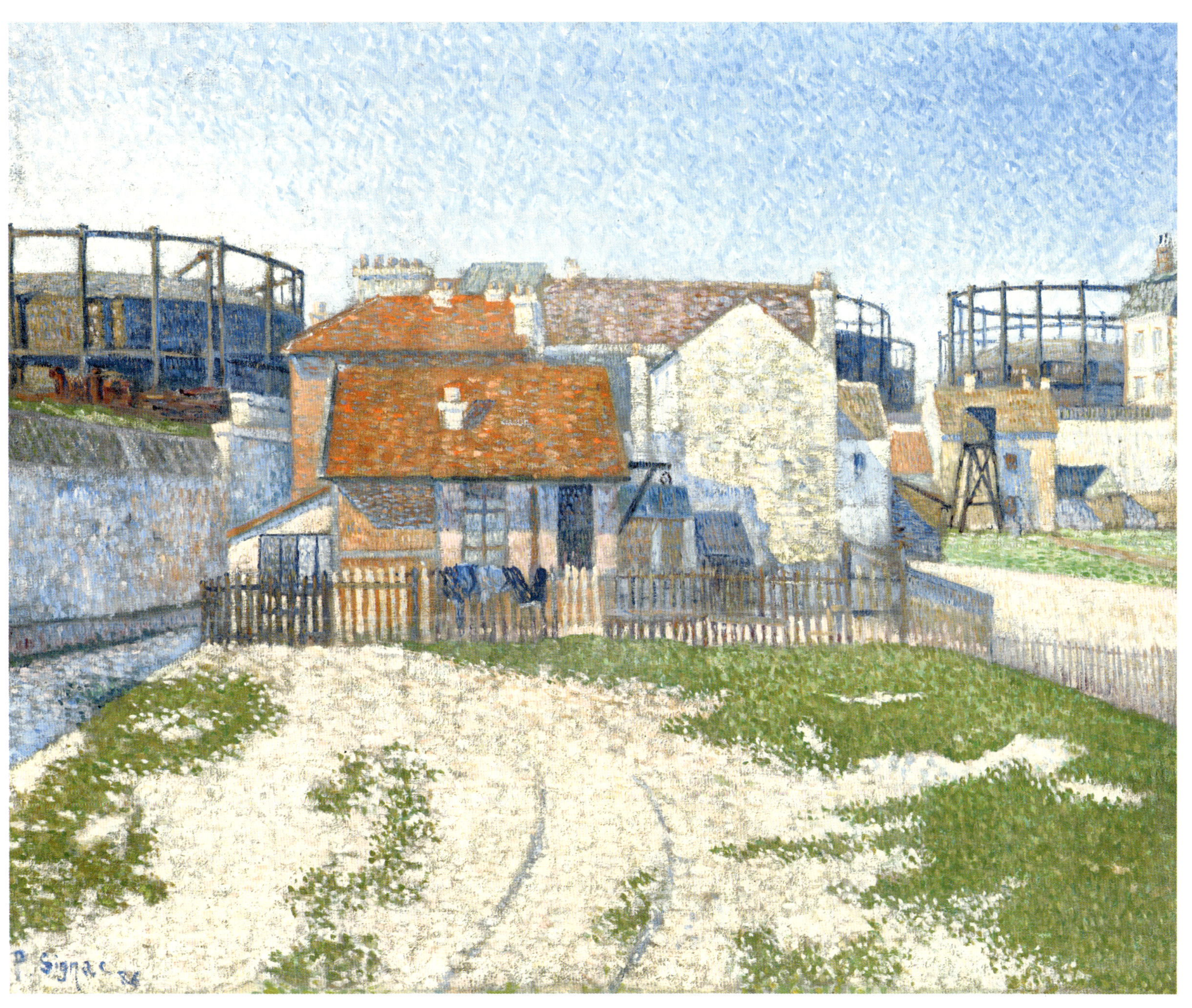
P. Signac 84

88. Claude Monet

France 1840–1926
Port-Goulphar, Belle-Île 1887
oil on canvas 81.0 x 65.0 cm
Art Gallery of New South Wales, Sydney
Purchased 1949 8356

Monet painted Port-Goulphar in autumn 1886 when he was staying on Belle-Île, an island off the Atlantic coast of Brittany, which he described as 'superb in its savagery, piles of terrible rocks, and a sea of incredible colours …'[1] He painted three versions of this view, part of a group of thirty-six paintings of cliffs, rocks and sea, which initiated his series of paintings of the same motif under different conditions of light and weather. He wrote:

> … to paint the sea truly, one must see it every day, at every hour, and at the same spot, to understand its life at that spot, thus I repeat the same motif four or even six times.[2]

A visitor saw Monet painting at his easel anchored to a cliff, lashed by wind and rain.[3] He had to work like this because his landscapes depended on direct contact with nature but, paradoxically, Monet's paintings are quite abstract; their colours are not those of nature, and the thick, pasty brushstrokes do not describe the appearance of rocks and sea, but rather draw attention to the way he represented *his* sensation of nature. He wrote: 'I – who am drawn to soft, tender tints – must make great efforts to paint sombre, to render these sinister, tragic aspects'.[4] In painting wild Belle-Île, he was not only challenging his own habits of seeing, but also experiencing emotions very different from those evoked by his familiar landscapes between the Norman coast and Paris.

In this painting, Monet used abstract scales of colour, rendering the sea in dominants of bright greens and blues, heightened by touches of tinted white, and weaving the blues and greens into the contrasting dark greens, puces, purples and rusty pinks of the rocky outcrops. The virtuoso display of brushstrokes includes small, curved strokes which register the ceaseless movement of the waves; stabbing brushstrokes shape the cliffs; long linear brushstrokes suggest the force-lines in rocks, and the dynamic interaction between the rocks and the eroding sea. These colours and the almost expressionistic brushstrokes embody both Monet's sensations and his emotional reaction to the 'sinister' and 'tragic' island.

The unusual composition in which Monet defied European linear perspective by tilting the plane of water up the picture surface, and placing the heaviest and most defined forms at the top of the painting was probably inspired by his long study of Japanese woodblock prints – in particular Hiroshige's and Hokusai's prints of similar subjects that hung on his walls at home. He was probably also influenced by the calligraphic brushstrokes and the spatial construction of Japanese scroll and screen paintings.[5]

As soon as Monet began to give shape to his perception of 'a moment of light' – as he called it – that moment was already passing, never to return. He lamented the endless changes of weather and of the sun's position as autumn advanced. He therefore had to alter his paintings, scrape them down, begin them again, extending his stay week after week. When he returned home to Giverny, he spent months working on the paintings in his studio. He exhibited ten of them (although not *Port-Goulphar*) in Paris, where they were well received by critics and sold well. But Monet's two months alone on the cliffs of Belle-Île were equally important because they allowed him to think himself into nature more profoundly than ever before.

Virginia Spate

1. Letter to Caillebotte, 11 October 1886, Daniel Wildenstein, *Claude Monet: biographie et catalogue raisonné*, vol. II, Paris: La Bibliothèque des Arts, 1979, letter 709.
2. Letter to Alice Hoschedé, 30 October 1886, Wildenstein, vol. II, letter 730.
3. The writer was Gustave Geffroy, see Virginia Spate, *The colour of time: Claude Monet*, London: Thames and Hudson, 1992, p. 178 and note 73.
4. Letter to Alice Hoschedé, 23 October 1886, Wildenstein, vol. II, letter 721.
5. Virginia Spate, *Monet and Japan*, Canberra: National Gallery of Australia, 2001, p. 3.

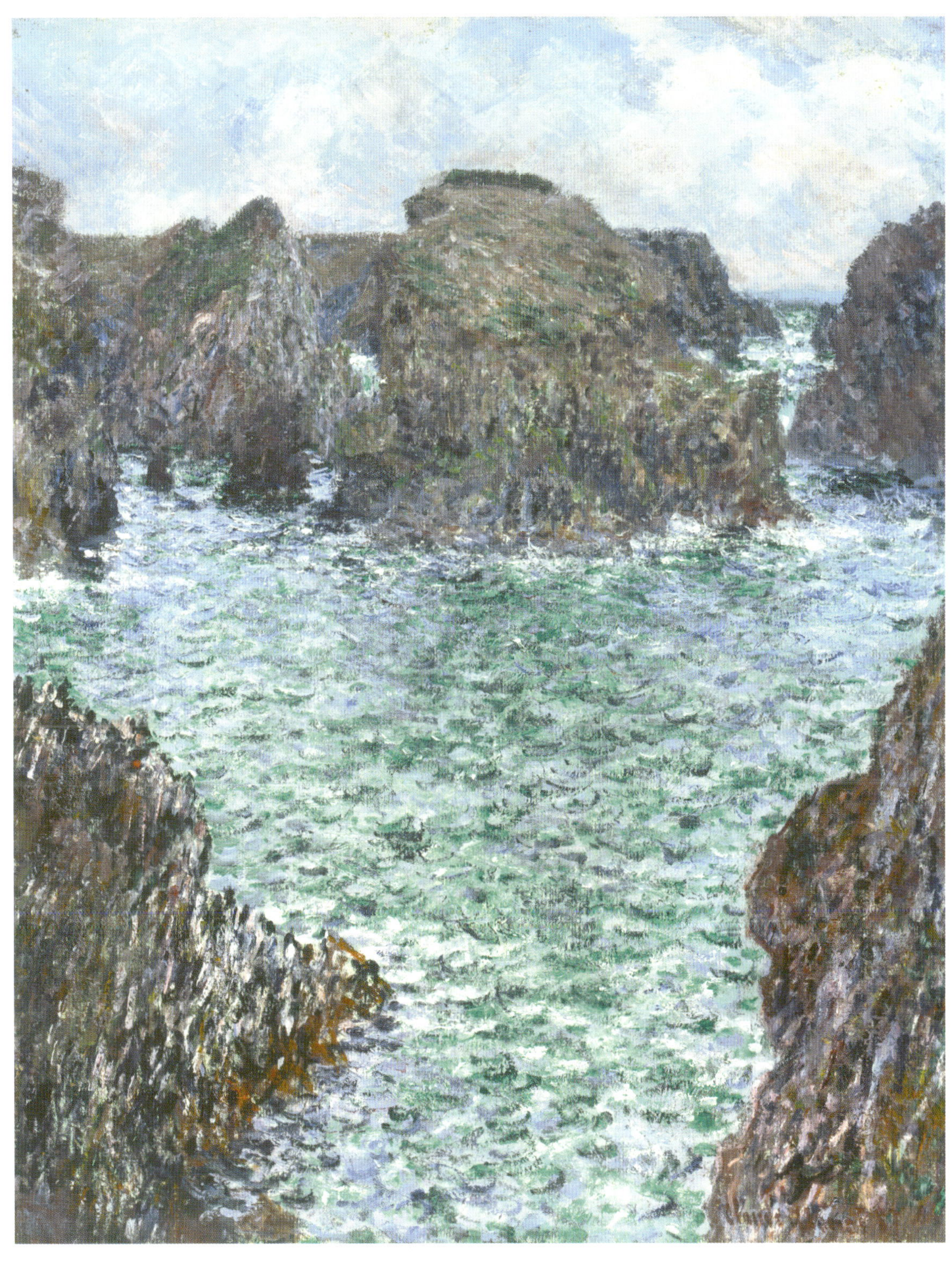

89. Claude Monet

France 1840–1926
***Haystacks, midday* [*Meules, milieu du jour*]** 1890
oil on canvas 65.6 x 100.6 cm
National Gallery of Australia, Canberra
Purchased 1979 1979.16

Long revered as Monet's most exquisite series, the *Haystack* paintings are remarkable for the range of light and weather conditions portrayed. In *Haystacks, midday* the edges of the stacks shimmer in the heat, and sunlight appears to radiate from the structures themselves. Elsewhere, in the snow scenes, the forms seem to absorb light. The practical nature of the stacks – a means of storing the harvest – receives less attention. When the sheaves of wheat or oats were cut, the cereal stacks were thatched with straw and left to stand until spring, and the arrival of the threshing machines that moved between villages. For a country still smarting from the effects of the Franco–Prussian war – and in a period when France seemed to be rapidly overtaken by industrialised Britain, Germany, the United States or even Russia – Monet's choice of motif, like the series of poplar paintings that followed, was reassuringly French. The haystacks resonate with notions of rural productivity and the relative harmony of country life.

Monet spent extended periods travelling and painting picturesque locations in and around France in the late 1870s to the 1890s – from Vétheuil on the Seine to the coasts of Normandy and Brittany, then London, Venice, Norway and the Mediterranean. Between late 1888 and February 1891 he painted at least thirty canvases of haystacks, of which fifteen were shown in May 1891 at Durand-Ruel's gallery.[1] This exhibition built on Monet's growing success: despite comparatively high prices, most of the *Haystacks* sold, many of them to American collections where they remain. In October 1890 he could afford to buy the house at Giverny that he had rented since 1883. Ten years later, Monet bought an adjoining field and, from the early 1900s, extended his famous garden with its bridges and ponds of waterlilies (fig. 22, p. 43).

Pissarro wrote that Monet's haystacks 'breathed' happiness, but at times the series caused the artist much anxiety.[2] In October 1890 he complained about the difficulty of his work, especially his frustration at the time it took to capture instantaneous effects of light.[3] *Haystacks, midday* is certainly the result of a 'long and continued effort' with its layered paint and compositional changes indicating successive reworking in the field and in the studio. Monet gradually incorporated more and more colour – red–orange at the top of the stack, pink that flecks the stubblefield, touches of orange in the sky, shimmering yellow outlining the trees – until the whole surface of the canvas vibrates in the haze of the midday heat. His sensitivity to rapidly changing light, developed during three decades painting *en plein air*, as well as the initial haystack paintings made in the previous eighteen months, meant that he was able to extend the series under a greater range of conditions. Clearly it was the changing effects of light, an atmospheric *enveloppe* around the forms, rather than the stacks themselves, that fascinated the artist. There is a small piece of grass imbedded in the lower right edge of the canvas – perhaps it serves as a reminder of the practical function of haystacks.

Lucina Ward

1. Daniel Wildenstein, *Monet, or, The triumph of Impressionism (catalogue raisonné)*, 4 vols, Cologne and Paris: Taschen and Wildenstein Institute, 1996, vol. 3, see cat. W1213–1217 for 1888–89 stacks, W1266–1273 for summer–autumn 1890 and W1274–1290 for 1890–91 winter stacks; the May 1891 exhibition comprised twenty-two works, of which fifteen were haystacks.
2. Camille Pissarro, letter to Lucien Pissarro, 5 May 1891, in Janine Bailly-Herzberg (ed.), *Correspondance de Camille Pissaro*, 5 vols, Paris: Presses universitaires de France, 1980–91, vol. 3, l. 658, p. 72.
3. Letter to Gustave Geffroy, 7 October 1890, no. 1076, Wildenstein, vol. III, p. 258.

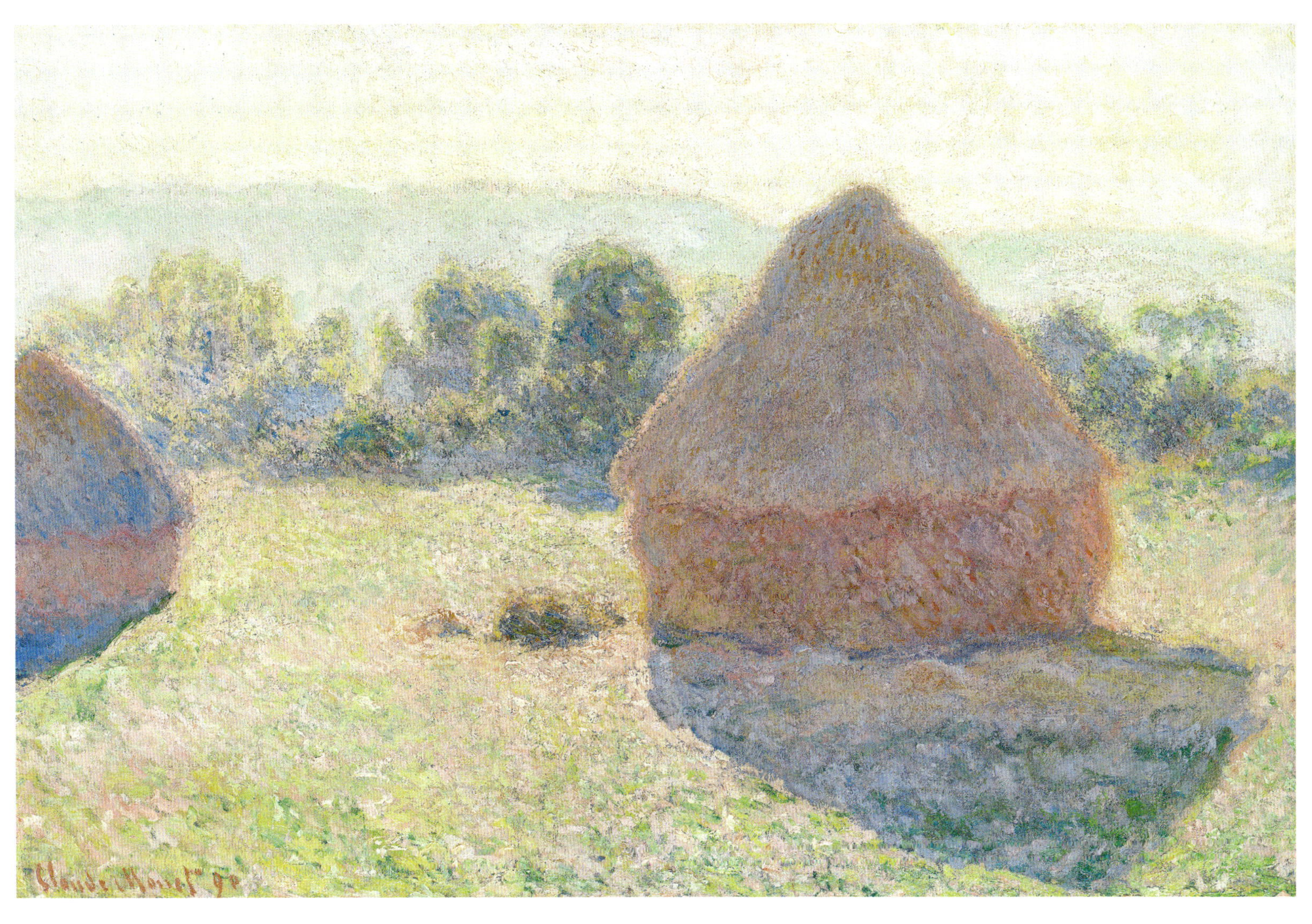

90. Vincent van Gogh

The Netherlands 1853 – France 1890
Undergrowth [***Sous-bois*** or ***Kreupelhout***] 1889
oil on canvas 49.0 x 64.0 cm
Van Gogh Museum, Amsterdam
Vincent van Gogh Foundation

All our emotional sensors come alert at the signal of van Gogh's name. Rather than looking purposefully at the paintings – his claim to immortality – we remember a short and tragic life. Vincent's story is so familiar that we refer to him by a signature first name, like Michelangelo or Leonardo. His paint-laden, radical canvases are perceived through psychological or biographical veils, points of view that may obscure or slant the reality of a great artist's work. Van Gogh's own voice can still be heard, in many letters written to his always-supportive brother. Theo was a moderately successful art dealer in England and France. The letters detail Vincent's everyday struggles, as well as his aesthetic dilemmas.

When *Undergrowth* is scrutinised as a work of art rather than a self-consciously rendered artefact of the artist's life, what do we see? A canvas has been filled from top to bottom and left to right by short strokes of paint. It is one of three versions of this motif made by van Gogh in the asylum garden at Saint-Rémy, where he produced 150 paintings in thirteen months. Lassaigne declares that the works:

> … show the continuing evolution of his art, even more striking than his progress at Arles. They have remarkable unity, for van Gogh was now at the very heart of nature, less preoccupied with its colours than with its vital forms.[1]

Van Gogh paints the woodland floor, rejecting or ignoring panoramas of horizon and sky, those traditional characteristics of landscape composition. As the end of the century approached, many landscape conventions were subverted and new ideas aired.

In *Undergrowth*, the viewer is forced to observe close up, an area that conventionally forms only the foreground of a landscape painting. Here, however, both middle and far grounds are excised. The artist employed secondary and tertiary hues, rather than the brighter primaries of red, blue and yellow. One of the lessons of Impressionism was to avoid black, a colour that does not occur in nature. Van Gogh outlines the tree-trunks with his darkest tones, animating them with dabs of yellow and blue. Light enters the wood gradually, filtered by vegetation, falling on tree-trunks, grass and ivy. His lighter palette is limited to blue, green and yellow, mixed with white for pale accents. Paint is applied mainly in quick, diagonal brushstrokes to create the animated effect of the dappled woods. The trees are not the main subject: rather van Gogh considers how we experience nature though time, colour and light.

Christine Dixon

1. Jacques Lassaigne, *van Gogh*, London: Thames and Hudson, 1972, p. 61.

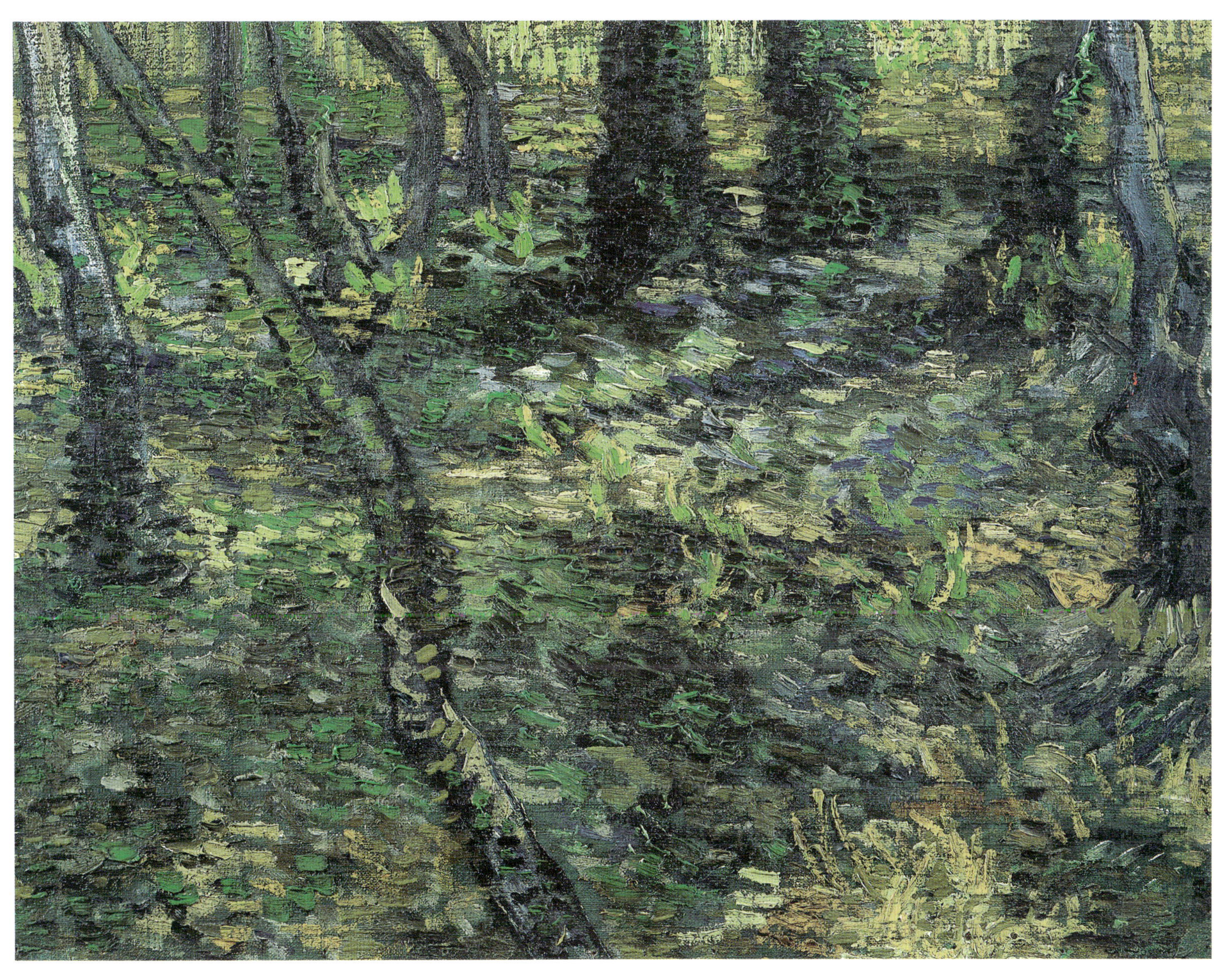

91. Vincent van Gogh

The Netherlands 1853 – France 1890
Tree trunks in the grass **[*Boomstammen in het grass*]** 1890
also known as ***Field of grass, with dandelions and tree trunks***
oil on canvas 72.5 x 91.5 cm
Kröller-Müller Museum, Otterlo
KM 100.189

Van Gogh's extraordinary and tragic life, his feelings and thoughts revealed in prolific correspondence, often overwrites the material reality of his paintings. He was a pioneer of modern art, using the genres of landscape, portraiture and still life to experiment with form and colour. Here, in an extraordinary close-up rendition of urban nature, *Tree trunks in the grass*, van Gogh reinvigorates the landscape format by looking down into it instead of outwards, and thus eliminates both horizon and sky.

He wrote about the painting in a letter to his brother Theo in early May 1890, in which he also details a planned journey from the asylum at Saint-Rémy to the care of Dr Gachet at Auvers-sur-Oise:

> … my work is going well, I have done two canvases of the fresh grass in the park, one of which is extremely simple, here is a hasty sketch of it. The trunk of a pine violet-pink and then the grass with white flowers and dandelions, a little rose tree and other tree trunks in the background right at the top of the canvas.[1]

By cropping the composition so radically, especially at the top and bottom, van Gogh shows how well he absorbed the strategies of Japanese woodblock artists. He combines these with the exemplar of photography, focusing on one part of an object to stand in for the whole. Verticals and diagonals struggle for dominance, with the main tree trunks sloping slightly, boldly placed off-centre. Our eye is led back by white accents from the foreshortened ground in a zigzag, and through the central field into the dappled lawn under the far trees. It lingers briefly, returning by means of blue marks, to the central motif.

In *Tree trunks in the grass,* the artist's palette is reduced to light shades of green, white and yellow, highlighted by blue and a little red, allowing tones to accentuate the texture of the main trunk. Other trunks are blue-black, dark against bright spring vegetation. Van Gogh's characteristically energetic paintstrokes, delicate in the flowers and thicker in the grass, become rugged in the bark of the trees. This landscape was observed close-to, painted on the spot in the asylum garden at the end of April 1890. Van Gogh is a specific, rather than a general, artist: that is, he uses the immediate to communicate larger themes. Looking at the painting, we feel the joy of being outdoors, where sunlight and flowered grass suffuse our senses.

Christine Dixon

1. Letter 631, *The complete letters of Vincent van Gogh*, 2nd edn, vol. 3, London: Thames & Hudson, 1959, pp. 265, 267.

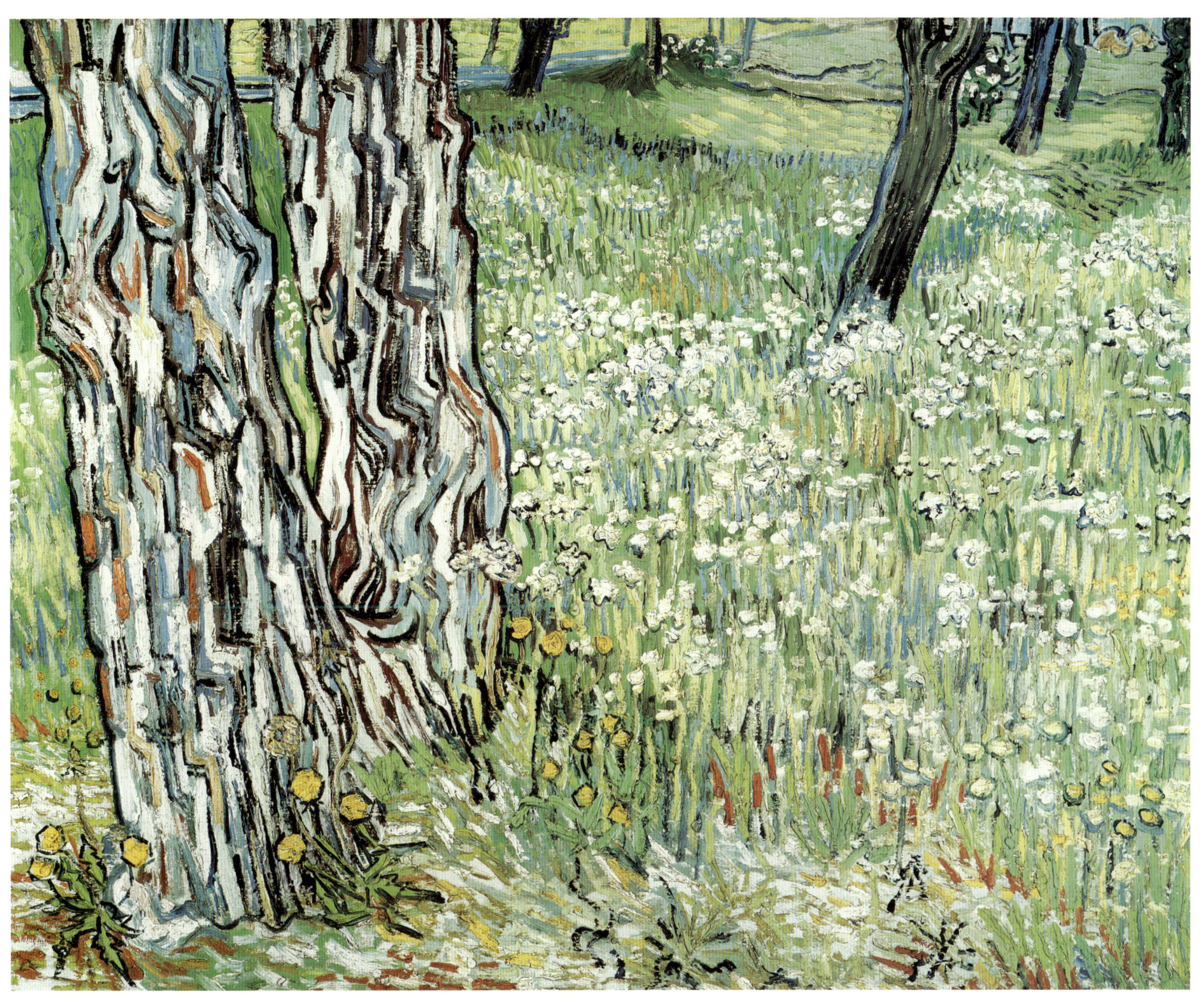

92. Paul Gauguin

France 1848 – Marquesas Islands 1903
Haystacks in Brittany [***Meules de foin en Bretagne***] 1890
also known as ***The hayricks*** and ***The potato field***
oil on canvas 74.3 x 93.6 cm
National Gallery of Art, Washington
Gift of the W. Averell Harriman Foundation
in memory of Marie N. Harriman 1972.9.11

Here in Brittany the peasants have a medieval air about them and do not for a moment look as though they think that Paris exists and it is 1889
Gauguin, letter to van Gogh, 1889[1]

Haystacks in Brittany is among a small number of works painted by Gauguin in 1890 at Le Pouldu, on the Breton coast. From July 1886 until his departure for Tahiti in March 1891, Gauguin travelled regularly between Paris and towns in Brittany and Provence – the latter the site of his notorious collaboration with van Gogh – searching for a way to consolidate his style, as well as a place to live cheaply. He stayed at Le Pouldu, some twenty kilometres south-west of Pont-Aven, late in 1889 and during 1890. The works he painted there, images of peasant life, the landscape and harvest scenes, are some of the most radically simplified of his career. Gauguin described how he 'scrutinised the horizons, seeking that harmony of human life with animal and vegetable life through compositions in which I allowed the great voice of the earth to play an important part'.[2]

Like many of his generation Gauguin recognised the strength of landscape painting at this time. His early works show the impact of Corot and other Barbizon painters; he painted in an Impressionist mode until the late 1880s and, introduced by Pissarro, was included in several Impressionist exhibitions. By 1885 Gauguin had started painting full-time and, from his first campaign in Brittany, reduced traditional modelling to a strict minimum: in his Pont-Aven and Le Pouldu works it is his combination of colour and form, rather than narrative or sentiment, which appeals to the viewer. Gauguin's absorption of the peasant traditions of the region, music and especially woodcarving, as well as the influences of 'primitive art' and Japanese prints, is apparent.[3] Having abandoned Pont-Aven – he complained that it was now too spoilt by crowds – Gauguin set off for the remote hamlet of Le Pouldu. The isolated region, with its dramatic rocky peninsula, windswept dunes, sandy beaches and scattered farms, suited Gauguin. At the *Buvette de la Plage* – an inn owned by a young local woman, Marie Henry – he was joined by Sérusier (cat. 93) and the Dutch painter Jacob Mayer de Haan (1852–1895).

Haystacks in Brittany has the structure of a traditional landscape. The painting is composed of a series of bands: the distant sky, fields in the mid-ground and crops of the foreground, with a frieze of cows and their female attendant in front. Despite its variant titles, it is not the agricultural land that is of interest here, but the rich patterns that Gauguin develops from various elements. The disjunction between the landscape's recession and the frieze-like procession of cows and cowherd emphasises the stained-glass qualities of *Haystacks in Brittany*. The previous year Gauguin had experimented with a technique he learnt from a restorer. The technique, using paste, newspaper and horn irons, produced a matt surface.[4] His *synthétiste* paintings and subsequent work in Tahiti appear to have benefited from this new process.

Lucina Ward

1. Written in Le Pouldu, c. 20 October 1889, to Vincent van Gogh, in Douglas Cooper, *Paul Gauguin: 45 lettres à Vincent, Théo et Jo van Gogh. Collection Rijksmuseum Vincent van Gogh, Amsterdam*, 's-Gravenhage: Staatsuitgeverij, 1983, no. 36.
2. Belinda Thomson, *Gauguin*, London: Thames & Hudson, 1987, p. 102.
3. Gauguin also made sculpture, ceramics and prints as well as carving in wood.
4. Thomson, p. 102.

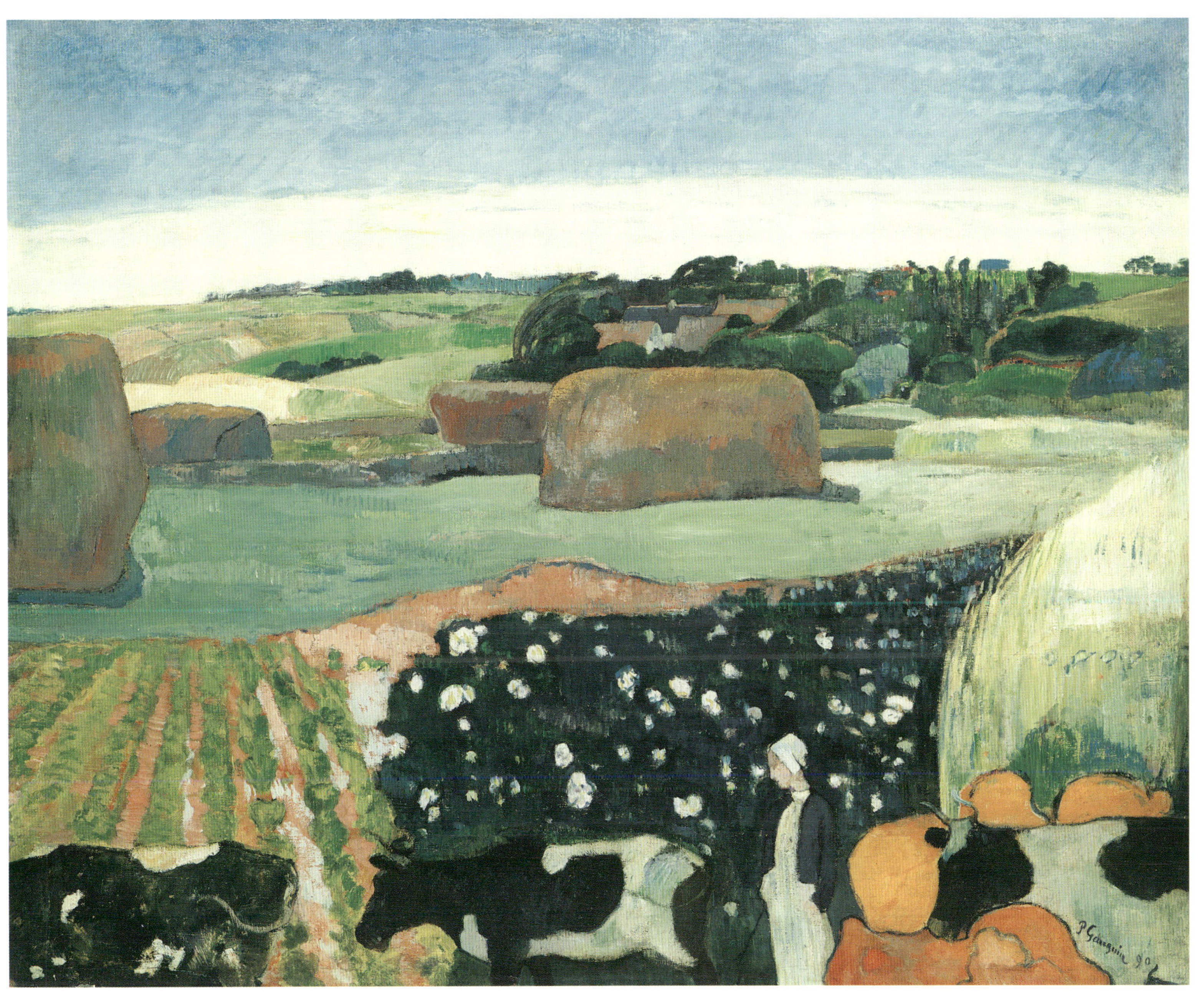
P Gauguin 90

93. Paul Sérusier

France 1864–1927
Mother and child in a Breton landscape
[***Une mère et son enfant dans un paysage Breton***] 1890
oil on canvas 73.2 x 60.0 cm
Kerry Stokes Collection, Perth

Sérusier's meeting with Gauguin and Émile Bernard at the popular artists' retreat at Pont-Aven in Brittany in the summer of 1888 radically changed the aesthetics of this promising young art student, who trained in Paris at the Académie Julian under Jules Lefebvre. Gauguin encouraged Sérusier to abandon the almost photographic realism of Lefebvre's bravura painterly technique, and employ pure colours to capture the subjective sensations and feelings that he experienced before nature.

In Paris, Sérusier shared these ideas with a circle of young painter friends who were seeking new intellectual directions in art. Along with Paul Ranson, Sérusier headed this group, who came to be known as the Nabis (a term coined by Sérusier, after the Hebrew word for prophet).[1] Gauguin's influence upon the group was soon noted by critics. In 1891 Alphonse Germain wrote:

> Gauguin's admirers called themselves Distorters [*déformateurs*] at first. Their goal: to carefully preserve an original sensation, and to depict it with exquisitely rare and harmonious lines and colours, but also via primitive methods and a free interpretation bordering on the strange, and the distorted.[2]

Sérusier again worked alongside Gauguin at Pont-Aven and Le Pouldu in the summers of 1889 and 1890, painting scenes of rural life in the countryside of Brittany, that drew inspiration from Gauguin's use of simplified forms and a restricted palette. In both subject matter and execution, *Mother and child in a Breton landscape* reflects the formative influence of the older artist. As Sérusier loved to recount, his mentor had encouraged him to paint his immediate colour sensations, no matter how strident they seemed, even using unblended pure pigments direct from the tube. The deep, rich greens and startling blue shadows employed here show Sérusier already moving towards a radical simplification of colour which he achieved just two years later. As he wrote to his friend the Dutch painter Jan Verkade in 1892:

> As for colour, I've given up using small delicate tints, amassed next to each other. While drawing attention to a particular section of a painting, they mar its overall effect. Three or four colours, carefully chosen, are enough, and quite expressive. Any more colours would only lessen the painting's impact.[3]

After Gauguin's departure for Tahiti in April 1891, Sérusier was still drawn to Brittany, settling there with brief return visits to Paris. For the next three years he lived at Huelgoat, a small village in the centre of the region, about sixty kilometres from Pont-Aven. Here he found an even more traditional and intact local culture than at Pont-Aven, and a landscape filled with ancient rocky outcrops and dark, mysterious woods. It was at Huelgoat that Sérusier developed his unique artistic personality, as his depictions of Breton peasant life increasingly blurred the boundaries between descriptions of traditional village practice and evocations of secret, druidic rites.[4] At this time Édouard Schuré's *Les grands initiés* (1889), a study of the world's ancient and modern religions, radicalised numerous-mystically inclined followers, Sérusier among them. His theories melded with the painter's fascination with Celtic Brittany's druidic past; Sérusier's Huelgoat paintings are replete with echoes of pre-Christian and Arthurian times.

Ted Gott

1. The Nabis circle included at various times Pierre Bonnard, Maurice Denis, Georges Lacombe, Aristide Maillol, Ker-Xavier Roussel, Édouard Vuillard and Félix Vallotton.
2. Alphonse Germain, *La Plume*, 1 September 1891, quoted in Marcel Guicheteau, *Paul Sérusier*, Paris: Éditions SIDE, 1976, p. 48.
3. Letter quoted in Joëlle Ansieau, *Georges Lacombe 1868–1916, catalogue raisonné*, Paris: Somogy, 1998, p. 61.
4. See Guicheteau, especially Chapter IV, 'Les trios étés à Huelgoat', pp. 63–79.

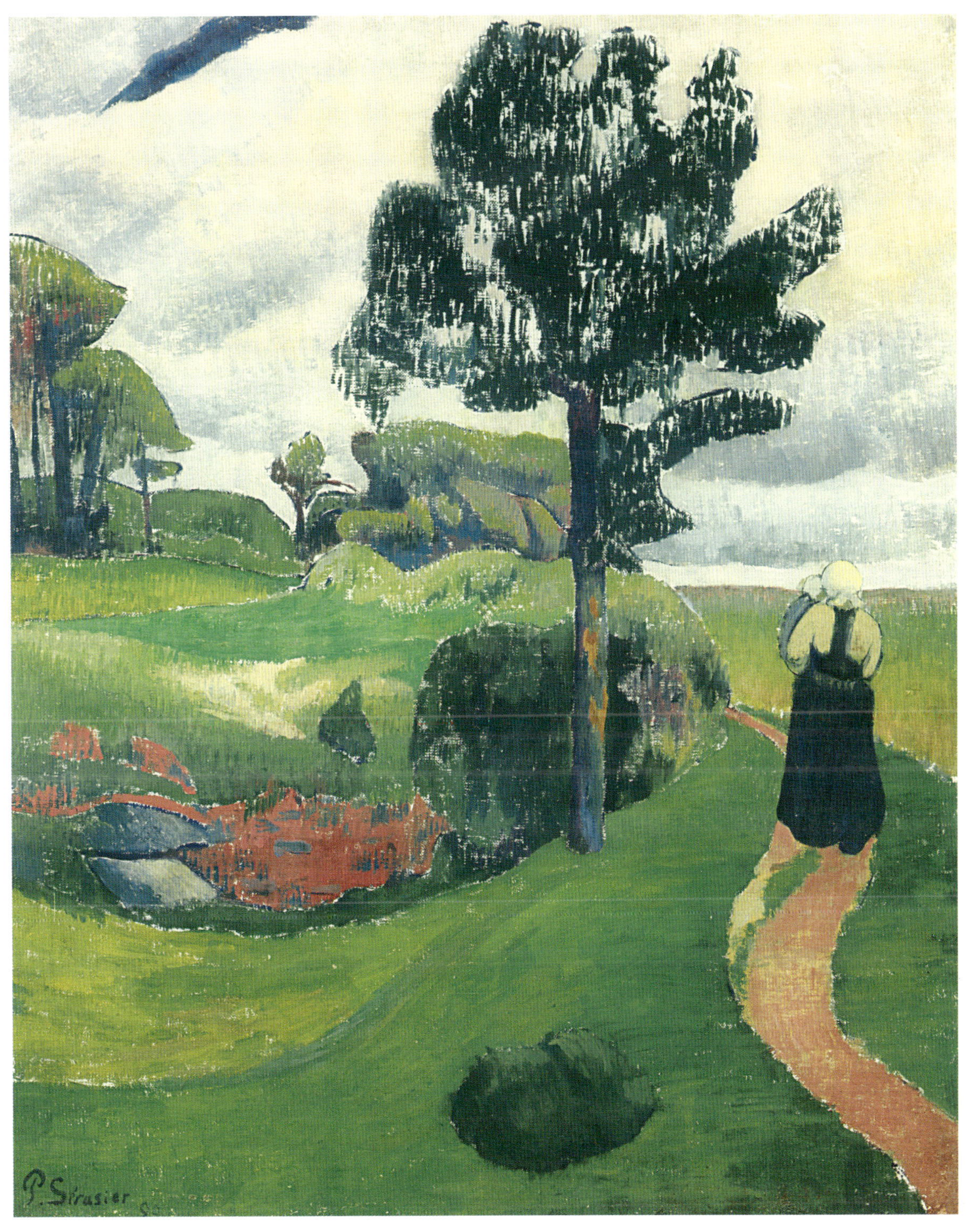
P. Sérusier

94. Charles Conder

Great Britain 1868–1909
Australia 1884–1890
Hayfield, France 1894
oil on canvas 60.3 x 73.5 cm
Art Gallery of South Australia, Adelaide
M.J.M. Carter, AO, Collection

Following Monet's example, Conder began making extended visits to Normandy from 1891. This northern region inspired Conder to produce some of his finest paintings over the ensuing years. He discovered a landscape that engaged him aesthetically, as had the Yarra Valley in Heidelberg, Melbourne, several years earlier.[1] Conder's enchantment was evident: 'I have so little desire to see Paris that I entertain no ideas of going back just yet for the countryside is a delight'.[2] Monet was also a critical influence during this period, as reflected in the subject and palette of *Hayfield, France*, but it was the landscape itself that rejuvenated Conder's painting practice. He used the captivating beauty of the countryside to evoke a sense of poetry and sometimes melancholy within his *plein-air* paintings, which he achieved through an aesthetic response to the landscape rather than seeking 'truth to nature'.

Seeing Monet's exhibition of *Haystacks* in February 1891 had a dramatic impression on Conder and renewed the way he looked at the landscape. He promptly wrote to Roberts:

> I only wish you could have seen some of his landscapes; *they lived* ... He paints a good deal still with pure colour, but you quite lose the paint at three or four yards (less). He takes you among hayricks and sunsets in the most natural way and then lets you see it as you have been used – not in his but in your own way.[3]

Under Monet's influence, Conder developed a heightened palette and loose, spontaneous brushwork of contrasting colours. He also used colour to define form and light, rather than tone, as in *Hayfield, France* where the transition out of full shadow into full sun is represented by starkly contrasting blues with greens.

It was not, however, Conder's intention to replicate Monet's technique or aesthetic. He did not apply Monet's complex structure of colour juxtapositions nor the variety of the master's palette. The sky, for example, was rendered with a smooth, relatively uniform expanse of blue. Even in the more radically worked foreground area, the canvas was thinly covered and not a richly textured paint surface, which one might expect. Conder continued to see the landscape according to his own aesthetic sensibility, *in his own way*, but enlivened it through an appreciation for Monet's use of colour and his ability to capture the evanescent qualities of light and atmosphere.

Conder uses the rhythm of colour and form as agents of lyricism in *Hayfield, France*. His palette is a harmony of pistachio and light citrus greens, cornflower and powder blues, custard cream and a pale strawberry-pink. These fresh, pastel colours create a hazy luminosity characteristic of the white misty glow that lingered until late morning during spring in Normandy. Light and colour are applied poetically to establish a sense of tranquillity and melody, rather than analytically developed in relation to one motif or view. Conder choreographs the composition so that the ribbons of colour, the meandering line of the foreground shadow and the various landscape motifs set a dreamy rhythm within the painting. He also employs certain accents, such as the solitary cloud mass floating in space or the arabesque branch motif in the upper left corner, to add an arresting ambiguity to the painting.[4]

Jane Messenger

1. Ann Galbally, *Charles Conder: the last bohemian*, Melbourne: The Miegunyah Press, Melbourne University Publishing, 2002, p. 98.
2. Letter from Conder to William Rothenstein, late March 1894, quoted in Galbally, pp. 115–16.
3. Conder, quoted from a letter dated 26 February 1891 in Galbally, p. 76.
4. The asymmetrical cropping and foreground placement of the branches reflect the influence of Japanese art as Conder would have understood it through James McNeill Whistler (1834–1903), whom he admired greatly, and Henri Toulouse-Lautrec (1864–1901), with whom he was closely associated during the early 1890s. They also reflect Conder's interest in design over representation.

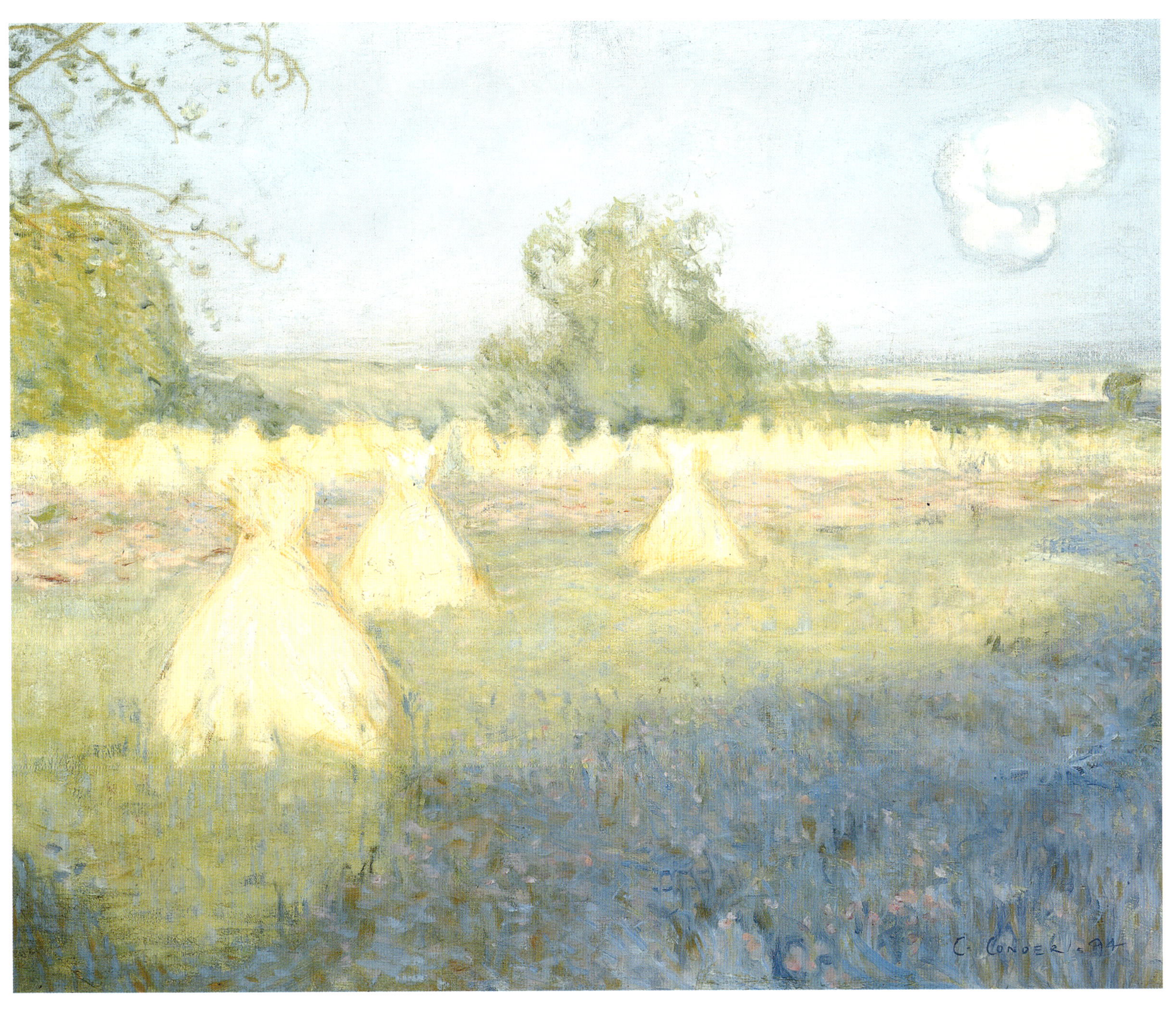
C. CONDER . 94

95. Philip Wilson Steer

Great Britain 1860–1942
Yacht racing on the Solent 1893
oil on canvas 60.3 x 75.9 cm
Art Gallery of Western Australia, Perth
Purchased in 1898 1988/00P1

The English painter and teacher Steer was a leading proponent of Impressionism in Britain. He developed an individual style using a flecked brushstroke to apply pure colour directly onto the canvas, through which he expressed the changing effects of light. After preliminary training in London, he studied art in Paris in the 1880s, where he saw works by James McNeill Whistler and Edouard Manet, but his real contact with Impressionism seems to have been through paintings he viewed in London exhibitions. His contemporary George Clausen (1852–1944) said that Steer concentrated 'on the problems of colour, almost to the exclusion of everything else' in order to realise 'the great forces of nature'.[1]

From 1884 to 1892 Steer regularly spent his summers in resorts on the English and French coasts, where he painted images of bathers and beaches. In the summer of 1892 he worked at Cowes on the Isle of Wight: it is likely that he painted *Yacht racing on the Solent* in his London studio the following year from sketches made on the spot. He drew many images of racing yachts on the Solent and related subjects in four pocket-sized notebooks, including detailed studies for the main yacht on the right, exploring whether to place the main sail on the right or on the left, and the patterns made by the sails.[2] He subsequently made several paintings of yachts in profile, including *A procession of yachts* 1892–93.[3]

Yacht racing on the Solent can be more closely linked to the drawings in the sketchbooks than *A procession of yachts* and therefore can be considered to have been painted first. It is also more freely painted and less decoratively arranged, which would also suggest it is the earlier version. It is likely that Steer was also influenced by Turner's images of a similar scene at Cowes, painted when he attended the regatta there in 1827. Steer would have known Turner's painting of this subject in the Tate's collection, which has a similar composition although a distinctly more choppy sea and cloudy sky than Steer's yacht race.

This is one of Steer's most Impressionist works. He used short flecks of colour – blues, greens and reds – with touches of creamy impasto to suggest the effect of sunlight flickering on the water. The areas of pure colour are echoed and varied throughout the image by secondary tones of ultramarine, russet, lilac–blue and apricot. He evoked a sense of the wind in the sails through his rhythmical arrangement of the sweeping forms of the sails and in his energetic brushstrokes.

Up to 1895 Steer painted modern pictures such as *Yachts racing on the Solent*, but afterwards radically changed his approach with a view to revitalising the English tradition, painting figure subjects and landscapes under the influence of eighteenth-century French and British art. But even as late as 1913 Steer was still painting atmospheric images of boats in the harbour, such as *Harbour at sunset, Harwich*.[4]

Anne Gray

1. D.S. MacColl, *Life work and setting of Philip Wilson Steer*, London: Faber and Faber, 1945, p. 27.
2. Bruce Laughton, *Philip Wilson Steer*, Oxford: Clarendon Press, 1971, p. 28. The note books are in the collection of the Victoria and Albert Museum, London (E304 – 1943, E305 – 1943, E306 – 1943, E307 – 1943).
3. Collection of the Tate Britain.
4. Collection of the Sterling and Francine Clark Institute, Williamstown, Massachusetts.

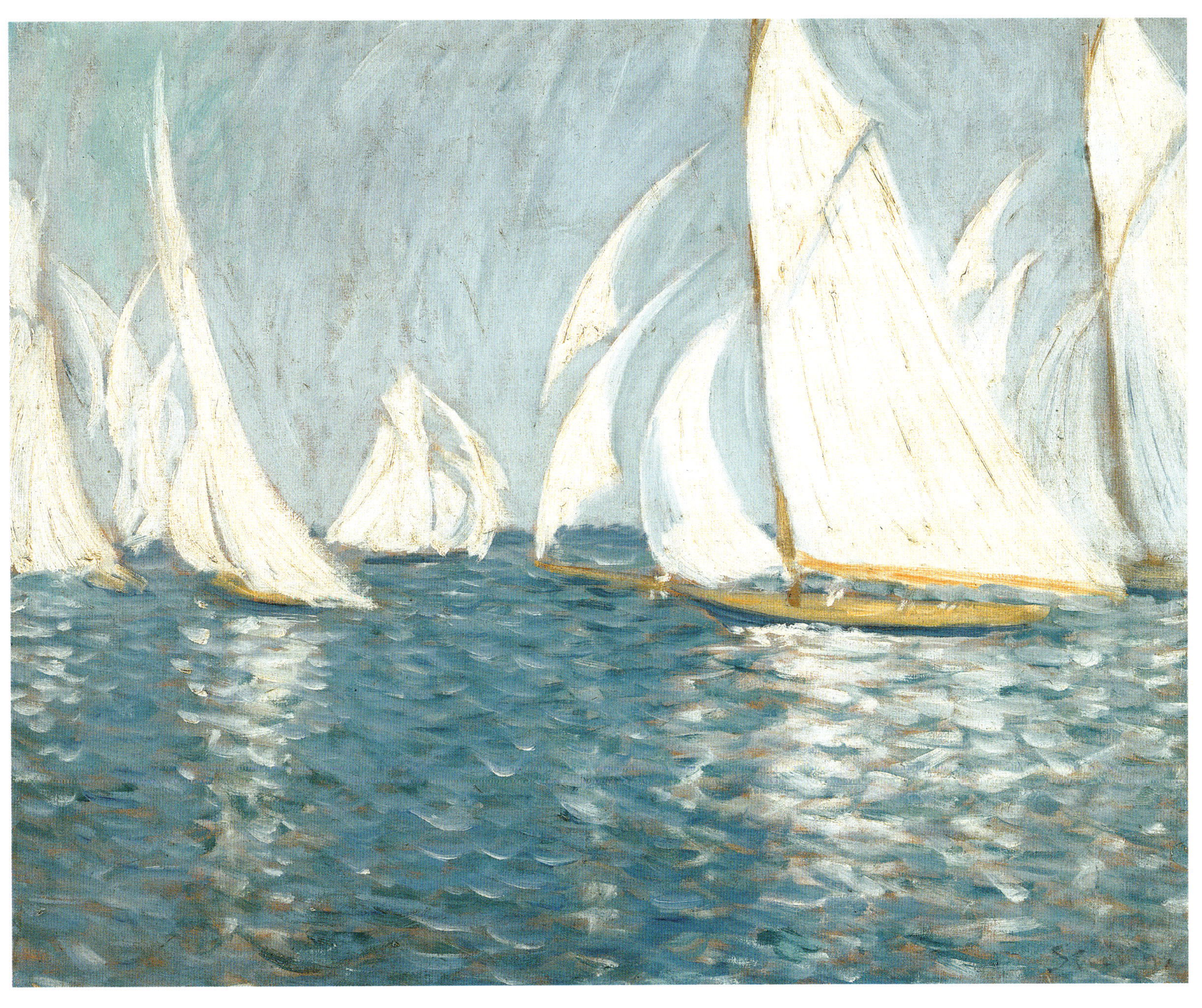

96. Maximilien Luce

France 1858–1941
Camaret, moonlight and fishing boats [***Camaret. Clair de lune et flottille de pêche***] 1894
oil on canvas 72.4 x 92.1 cm
Saint Louis Art Museum, Missouri
Museum Purchase, Museum Shop Fund, and funds given by Gary C. Wolff, the Stephen F. Brauer and Camilla T. Brauer Charitable Trust, the Pershing Charitable Trust, the Kate Stamper Wilhite Charitable Foundation, the William Schmidt Charitable Foundation, the John R. Goodall Charitable Trust, Nooter Corporation, Eleanor C. Johnson, Mrs Winifred Garber, Hunter Engineering, the Joseph H. & Elizabeth E. Bascom Charitable Foundation, the Stephen M. Boyd Fund, Robert Brookings Smith, Irma Haeseler Bequest, BSI Constructors Inc., Mr and Mrs Thomas Latzer, Samuel C. Davis Jr, Dr and Mrs William H. Danforth, Mr and Mrs George Conant, Mr and Mrs Michael Cramer, Dr and Mrs David M. Kipnis, Mr and Mrs John O'Connell, Edith B. Schiele, and donors to the Annual Appeal 29:1998

Luce used landscape compositions such as *Camaret, moonlight and fishing boats* to explore formal issues of colour and light as well as his own political concerns. The painting depicts fishing boats at night in the protected harbour of Camaret, a small fishing village in Brittany on the Atlantic coast. It is executed in Luce's characteristic divisionist style, distinguished by the building up of the painted surface using separate brushstrokes of colour. The artist employs varying shades of green and periwinkle blue, along with pink and yellow for the night sky. Violet, blue, turquoise and deep pink splotches, along with green and lemon-yellow strokes serve for the areas of shadowed and moonlit water. Deep blues, purples and near-blacks make up the silhouetted shapes of the fishing boats.

By 1887 Luce had adopted the divisionist technique first developed by Seurat, a fellow French Neo-Impressionist artist. The technique was based on theories about colour and seeing, which asserted that the eye would blend colours juxtaposed on the canvas. The adjacency of complementary strokes of colour would produce a brilliant effect, closely approximating the appearance of natural light. This effect was well suited to Luce's project here, of representing the luminosity of moonlight on calm water.

Luce also began showing with other Neo-Impressionists in 1887, contributing to their third independent exhibition in Paris. In addition to a commitment to colour theory, Luce shared with some of these artists a dedication to the tenets of Anarchism. The form of Anarchism he endorsed was an idealistic socialism, involving precepts of social harmony and the absence of a centralised government.[1] His convictions included an abiding interest in the condition of the working class, whose members and places of employment occasionally appear in his paintings. Luce often portrayed modern industrial work sites as locations of strenuous labour or intrusion into the landscape.[2] In *Camaret, moonlight and fishing boats*, however, he depicts the boats as representatives of a more traditional livelihood. They are presented in a moment of quiet restfulness, fully integrated with the other elements in the scene. The repeated forms of hulls and bare masts become a decorative pattern against the variegated colours of the sea.

Janeen Turk

1. Joachim Pissarro and Eliot W. Rowlands, *Maximilien Luce, 1858–1941: the evolution of a Post-Impressionist*, New York: Wildenstein, 1997, pp. 12–14, 20.
2. Anne-Claire Ducreux and Aline Dardel, *Maximilien Luce: peindre la condition humaine*, Paris: Somogy Editions d'Art 2000, pp. 72–87; Denise Bazetoux, *Maximilien Luce: catalogue raisonné de l'oeuvre peint*, vol. 2, Paris: Editions JBL 1986, cats 799–951, 1046–65.

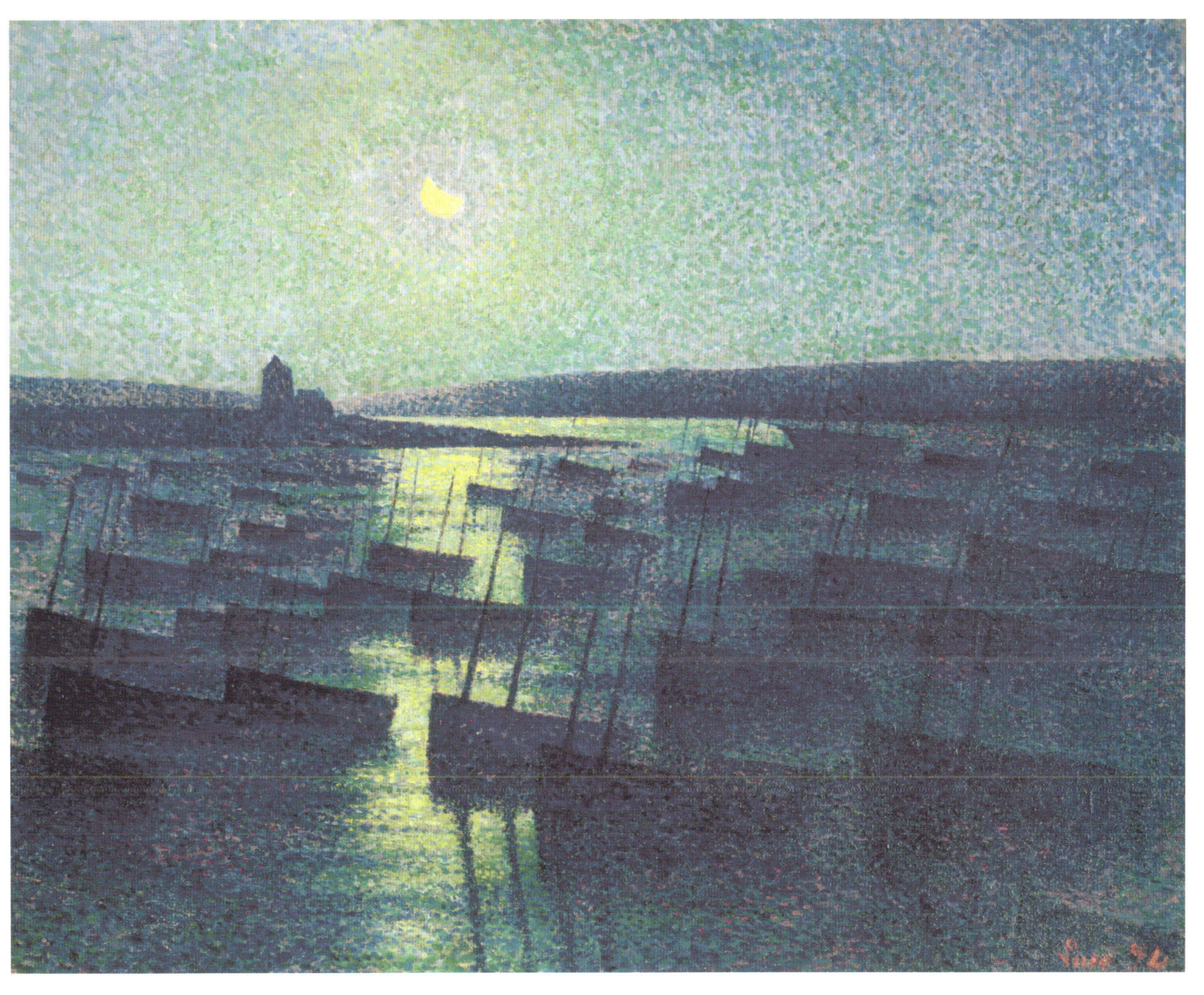

97. Claude Monet

France 1840–1926
***Morning haze* [*Matin brumeux, débacle*]** 1894
oil on canvas 65.7 x 100.3 cm
Philadelphia Museum of Art, Philadelphia
Bequest of Mrs Frank Graham Thomson, 1961 1961-48-2

For me, a landscape does not exist in its own right, since its appearance changes at every moment; but its surroundings bring it to life – the air and the light, which vary continually … For me, it is only the surrounding atmosphere which gives objects their true value.
Monet 1891[1]

As he matured as an artist, Monet returned to the same motif with endless variations: Rouen Cathedral, poplars, haystacks, waterlilies. It was only in this way that he could seek to capture differing effects of light on objects, and changing times of day, as the nominal theme and composition differed only to a small degree. In the ice-floe paintings he made in and after the severe winter of 1892–93, there are even fewer variables, as the dazzlingly colourful effects of sunlight on vegetation or stone surfaces have been eliminated.

Monet had addressed the subject of ice breaking up on the Seine – the 'débacle' of the title – at least twice before, in 1868 at Bougival, and in 1879–80 at Lavacourt, near Vétheuil. The thirteen Giverny paintings of 1893–94 were composed and begun at the small village of Bennecourt near his house.[2]

> Having swept along its ice floes for several days, the Seine finally froze over in mid-January, 1893. Monet set up on the Bennecourt bank and painted the river looking towards the hills on the left bank.[3]

The date 1894 written on the canvas, a year after the freezing flood, puts firmly to rest the myth that Monet always painted out of doors: like almost all artists he finished works in the studio, sometimes large parts of them.

In *Morning haze* Monet's subject is the disappearance of form and colour under nature's wintry grey and white coverings of snow and fog on a river. Like Turner, Monet attempts to paint the ineffable appearance of light and water, the infinite array of snow, river, vapour and sky. The tonal spectrum he employs is small, varying from very light to middle tones, while his palette is limited to mixed hues of white and the palest shades of grey and purple. But the skin of paint is robust, built up in layers like masonry. The way mist dissolves material reality is evoked by a haze of paint. The bright snow on the bank emphasises the snow on the ice floes, while the river's surface reflects the mist and sky, as well as the trees on the far bank and on the little islets. By cutting off the foreground, Monet allows the river to flow out of the canvas, encroaching into the viewer's world. As so often in Monet's painting, his experience of transience, of recording an instant, implies time passing and the inevitability of change.

Christine Dixon

---

1. Said by the artist to a visitor to his *Haystacks* exhibition in 1891, see W.G.C. Bijvanck, 'Une Impression (Claude Monet)' in his *Un Hollandais à Paris en 1891*, Paris: Perrin, 1892, p. 177, quoted in John House, *Monet: nature into art*, New Haven: Yale University Press, 1986, pp. 28–9.
2. Daniel Wildenstein, *Claude Monet: biographie et catalogue raisonné*, Lausanne: La Bibliothèque des arts, 1974–1991, 5 vols, cat. 1333–1344, see vol. III, pp. 542–6.
3. Wildenstein, vol. III, pp. 542–3.

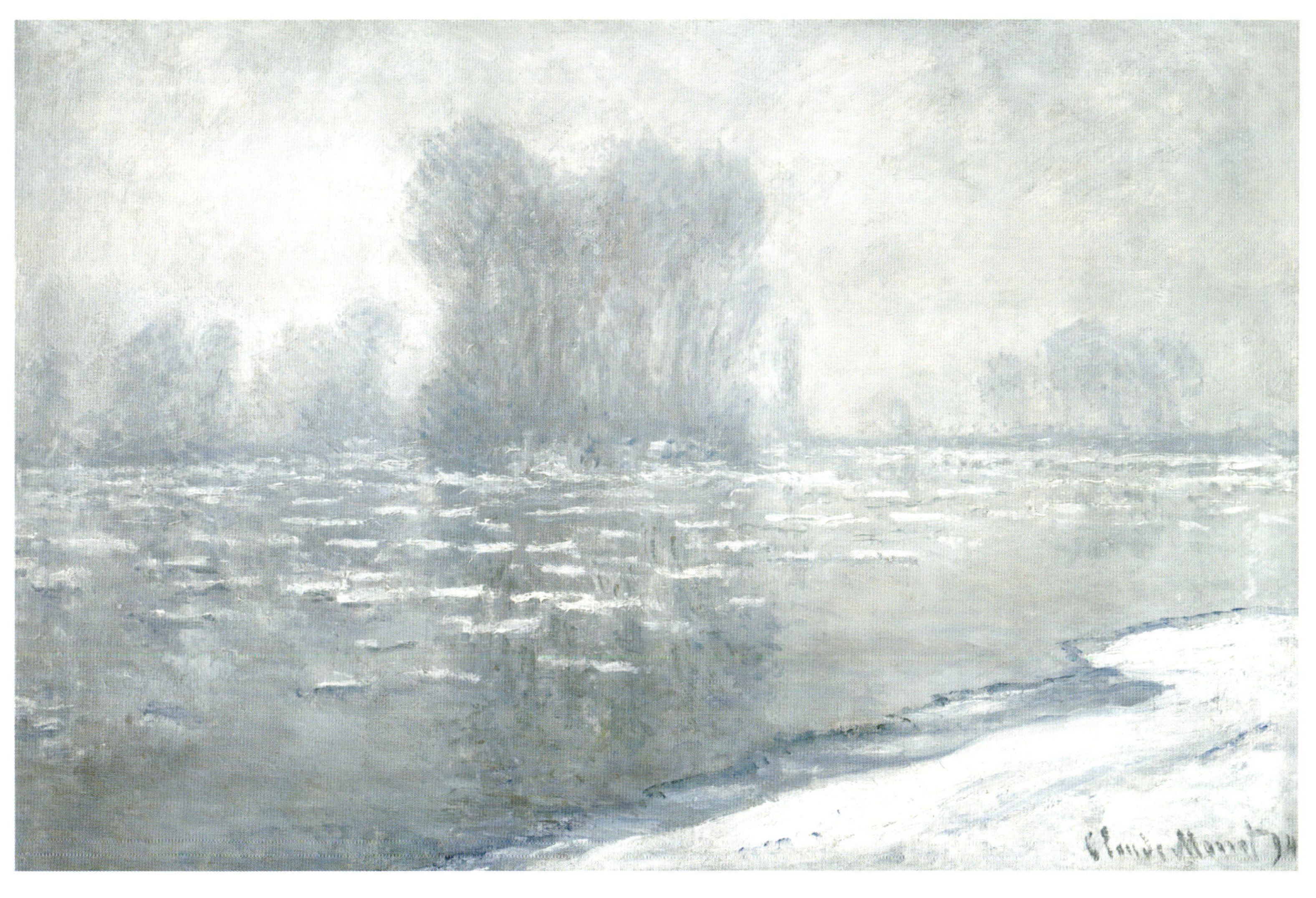
Claude Monet 94

98. Jan Toorop

Indonesia 1858 – The Netherlands 1928
***The sea* [*De zee*]** 1899
oil on canvas 46.0 x 50.5 cm
Kröller-Müller Museum, Otterlo
Purchased with support from the Rembrandt Society KM 101.352

The pastel striations of Toorop's painting of sky, sea and sand stretch horizontally across the canvas. All is pale, almost featureless, except for a strip of rich blue indicating deeper ocean. Above the sea's horizon is a suggestion of clouds in the lavender sky. Barely distinguishable, some boats sail towards the ocean, having traversed the shallows where white-tipped waves advance towards us hypnotically – light green, yellow, changing again to blue and mauve onto the pallid pink and beige beach.

Among the foremost Dutch exponents of modernism, Toorop was a highly experimental artist: Neo-Impressionism was one of many styles with which he experimented in the last decades of the nineteenth century. Sent to the Netherlands from his homeland of Java at the age of fourteen, the young artist studied in Delft, Amsterdam and Brussels from 1876 to 1885. Working first in a Realist and then an Impressionist manner, Toorop became a founder member of the Belgian proto-Symbolist group Les XX (The Twenty) in 1884. Here his main influence was James Ensor (1860–1949), who advocated white as a newly dominant value in painting. The artist incorporates Ensor's ideas in *The sea*, using the foamy waves as a vehicle for the application of luminous white highlights. No black, no darkness remain.

The artist animates the flat surface of *The sea* by using short brushstrokes in a way that was characteristic of contemporary Neo-Impressionist painters in Paris. We are reminded particularly of Divisionist artists such as Seurat and Signac, and their followers. Toorop was exposed to Signac's paintings in Brussels at the exhibitions of the avant-garde society La Libre Esthétique.

Also manifest in Toorop's seascape is the influence of Japanese woodblock artists, which pervaded Western Europe during the second half of the nineteenth century. The artist's adoption of a bold, frontal viewpoint in *The sea* emulates the radical compositional strategies of Japanese printmakers, especially Hokusai's and Hiroshige's daring images. No-one is invited into Toorop's scene through the angled entry of conventional perspective. Instead the image is isolated, cut off on both sides, and cropped at the top and bottom – a compositional device that might echo a photographer's point of view.

Neo-Impressionism's abstract qualities were linked to Symbolist aesthetic theories and, often, anarchist politics. Allusive, evocative, radical: the apparent subject of a Symbolist work did not necessarily represent its entire meaning. Toorop's meditation on a banal Dutch seaside scene holds other possibilities; he suggests hidden spiritual and mystical experiences of life through symbolic forms, in particular the synaesthesia of music, rhythm and colour. While the ebbing tide has its own unique forms, as each wavelet is shaped differently, the movement of the sea is eternal.

Christine Dixon

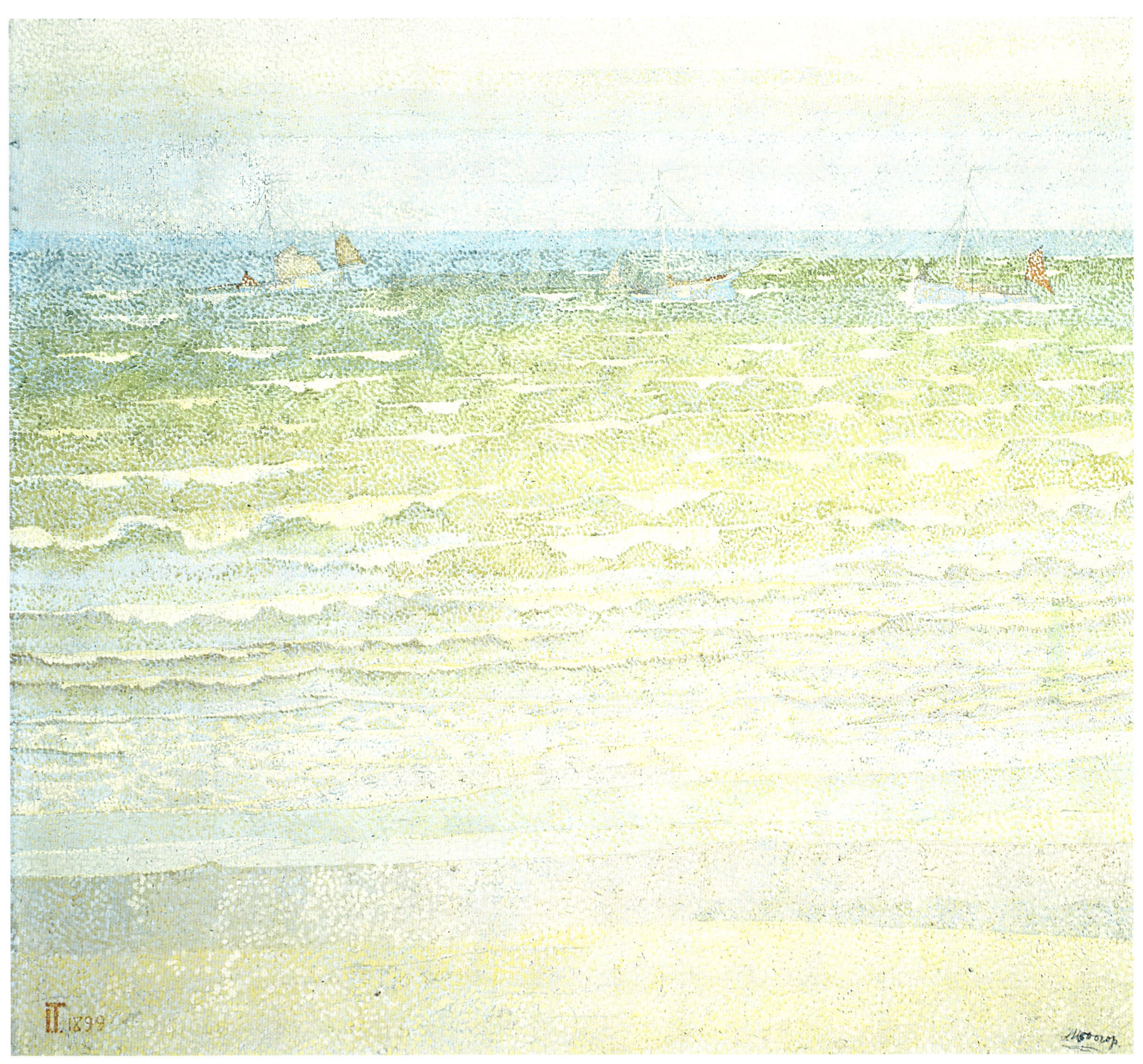

99. Paul Gauguin

France 1848 – Marquesas Islands 1903
Landscape with a horse [***Paysage avec un cheval***] 1899[1]
oil on burlap 70.8 x 44.5 cm
Saint Louis Art Museum, Missouri
Gift of Sydney M. Shoenberg Sr. 27:1974

Gauguin's *Landscape with a horse* immerses the viewer in a lush, tropical world where humans are virtually absent. A tall tree dominates the composition, emphasising the verticality of the picture. This choice, as opposed to the more conventional horizontal orientation for landscape paintings, underscores Gauguin's innovative approach to the genre. The painting's surface does not conceal the rough texture of the burlap support, which is visible along the edges, adding to its modernist vigour and intentional lack of refinement.

The landscape subject provides a vehicle for Gauguin's exploration of rich, saturated colour. He structures the composition so that the hot orange and pink tonalities of the middle ground are framed by the verdant foreground and the cool blue of the sky, punctuated by leafy trees and billowing clouds. The horse grazes peacefully, anchoring the composition in the centre and drawing attention to the low-slung houses behind it. The titular horse does not carry much narrative weight, but may refer to the idea of a journey, which was a prevalent theme in Gauguin's later work. A letter he wrote in 1899 evokes the painting's mood:

> Here in my cabin, in complete silence, amid the intoxicating perfumes of nature, I dream of violent harmonies. A delight enhanced by I know not what sacred horror I divine in the infinite. An aroma of long-vanished joy that I breathe in the present. Animal figures rigid as statues, with something indescribably solemn and religious in the rhythm of their pose, in their strange immobility. In the eyes of that dream, the troubled surface of an unfathomable enigma.[2]

Indeed, the landscape and culture of Tahiti fuelled the artist's pictorial imagination during the years he spent there, and until his death in 1903.[3] In Tahiti Gauguin achieved his mature style, as well as a rich vein of new subject matter that was transformative for his art and life. He first arrived in 1891, returned to France in 1893 for two years, and made his final trip in 1895.[4] The works he made in Polynesia were destined for European audiences, so Gauguin's professional ambitions remained in France while his artistic life unfolded half a world away.

Gauguin was a polymath in terms of media and subject matter: throughout his career, from his amateur days in the 1870s into his maturity as an avant-garde artist in the 1890s and first years of the 1900s, he made paintings, sculptures, ceramics, drawings, and prints, of portraits, genre scenes, landscapes and still lifes (cat. 92). Gauguin was an experimenter by nature, fearless in pursuit of the new. His sojourns to Polynesia provided endlessly fascinating subjects that were perfect vehicles for his fascination with rich, saturated colour and for depicting landscapes that were both observed and imagined.

Charlotte Eyerman

1. The inscribed date on the canvas has also been read as '1891' though 1899 is the accepted date. The painting was purchased by the Parisian art dealer Ambroise Vollard (1867–1939) directly from the artist in 1900 and resold shortly thereafter (SLAM document files).
2. Paul Gauguin, 'Letter to Monsieur Fontainas', March 1899, in Linda Nochlin (ed.), *Impressionism and Post-Impressionism, 1874–1904*, Englewood Cliffs, New Jersey: Prentice-Hall, 1966, p. 179.
3. See George T.M. Shackelford and Claire Frèches-Thory et al., *Gauguin Tahiti*, Boston: Museum of Fine Arts, 2004.
4. See Richard R. Brettell et al. (eds), *The art of Paul Gauguin*, Washington: National Gallery of Art, 1988, for the period 1893–95, pp. 291–5; for 1895–1903, pp. 379–87.